Arming Slaves

Since its founding in 1998, The Gilder Lehrman Center for the Study of Slavery, Resistance, and Abolition, which is part of the Yale Center for International and Area Studies, has sponsored an annual international conference on major aspects of the chattel slave system, its ultimate destruction, and its legacies in America and around the world. The Center's mission is, one, to increase knowledge of this story across time and all boundaries, and, two, to reach out to broader publics which demonstrate a growing desire to understand race, slavery, abolition, and the extended meanings of this history over time. Because the research, discoveries, and narratives presented at our conferences do so much to enrich our knowledge of one of humanity's most dehumanizing institutions and its place in the founding of the modern world, as well as of the first historical movements for human rights, we are immensely grateful to Yale University Press for engaging in this joint publication venture. The Gilder Lehrman Center is supported by Richard Gilder and Lewis Lehrman, generous Yale alumni and devoted patrons of American history. The Center aspires, with Yale University Press, to offer to the broadest possible audience the best modern scholarship on a story of global and lasting significance.

DAVID W. BLIGHT, Class of 1954 Professor of History at Yale University, and Director, Gilder Lehrman Center for the Study of Slavery, Resistance, and Abolition

Edited by
CHRISTOPHER LESLIE BROWN
and PHILIP D. MORGAN

Arming Slaves

FROM CLASSICAL TIMES TO

THE MODERN AGE

Yale University Press
New Haven &
London

Published with assistance from the foundation established in memory of Philip Hamilton McMillan of the Class of 1894, Yale College.

Set in Sabon Roman types by Keystone Typesetting, Inc.

Printed in the United States of America.

Library of Congress Cataloging-in-Publication Data

Arming slaves : from classical times to the modern age / edited by Christopher Leslie Brown and Philip D. Morgan.

p.   cm.

Based on lectures from a conference in Fall 2000 at the Gilder Lehrman Center for the Study of Slavery, Resistance, and Abolition at Yale University

Includes bibliographical references and index.

ISBN-13: 978-0-300-10900-9 (pbk. : alk. paper)

ISBN-10: 0-300-10900-8

1. Slave soldiers — History. I. Brown, Christopher Leslie. II. Morgan Philip D., 1949– III. Gilder Lehrman Center for the Study of Slavery, Resistance, and Abolition.

UB416.A86 2006

355.3'308625 — dc22

2005026285

A catalogue record for this book is available from the British Library.

10 9 8 7 6 5 4 3 2 1

In memory of Thomas E. J. Weidemann

Contents

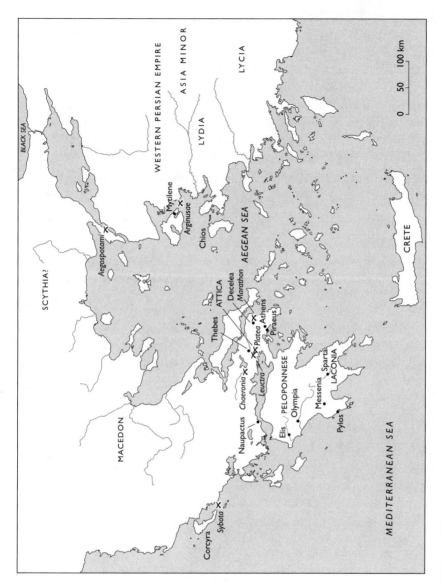

Classical Greece

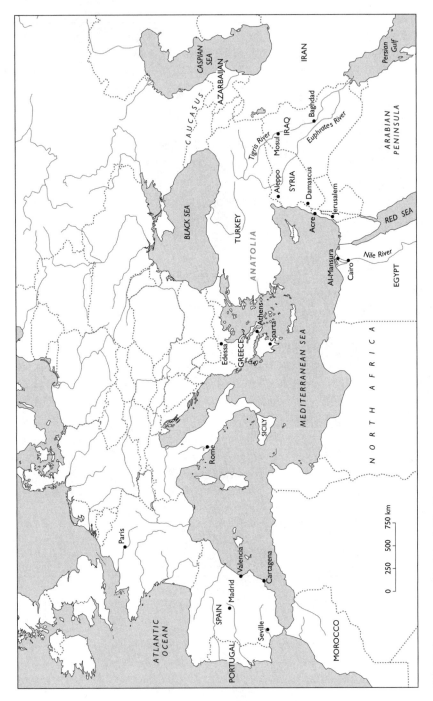

The Mediterranean and the Islamic World

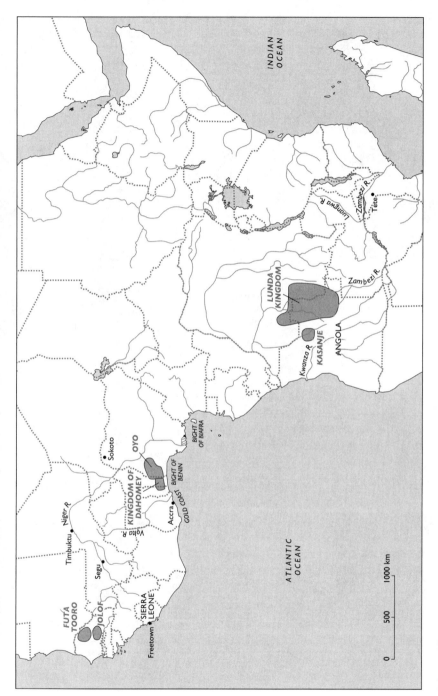

Atlantic Africa

South America

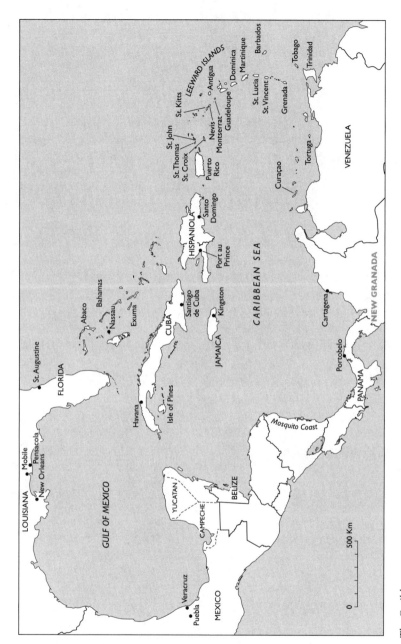

The Caribbean

Acknowledgments

This book has its origins in a conference held at the Gilder Lehrman Center for the Study of Slavery, Resistance, and Abolition at Yale University in the fall of 2000. We thank its former director, David Brion Davis, Sterling Professor of history emeritus, for inviting us to edit this book and allowing us to expand its scope beyond the original set of papers delivered at the conference. The contributors to this volume took on their assignments with energy and good cheer and have awaited the results with patience. We deeply appreciate their commitment to seeing this project through to completion.

Along the way we have received valuable assistance from the administrative staff in the History Department at The Johns Hopkins University, in particular Clayton Haywood, Shirley Hipley, and Ayanna Teal. Jessica Roney provided editorial assistance at a crucial stage. At Yale University Press, Larisa Heimert, Molly Egland, and Margaret Otzel offered enthusiastic support for this project from the beginning and outstanding professionalism throughout. Bill Nelson graciously and expeditiously assisted us with the maps. Our superb copyeditor, Jane Zanichkowsky, attended to the manuscript with expert care.

The premature death of Thomas E. J. Weidemann, professor of Latin and founder of the Institute for the Study of Slavery at Nottingham University, robbed the international community of scholars of a leader. Although he did not live to see this book in print, we hope that he would have approved.

Hilary-Anne Hallett and Barbara Morgan know well enough the labors that made this book possible. We thank them for their wisdom, encouragement, love, and support.

Introduction

DAVID BRION DAVIS

To many readers, the subject of this book — arming slaves — may seem self-contradictory, an oxymoron. If household slaves in Renaissance Italy and Spain were customarily referred to as "the domestic enemy," why would the master class ever dream of supplying such inherent enemies with arms? At first thought, the very idea seems equivalent to providing the convicts in our maximum-security penitentiaries with submachine guns and hand grenades.

But in addition to this fear of an armed Spartacus (the famed leader of a Roman slave revolt) or of a Toussaint Louverture (who was called "the black Spartacus"), slaves had often been stereotyped as cowardly "Sambos" who were even less capable of combat than were the frail ladies of the house. Such feminization or infantilization of male slaves was long used to reassure whites in the American South. This ideology, combined with fear, long prevented the Confederate government from seriously considering the arming of slaves until the last months of the American Civil War. As Howell Cobb, a former senator from Georgia and a Confederate major-general, put it: "The moment you resort to negro soldiers your white soldiers will be lost to you. . . . The day you make soldiers of them is the beginning of the end of the revolution. If slaves will make good soldiers our whole theory of slavery is wrong."[1]

Yet in Ira Berlin's prize-winning book *Many Thousands Gone,* we read that English officials in colonial South Carolina, like their Spanish counterparts in

Florida, drafted slaves in time of war and regularly enlisted them in the colony's militia. Indeed, Berlin writes that between the settlement of the Carolinas in the late 1600s and the conclusion of the Yamasee War almost fifty years later, black slave soldiers helped repulse every Spanish and Indian attack on the colony.[2] This dramatic contrast between early colonial experience and a Confederate policy based on a profoundly racist theory of slavery is precisely the kind of subject we need to explore if we wish to understand both the extraordinary importance and the complexity of the institution of slavery in human history.

Because the chapters in this book consider examples that extend over thousands of years and that move from the ancient Mediterranean and early Islamic states to Africa, South America, the Caribbean, and on to the American Civil War and to anticolonial insurgency in late nineteenth-century Cuba, they illuminate some highly revealing samples taken from relatively unexplored territory, a rich resource for the social and cultural understanding of human nature.

Instead of attempting to summarize all the chapters, which bring continuing surprises and even amazement, I would like to use some of them in a preliminary way to consider why some slaves would choose to fight for their masters and how the arming of slaves, or the refusal to do so, deepens our understanding of the most exploitative of human institutions. Other major questions raised by the chapters in this book are why the large-scale enlisting of slave soldiers did not undermine slavery itself and whether the practice did finally help destroy slavery after the Western world had begun to embrace a revolutionary ideology of individual freedom.

Slavery first appeared in human history, according to the classical account, when warriors realized that it would be more advantageous to secure the services of captives than to kill them. The connection between homicide and slavery persisted, however, since the slave might at any moment resume the warfare that his capture had suspended, and the master might choose to kill his slave for disobedience.[3]

This image of warfare was the ground for John Locke's famous defense of slavery in his *Two Treatises of Government*. According to Locke, who in another section referred to slavery as "so vile and miserable an Estate of Man . . . that 'tis hardly to be conceived that an *Englishman* much less a *Gentleman*, should plead for 't," the origin of the institution was entirely outside the social contract. When any man, by fault or act, forfeited his life to another, according to Locke, he could not complain of injustice if his punishment was postponed by his being enslaved. If the hardships of bondage should at any time outweigh the value of life, he could risk suicide by resisting his master and probably receiving the death he had all along deserved: "This is the perfect condition of *Slavery,*" Locke wrote, "which is nothing else, *but the state of War continued, between a lawful Conquerour, and a Captive.*"[4]

Thus the relation between master and slave was one in which the obligations of the social compact were entirely suspended. And for Locke, presumably, it would be unthinkable in any situation for the "lawful Conquerour" to provide arms to his captives, though on a less philosophical level Locke was an investor in the slave-trading Royal African Company and corresponded with Sir Peter Colleton, a resident of Barbados and a proprietor of the Carolinas. Thus Locke, while drafting what might well be termed a proslavery constitution for South Carolina, may have been aware of the military prowess of many Africans and of what legal scholars term "the doctrine of necessity," or the precedence of self-preservation over all other principles. At critical moments in warfare, self-preservation might demand the risky enlistment of armed slaves.

For example, the ancient view of slavery as a continuation of warfare is evident when the Spartans felt it necessary to formally declare war once a year on the defeated and slavelike Helots, presumably to remind the Helots of their inferiority and subjugation. That said, as Peter Hunt's chapter points out, the Spartans *did* enlist many Helot "slaves," despite their reputation for rebelliousness, as soldiers in land armies, especially in campaigns far from home.

As we learn from the thought-provoking chapters in this book, the doctrine of necessity was often of ruling importance. As Hunt indicates, the ancient Greeks and Romans often expressed a strong ideological aversion to enlisting slaves in their armies, which were supposed to be composed of citizen soldiers — in the case of Athenians, "hoplites," or independent farmers who were known for their courage and reliability. Yet there were continuing emergencies and manpower shortages that prompted the Greeks and especially the Romans to free slaves and then draft them for military service. Whether slaves were used as rowers in the Athenian navy, as carriers of their hoplite owners' shields and armor, or as combat troops and looters, they became a source of indispensable manpower, especially in long and desperate wars.

Aside from security, there was often a bitterly controversial conflict between the interests of individual slave owners and the military needs of a government that might deprive such owners of their property — a form of tension that would extend down through the ages to nineteenth-century wars.[5] Another barrier to the enlistment of slaves, going back at least to the time of ancient Greece, was the widespread stereotype of slaves as the personification of childishness and cowardice. Yet even in the ancient world warring states did their best to incite the rebellion or desertion of their enemy's slaves, tactics that suggested, at least, that slaves were "domestic enemies" who only needed to be roused from their feelings of helplessness and defeat.

Moreover, as Allen Isaacman and Derek Peterson show in their chapter about the "Chikunda," or military slaves in southern Africa from 1750 to 1900, the Portuguese and their descendants succeeded in creating a traditional class of African slaves who saw themselves as fierce conquerors. Facial tattoos, special clothing, and body language reinforced the Chikundas' celebration of themselves as macho warriors, unrivaled in their courage, physical prowess, and arrogance. Torn away and wholly separated from their natal families and tribes, the Chikunda expressed bitter contempt for local indigenous groups; as sharply defined outsiders, they were used not only in combat but in raids to collect a continuing supply of slaves to ship to Brazil, as policemen and overseers, and as expert elephant hunters who could help meet the rising world demand for ivory. But despite their bravado and seeming power, the Chikunda were still slaves who lived and obeyed orders in a highly regimented world.

A few years ago, when I was an outside reader for a University of Toronto doctoral dissertation subtitled "Muslim, Eastern, and Black African Slaves in Fifteenth-Century Valencia," I was very surprised to find that in late medieval Spain black slaves frequently served as armed personal bodyguards. Debra G. Blumenthal, the author, points out that unlike the numerous Moorish slaves, the black Africans could not be redeemed by nearby brethren or assimilated into Valencian society. This natal alienation and social death, to use Orlando Patterson's terms, made the blacks ideal bodyguards for their honor-obsessed masters.[6] According to Blumenthal, "contemporary testimony reveals that fifteenth-century Valencians could not conceive of anyone more 'base' or 'vile' than a black male slave." Therefore, in order to degrade their white enemies, white masters would order their black bodyguards to ridicule, assault, and batter their rivals or foes. Black slaves were also used to commit various crimes for their masters.[7]

I have now learned from some of this book's chapters as well as from other works that Valencia's black bodyguards were by no means exceptional. The Julio-Claudian Roman emperors of the first century of the Common Era were served by slave bodyguards taken from what is now Holland, at the fringe of the empire. And as a protective empire disappeared in late Roman times, the well-to-do increasingly relied on armed slaves as personal bodyguards, preferably slaves from distant regions (thus separating the slaves from families and clans). Much later this practice spread to Brazil and to Spanish America. Instead of conforming to Locke's picture of the slave as a defeated soldier in a "state of War continued," such bodyguards suggest Aristotle's concept of the slave as a tool or instrument, analogous to a loyal dog, carrying out his master's will. They also bring to mind the Arabs' and the Turks' almost total reliance on armies of generally loyal slaves purchased as children or adolescents from the distant Caspian and Black Sea regions and then trained to be devoted protectors.

As the chapter by Reuven Amitai makes clear, these mamlūks represented a highly distinctive kind of slavery even though they were bought and technically owned as property. If they were exploited as life-risking soldiers, the mamlūk institution showed little intent to dehumanize the young warriors who were highly disciplined in such arts as horsemanship and archery. Deprived of any family or tribal identity, they were expected to bond with one another and especially with a patron or sultan to whom they would express unconditional loyalty.

Unlike the ancient Greeks and Romans, or the many European peoples that colonized the New World, the Muslims, beginning in the eighth century of the Common Era, seemingly had no fear of or deep misgivings about the arming of such preconditioned slaves. Like the later Chikunda, they were alienated by origin, language, and upbringing from local indigenous populations. And Muslim authorities continued to rely on fresh young recruits, not on the supposedly sedentary offspring or descendants of the mamlūks, who were male by definition and in the beginning were mainly obtained from Anatolia (before it became Turkey) and then from the Caucasian region between the Caspian and Black Seas.

These Turkish and Caucasian troops played a decisive role in defeating the Byzantine Christians, in conquering and "creating" Turkey, in fighting and ultimately repelling European Crusaders from Egypt and the Holy Land, and in stopping the invasions of Mongols (who nevertheless furnished more Caucasian slaves to Christian merchants as well as to Muslims). Even though some mamlūks revolted and seized power for several centuries in northern India and in Egypt and Syria (from the mid–1200s to the early 1500s), this acquisition of political authority failed to weaken the institution of slavery, which was sanctioned by Islamic law and persisted in various forms through much of the twentieth century. Indeed, the Muslim Arabs and the Berbers were the ones who initiated the long-distance trade in sub-Saharan African slaves. Over a period of at least eleven centuries their desert caravans and Indian Ocean ships transported untold millions of black slaves to the Mideast, northern Africa, Sicily, and Spain.

Given the Moors' long occupation of Portugal and Spain, the Iberian Christians could hardly have been better informed about the Muslim experience in arming slaves and in developing a kind of proto-racism with regard to blacks. And one can hardly exaggerate the importance of the fact that it was the

Spaniards and the Portuguese who first explored, conquered, settled, and developed the Western Hemisphere. I refer to peoples who in 1492, with the capture of Granada, the Moors' last southern outpost in Spain, had just completed many centuries of so-called holy reconquest, often fighting armies that included large numbers of black slaves; a people who expelled Jews, Moors, and eventually Moriscos, or converted Muslims, while also enslaving and exterminating the Guanches, or natives of the Canary Islands; a people who had imported by sea thousands of black slaves from Africa and had established slave-worked sugar plantations in the so-called Atlantic islands west of Africa's coast; a people who would soon lead the Counter-Reformation and do their best to prevent Protestant Dutch, English, and Scandinavian explorers from establishing bases in the New World.

As the chapters by Jane Landers and Hendrik Kraay demonstrate, the Iberians armed slaves and free blacks and mulattoes from the very beginnings of their New World conquests and settlements. In the sixteenth, seventeenth, and eighteenth centuries the English, the Dutch, and the French similarly made alliances with groups of black maroons who had escaped the Spaniards and also recruited free blacks and slaves for naval warfare and raids on key Spanish settlements such as Cartagena. The Caribbean was a major theater of warfare and piracy as well as a growing source of immense wealth as northern European ships sought out Spanish galleons loaded with gold and silver and as planters began to discover the enormous multinational market for slave-grown sugar, tobacco, coffee, chocolate, and cotton. French, English, and Dutch privateers also captured many tons of sugar from Portuguese ships off the Brazilian coast.

Because the Spanish lacked the European manpower to settle and defend their vast territories from Florida to New Spain (Mexico) and Chile, they relied on armies partly comprised of free and enslaved blacks as well as Indians, Moriscos, and even gypsies. As Landers points out, the tradition of Roman law and the thirteenth-century *Siete Partidas* legitimated slavery but also encouraged manumission as a reward for meritorious service to the state. Thus many black slaves embraced military service as a route to freedom and assimilation, and despite protests from white planters and soldiers, large numbers of free and enslaved militiamen defended Spain's interests from Cuba to Peru. Spanish authorities freed British slaves who fled from South Carolina to Florida and from Jamaica to Cuba and also paid compensation to the Spanish owners of slave soldiers killed in battle.

Although Spain, unlike revolutionary France, never moved toward a repudiation or even a serious questioning of slavery until after the American Civil War, three of the black leaders of the Haitian Revolution (1791–1804) forged an alliance with Spain and fought valiantly against the French. Toussaint Louverture soon switched sides, but Biasou won medals for his bravery and moved on to Spanish Florida, where he and other freed blacks could look with contempt on the many white Spanish slaveholders.

Despite Spain's use of armed slaves from the very beginning of its conquests in the New World, racial slavery continued to flourish in Spanish Cuba and Puerto Rico until the 1880s. But the practice of arming and freeing slaves had very different consequences in the Spanish colonies that fought for independence much earlier in the nineteenth century. As Peter Blanchard's chapter shows, the arming of large numbers of slaves by both sides in the Spanish-American wars of independence helped undermine the institution from Mexico and Central America to Chile. Yet the proportion of slaves in most of the Spanish colonies was roughly similar to that in the northern American states, and the process of very gradual emancipation, following wartime and postwar commitments, took about the same length of time in both regions.[8]

The Portuguese, whose gigantic colony of Brazil absorbed more slaves from Africa than did all the Spanish colonies combined, were far more reluctant to create armies filled with slaves or newly freed slaves. As a true "slave society," whose massive production of sugar and coffee depended entirely on slave labor and on the continuing importation of slaves from Africa, Brazilian officials were eager to prevent slaves from acquiring or carrying weapons, especially in the aftermath of slave insurrections. But Kraay also observes that the private arming of slaves by their owners became routine on the lawless frontiers and during the hectic gold rush period in Minas Gerais. Yet even during Brazil's prolonged war with Paraguay from 1865 to 1870, the government exercised great caution in arming freed slaves, which by then many saw as a step toward emancipation, and the government also recognized the need to compensate slaveowners, who were supposedly the only ones who could actually grant slaves freedom.

Most of the high points of arming Caribbean and North American slaves came with the Seven Years' War, the American Revolution, and then the French Revolution and the Napoleonic Wars. Philip D. Morgan and Andrew J. O'Shaughnessy point to how close the British came, in the American War of Independence, to an enlistment of manumitted West Indian slaves and to the use of some kind of emancipation proclamation to subvert what seemed to them the most hypocritical cause, with "the loudest *yelps* for liberty," as Samuel Johnson famously put it, coming from "the drivers of negroes." In retrospect, it would appear that the American rebellion could have been demolished if Britain had turned to a massive and unqualified antislavery policy. Yet with regard to hypocrisy, Britain was the world's greatest slave-trading nation in the eighteenth century, and the government could hardly ignore the pressures from merchants, West India planters and their agents, or loyalist slaveholders in the American South. As Morgan and O'Shaughnessy make evident, the war devastated large regions of the South and led to the conscription of large numbers of slaves in the British West Indies, many for duty on British warships. Many thousands of American slaves deserted their owners and won a dubious freedom, ending up, if they lived long enough, in Sierra Leone. Other slaves, especially in the Upper South and the North, won manumission as a reward for fighting against the British. Yet in 1790 and especially 1800 slavery was far stronger and more deeply entrenched in the United States than it had been at the start of the Revolution (except in the Northern states).[9]

In the Caribbean and Latin America, in striking contrast to post-seventeenth-century North America, an immense gap in status usually separated slaves from the often lighter-colored freedpeople. This meant that the liberation and enlistment of selected slaves posed less danger to the institution of slavery and did not enlarge a degraded and rootless population that whites longed to deport or "colonize," as in the United States. Moreover, there were many black or colored *slaveholders* throughout the Caribbean, Latin America, and Louisiana (and a few even in South Carolina).

But the central point, in my opinion, is that the increasing use of armed blacks from the early sixteenth to the early nineteenth century did not prevent or appreciably slow down the development of an enormous plantation system from Brazil to the Chesapeake and the Mississippi Valley. Indeed, beginning in 1795, as Roger Buckley, David Geggus, and other scholars have shown, Britain's black West India Regiments, including many Africans who had just arrived on slave ships, saved and even expanded the British Caribbean slave colonies during the Haitian Revolution and the Napoleonic Wars.[10]

This startling and counterintuitive conclusion raises two important questions. First, why were European combatants willing to rely so heavily on slave or former slave troops when British planters, for example, protested and predicted an undermining of the entire plantation system? Second, why were black slaves and ex-slaves willing to fight for the slave regime after the Haitian Revolution had begun? As David Geggus vividly shows, the British and the Spanish were able to recruit large numbers of slaves even in Saint Domingue, where blacks and free coloreds long fought on all sides.

After reading the chapters by Geggus and by Laurent Dubois, it would appear that except for the final years of the Haitian Revolution, combatants and potential combatants in the Caribbean perceived no clear line dividing whites from blacks—a line equivalent to that dividing slaves from free persons. In part, I suspect that this lack of a clear racial distinction can be attributed to the large and expanding Caribbean populations of free coloreds, to the natal alienation of slavery, and to the absence of any African nationalism that would unite peoples of diverse African ethnic and linguistic backgrounds.

In any event, as several of the chapters inform us, the white leaders in the Caribbean faced a growing crisis as appalling numbers of European soldiers died from tropical diseases that had far less impact on people of African descent. Europeans also discovered with some dismay the military skills of Africans, who knew the tactics of guerrilla warfare, especially in jungles and mountainous regions. In theory, African capability meant that European forces might have been crushed by a united African effort, as they eventually were in Saint Domingue. But as it happened, skin color provided neither ethnic nor racial unity, and black maroons, slaves, and former slaves could be enlisted to hunt down fugitives or suppress the revolts of other maroons or slaves.

For slaves, military duty offered a welcome escape from the misery of plantation labor. The allure of a promise of freedom also entailed upward mobility, dignity, prestige, and the chance to prove one's manhood and to receive awards that would impress one's peers as well as white authorities. For blacks who had already spent significant time in the New World, there were also motives to defend one's home, family, and even paternalistic whites. During the American Civil War, after nearly a century of antislavery agitation, the former slave Frederick Douglass expressed alarm about reports that the Confederacy might begin to arm slaves with the promise of freedom. Douglass, who had written about his own experience of being "broken in body, soul, and spirit" — of being "transformed into a brute" — was convinced in January 1865 that a significant number of southern slaves would fight to defend the South, and thus slavery, if they could be assured their own liberty: "Into which scale the black man goes there goes victory. I am not at all of the opinion of some of the Anti-Slavery press that the slaves of the South will not fight in the interests of the South. I am inclined to think that such is the power of the slave-masters over their slaves, such is the confidence they can inspire, that if Jeff. Davis earnestly goes about the work to raise a black army in the South, making them suitable promises they can be made very effective in a war for Southern independence."[11] Fortunately, as Joseph P. Reidy explains in a chapter that I discuss below, the Confederate government disagreed with this conclusion until it was far too late.

I know that a Whiggish or teleological historian might well see the American Revolution and especially the French Revolution as the beginning of an inevitable chain of events leading to the abolition of slavery in the Western Hemisphere. Certainly these revolutions led to the beginnings of antislavery movements. And without these movements, converging much later with unpredictable events such as the Latin American wars of independence, British parliamentary reform, and the revolutions of 1848, the eradication of New World slavery would have been impossible. But even recognizing the supreme importance of the French slaves' self-emancipation in Haiti, to say nothing of the French emancipation decree of 1794, which in effect was negated in 1802 by Napoleon, what impresses me the most about the period from 1775 to 1865 is the remarkable strength and durability of the New World's plantation systems. Today we find it almost impossible to understand how an average of 1.5 or two white males could successfully manage a plantation, often quite isolated, with fifty or one hundred or more slave laborers. It is no less difficult to imagine how the highly productive and profitable slave systems managed to survive the disruption of major wars. Moreover, in the American South, where slaves commonly supplemented their diets by hunting and fishing, gun ownership was sometimes fairly common despite laws to the contrary.

As Frederick Douglass suggested, the climax of our story, even for the late nineteenth-century Cuba described by Ada Ferrer, came with the great debate in the American Civil War, first in the North and finally in the South, about freeing and enlisting blacks as combat troops. One new and often overlooked aspect of the question was the immense monetary value of young male slaves. In the West Indies and elsewhere owners had commonly been reimbursed for slaves who were killed, badly wounded, captured, or lost in some other way. But by 1860 a strong young field hand could sell in New Orleans for $1,800, or at least $50,000 in today's currency. And southerners continued to pay even more as slave prices increased during the first part of the war. The Confederacy would have had a difficult time, to say the least, in paying the price for any significant compensated emancipation.

For the Union, captured or fugitive slaves were first termed "contraband" and compensation, except for border state slaveholders, was soon out of the question. Despite Lincoln's early reluctance to enlist blacks or former slaves, by the spring of 1863, after years of prodding from more radical army officers and politicians, he was urging the massive enlistment of black troops and told Andrew Johnson, the war governor of Tennessee, that "the bare sight of 50,000 armed and drilled black soldiers on the banks of the Mississippi would end the rebellion at once." As things turned out, the Union enlisted about two hundred thousand black troops and sailors, most of them freed slaves, and the Union army became in effect an army of liberation.

As Reidy indicates, the Confederacy relied on slaves from the outset "as unskilled field hands and laborers, growing foodstuffs, transporting military goods, and otherwise working to support soldiers in the field and civilians on the home front." But despite early calls for the enlistment of slaves in the Confederate army, a century of increasing racism combined with fear of abolitionist ideology apparently had repressed memories of the successful arming of black slaves in the colonial era and in the British Caribbean. Antislavery and proslavery ideologies had transformed the meaning of arming slaves by the time of America's Civil War, the outcome of which would surely influence the destiny of slavery in Cuba and Brazil. It was not until early in 1865 that Secretary of State Judah P. Benjamin succeeded in persuading President Jefferson Davis and Robert E. Lee to poll Confederate soldiers on the issue of arming and freeing slave soldiers. By that time the Confederacy had suffered a series of decisive defeats and faced a critical shortage of manpower. But while most army units favored the radical step, political opposition remained intense. It was only in March 1865 that the Confederate Congress passed legislation freeing some slaves to fight for Confederate independence. Hence before the government evacuated Richmond, one company of blacks had been recruited to train for war and soon a few hundred freed slaves wore Confederate uniforms.

Given the evidence that Reidy and other historians have presented, it would appear that the Union forces could not have won the Civil War without the support of a significant number of African American soldiers and sailors. Reidy goes on to observe that when most of these black veterans returned to their southern home states, they took pride in having helped destroy slavery and save the Union. They formed the "backbone of the Republican party" and gave indispensable support to black male suffrage and the other measures during Reconstruction. But like so much that is related to slavery and the Civil War, this crucial contribution to the new, revolutionized United States, "dedicated," in Lincoln's words, "to the proposition that all men are created equal," was seldom honored and was soon repressed from white Americans' collective memory. And if the Confederacy, like innumerable governments from ancient Greece to Napoleonic Britain, had taken the risk of freeing and arming large numbers of slaves — as early, say, as the spring of 1862 — the slavocracy might well have won its independence, with an outcome that is almost impossible to predict. The possibility that black veterans would then have overthrown their masters is somewhat lessened when we look at the fate of the enormous number of black veterans after World War I.

Notes

1. Quoted in James M. McPherson, *Battle Cry of Freedom: The Civil War Era* (New York: Oxford University Press, 1988), p. 835.

2. Ira Berlin, *Many Thousands Gone: The First Two Centuries of Slavery in North America* (Cambridge: Harvard University Press, 1998), pp. 66–67. Although it was customary throughout history to offer enlisted slaves the reward of freedom, Berlin notes that in the Carolinas "only a handful of slaves won their freedom through military service, and the English never formally incorporated black men into a regularly constituted militia as did the Spanish." In other regions slaves were often freed *before* they took up arms, but the Muslim mamlūks had been enslaved *in order* to serve as soldiers and were very rarely emancipated. This is a major difference between Christian and Muslim societies. See also Keith R. Bradley, "The Roman Slave Wars, 140–70 B.C.: A Comparative Perspective," in *Forms of Control and Subordination in Antiquity*, ed. Toru Yuge and Masaoki Doi (Leiden: Brill, 1988), pp. 369–376.

3. I explore aspects of this theme in *From Homicide to Slavery: Studies in American Culture* (New York: Oxford University Press, 1986), and in my introduction to *A Historical Guide to World Slavery*, ed. Seymour Drescher and Stanley L. Engerman (New York: Oxford University Press, 1998), pp. ix–xvii. With regard to primitive combat and enslavement, see the biblical story of David and Goliath: I Samuel 17:1–51. As the armies of Israelites and Philistines face each other, the towering and gigantic Goliath shouts out: "Choose one of your men and let him come down against me. If he bests me in combat and kills me, we will become your slaves; but if I best him and kill him, you shall be our slaves and serve us."

4. John Locke, *Two Treatises of Government*, ed. Peter Laslett (Cambridge: Cambridge University Press, 1960), pp. 297–302, emphasis in original.

5. Note that the first serious philosophical attack on the very principle of slavery came from the late sixteenth-century defender of authoritarianism Jean Bodin, who held that the rights and powers of a slaveholder undermined the absolute sovereignty of a monarch.

6. Orlando Patterson, *Slavery and Social Death: A Comparative Study* (Cambridge: Harvard University Press, 1982), passim.

7. Debra G. Blumenthal, "Implements of Labor, Instruments of Honor: Muslim, Eastern and Black African Slaves in Fifteenth-Century Valencia" (Ph.D. diss., University of Toronto, 2000), pp. 216–221.

8. In a few smaller states, such as Vermont and Massachusetts, and in Central America, emancipation was almost immediate. By the time of its independence, Mexico had relatively few slaves, and it freed them in 1829.

9. Few if any historians have noted that Alexander Hamilton not only favored the arming of slaves during the War of Independence, in conformity with the well-known plan that John Laurens tried without success to sell to South Carolina's governor and legislature, despite its approval by the Continental Congress. Hamilton also saw the enlistment and arming of thousands of South Carolina's slaves as an entering wedge for total emancipation, if only the barrier of racial prejudice could be overcome: "I foresee that this project will have to combat much opposition from prejudice and self-interest. The contempt we have been taught to entertain for the blacks, makes us fancy many things that are founded neither in reason nor experience; and an unwillingness to part with property of so valuable a kind will furnish a thousand arguments to show the impracticability or pernicious tendency of a scheme which requires such a sacrifice. But it

should be considered, that if we do not make use of them in this way, the enemy probably will; and that the best way to counteract the temptations they will hold out will be to offer them ourselves. An essential part of the plan is to give them their freedom with their muskets. This will secure their fidelity, animate their courage, and I believe will have a good influence upon those who remain, by opening a door to their emancipation. This circumstance, I confess, has no small weight in inducing me to wish the success of the project; for the dictates of humanity and true policy equally interest me in favor of this unfortunate class of men" (Alexander Hamilton to John Jay, March 14, 1779, in *The Papers of Alexander Hamilton*, ed. Harold C. Syrett, 24 vols. [New York: Columbia University Press, 1961–1987], 2:17–18). I am indebted to Philip Ziesche, a Yale University graduate student, for this information.

10. Although there is some evidence that the enlistment of black soldiers lessened racism in Latin America, and we have much evidence that racial integration has succeeded in America's present military forces, I myself witnessed the most extreme racism and bloody racial conflict in the segregated American army of 1945–1946. See my essay "The Americanized Mannheim of 1945–1946" in *American Places: Encounters with History; A Celebration of Sheldon Meyer*, ed. William E. Leuchtenburg (New York: Oxford University Press, 2000), pp. 79–91.

11. Douglass, "Black Freedom Is the Prerequisite of Victory: An Address Delivered in New York, New York, on January 13, 1865," in *The Frederick Douglass Papers*, ser. 1, *Speeches, Debates, and Interviews*, vol. 4, *1864–80*, ed. John W. Blassingame and John R. McKivigan (New Haven: Yale University Press, 1991), pp. 55–56. Douglass continued: "If Jeff. Davis will hold out to the blacks of the South their freedom, guarantee their freedom, the possession of a piece of land, and the elective franchise, I should say that the negroes of the South would be acting unwisely if they do not fight, and fight valiantly, for this boon, if on the other hand, the North is unwilling to concede those rights and guaranties."

Arming Slaves and Helots in Classical Greece

PETER HUNT

The independent Greek city-states of the classical period, 500–338 BC, fought many wars against each other, individually or in various combinations. Many of the most important city-states were also slave societies: their numerous slaves were crucial to their agriculture and to their urban economies. In response to this pair of circumstances, cities sometimes encouraged their opponent's slaves to desert. They also mobilized their own slaves in a variety of ways ranging from emergency infantry service with the promise of freedom to regular mobilization with pay in the navy.

Warfare between the independent city-states of Greece in the archaic period, 750–500 BC, was limited and convention-bound.[1] This type of warfare is sometimes called *agonal* because it resembled a contest with set rules, an *agon:* a single battle resulted in a clear winner and decided the war. The heavy infantry, the *hoplites,* who determined the battle's outcome, provided their own metal armor and thus came from the richer part of the population. This warfare regime left little scope for arming slaves, because only a fraction of the free population was armed, and inviting the desertion of an enemy's slaves would result only in retribution and contribute little to the single battle that counted.

In the classical period, some wars became more intense and lasted longer.

They were decided not by single battles but sometimes by lengthy campaigns. Wars were no longer fought over disputed borderlands, but more often a state's independence and even its system of government were at stake. On occasion, a city's very existence could be at risk: the adult men could be killed and their women and children sold into slavery. Athens, the most populous city in the Greek world, came close to such a fate at the end of the Peloponnesian War, a particularly bitter conflict. Naval warfare, whose importance grew with the increasing importance of trade, demanded material and financial resources, centralized planning, and manpower well beyond those required by hoplite warfare. In the context of more intense wars, often involving large navies, states used every available source of manpower including their slaves. As attacks on an enemy's economy became more common, states were often tempted to try to get the slaves of their opponents to rebel or, more often, simply to desert.

Ancient Greek city-states typically possessed significant populations of chattel slaves.[2] The commercial and prosperous islands of Chios and Corcyra seem to have had particularly numerous slaves, but agrarian Elis and Thebes had many also. Plausible estimates of the number of slaves in classical Athens range from forty thousand to more than one hundred thousand at the time of the Peloponnesian War. Since the population of Athenian adult male citizens was between thirty thousand and sixty thousand at this time, the military potential of slave manpower was obvious.

Greek agriculture was mixed, intensive, and dominated by mid-sized farms with a few slaves on each. Slaves were even more prominent in urban crafts, commerce, and mining. The greatest concentrations of slaves were employed in these sectors: one hundred slaves working in a shield workshop or a thousand owned by a single man and rented out to work in the silver mines of southern Attica, which may have employed more than twenty thousand slaves at their height.[3] But, perhaps more typically, craftsmen worked together with a single slave or a handful of slaves. Overall, slave ownership was more widely distributed among the free than in New World slavery: at the height of Athenian wealth, fully a third of the male citizens probably owned at least one slave; very few owned large numbers of slaves, that is, more than thirty. The politics of arming slaves was influenced by this pattern of ownership within different classes. Although the common people held sway in Athens' direct democracy, widespread slaveholding meant that only in extreme emergencies would the emancipation of slaves for military service be contemplated — and even then it was controversial.[4] As we shall see below, the regular use of slaves in the navy did not usually infringe on the interests of slave owners.

The Evidence and Its Difficulties

Our sources of information about the role of slaves in ancient Greek warfare are pitiful.[5] Two examples show the grand scale of Greek slave recruitment and our paltry evidence for the practice. Aegospotami, the last and decisive battle of the Peloponnesian War, 431–404 BC, was fought between the navies of the Spartan-led Peloponnesian league and of the Athenian Empire. These navies together were manned by more than sixty thousand men including slave rowers. We have to guess, however, at the proportion of slaves in their crews and with little firm ground on which to base our speculation: at most we possess six scraps of evidence relevant to the proportion of slave rowers.[6] Each must be squeezed to produce a possible estimate for the proportion of slaves in a particular navy. And this information is for all of Greece during the entire classical period. None of this evidence pertains specifically to the battle of Aegospotami. So the number of slaves at this battle may have been anywhere from ten thousand to forty-five thousand. We know that slaves took part in this decisive battle on a large scale, but theories about their origins, means of recruitment, and fate depend on arguments from probability — and sometime tenuous ones — rather than on hard evidence.

The second example concerns slave desertion, again in the Peloponnesian War. Thucydides mentions briefly that more than twenty thousand slaves, most of them skilled workers, ran away from their Athenian masters and escaped to a fort established by the Spartans in Athenian territory at Decelea.[7] Whether these slaves escaped to freedom or to reenslavement under different masters or ended up as rowers in the Peloponnesian Navy is unknown. Nor does Thucydides explicitly say that the Spartans promised freedom to the slaves, although this is most likely what motivated them to desert in such large numbers.[8]

In part, the lack of detailed information is a problem common to all ancient history: our sources are scarce and difficult to interpret even when compared to the high Middle Ages and are far inferior to the evidence for any modern period. Crucial events, matters of common knowledge and great interest throughout Greece, are insecurely known. For example, the mid-fifth-century treaty that formally ended the great Persian Wars, the Peace of Kallias, is so insecurely attested that many scholars doubt its very existence.[9]

When, however, we consider the Peloponnesian War, we might expect our information to be much better, since we possess the long and meticulous account of Thucydides and its admittedly less competent continuation by Xenophon. But another difficulty now presents itself. Greek historians assumed informed Greek readers. They did not always detail standard practices that their readers understood already. Rather, they focused on the course of events, on its explanation, or on exceptional practices. Certain uses of slaves in war may have been taken for granted and therefore neglected.

This explanation for ancient reticence is still not quite sufficient: Thucydides would never have let the fate of twenty thousand Athenian citizens go unstated as he does the fates of the slaves who fled to Decelea. A systematic neglect of slaves mars our sources. To begin with, slaves were less important than citizens and thus less worthy of report. But even this explanation is too neutral; slave soldiers were not merely unimportant but a particularly awkward topic for two main reasons. First, classical Greece emphasized more than most other societies the importance of military service in judging a man and specifically his claims for political rights. Second, in common with a variety of slave societies, free Greeks affected to despise their slaves for a variety of faults, several of them incompatible with the virtues of a brave soldier.

From the time that the *Iliad* was written down, around 700 BC, a strong stream in Greek thinking put a high value on fighting for one's city and linked it with social status. Homer's aristocrats encourage each other to fight as follows:

> Therefore it is our duty in the forefront of the Lykians
> to take our stand, and bear our part of the blazing battle,
> so that a man of the close-armoured Lykians may say of us:
> "Indeed, these are no ignoble men who are lords of Lykia,
> these kings of ours, who feed upon the fat sheep appointed
> and drink the exquisite sweet wine, since indeed there is strength
> of valour in them, since they fight in the forefront of the Lykians."[10]

When hoplites came to dominate warfare in the course of the seventh century BC, military service became associated with the citizenship of the independent farmers who made up the hoplites, rather than the aristocrats of Homer.[11] Even in classical Athens, a man could lose his rights as a citizen for cowardice in battle.[12] Not only political rights but also basic worth depended on one's fighting ability and courage: Tyrtaeus' archaic paean to the absolute primacy of the virtues of a good hoplite was still well-known in the fourth century:

> I would not say anything for a man nor take account of him
> for any speed of his feet or wrestling skill he might have . . .
> not if he were more handsome and gracefully formed than Tithónos,
> or had more riches than Midas had, or Kínyras too,

not if he were more of a king than Tantalid Pelops,
or had the power of speech and persuasion Adrastos had,
not if he had all splendors except for a fighting spirit . . .
Here is courage, mankind's finest possession, here is
the noblest prize that a young man can endeavor to win.[13]

Tyrtaeus specifies that it is fighting at close quarters in the infantry that reveals
the worthy man. Classical Athens, however, depended more on its navy than
its hoplites. But despite some aristocratic contempt for the naval mob, the
connection between military service and rights remained strong.[14] A fifth-
century critic of Athenian democracy had to admit that the common people
deserve their power because "it is the ordinary people who man the fleet and
bring the city her power."[15] Although Tyrtaeus' poem manifestly oversimpli-
fies the actual complexity of social status in Greece, the military virtues played
an unusually large role in the Greek spectrum of values. Accordingly, the
question of arming slaves was always a political and ideological one as well as
a practical one.

All sorts of military service, therefore, even rowing for the navy, were associated with rights that slaves manifestly did not have and, to Greek thinking,
should not have. Slaves were sometimes Greek prisoners of war, but more
often they came to Greece via trade from areas in the northern Aegean, around
the Black Sea, and the coasts of Asia Minor and Syria. The circumstances of
their original enslavement are largely unknown. Slaves were seen as inferior,
having been defeated in war or coming from "barbarian" peoples. They were
seen as childish and cowardly and as the polar opposites of the citizens.[16] None
of these ways of viewing slaves could easily be reconciled with their playing an
important role in warfare, an activity so central to the self-definition of the
male citizen.

The juxtaposition of this seemingly overwhelming ideology and the barely
mentioned participation of slaves in warfare have resulted in two very different historical approaches. Some scholars have played down the evidence for
slave participation, since such a practice was incompatible with Greek thinking. They tend to argue that a handful of exceptional cases constitute the
whole of slave use in classical Greek warfare. I have recently argued for the
opposite approach. Rival cities at war often had no choice but to press every
advantage including the recruitment of slaves — and inciting desertion among
their enemies. Contemporary Greek historians were not similarly constrained
in what they chose to report or focus on. They could neglect slave participation or focus on other issues. So, far from looking askance at brief references
to arming slaves on the grounds that such a practice was incompatible with

Greek thinking about slaves and military service, we should take full account of this evidence. Indeed, other cases have very probably been completely lost from the record.

Types of Slave Use

Rather than go through the scattered individual cases of arming of slaves in the many wars of classical Greece, it is perhaps more useful first to sketch out typical practices in broad strokes. It is readily admitted that such a general picture, faute de mieux, is not as solid as one built up by the consideration of many detailed narratives. We have a few pieces of a jigsaw puzzle and are trying to put them together, knowing full well that they may belong to different puzzles and simply hoping that the puzzles resemble each other, that is, that a Peloponnesian navy of 405 will resemble one of 411. This general overview focuses on three cases: slaves from Scythia, archers, who performed police functions within Athens; slaves who accompanied hoplites on campaigns but were not armed; and slaves who were occasionally armed as infantry soldiers. Then I consider in greater detail two cases that were of great military importance and about which the evidence allows more insight into the practical problems, politics, and effects of arming slaves: the military roles of Sparta's serflike Helot population and the use of slaves in the Athenian navy during the Peloponnesian War.

Athens did not have a police force; its legal system depended a great deal on self-help and social pressure.[17] In order to maintain order in the courts and assemblies and to assist certain magistrates, Athens, in the fifth century, bought a force of three hundred Scythian slaves, armed with the traditional Scythian bow. These slaves carried these lethal weapons among an unarmed populace, but they seemed to have performed their jobs smoothly and did not evoke fears of a slave revolt. Despite being the butt of various xenophobic jokes in comedies,[18] the archers were a favored group of slaves. Because of their homogeneity and their weapons, their lives were perhaps more like those of mercenaries — or of Muslim slave soldiers — than of individual chattel slaves. These archers may have provided a bulwark for the democracy against the possibility of coups by the oligarchs, which often depended on a surprise attack in concert with mercenaries. The Scythian archers also strengthened the state's power while maintaining equal rights among the citizens: such equality was felt to be offended if a citizen, even in the role of policeman, laid hands upon another.[19] The Scythian archers were armed slaves, but they were armed for internal rather than external purposes.

Each hoplite, often an independent farmer, typically brought one of his slaves with him on a campaign. Such attendants played a key support role in warfare. In particular, they helped carry the hoplite's armor, which weighed up to sixty pounds and was uncomfortable in the summer heat, and thus not put on until the last possible moment. The attendants might also help plunder or ravage the enemy's countryside, throw stones at the enemy, and carry and care for the wounded. They seem not to have played a large role in battle itself and did not present the threats, both practical and ideological, that slaves in combat did. Although such slaves might take the opportunity to desert, they might also render their masters exceptional service and receive commensurate rewards, such as their freedom, or at least public commemoration if they died.[20] More commonly they did hard but inglorious work on a campaign and returned to their previous duties afterwards.

On occasion, slaves were armed as infantry soldiers. A variety of factors limited the usefulness of this policy. Although chattel slave revolts were almost unheard-of in the classical Greek world,[21] the Greeks often viewed their slaves as intrinsically hostile to the free: Xenophon argues that the free citizens provide a bodyguard for each other so that they are not murdered by their slaves.[22] Therefore, slaves who fought in the infantry were typically either promised or given their freedom to assure their loyalty. Rarely were they made citizens, a closely guarded prerogative; rather, they became *metics*, resident aliens, liable for military service and subject to a special tax but also free to leave the city. Thus, the policy of freeing slaves to fight was expensive, unrepeatable, and usually reserved for emergencies. For example, after Philip of Macedon defeated the Athenians and their allies at the battle of Chaeronia, 338 BC, the Athenians voted, among other emergency measures, to free and arm their slaves, presumably to man the extensive walls of Athens and its port, the Piraeus.[23] When they discovered that Philip was willing to offer them peace terms instead of attempting to storm the city, they rescinded their offers and decided to make peace instead. Hyperides, who proposed the motion to arm the slaves, was put on trial. He defended himself on grounds of necessity alone: "It was not I who wrote the decree; the battle of Chaeronia did."[24] Earlier, during the Peloponnesian War, an Athenian general armed the crews of his navy as javelin throwers, a type of light infantry.[25] These crews included slave rowers, but, as we shall see, such slaves probably enjoyed an above-average status and incentives for good behavior, including the hope of eventual manumission. So they could be used as infantry almost as easily as they could serve as rowers.

In neither of these cases did slaves serve as hoplites, the heavy infantry who dominated Greek battles. An ideological factor made the arming of slaves as hoplites particularly unpalatable: all military service gave some claims to those who performed it, but the hoplite was the soldier most closely associated with citizenship. Thus, the hoplites remained primarily citizen amateurs in the fourth century, when the use of mercenaries had become common for other types of soldiers.[26] The hoplites formed the branch of the armed forces from which slaves ought especially to have been excluded.

In addition, the hoplites only came from the richer half or third of the male citizens, and class imperatives often influenced the decision of whom to arm. If a city had extra hoplite weapons and armor on hand, it could, if it wished, arm its poorer citizens. In some cases, class tension among the citizens made this option unappealing — on one occasion the poor overruled an oligarchic government as soon as they were given hoplite weapons.[27] The Athenians reportedly armed three hundred slaves, probably as hoplites, to fight at the battle of Marathon against the Persians, 490 BC.[28] They did so although they had thousands of poorer citizens, the *thetes,* available. Presumably, the rich and middling farmers, the hoplites, wanted to maintain their monopoly of the prestige of defending the city. They were willing not only to risk their lives to justify their prerogatives — as they had for centuries — but also to give the available extra armor to their slaves rather than to the thetes, who were perhaps considered more of a threat to their dominance. The promise of freedom for the slaves could be considered another act of laudable public spirit on the part of the slave owners, since they were making a financial sacrifice for the community's benefit.

Sparta's Rebellious Helots

For deeper insight into the practical problems, politics, and effects of arming slaves, the military roles of Sparta's serflike Helot population deserve special mention. Spartans maintained their status as leisured professional soldiers by means of their exploitation of a large population of unfree peasants called Helots.[29] The origins of Helotry in the Spartan homeland, Laconia, is obscure, but many of the Helots inhabited the territory of Messenia, conquered by Sparta in the early archaic period. These owed to the Spartans a proportion, probably half, of their produce. They might have been required to perform personal service as well, for example, as hoplites' attendants. The Spartans called them their "slaves," and they are so described even in treaties.[30] This designation was an attempt to assimilate Sparta's controversial subjection of an entire Greek people to the accepted system of slavery, which usually involved non-Greek individuals. The Helots were not, however, chattel slaves. They could not be bought or sold individually. Many lived within their own villages and with their own families.

The Helots, especially those of Messenia, were notorious for their rebelliousness. Messenia had attempted and failed to free itself in a bitter war in the seventh century. Messenian exiles, attested in the mid-sixth century, suggest further disturbances. Another revolt is likely to have occurred in 490.[31] Sparta required the aid of allies throughout Greece — and may have taken years — to put down a large Helot insurrection in the mid-fifth century. Indeed, Spartan treaties sometimes specified that Sparta's allies must come to its aid in case the "slaves rose in rebellion."[32] In addition to these particular incidents, an atmosphere of suspicion and brutality between Spartans and Helots is well attested. The constant military training and totalitarianism of the Spartans were aimed as much at the danger within as at any external Greek enemy.

These two threats combined when Sparta's enemies tried to take advantage of Helot discontent. Athens gave Naupactus, a city it had conquered and later used as a naval base, to the Messenian refugees who had left the Peloponnese on a safe-conduct at the end of the mid-fifth-century revolt. These Messenians became particularly brave and loyal allies of the Athenians during the Peloponnesian War and afterwards. It was probably at their suggestion that in 425 Athens built a fort at Pylos, on the Messenian coast, in order to attract deserters and incite Helot rebellions. This fort was later manned by the Messenians from Naupactus, who were particularly effective at inciting their countrymen to rebel.

By climbing apparently insurmountable cliffs and appearing unexpectedly at the Spartans' rear, they also played a key role in forcing the surrender of several hundred Spartans trapped on the island of Sphacteria.[33] These Messenians even dedicated a beautiful victory statue, now known as the Nike of Paeonius, at Olympia taken from "the spoils of their enemies."[34] Although the Spartans were not named as the defeated enemies, the presence of a dedication by the Messenians — the very name was unpalatable for Sparta and its sympathizers — at the Panhellenic center of Olympia was, no doubt, hard for the Spartans to swallow.[35]

Late in the war, the Spartans besieged Pylos and recaptured it after letting the garrison of Messenians from Naupactus and Helot deserters leave under a safe conduct.[36] The Athenian defeat in the Peloponnesian War allowed the Spartans to captured Naupactus.[37] A generation later, however, Thebes, after defeating the Spartans at Leuctra in 371 BC, invaded Messenia and helped the Messenians build a walled city there. After three centuries of large and small rebellions, the Messenians gained their freedom with the intervention of Thebes. Sparta continued to possess Helots in its home territory, but it never again subjected Messenia nor played a major role among the important Greek city-states.

The sudden conversion of the majority of Sparta's "slaves" into a Greek city-state sparked considerable controversy. Most interesting for our purposes are the two types of arguments employed by pro-Messenian propagandists. The more radical and ultimately less influential approach accepted that the Messenians had been slaves and so denounced slavery: it was in a work about Messenia that Alcidamas, a sophist and rhetorician, argued — in one of the very few criticisms of slavery to survive from ancient Greece — that "god made all men free; nature has made nobody a slave."[38] The other approach had begun well before Messenia had been freed.[39] This was to separate the subjection of Messenia from usual chattel slavery: the Messenians were not like slaves at all but were Greeks with their own mythical history going back to Nestor in the *Iliad*. This approach ended up prevailing because it reconciled the liberation of Messenia with its eventual position as a regular Greek city-state, led by slaveholders, which had been freed by another city, Thebes, led by slaveholders. Thus the epitaph of the great Theban general Epaminondas stated, "By my plans Sparta was deprived of its glory / And holy Messene received back its children at last /... / All Greece was independent and free."[40] Although all Greece was "free," the epitaph did not imply that any slaves had been freed or needed to be freed but rather that the Messenians had been restored to their rightful position.

Helot Soldiers

Among the Athenian forces, whose expedition against Syracuse ended in disaster in 413, Thucydides lists a contingent of Messenians from Naupactus and Pylos.[41] The Spartan general Gylippus, whose arrival in the nick of time kept Syracuse from surrender, came with one thousand men from the Peloponnese and a unit of six hundred men picked from among the Helots and the Neodamodeis, the latter being Helots freed for military service.[42] In a pattern that will become less surprising as the reader continues through this book, Helots were used extensively in Spartan land armies despite their well-earned reputation for discontent and rebelliousness.[43]

Sometimes Helots were used in large numbers for short campaigns. At the battle of Plataea, Herodotus reports, Helot soldiers outnumbered the Spartans by seven to one: there were thirty-five thousand Helots to five thousand Spartans.[44] I have argued elsewhere that at Plataea the Spartans, professional soldiers with a fearsome reputation, fought in the front rank while the Helots made up the rear seven ranks of a typical Greek phalanx. Traditional scholarship, on the other hand, assigns the Helots a less important role as lightly armed troops on the periphery of the battle.[45] In later campaigns in the Peloponnese, the Helots were again mobilized en masse, along with the

Spartans.[46] It is not clear whether these Helots served in the same formation as the Spartan hoplites, although at other points we definitely hear of Helot hoplites.[47] Again our information about these mobilizations is scanty, deriving in each case from a few words in Thucydides. Such mobilization was probably an unrewarded obligation, although occasionally Helots gained or hoped for rewards for particularly meritorious service.[48]

In a different pattern of mobilization, the Spartans recruited smaller numbers of Helots as professional hoplites for distant and lengthy campaigns. These Helot soldiers were typically rewarded, either before or after their service, with freedom from the obligations of Helotry. They served in separate units in armies consisting typically of a few Spartan leaders, mercenaries, and allies. At the peak of Spartan imperial power, in the early fourth century, the Spartans had at least as many armed Helots in service at a time, probably three thousand, as they had full citizens in total.[49] These Helot soldiers allowed Sparta to fight the long and distant campaigns it was unwilling to undertake otherwise.

Ironically, the Spartans were unwilling to leave the Peloponnese in force because of their fear of Helot rebellions. By promising freedom to some Helots and having them fight distant campaigns for them, the Spartans selected and co-opted — or at least removed — some of the most martial Helots. The Spartans were also able to stay near home and supervise the rest more closely. The loyalty of Helot soldiers is impugned in a couple of the sources,[50] but neither rebellions nor large-scale desertions seem to have occurred during the five decades when they were a pillar of Sparta's military presence abroad. Sparta may have finally gone too far when it promised freedom to several thousand Helots to help fight against the Theban-led army that was to liberate Messenia; many of these Helot soldiers deserted to the enemy.[51]

The organization of Helot society, with its families, local communities, and traditions, made the Helots a greater threat than the chattel slaves of other Greek states. Indeed, other cities were advised not to import too many slaves from one place.[52] The factors that made Helots safer to arm than chattel slaves were also no doubt complex. Two deserve mention. First, the state, as a representative of the community of Spartans with full citizenship, was very powerful in comparison to the individual. Therefore, individual Spartans had less power or will to oppose the mobilization of Helots from their estates. Second, the home ties that Helot soldiers possessed could also serve as pledges of their good behavior. Thus their rebelliousness and their military service for Sparta were not irreconcilable poles of Helot behavior but were linked by their special position as subjected but not quite enslaved Greeks.

Slaves in the Athenian Navy

Slaves were much more commonly used in the navy than as foot soldiers. Naval warfare required far larger numbers of people than land warfare. Athens never managed to field more than sixteen thousand hoplites at any one time, but its largest naval effort required fifty thousand crew members. So whereas hoplite service was not imposed on the poorer half of the citizen population, mobilizing a navy required large numbers of poor citizens, resident aliens, foreign mercenaries, and slaves. The vast majority of these men were rowers: one hundred and seventy of a trireme's crew of two hundred pulled at the oars. The experience, strength, skill, and morale of these rowers were central to a ship's success. Rowing in a trireme required at least as much skill as did fighting as a hoplite: each person manned his own oar, and precise coordination among rowers was crucial. Classical sea battles depended on maneuvering and ramming rather than on boarding enemy ships or on missiles launched from the decks. The pride of the unmatched Athenian navy was its skill at the maneuvers that set up ramming opportunities: the *periplous* (the sailing-around) and the *diekplous* (the sailing-through-and-then-out). In contrast, navies that depended on the fighting men on their decks could be considered old-fashioned, if not incompetent.[53] The ship itself with its metal ram was the main weapon of naval warfare, and it was the rowers who wielded it. Rowers did not individually possess weapons, and thus slave rowers did not present the threat or require the rewards that slave infantry usually did. But rowers more than anybody else were the fighters in naval battles—and were acknowledged as such in contemporary sources.[54]

Although this naval role was their most important role, evidence for the practice is brief and scattered.[55] For example, of one thousand prisoners captured from the navy of Corcyra at the battle of Sybota in 433 BC, eight hundred were slaves.[56] Later, the Athenian general Phormio brought back to Athens the "free men out of the captives from the naval battles" against a mainly Corinthian navy.[57] Among the half-dozen other pieces of evidence for slave rowers, one stands out: in a large allied navy under Spartan leadership in 411, the Syracusan and Thurian crews demanded their back pay most vociferously, because they "were mostly free men."[58] This statement implies two things: the Syracusan and Thurian crews contained slaves and, more startling, the crews of the other ships contained more slaves than free sailors.

The Athenian navy, about which the most is known, was no exception to the practice of using slaves as rowers. The two official state ships are described as "having only free citizens in their crews," marking them out as exceptions.[59]

Our only Athenian crew roster, although fragmentary, records the names and status of a squadron's crew members.[60] Between 20 and 40 percent of the rowers on the different ships were slaves. Rather than being a record of the exceptional use of slaves, as some scholars have argued, this inscription confirms that Athenian ships, like those of every other Greek navy, had a significant proportion of slaves among their rowers. Nevertheless, the Athenian ships were not "slave galleys." The majority of the crew was made up of free Athenian citizens or foreigners, mainly from the subject cities of the Athenian Empire. The slaves were not chained to their benches nor driven by the whip.

How did a promiscuous group of slaves, citizens, and foreigners end up providing the crews for the Athenian navy? Two patterns emerge: first, a proportion of slaves served regularly in the typically dominant Athenian navy; second, in the desperate circumstances of the Arginusae campaign, late in the Peloponnesian War, the Athenians needed to mobilize their slaves en masse for a relief force. In order to accomplish this they promised them freedom and eventually gave them citizenship, a far more disruptive and controversial practice.

To muster a large navy was an ambitious undertaking for the rather rudimentary classical state, most of whose officials were chosen annually by lot.[61] The ships were manned using a complex process that was anything but uniform. The officers, archers, and hoplite marines were provided by the state. The captain of a trireme, the trierarch, was chosen not for his nautical skill but for his wealth: he was financially responsible for the ship. The state provided a hull, necessary equipment, and the base salary for the crew, but the incidental expenses and final responsibility for outfitting and manning a ship were the trierarch's. In some cases, trierarchs recruited volunteers and paid bonuses to attract skillful rowers. In other cases, the state drafted citizen rowers and assigned them to different ships.[62] These draftees did not make up the full complement of rowers, and one trierarch claimed in court that because many of them were of inferior quality, he was forced to hire good men in their place.[63]

Hence, the type of people who rowed in triremes was not a matter of state policy. Rather, the use of slaves might be at the discretion of an ambitious trierarch trying to put together a crew to do him credit—there were races at the start of naval expeditions, and having the admiral choose to ride on a particular trireme was a great honor. Or a thrifty trierarch might try to minimize his expenses but still fill the benches. In either case, the officers and marines were usually citizens drawn from the richest one-third of the citizen body and used to having slaves with them. The lone surviving crew roster indicates that many of the slaves on board belonged to these citizens. So in manning a trireme, a trierarch would hire as rowers some slaves of the officers who had been assigned to him. There were also slaves who belonged to other rowers, probably urban artisans or farmers put out of work by the war; both of these classes often owned slaves.[64]

Finally, there seem to have been some slaves without masters on board the warships. Their supervision may have been informally assigned to a relative or friend of their master — and the whole crew had a stake in a full and competent complement for maximum speed in battle and cruising. Nevertheless, such slaves were trusted in situations in which flight was relatively easy, since triremes, built for mobility and little else, pulled ashore every night and often did so for lunch. Family ties might keep some of them loyal. Early in the war, fugitive slaves might well be enslaved again if they appeared, speaking broken or accented Greek, in another city-state's countryside. When the Spartan alliance, with Persian financing, started manning a large navy and needed crew members of whatever provenance, and when desertion to this outfit became easier with the establishment of the Spartan fort at Decelea in Attica, masters were under more pressure to grant their slaves significant incentives or lose them.

As in many urban commercial slave systems, monetary incentives with the possibility of eventual manumission were a crucial part of the control a master could exert over his slaves.[65] How might such a system work for slave rowers? To begin with, they were paid at the same rate as the free. A fifth-century passage, although difficult to interpret, suggests that, as in many such societies — compare the *jornal* system of Latin American slavery — masters allowed their slaves to keep some of their wages and eventually buy their freedom: "In a state relying on naval power it is inevitable that slaves must work for hire so that we may take profits from what they earn, and they must be allowed to go free."[66]

Although we have no evidence about the way a Greek slave's wage was split between master and slave, we know or can estimate the usual pay for a rower, the cost of subsistence, the length of the sailing season, and the replacement cost of an average slave. A reasonable guess — and it is no more than that — might also assume a master interested in profit but also in a motivated rather than a desperate slave. In such a case, a slave rower who brought in no additional cash during the off-season might be allowed to keep one-sixth of his gross salary. He could then afford his freedom after about seven years. His master would pocket twice as much in profit each year and recoup the slave's price when the slave paid for his freedom.[67]

The closest parallel in Athens to the mixed crews of triremes appears in the work records for the construction of the Erechtheum temple, which also took place during the late Peloponnesian War.[68] There we find slaves, foreigners, and citizens in ratios similar to those on the crew list. The three different classes again received equal pay for equal work—something slave masters probably insisted on. Although a few managerial jobs were reserved for citizens, slaves typically followed the trades of their masters.

The only distinction between skill and wages among rowers was that between the men in the highest row of oarsmen, the *thranitai,* and the men in the other two rows. The thranitai, sitting on outriggers above the second row, had the most difficult rowing job. Aristophanes singles the thranitai out for praise as the saviors of the state while, in another play, he has fun at the expense of the lowest row, who, he says, were farted upon.[69] Thucydides mentions that trierarchs paid bonuses to attract the best thranitai.[70] If there were any distinction between slave and free among the rowers on a trireme, it might be that the thranitai tended to be free while slaves were relegated to the lower rows. In the absence of evidence either way, such a hierarchy among the rowers cannot be ruled out. The demands of military efficiency, however, can also be compelling: one can easily imagine sloppy, weak, or ill free thranitai being sent down in favor of fit slaves. In any case, the numbers probably never worked out exactly enough to allow a consistent distinction between slave and free rowers.

This system did not always produce ideal crews. When the Athenians on the Sicilian expedition captured the town of Hyccara, they enslaved the population. Some rowers bought these slaves—slaves were typically cheap at the time of capture—and convinced their trierarchs to take them as substitutes for themselves.[71] Experienced rowers therefore left the foundering Athenian expedition against Syracuse. The ships were stuck with extremely unmotivated slave rowers without individual masters responsible for them and with no training or experience in naval warfare. Moreover, other slave rowers were deserting.[72] But the fleet's disintegration included problems not only with the slaves but also with the Athenian allies who came on the campaign "expecting to make money rather than to fight" and who were also deserting.[73] As the Athenians' prospects in Sicily faded, anybody who could abandon them did so. Until this point, the mixed crews of slaves, foreigners, and Athenians seem to have functioned perfectly well.

This regular and usually uncontroversial use of slaves in the Athenian navy seems worlds away from the tension and conflict usually associated with arming slaves—often in the teeth of violent opposition from slave owners. Indeed, Athenian practices did not disrupt the system of slavery but were integrated into a pattern of incentives mainly intended for skilled urban slaves. The factors that made this system work were several. There was plenty of rowing—or better-paid work — to go around in imperial Athens. Citizens sometimes had to be drafted for the navy and supplemented with foreigners as well as slaves. Therefore, the free poor, whose clout in democratic Athens was considerable, were not typically deprived of jobs by slave rowers. Seasonal naval service allowed slave owners to keep their slaves more fully employed, and the wartime interruption of agriculture meant that farmers, too, were happy to have paying work for their slaves rather than being upset about losing needed labor.

From the slave's point of view, to be a rower was to earn a wage in a society with no sanctions against manumission. The power of the Athenian navy was also a significant factor. For much of the classical period, and especially in the first seventeen years of the Peloponnesian War, the Athenian navy rarely faced a significant challenge to its supremacy, so rowing in the navy may have seemed a job like any other.

Arginusae and Its Aftermath

Near the end of the Peloponnesian War, different circumstances evoked a categorically different pattern of recruitment, bitterly contested and disruptive of Athenian slavery. Athens, having already lost two large navies in Sicily and with much of its empire in revolt, was challenged at sea by a Spartan-led navy subsidized by the Persian king. In 407 the Spartans began to pay a higher salary and thus to outbid the Athenians for foreign rowers, probably the most numerous class of rowers in the Athenian navy. They probably also recruited many of the more than twenty thousand slaves who had fled from Athens to Decelea but no longer had a home to which they could easily return.[74] Experienced slave rowers may also have deserted directly from the Athenian to the Peloponnesian fleet, where they would be free men and might hope to keep all of their pay. So, in the spring of 406, the Athenian fleet was able to man only 70 ships instead of the more than 100 in use the previous year; the Spartan fleet grew from 90 to 140 and then to 170.[75] The Spartans chased and then blockaded the smaller Athenian fleet at Mytilene. A single Athenian trireme managed to run the blockade and get the news to Athens.

At this point, Athens was no longer able to man a fleet by its usual methods; rather, "they voted to go to the rescue with one hundred and ten ships, putting aboard all who were of military age, both slave and free; and within thirty days they manned the one hundred and ten ships and set forth. Even the cavalry class went aboard in considerable numbers."[76] Despite having only a few weeks' training, this fleet won a major victory over the Peloponnesian fleet at the battle of Arginusae. They destroyed or captured almost two-thirds of the enemy fleet and relieved the blockade of their own navy.

In order to accomplish this feat, the Athenians had to promise freedom to their slave rowers. And, even more startling, they had to grant citizenship to them. To be precise, they made the slaves "Plataeans" by giving them the same citizenship — without the right to certain hereditary priesthoods — with which they had honored their loyal Plataean allies when the latters' city was destroyed by the Spartans. Otherwise citizenship was ideally a strictly guarded prerogative requiring proof of Athenian descent on both sides. The Athenians, however, had to take these dramatic and unusual measures to overcome two major problems they faced in 406.

First, they needed to motivate a larger, different, and less tractable group of slaves to train as rowers and then to fight. When the cavalry class embarked on the ships, along came their numerous slaves. These belonged to larger households and often worked farms for masters who lived in the city. They generally had had little personal contact with their masters. Even more alienated were the slaves who worked in the appalling silver mines in southern Attica.[77] These mines seem finally to have stopped production at this point in the war; the most likely cause was the recruitment en masse of their slave workers to provide rowers for the Arginusae fleet. Promising them freedom was the only way to motivate these slaves. Some small portion of a rower's wage — which Athens paid less and less regularly as the war dragged on — would no longer do the trick.

Second, the Athenians needed to keep their crews. Winning the battle could not effect a lasting change in Athens' prospects as long as its rowers were deserting to the enemy for higher pay. The grant of citizenship in democratic Athens probably made staying with the Athenian navy a much more attractive option for the slaves. For slaves to return home would often be impossible after a lengthy absence — one often originally due to poverty or a military or political defeat — and would almost never entail the rights and security that an Athenian citizen possessed. The granting of freedom and citizenship solved Athens' manpower problems, if not its financial ones, for the rescue campaign and for the rest of the war — which ended in 404 BC after a crushing defeat and a horrific siege.

Many patriotic Athenians may have seen the necessity — and the fairness — of rewarding their slave rowers. The reaction of other slave owners, whose valuable property had been converted into fellow citizens, was probably one of outrage. Athens did not have many regular taxes and depended on special wartime taxes on capital and on liturgies such as the trierarchy, which could be extremely expensive. This wholesale liberation of Athenian slaves was nevertheless an extreme imposition.

In more modern cases, we often have copious evidence of planters' outrage at far less liberal policies than this. In the case of Athens, we are probably right to assume similar attitudes on the part of, for example, men whose fortunes were invested in mine slaves.[78] Unfortunately, our only hard evidence consists of an ambiguous couple of lines in a contemporary comedy, the *Frogs* by Aristophanes. The *parabasis* of a comedy, in which the author spoke in his own voice, sometimes contained serious advice.[79] Aristophanes begins the parabasis of *Frogs* by saying that it is "shameful" for men who have fought in only one naval battle to be straightaway Plataeans and masters instead of slaves.[80] Thus, he expresses slaveholders' dismay at the liberation and enfranchisement of the Arginusae slaves. Then, however, he retreats and claims that he approves of this policy. His real goal, it turns out, was not to overturn a *fait accompli* but rather to urge that the Athenians implicated in the oligarchic coup of 411 have their full citizens' rights restored. He points out that they fought in many naval battles and not just one, as many of the freed slaves had. He sums up with the argument that all who fight battles in the Athenian navy should be citizens with full rights. Thus, he includes both the Arginusae slaves and the suspected oligarchs in an argument based on a militaristic justification of political status.

There is little evidence that the liberation and enfranchisement of the Arginusae slaves prompted a reevaluation of slavery. Athens was, no doubt, short of slaves, especially males, by the end of the Peloponnesian War. Nevertheless, the economic and political impetus behind the institution of slavery had not changed, and in the fourth century Athens recovered and continued to be a slave society; mining activity reached its peak during that time. A distinguished scholar has suggested that Aristophanes' *Frogs* may mark the introduction of a new and much more active type of slave character into Athenian comedy and that this may best be understood in the context of the rewards bestowed on the Arginusae slaves the previous year.[81] All in all, Greek thinking about slaves, although it made the mobilization of slaves awkward, was flexible enough to tolerate granting citizenship to some slaves who had proved themselves worthy men. Greek ethnocentrism was not as systematic as some modern forms of racism, nor were the negative stereotypes of slaves absolute: some slaves could simply be normal people who had suffered a terrible fate.[82] Thus the triumph of the Arginusae slaves was quickly forgotten or explained away.

Perhaps the most significant change in attitude due to the use of slaves — and also mercenaries, often from areas considered half-barbarian — in the military was not a raising of their status but rather a demotion of the importance of military virtues as the final test of worth. Admittedly, this shift was a matter of degree rather than a complete rejection of the congruity of social and military status.[83] But Plato, for example, in the mid-fourth century takes aim at the words of Tyrtaeus, discussed above. He points out that many people who are good fighters are, in fact, stupid and brutish and that success in warfare cannot be the criterion for the judgment of individuals or of states.[84]

At first glance, the enfranchisement of the Arginusae slaves may seem one of the greatest benefits that the war brought to chattel slaves. A garbled version of the battle is found in one of the scholia to Aristophanes: "The slaves went out and defeated the Lacedaimonians near Arginusae and recovered the bodies of the slain. As a result they were freed and nobody was allowed to hit slaves."[85] It is hard to imagine an actual law forbidding masters to hit their own slaves, but already in the early Peloponnesian War, the mere threat of flight is supposed to have had a similar effect: *Clouds* begins with Strepsiades complaining that because of the war he can no longer beat his slaves — and thus they are sleeping late.[86]

The course of events, however, did not long favor the slaves of Arginusae. The navy remained in commission, and so few of the slaves are likely to have had a chance to be enrolled officially as citizens. In the following year, the Athenian navy was almost completely destroyed by a surprise attack while beached with its crews dispersed. Only nine of one hundred and eighty ships escaped. The Athenian citizens who were captured, two thousand of them, were massacred. Presumably, many of the Arginusae slaves did not choose to assert their citizenship at this particular juncture, although the alternative was likely reenslavement.

Indeed, there are only a few traces in the aftermath of the Peloponnesian War of slaves who had been freed for military service, although the numbers of slaves used on both sides must have surpassed ten thousand.[87] When the Sparta-backed oligarchy of the Thirty was ousted in 403, a proposal to grant citizenship to the non-Athenians who had helped restore the democracy was passed. The motion was blocked by a jury-court decision on the grounds that the proposal was unconstitutional owing to a procedural irregularity. Contributing to this reversal was the consideration that many of those to be enfranchised were "manifestly slaves."[88] We also possess an odd speech against a certain Pancleon, who returned to Athens after a lengthy absence in the 390s.[89] Pancleon claimed to be a Plataean — which could mean that he was an exile from Plataea or a slave of Plataean status like those of Arginusae — but two people claimed him as their slave. Although we have no record of the case's outcome, Pancleon may have depended too much on an emergency decree from a lost war, underestimated his owners' memories and power, and possessed no proof that he had been a beneficiary of Athens' brief generosity.

Two former slaves turned up in the Ten Thousand, the army of Greek mercenaries that fought for Cyrus in his abortive attempt to seize the throne of

Persia in 401 and then had to fight their way out of the center of the Persian Empire. Xenophon, an Athenian mercenary who recounted the expedition, mentions a certain Apollonides, an officer of Lydian origin, whose Greek was the dialect spoken in Thebes.[90] The likeliest explanation of this description is that Apollonides was a Theban slave imported from Lydia, a common source of slaves, who had won his freedom or escaped during the war. Without a home to return to, but apparently having enough military experience to be an officer, he had joined the mercenary force raised by Cyrus.

At another point the Ten Thousand were on the verge of attacking a people called the Macronians, who were defending a stream crossing located in difficult terrain.[91] An unnamed ex-slave from Athens, a member of the light infantry, stepped forward. He had realized that this was his original homeland and that the Macronians were his people. He arranged a truce and a safe-conduct for the army. Xenophon did not record whether he continued with the mercenaries or decided to stay with the Macronians. The chain of events that led a slave from Athens to be a soldier with the Ten Thousand might have involved the rewards to the Arginusae rowers or the desertion to Decelea or the arming of baggage carriers during the march of the Ten Thousand. As a slave soldier, at whose no doubt fascinating story we can only guess, he provides a fitting end for this account of the classical period.

Conclusion

The arming of slaves in classical Greece took many forms. Slaves served as armed police and unarmed hoplite attendants. They were armed as foot soldiers in crises, especially during sieges but occasionally as hoplites themselves. The discontent of Sparta's Helots was taken advantage of by its enemies; at the same time, Helot soldiers were crucial in its land forces, fighting regularly as hoplites and allowing Sparta to undertake lengthy and distant campaigns. Slaves rowed in Greek navies, both as a regular practice and in mass levies in emergencies. Although the participation of slaves in the military went against a strong strain of Greek thought that stressed a link between military service and political right, in extremis, Greek states did not hesitate to enlist their slaves. Such practices, so contrary to Greek citizen militarism, tended to be neglected in the extant sources.

The Macedonians' defeat of Athens and its allies at the battle of Chaeronia in 338 BC brought the Classical period to an end. The old Greek city-states entered a period of domination by large kingdoms and their professional or mercenary armies. The Hellenistic kingdoms resulting from the conquests of Alexander the Great were not essentially slave societies. Their Greek-speaking elite still owned slaves, but the rural economy was dominated by a dependent peasantry. Patterns and consequences of arming slaves changed as a result.[92] The Roman Empire, which eventually subjugated the Hellenistic kingdoms and united the Mediterranean, has its own long and complex history of arming slaves spanning more than seven centuries.[93] Roman slaves managed to stage massive slave revolts.[94] They were nevertheless occasionally freed for emergency infantry service, used regularly in the navy, and involved in civil wars. Although some continuities are obvious, differences in the scale of the Roman Empire, the distribution of slave ownership, military forces, and ideology about slavery and citizenship meant that the conditions and consequences of arming slaves were quite distinct from those in the small, independent city-states of classical Greece.

Notes

1. Greek warfare: Victor Hanson, *The Western Way of War: Infantry Battle in Classical Greece* (New York, 1989) and the essays collected in Victor Hanson, ed., *Hoplites: The Classical Greek Battle Experience* (London, 1991) provide a good introduction to hoplite warfare. W. Kendrick Pritchett, *The Greek State at War*, 5 vols. (Berkeley, 1971–1991) covers a large range of topics. J. K. Anderson, *Military Theory and Practice in the Age of Xenophon* (Berkeley, 1970) is an admirably readable and concise introduction. Josiah Ober, "Classical Greek Times," in *The Laws of War: Constraints on Warfare in the Western World*, ed. M. Howard, G. J. Andreopoulos, and M. R. Shulman (New Haven, 1994) and Victor Hanson, *The Other Greeks: The Family Farm and the Agrarian Roots of Western Civilization,* 2nd ed. (Berkeley, 1999, 219–286) provide explanations of the archaic limits and conventions in terms of the structure of Greek society. Peter Krentz, "Deception in Archaic and Classical Greek Warfare," in *War and Violence in Ancient Greece,* ed. Hans van Wees (London, 2000) and Hans van Wees, "Politics and the Battlefield: Ideology in Greek Warfare," in *The Greek World,* ed. A. Powell (London, 1995) make significant criticisms of this model.

2. Greek slavery: The seminal works of M. I. Finley — *Ancient Slavery and Modern Ideology* (Harmondsworth, 1980) and the articles collected in B. Shaw and R. Saller, eds., *Economy and Society in Ancient Greece* (New York, 1982) — still provide much of the conceptual framework for more recent research. N. R. E. Fisher, *Slavery in Classical Greece* (London, 1993) provides a balanced introduction with bibliography. Yvon Garlan, *Slavery in Ancient Greece,* trans. Janet Lloyd (Ithaca, NY, 1988) is another excellent overview from a Marxian perspective. T. E. J. Wiedemann, *Greek and Roman Slavery* (London, 1981) is a useful collection of translated ancient sources. On the controversial role of slaves in agriculture see Michael Jameson, "Agriculture and Slavery in Classical Athens," *Classical Journal* 73 (1977–1978): 122–141; Michael Jameson, "Agricultural Labor in Ancient Greece," in *Proceedings of the Seventh International Symposium at the Swedish Institute at Athens,* ed. B. Wells (Stockholm, 1992); Hanson, *Other Greeks* , 63–70; contra Ellen M. Wood, *Peasant-Citizen and Slave* (New York, 1988).

3. Lysias 12.19; Xenophon *Ways and Means* 4.14–15.

4. See Peter Hunt, "The Slaves and the Generals of Arginusae," *American Journal of Philology* 122 (2001): 359–380.

5. General studies of slaves in Greek warfare: Garlan, *Slavery in Ancient Greece,* 163–176, provides an English-language summary of many of the conclusions of his earlier articles. Karl-Wilhelm Welwei, *Unfreie im Antiken Kriegsdienst,* vol. 1, *Athen und Sparta* (Wiesbaden, 1974) is the only comprehensive treatment of the subject. My recent book, Peter Hunt, *Slaves, Warfare, and Ideology in the Greek Historians* (Cambridge, UK, 1998), argues for greater slave participation than Garlan and Welwei accept and discerns a pattern of neglect in our sources. Detailed reactions are found in the reviews by Paul Cartledge in *Slavery and Abolition* 20 (1999): 137–138, by Jonathan Hall in *Classical Philology* 94 (1999): 461–466, and by N. R. E. Fisher in *American Historical Review* 106 (2001): 235–236. Studies of specific cases of arming slaves and related issues appear in the relevant footnotes below.

6. *IG* I³.1032; Thucydides 1.55.1, 8.84.2; Herodotus 6.15; Diodorus 14.58.1, Decree of Themistocles, printed in Michael Jameson, "The Provisions for Mobilization in the Decree of Themistocles," *Historia* 12 (1963): 385–404. The proportions of slaves implied, more or less firmly, in these sources are as follows: more than 20 percent, about 80 percent, more than 50 percent, more than 80 percent (?), and 50 percent (?), respectively — see text at note 60 for a discussion of some of these passages. My minimum of ten thousand of sixty thousand, 17 percent of the total, is conservative.

7. Thucydides 7.27.5.

8. Hunt, *Slaves, Warfare, and Ideology,* 108–115.

9. D. M. Lewis, "The Thirty Years' Peace," in *The Cambridge Ancient History: The Fifth Century,* 2nd ed., ed. D. M. Lewis, J. Boardman, J. K. Davies, and M. Ostwald, 2:121–127 (Cambridge, UK, 1992), surveys the controversy.

10. Homer *Iliad* 12.315–321. See *The Iliad of Homer,* translated with an introduction by Richmond Lattimore (Chicago, 1951).

11. Hanson, *Other Greeks,* 219–242, provides a lucid introduction with bibliography to the complex and contested relation of military change and the expansion of political rights. See also Yvon Garlan, *War in the Ancient World: A Social History,* trans. Janet Lloyd (London, 1975).

12. Lysias 10.1.

13. Tyrtaeus 1 in Richmond Lattimore, trans., *Greek Lyrics* (Chicago, 1949), 14.

14. See most recently Barry Strauss, "The Athenian Trireme, School of Democracy," in *Demokratia: A Conversation on Democracies Ancient and Modern,* ed. J. Ober and C. Hedrick (Princeton, 1996); Barry Strauss, "Perspectives on the Death of Fifth-Century Athenian Seamen," in *War and Violence in Ancient Greece,* ed. Hans van Wees (London, 2000); and David Pritchard, " 'The Fractured Imaginary': Popular Thinking on Military Matters in Fifth-Century Athens," *Ancient History: Resources for Teachers* 28 (1998): 38–61.

15. Xenophon [pseud.], *The Constitution of the Athenians* 1.2.

16. The scholarship on Greek attitudes toward slaves is huge. My views can be found in Hunt, *Slaves, Warfare, and Ideology* (with bibliography), 126–138 (polar opposites to citizens), 146–160 (defeated in war), 160–164 (childish and cowardly), 48–50 and 158–159 (inferior foreigners).

17. See David Cohen, *Law, Violence, and Community in Classical Athens* (Cambridge, UK, 1995) on the maintenance of order within Athens. See Oscar Jacob, *Les esclaves publics a Athènes* (New York, 1979), 53–78, on the Scythian slaves.

18. For example, Aristophanes *Thesmophoriazusae* 1082–1135, 1176–1226.

19. Paradoxically, this sensitivity probably derived from the Athenian practice of slavery: to be answerable with one's body was the mark of a slave (Demosthenes 22.55, 24.166–167). I owe this interpretation of the Scythian slaves to Margaret Imber, "Cops and Robbers and Democratic Ideology," paper presented to the annual meeting of the American Philological Association, San Diego, December, 1995.

20. Thucydides 7.75.5; cf. Pausanias 1.29.7 with D. W. Bradeen, "The Athenian Casualty List of 464 BC," *Hesperia* 36 (1967): 321–328.

21. On slave revolts see M. Fuks, "Slave War and Slave Troubles in Chios," in *Social Conflict in Ancient Greece* (Leiden, 1984); Paul Cartledge, "Rebels and Sambos in Classical Greece: A Comparative View," in *Crux: Essays in Greek History Presented to G. E. M. de Ste. Croix,* ed. Paul Cartledge and F. D. Harvey (Exeter, 1985); Garlan, *Slavery in Ancient Greece,* 176–191.

22. Xenophon *Hiero* 4.3; see also *Hiero* 10.4, Plato *Republic* 578d–579b, and Kenneth J. Dover, *Greek Popular Morality* (Oxford, 1974), 114 on this attitude.

23. A Hellenistic writer, Philon of Byzantium (5.4.14–15), advises that it's a good idea for besieging armies publicly to promise freedom for deserting slaves. Then the defenders will not be able to arm their slaves for fear of desertion or rebellions. They will also have to feed their slaves better and will run out of food sooner.

24. Hyperides fragment 28 in C. Jensen, *Hyperidis Orationes Sex* (Leipzig, 1917).

25. Xenophon *Hellenica* 1.2.1.

26. Hunt, *Slaves, Warfare, and Ideology,* 190–194; Leonhard A. Burckhardt, *Bürger und Soldaten: Aspecke der Politischen und Militärischen Rolle Athenischer Bürger im Kriegwesen des 4 Jahrhundert v. Chr.* (Stuttgart, 1996), 104, 114, 140.

27. Thucydides 3.27.

28. Hunt, *Slaves, Warfare, and Ideology,* 26–28. Almost all scholars accept the story of armed slaves at Marathon, since it is hard to imagine a reason for the story to be invented.

29. See Paul Cartledge, *Agesilaos and the Crisis of Sparta* (Baltimore, 1987) and Jean Ducat, *Les Helots* (Paris, 1990) on Helots. The articles about Sparta collected in Anton Powell, ed., *Classical Sparta: Techniques Behind Her Success* (Norman, OK, 1988), Anton Powell and Stephen Hodkinson, eds., *The Shadow of Sparta* (London, 1994), and Stephen Hodkinson and Anton Powell, eds., *Sparta: New Perspectives* (London, 1999) give an ample and up-to-date bibliography.

30. Thucydides 4.118.7, 5.23.3.

31. Hunt, *Slaves, Warfare, and Ideology,* 26–31.

32. Thucydides 5.23.3.

33. Thucydides 4.36.

34. Russell Meiggs and David Lewis, *A Selection of Greek Historical Inscriptions to the End of the Fifth Century BC,* rev. ed. (Oxford, 1988), 223–224 (no. 74).

35. For the controversial nature of the expression "Messenian" see Hunt, *Slaves, Warfare, and Ideology,* 68–69, 181.

36. Diodorus 13.64.5–7; Xenophon *Hellenica* 1.2.18.

37. An Athenian general still possessed an overenthusiastic bodyguard of Messenians in the 390s: *Hellenica Oxyrhnchia* XX (XV) 3.

38. Alcidamas, in scholia to Aristotle *Rhetoric* 1373b18. See J. Vogt, *Ancient Slavery and the Ideal of Man*, trans. T. Wiedemann (Cambridge, 1975), G. Cambiano, "Aristotle and the Anonymous Opponents of Slavery," in *Classical Slavery*, ed. M. I. Finley (London, 1987), and, most recently, Peter Garnsey, *Ideas of Slavery from Aristotle to Augustine* (Cambridge, 1996) for Greek criticisms of slavery. See Hunt, *Slaves, Warfare, and Ideology,* 177–184, for more details about the liberation of the Helots and its effect on thinking about slavery.

39. On early indications of Messenian mythology see Hunt, *Slaves, Warfare, and Ideology,* 76–79.

40. Pausanias 9.15.6.

41. Thucydides 7.57.8.

42. Thucydides 7.19.3, 7.58.3.

43. For interpretations of this phenomenon see R. J. A. Talbert, "The Role of the Helots in the Class Struggle at Sparta," *Historia* 38 (1989): 22–40; Paul Cartledge, "Richard Talbert's Revision of the Spartan-Helot Struggle: A Reply," *Historia* 40 (1991): 379–381; Hunt, *Slaves, Warfare, and Ideology,* 38–39, 115–120.

44. Herodotus 9.10.1, 9.28.2, 9.29.1.

45. Peter Hunt, "The Helots at the Battle of Plataea," *Historia* 46 (1997): 129–144, includes a discussion of previous scholarship.

46. Thucydides 5.64.2, 5.57.1.

47. Thucydides 7.58.3.

48. Thucydides 4.26.5, 4.80.3.

49. See Talbert, "Role of the Helots," 26, for the numbers of Neodamodeis; see Cartledge, *Agesilaos*, 38, 167–168, for the number of Spartans.

50. Xenophon *Hellenica* 3.3.6, 6.1.14; Xenophon *Agesilaus* 2.7–8.

51. Xenophon, a contemporary with Spartan connections, claims that Sparta enlisted six thousand Helots (Xenophon *Hellenica* 6.5.28–29; cf. Diodorus 15.65.6), but there were many desertions (Plutarch *Agesilaus* 32.7).

52. Plato *Laws* 777c–d; Aristotle *Politics* 1330a25–28.

53. Thucydides 1.49.1–3.

54. For example, Aristophanes *Wasps* 1097, 1118–1119; Xenophon [pseud.], *Constitution of the Athenians* 1.2. See Hunt, *Slaves, Warfare, and Ideology,* 124–126, for further examples and discussion.

55. Regular use of slaves in the navy: Hunt, *Slaves, Warfare, and Ideology,* 83–101; Hunt, "Slaves and the Generals"; A. J. Graham, "Thucydides 7.13.2 and the Crews of Athenian Triremes," *Transactions of the American Philological Association* 122 (1992): 257–270; Graham, "Thucydides 7.13.2 and the Crews of Athenian Triremes: An Addendum," *Transactions of the American Philological Association* 128 (1998): 89–114. Contra: M. Amit, *Athens and the Sea: A Study in Athenian Sea Power* (Brussels, 1965), 33; Lionel Casson, "Galley Slaves," *Transactions of the American Philological Association* 97 (1966): 35–44; J. S. Morrison, J. F. Coates, and N. B. Rankov, *The Athenian Trireme: The History and Reconstruction of an Ancient Greek Warship,* 2nd ed. (Cambridge, 2000). Welwei, *Unfreie im Antiken Kriegsdienst,* 65–104, takes a middle position.

56. Thucydides 1.55.1.

57. Thucydides 2.103.1.

58. Thucydides 8.84.2.

59. Thucydides 8.73.5.

60. This inscription, originally *IG* 2².1951, is now *IG* 1³.1032. The most complete discussion is still D. R. Laing Jr., *A New Interpretation of the Athenian Naval Catalogue IG II² 1951* (Ann Arbor, 1966), but Graham, "Thucydides 7.13.2" and Graham, "Thucydides 7.13.2: Addendum," focus on the slaves and include recent bibliographies.

61. Vincent Gabrielsen, *Financing the Athenian Fleet: Public Taxation and Social Relations* (Baltimore, 1994).

62. Regular conscription of citizens for naval service is mentioned in the fourth century: Demosthenes [pseud.] 50.6, 50.7, 50.16. The inscription, *IG* 1³.1127–1131, suggests a regular draft of citizens — as opposed to emergency levies — already in the fifth century. See Mogens Hansen, *Demography and Democracy: The Number of Athenian Citizens in the Fourth Century B.C.* (Herning, Denmark, 1985), 23–24.

63. Demosthenes [pseud.] 50.7.

64. Graham, "Thucydides 7.13.2: Addendum," 98–102, is the most recent treatment of the ownership of slave rowers. See Vincent Rosivach, "Manning the Athenian Fleet, 433–426," *American Journal of Ancient History* 10 (1985): 41–66 on the types of free rowers in different navies.

65. Compare Keith Bradley, *Slaves and Masters in the Roman Empire: A Study in Social Control* (Oxford, 1987), 81–112, for Rome.

66. Xenophon [pseud.] *Constitution of the Athenians* 1.11.

67. These rough calculations for the classical period require several assumptions, which I regard as likely enough but neither certain nor applicable to all cases: A rower's full wage at the beginning of the Peloponnesian War was 6 obols per day. I assume 3 obols per day for the slave's living expenses. Although we have references to 2 obols per day as a subsistence wage, I allocate a bit of extra money for clothes and incidental expenses. So 6 − 3 = 3 obols to be divided by master and slave. Our hypothetical master takes 2 obols per day and the slave 1 obol per day. A sailing season of 100 days — assuming the slave is with a large summer navy rather than a smaller year-round squadron — yields the slave 100 obols per year. An average slave price is 750 obols, so a thrifty slave can afford his freedom after seven and one-half years of rowing. On rowers' wages see the discussion and bibliography in Margaret L. Cook, "Timocrates' 50 Talents and the Cost of Ancient Warfare," *Eranos* 88 (1990): 69–97. On the sailing season see Rosivach, "Manning the Athenian Fleet," 41–44. See Hanson, *Other Greeks,* 68–69, 351 n. 34, for bibliography regarding slave prices.

68. R. H. Randall, "The Erechtheum Workmen," *American Journal of Archaeology* 57 (1953): 199–210.

69. Aristophanes *Acharnians* 161–162; Aristophanes *Frogs* 1074.

70. Thucydides 6.31.3.

71. Thucydides 7.13.2. Note that these replacements were done entirely on the authority of the trierarch against the will of the general in charge.

72. See Graham, "Thucydides 7.13.2," 257–259, on Thucydides 7.13.2.

73. Thucydides 7.13.3.

74. Hunt, *Slaves, Warfare, and Ideology,* 111–114.

75. Xenophon *Hellenica* 1.5.4–8, 1.5.10, 1.5.15, 1.5.20, 1.6.3, 1.6.16.

76. Ibid., 1.6.24 (trans. Brownson). See Hunt, "Slaves and the Generals," for a full treatment of the slaves in the Arginusae navy and the issues raised by their use.

77. On slave miners in Attica see Siegfried Lauffer, *Die Bergwerkssklaven von Laurion,* 2nd ed. (Wiesbaden, 1979). For a brief overview of slave miners in ancient Greece and Rome see Peter Hunt, "Greek and Roman Mines," in *The Macmillan Encyclopedia of World Slavery,* ed. P. Finckleman and J. C. Miller (New York, 1998).

78. In Hunt, "Slaves and the Generals," I argue that the resentment at the liberation of the Arginusae slaves may have contributed to the unfair trial and execution of the victorious Athenian generals after the battle .

79. Indeed, the Athenians took some of the advice in Aristophanes' *Frogs* and honored him for giving it. W. Geoffrey Arnott, "A Lesson from the *Frogs,*" *Greece and Rome* 38 (1991): 18–23.

80. Aristophanes *Frogs* 692–702.

81. K. J. Dover, *Aristophanes: Frogs* (Oxford, 1993), 50.

82. Bernard Williams, *Shame and Necessity* (Berkeley, 1993), 106–118, presents an interesting analysis of this strain of thought but does not sufficiently acknowledge Greek prejudice against slaves (see Hunt, *Slaves, Warfare, and Ideology,* 160 n. 85).

83. See Burckhardt, *Bürger und Soldaten.*

84. See Hunt, *Slaves, Warfare, and Ideology,* 194–202, on Plato *Laws* 629a–630b and Aristotle *Politics* 1255a13–16.

85. Scholia to Aristophanes *Clouds* 6 in D. Holwerda, *Prolegomena de Comoedia; Scholia in Acharnenses, Equites, Nubes,* vol. 3, pt. 1 (Groningen, The Netherlands, 1977), 9.

86. Aristophanes *Clouds* 6–7. Compare Aristophanes *Peace* 451.

87. See note 6 above and accompanying text for the minimum number of ten thousand slaves. A list of slaves from Chios, probably freed for Peloponnesian military service, has been found: L. Robert, "Sur des inscriptions de Chios," *Bulletin de Correspondance Hellénique* 59 (1935): 453–470. Sparta, too, freed Helots for naval service.

88. Aristotle *Ath. Pol.* 40.2. See also Phillip Harding, "Metics, Foreigners or Slaves? The Recipients of Honours in *IG* II².10," *Zeitschrift für Papyrologie und Epigraphik* 67 (1987): 176–182.

89. Lysias *Against Pancleon* (23). See also Lysias *Against Simon* (3) 5, 33.

90. Xenophon *Anabasis* 3.1.26, 3.1.31.

91. Ibid., 4.8.4.

92. Karl-Wilhelm Welwei, *Unfreie im Antiken Kriegsdienst,* vol. 2, *Die kleineren und mittleren griechischen Staaten und die hellenistischen Reiche* (Wiesbaden, 1977).

93. Karl-Wilhelm Welwei, *Unfreie im Antiken Kriegsdienst,* vol. 3, *Rom* (Wiesbaden, 1988); Norbert Rouland, *Les esclaves Romains en temps de guerre* (Brussels, 1977).

94. Keith Bradley, *Slavery and Rebellion in the Roman World, 140 BC–70 BC* (Bloomington, 1989).

The Mamlūk Institution, or One Thousand Years of Military Slavery in the Islamic World

REUVEN AMITAI

Introduction

The importance, scope, and duration of military slavery in the Islamic world have no parallel in human history. From the early ninth century CE to the first decades of the nineteenth, from Egypt to the edges of Central Asia and India, military slavery was often the primary form of military organization. Even when military slaves — usually known as *ghulāms* or *mamlūks* — did not constitute the majority of the army of a Muslim state, they often formed its predominant element. At times, and for long periods, military slaves exploited their prowess and importance to achieve political influence, more than occasionally becoming the de facto and even de jure rulers of the state. This chapter attempts an overview of this important topic, discussing the origins of military slavery in the Islamic world, its development, crystallization, and eventual disappearance.

Although there has never been a single work devoted to the phenomenon of Muslim military slavery, it has received much attention within the framework of general histories of medieval and early modern Islam. Furthermore, particular aspects of Islamic military slavery or periods when military slaves were of exceptional importance have been the subject of specialized books and articles.[1] Readers who have some familiarity with medieval Muslim history — and the matter of military slavery in particular — will note my debt to the works and thinking of the late David Ayalon. Although the Ayalonian model of military slavery needs refinement and expansion, I find that on the whole it provides a satisfying framework for the examination of the phenomenon, certainly for the later Middle Ages.[2] Saying this, I should mention the important observation of Jürgen Paul, who has drawn attention to the difficulty of generalizing on the subject of Islamic military slavery given the dearth of detailed studies of specific periods.[3] His caveat can be taken to heart, but with due caution I will forge ahead, attempting an overview that I hope will convince historians from other fields of the significance of military slavery in Islamic history. This is in light of some recent general works about slavery that give little space to military slavery in general and hardly mention its decisive role in the political, social, and economic development of the Islamic Middle East.[4]

Given limitations of space, this chapter is both a survey and an interpretive essay that puts military slavery front and center in the history of Islam. While not neglecting the internal dynamics of the institution, I emphasize showing the decisive role often played by military slaves, mostly Turks, in Middle Eastern history. There is less reference to primary sources than to the works of modern scholarship. Considering that we are dealing with about a thousand years of history for most of the Muslim world, it could not be much different in the framework of a chapter in a collected work. Some emphasis is placed on the origins of the institution in the ʿAbbāsid Caliphate of the early ninth century. Relatively wide coverage is also devoted to the so-called Mamlūk Sultanate, which ruled Egypt and Syria from the mid-thirteenth century until the coming of the Ottoman Empire to the region in 1516–17. The Mamlūk Sultanate, in which mostly mamlūks ruled in name and not just behind the scenes, commands special attention for at least two reasons. The first is the pivotal role of this state in world history, not least for having stopped the Mongol conquests in the Middle East and having eradicated the Crusader presence in the Levant. Second, owing to the rich historical writing issuing from the sultanate, the mamlūk phenomenon is best documented for this period. With necessary caution, one might apply some of the insights derived from this era to earlier periods.

I would like to emphasize one point at this stage: there is little that is particularly Islamic about this large-scale military slavery. Rather, I am discussing a social and military institution within the premodern Islamic world. Although slavery, and by extension military slavery, is recognized by Islamic law,[5] there is nothing inherently Islamic about the institution from a religious point of view. We might identify antecedents to the phenomenon in pre-Islamic and early Islamic society and note certain factors in the Muslim state that contributed to its rise, but the emergence of military slavery was not an a priori necessity dictated by early Muslim religion, law, or society. Rather, as I hope to show, a marriage of circumstances (whether happy or not is another matter) took place, to which were added deliberate decisions by certain rulers. Once established, military slavery in the Islamic world took on a dynamic of its own, although individual rulers could indeed contribute to its growth and exact form. Only when it had clearly outlived its usefulness, and because of its obvious burden on rulers and on society at large, was military slavery, by now somewhat trans-formed from the original "medieval" model, finally eradicated.[6]

The Origins of Military Slavery in the Caliphate

The appearance of large-scale military slavery in the Islamic world is justifiably connected with the name of the ʿAbbāsid caliph Abū Isḥāq al-Muʿtaṣim (r. 833–42), the third son of the famous Hārūn al-Rashīd (r. 789–809) to take the throne. Although during his rule the phenomenon appears to have been full-blown, the antecedents go back some time. In order to best illuminate Islamic military slavery, I first trace briefly the development of the army of the Islamic state in its first two centuries of existence.

The Muslim army that burst out of the Arabian Peninsula in the 630s was composed almost exclusively of Arab tribesmen, not all of whom, however, were nomadic bedouin. Led by capable commanders and faced with enemies in relative disarray (the Byzantine and Sassanian Empires), these forces suc-ceeded in the space of a generation in conquering Syria, Egypt, Iraq, Iran, and much of the Caucasus and North Africa. Already in this early period, non-Arab elements — mostly from Iran — were integrated into the army of the ex-panding Muslim Empire, which was strapped for suitable manpower. Under the Umayyads (661–750) the army remained mainly Arab but was increas-ingly professionalized and limited to troops from Syria, the stronghold of the dynasty.[7] The coming of the ʿAbbāsids, whose armed revolution against the Umayyads was successfully launched from Khurasan in northeastern Iran,[8] heralded a fundamental change in the composition of the army. This trans-formation was probably not immediately discerned, since Arab tribes sta-tioned in the east and, in particular, Arab commanders were among the major elements in the ʿAbbāsid revolutionary armies.[9] But Abū Muslim, the com-mander of the revolutionary forces, had already instigated an important change by registering the non-Arab troops in the *dīwān* (the payment list) not by genealogy (that is, tribe) but by residence, thereby facilitating the de-cline and eventual disappearance of the Arab tribal component of the caliphal army.[10] Early on, part of the ʿAbbāsid army was composed of mixed Arab-

Iranian troops from Khurasan, some no longer speaking Arabic. These troops were known as Abnā' ("sons of") Khurāsān, although the appellation may have been initially applied also to the Arab tribal forces who had been stationed in Khurasan. Successive waves of Abnā' Khurāsān in the first seventy years or so of 'Abbāsid rule contributed to the ever-growing non-Arab composition of the army. These newer Abnā' contingents were also supplemented by converted Iranians from Transoxania (mainly modern Uzbekistan), which had been decisively conquered in the late Umayyad period. These Transoxanian forces, which may have contained some Turkish elements, were valued for their military skills because they had competed for generations with the Turkish tribes of the nearby Eurasian steppes.[11] Thus, during the early 'Abbāsid period, an increasing proportion of the Muslim army originated in the eastern part of the empire and beyond. From a military point of view, at least, the eyes of the Muslim political establishment were looking east and were soon to fall squarely on the Turks, to whom I have just alluded.

The Arab component in the army declined in turn. As stated above, much of the actual fighting done on behalf of the 'Abbāsids during their revolution (747–750) was conducted by Arab tribesmen, and Arabs had remained a force of some importance even in the civil war (811–813) between the two sons of Hārūn al-Rashīd, al-Amīn (809–813) and al-Ma'mūn (813–833).[12] Yet gradually the Arabs had been shunted aside in the military. During the reign of al-Ma'mūn, they were steadily removed from the *dīwān*.[13] Two factors seem to account for this development. First, large swaths of the Arab population had settled in the towns and cities (and perhaps also in the countryside), adopting a sedentary lifestyle and mixing with elements of the indigenous population that had converted to Islam. By settling, these Arabs had gradually lost their warlike qualities, or at least their desire to go to war. Second, the Arab populations, both the settled Arabs and those who remained nomads, had tribal, political, and religious agendas that competed with the interests of the ruler. Their loyalty, as a consequence, was often far from assured.

Another antecedent to military slavery was the institution known as the *mawālī*. The term *mawālī* (plural of *mawlā*) is used in several ways in early Islamic history, leading to some confusion among generations of modern students and scholars. It was applied originally to clients of Arab tribes, then to the earlier converts to Islam, who had indeed also become clients of Arab (now Muslim) tribesmen, and subsequently to all converts to Islam among the conquered population. By the early 'Abbāsid period it was being used in this last-mentioned sense less and less: with the exponential increase in converts and the increasing mixing with Arab Muslims, a distinctive term was thus unnecessary. *Mawālī* then became more frequently applied to one particular type of convert: the former prisoners of war and freed slaves, often from faraway lands, who at some point converted to Islam and upon their release remained loyal to a patron, often the ruler. These freedmen, whom Ayalon called "imported *mawālī*" to distinguish them from mawālī who were local converts, appear to have been predominantly of an eastern provenance, that is Iranians, Transoxanians, and even Turks. There were many hundreds of them at the ʿAbbāsid court, where they were cultivated and given great responsibility, even fulfilling at times a military role. These imported mawālī, certainly when they were fighting mawālī, represent a kind of proto-mamlūk institution and display most of the characteristics of military slavery: isolation and alienation from the local population, along with loyalty to and dependence on a patron, not necessarily a royal one.[14] As Ayalon noted, "the ties between a slave and patron were not severed with the slave's manumission. Mutual loyalty (*walāʾ*) constituted the basis of their relations."[15]

One notable example of these fighting mawālī can be seen from a passage by the historian al-Ṭabarī (d. 923) describing the behavior of a senior officer's entourage of freedmen during the civil war between al-Amīn and al-Maʾmūn. The former's governor in the province of Ahwāz in southwest Iran, one Muḥammad b. Yazīd al-Muhallabī, found himself in a losing battle and told his mawālī to flee. They refused, replying: "By God! If we do so, we would cause you great injustice. You have manumitted us from slavery, and elevated us from a humble position and raised us from poverty to riches. And after all that, how can we abandon you and leave you in such a state. Oh no! Instead of that we shall advance in front of you and die under your steed. May God curse this world and life altogether after your death." There upon the mawālī hamstrung their horses and fought together with their patron until they were all killed.[16]

Abū Isḥāq al-Muʿtaṣim's creation of the first mamlūk "regiment" occurred during the second decade of the eighth century, early in the reign of his brother al-Maʾmūn, a caliph known for his efforts to create a more centralized state. During his twenty-year reign al-Maʾmūn must have at least tacitly agreed to the establishment of a new and somewhat different fighting force, one composed exclusively of Turkish slaves. This unit, numbering about three thousand to four thousand troops, was a decisive factor behind Abū Isḥāq's success in gaining the throne at his brother's death. Their role, however, was not only internal politics and security, although this was evidently their initial purpose. The mamlūk regiment also eventually played an important part in some of the later campaigns against the Byzantines on the northern Syrian–eastern Anatolian frontier.[17]

The establishment of the first large-scale royal mamlūk formation represented a convergence of several factors. The first is the mawālī system, combining alienation from the local population, patron-client relations, and usually eastern provenance. To this was added the element of slavery (*riqq*), an institution with pre-Islamic Arabian and Near Eastern antecedents that had been further legitimized and crystallized in early Islam.[18] According to Hugh Kennedy, that these Turks were slaves was not the decisive factor; rather what was important was that they were from the periphery; he compares them with the armies of other states where military forces were composed of marginal elements.[19] Kennedy is correct, of course, to stress the peripheral nature of the mamlūks, to whom I will refer henceforth as the military slaves of the caliphate.[20] It may be, however, that he has gone too far in downplaying the significance of their passing through slavery. Rather, this status institutionalized their subservient position vis-à-vis their patrons and their difference from the indigenous population, and it facilitated their importation from far away. That military slavery in some form was to be found for a thousand years — in spite of a modification of the system — indicates the importance attributed to it in political and military circles.[21]

The third significant factor was the decisive inclusion of the Turks, who at this point entered the Islamic Middle East for the first time in relatively large numbers.[22] Muslim rulers and generals had been looking eastward for some time, and quality military manpower had long been imported from the regions near the Eurasian steppe. In an early example, the governor of Iraq, ʿUbaydallāh b. Ziyād b. Abīhi, had brought in a large number of Bukharans from Transoxania in 686 to serve in his army.[23] Apparently, the peoples of Transoxania and Khurasan had achieved this reputation because of the expertise that they had achieved fighting the Turks, then living in the steppe north of the Jaxartes (Sir Darya) River. In the early ninth century, the decision was made to seek what appears to have been the best available soldiers. The Turks had numerous advantages, not the least being that they were pagans and thus could be enslaved with legal ease.[24] Evidently they were also available in relatively large numbers.[25] Most important, however, the Turks of the steppe were well known for their outstanding military qualities, such as fortitude and discipline, as well as for horsemanship and archery. Relatively recent arrivals in this part of the Eurasian steppe, they were heirs to a centuries-old military tradition going back to the Scythians and beyond, which combined mobility with "firepower." The former was directly derived from their lifestyle of nomadic pastoralism, which was facilitated by the domestication of the horse. Inhabitants of the steppe were by definition potential cavalrymen. "Firepower," anachronistic as it may initially appear, accurately describes the effect of massed and disciplined archers using the composite bow to great effect.

This combination of cavalry and archery had made nomads from the Eurasian steppe — including those who came before and after the various Turkic group-ings — the scourge of much of the adjacent sedentary world: China, Iran, Asia Minor, and Europe. The introduction of the stirrup in the early modern period only contributed to the effectiveness of Eurasian mounted archery.[26]

Many contemporary (or nearly contemporary) Muslim sources waxed effu-sive about the martial qualities of the Turks. Several examples will illustrate these characteristics and the way they were perceived by a few contemporary and slightly later Muslim observers. The tenth-century geographer al-Iṣṭakhrī wrote: "And the Turks constituted [the caliph's] armies because of their superi-ority over the other races in prowess, valour, courage and intrepidity."[27] Al-Jāḥiẓ, a ninth-century bellettrist from Baghdad, writes that [the Turks] "be-came to Islam a source of reinforcement and an enormous army, and to the Caliphs a protection and a shelter and an invulnerable armour as well as an innermost garment worn under the upper garment."[28] Another tenth-century geographer, Ibn Ḥawqal, says of the Turks: "The most precious slaves are those arriving [in Khurasan] from the land of the Turks. There is no equal to the Turkish slaves among all the slaves of the earth."[29] The last passage is short on details regarding the advantages of the Turks, but it does provide a further indication of the esteem in which they were held.

The idea behind the system of military slavery enacted by al-Muʿtasim, perhaps abetted by al-Maʾmūn, was to take this quality military manpower as a sort of raw material. Little is known of the actual working details of this incipient system, but I might extrapolate from the mamlūk sultanate of several centuries later, aware that I may well be anachronistic. Young Turks were enslaved and imported at a relatively young age (probably eight to twelve years), when they had been somewhat formed by their environment and so-ciety and had picked up the rudiments of riding and archery. They were con-verted to Islam, given some basic religious instruction, and more military training over several years, raising their nascent skills to a high level. Being isolated by origin, language, and location from the local population, they focused their loyalty on their patron.[30] These first mamlūks were, of course, loyal to their patron, Prince Abū Isḥāq, soon to become Caliph al-Muʿtasim.

This reconstruction of the origins of the institution of military slavery in Islam is at variance with that offered by some scholars. Muhammad Shaban has called into question the importance of the Turkish element, seeing *Turk* as a general appellation for a hodgepodge of peoples from the periphery of the Islamic world and beyond. In addition, he doubted the importance of the role of slavery, noting that several significant Turks were in fact free and of noble background.[31] Similarly, Christopher Beckwith suggested that the origin of the mamlūk institution was not in slavery; rather, it was the custom of Central Asian rulers to surround themselves with entourages of "youths" culled from the sons of noble retainers and allies.[32] Both of these approaches have been cogently rebutted by Matthew Gordon, who in his recent book *The Breaking of a Thousand Swords* shows inter alia that we are indeed dealing with a large number of Turkish-speaking slaves. Gordon states that both authors fail to discuss "the body of evidence indicating an early, servile/slave status on the part of the Turks serving al-Muʿtaṣim. . . . There is no question but that many of the Samarran Turks, at an initial stage, were both slaves and soldiers: again, it would be perverse not to relate their history closely to the *Mamlūk* institution."[33]

Not long after ascending to the throne, al-Muʿtaṣim took the radical step of establishing a new capital, Sāmarrā, about one hundred and twenty kilometers north of Baghdad and also along the Tigris River. The caliph seems to have had two goals: first, to isolate his guard corps, in the hope of keeping these troops as "uncontaminated" as possible by the local population and its preoccupations, and second, to defuse intensifying opposition from other units of the ʿAbbāsid army and the inhabitants.[34] Sāmarrā was to remain the caliphal capital for more than fifty years. Built ex nihilo, the capital featured an enormous hippodrome constructed to train the mamlūks in horsemanship, including attacking in small tactical units while shooting arrows, before wheeling around and permitting the approach of another unit.[35]

Eunuchs played an important role in the training of the young mamlūks. In a posthumously published study Ayalon suggested that eunuchs contributed indirectly to the introduction of military slavery. A large body of royal eunuchs had long been in existence at the caliphal court (even before the ʿAbbāsids). The ruler placed great trust in this group (primarily as guardians of his harem), who in a sense were already involved in education (of the children in the harem), making them ready-made educators of the young mamlūks. Their particular physiognomy perhaps also made them natural preventers of sexual harassment from older mamlūks. With such educational infrastructure already in place, the establishment of a large unit of military slaves was greatly facilitated. In short, many eunuchs continued to serve in the harem in addition to being the "training sergeants" of the mamlūk corps, a position they were also to enjoy later in the mamlūk sultanate of Egypt and Syria. In court politics, eunuchs were also to play a key role as intermediaries between the mamlūks and the royal harem, particularly at times of political instability.[36]

Although some young slaves might be picked up as captives in the intermittent warfare on the northeastern frontier of the caliphate, other long-term arrangements had to be established to enable the regular supply of candidates for the royal guard corps. A supply system based on independent trading (but enjoying royal patronage) was soon established. This system depended on cooperation in the steppe society. A large number of young male slaves could be provided either by local princes or by tribal leaders raiding other tribal groups and taking young men as captives, or by the families and tribal groups themselves selling their sons, particularly in difficult times, such as famines. As the geographer Yāqūt (d. 1229) writes: "If a man [of the Kimik tribe of Turkey] begets a son, he would bring up and provide for him and take care of him until he attains puberty. Then he would hand [his pubescent son] a bow and arrows and would drive him out of his abode telling him: 'fend for yourself!,' and he would treat him [henceforth] as a stranger and foreigner. There are amongst [the Kimik] those who sell their sons and daughters in order to cover their expenses."[37] Thus at about the onset of puberty the bonds between father and son among at least some of the Turks were weakened, enabling the latter's separation and sale; in addition, tribesmen would sell their progeny when in economic distress.

The need for an ongoing trade in young mamlūks touches on another matter of significance. Al-Muʿtaṣim evidently had toyed with the idea of mating his Turkish military slaves with Turkish women, thus creating a self-propagating mamlūk ethnicity.[38] This idea was, however, soon abandoned (although not by al-Muʿtaṣim): the Muslim political and military elite evidently understood that the sons of mamlūks did not enjoy the qualities of their fathers. Growing up in the caliphal capital far from the milieu of the steppe made them less hardy, as well as less naturally exposed to the basic skills of riding and archery. Perhaps more important, no matter how hard the authorities tried, the sons of the mamlūks could not be cut off from the local people with their religious and political allegiances. Another focus of loyalty would be their family. It soon became clear that the preferred way to maintain the system of military slavery in the caliphate was not to base it on the progeny of the mamlūks but continually to bring in fresh recruits from the steppes, thus necessitating the trade system described in the previous paragraph. The famous North African historian Ibn Khaldūn (d. 1406) gave expression to the nature of this continually replicating military elite in a famous passage on the mamlūk system (cited at length at the end of this chapter): "Thus, one intake comes after another and generation follows generation, and Islam rejoices in the benefit which it gains through them, and the branches of the kingdom flourish with the freshness of youth."[39]

What happened to the sons of mamlūks? It appears that many of them, perhaps most, were absorbed by the larger society, some even becoming religious scholars. They might enter the army but usually were not members of prestigious units. On occasion, however, a very talented or well-connected son of a mamlūk, in particular a senior officer, might achieve high administrative or military office; this was an individual achievement and not representative of his social group.[40] One notable example is Aḥmad b. Ṭūlūn, who received the governorship of Egypt in 868 and turned the country into a virtual independent polity, until his descendents were removed from power in 905. Although of Turkish mamlūk descent, Ibn Ṭūlūn established neither a Turkish nor a mamlūk state. It was simply one of several all-but-independent provinces that emerged from the fragmenting ʿAbbāsid caliphate from the mid-ninth century onward. In this case, it just happens that the founder of the "state" had a father who had been a Turkish mamlūk.[41]

In theory, this system of military slavery had two major advantages: loyalty to the patron, still the caliph, and the maintenance of a high level of military skills based on the use of disciplined mounted archery. On the whole, this newly constituted guard corps proved itself in the first generation of its existence and certainly did so during the reign of al-Muʿtaṣim, giving him political support and fighting well on the frontier against the Byzantines (although there was not a major breakthrough on that front). Yet, while the loyalty of mamlūks to their patron was a given that generally proved itself over time, it was far from certain that this fealty would pass to his son or any other successor. The mamlūks, as individuals and as units, had economic and political interests that were usually furthered by their patrons but often not by his successors, who frequently chafed under the tutelage (not necessarily a tacit one) of the veteran mamlūk officers. To this can be added the new ruler's desire to further the interests of his own mamlūks, who in turn were expected to strengthen their patron's position. The result was potential conflict over matters of political and economic control, in particular, jobs, revenue-generating lands, and the state's resources in general.[42]

This seems to be the background of the crisis of 861, when Caliph al-Mutawakkil was murdered by a group of senior Turkish officers, most of them having had slave status.[43] This event led to the onset of political instability in the capital and the central province of Iraq, which in turn led to the gradual disintegration of the empire, with first far-flung provinces and then those closer to home becoming increasingly independent (although most maintained titular loyalty to the caliphate). The various units of Turkish slave soldiers, each commanded by their officer, who was usually himself of slave origin, played an important role in this political confusion, which often erupted in street fighting or in warfare in the surrounding countryside. The results of these struggles for power and resources, involving ever-changing coalitions of officers (mostly Turkish), bureaucrats, members of the royal family, women from the harem, and other figures, were continual weakening of the caliph's power even in Baghdad and the gradual separation of de facto and de jure rule. During this time mamlūks often acted as condottieri in Iraq and western Iran, wandering around following only their commander and looking out solely for their own material welfare. Only in 944, with the coming of the Buwayhids (or Būyads), Shiʿi Iranian freebooters from the hills of Daylam, to the south of the Caspian Sea, was some semblance of order restored in the central provinces of the ʿAbbāsid state. The caliph remained but was henceforth little more than a puppet.[44]

Slave Soldiers in the Era of Caliphal Disintegration

Besides mamlūk units remaining in what was left of the caliphal armies and freebooters of mamlūk origin, soldiers who were of military slave origin were found in the armies of the various "independent" dynasties that arose throughout the empire. Perhaps the most important of these states were those of the Sāmānids, a family of relatively noble Iranian origin from Transoxania who became the rulers of this region along with Khurasan at the end of the ninth century, holding effective control for about a hundred years (and continuing to rule over smaller regions until 1005). Before their rise to virtual independence, the Sāmānids had been one of the leading families in the region, being, inter alia, purveyors of mamlūks to the caliphal court.[45] The strategic position of the Sāmānids' state, straddling the trade routes from the Eurasian steppe, enabled them to monopolize the trade in young military slaves. This monopoly gave them two advantages: first, the ability — exploited at times — to put pressure on the caliphate, and second, the chance to pick the best slaves for their own army. Indeed, units of mamlūks formed an increasingly dominant component of their army, thus helping to weaken the role of the "volunteer" *jihād* fighters in the army and contributing to a growing alienation of the civilian elite from the state.[46]

The Ghaznawid state, the successor of the Sāmānids in Khurasan, is an important link in the history of the institution of military slavery and the Islamic state of the Middle Ages. Founded in the last third of the tenth century by a Sāmānid ghulām, the Ghaznawid state (centered in Ghazna, in modern-day Afghanistan) contributed to the military expansion of Islam into northern India and the Punjab. Its administration was a further development of Iranian-Islamic bureaucratic methods, which were to have a long-term impact on a larger area (via their successors in the Seljuq dynasty). Certain Turkish elements can also be discerned, in for example, titles and other forms of legitimization. Because of the origin of the dynasty and the proximity of the state to Central Asia, it should come as no surprise that Turkish slave soldiers played a major role in military affairs (and, indirectly, in political life), although other elements such as the Iranian Ghurids were also prominent. In spite of its mamlūk origins, it would be premature to call the Ghaznawid kingdom a mamlūk state: slave soldiers may have been the dominant military element, but one cannot yet speak of a class of mamlūk officers running the state, in name or in practice.[47]

Slave soldiers continued to play a significant part in the Ghaznawid's successor state, the Seljuq Empire, which eventually stretched, albeit for a relatively short time, from the Oxus to the Mediterranean Sea. The Seljuqs (perhaps more properly: Selchüq) were a leading family of the Oghuz peoples (rendered *Ghuzz* by Muslim writers), a Turkish-speaking tribal federation. Leading their Turcoman[48] followers into Transoxania and then Khurasan at the beginning of the eleventh century, they soon overcame the Ghaznawids (who were pushed into modern-day eastern Afghanistan and northwestern India) in the aftermath of the battle of Dandānqān in 1040.

Although the exact dates and circumstances of the Seljuq family's conversion to Islam are unclear,[49] there is no doubting their commitment to the new faith as they understood it. The Seljuqs quickly adopted from their Ghaznawid predecessors many aspects of the long-established Iranian-Islamic administrative culture, which they were to further develop, and which was to spread subsequently to areas west of Iran. Among the matters that they adopted from the Ghaznawids was a commitment to a militant Sunni Islam, which is certainly one reason behind their *Drang nach Westen*: Seljuq expansion into western Iran and Iraq was at least partially motivated by their desire to liberate the ʿAbbāsid caliph from the patronage and control of the Shiʿi Buwayhids. In this they succeeded in 1055, subsequently eliminating Buwayhid power throughout the region. The Seljuq leader, Alp Arslan (1063–1072), behaved with more courtesy toward the caliph and provided him with greater financial and political leniency, but it was clear that the latter figure was still mainly a de jure ruler. Real power remained in the hands of Alp Arslan, who was granted the title of *sulṭān,* which up to that time had generally meant "rule" or "authority" but henceforth could be understood to mean the de facto ruler, ostensibly appointed by the caliph to rule in his name.[50]

The expansion westward was also accompanied by structural changes within the Seljuq state, the foremost among which were military reforms. Although the mainstay of the Seljuq army had hitherto consisted of the Turcoman tribes, this was becoming increasingly problematic. The tribal leadership was chafing under the Seljuq administration, which saw itself more and more as a traditional Muslim state that guaranteed security for the entire population (which in turn encouraged higher tax receipts). The Seljuq family was no longer satisfied with the traditional role reserved for the tribal chieftain among the Turkish tribes on the Eurasian steppe, a role that left a great deal of autonomy to smaller tribal units. The tribes themselves were dissatisfied with the centralized regime, which worked to restrict the freedom of the nomads, preventing unbridled raiding, foraging, and pasturing. Both sides were thus in a sense relieved when the Turcomans began moving to the northwestern region of Iran, known as Azerbaijan.[51] The Turcomans found an area with large, well-watered pasturelands with climatic conditions somewhat similar to those of the Eurasian steppe and thus appropriate for their livestock. At the same time, the proximity of the Byzantine Empire could give free rein to the desire for raiding, now done under the guise of holy war. The Seljuqs, on the other hand, had gotten the Turcomans out of their hair. The tribes, however, were retrievable if needed for a campaign.[52]

The withdrawal of the Turcomans necessitated the creation or the calling-in of an alternative military force, for both internal political and external security needs. The Seljuqs looked no further than the already tried institution of military slavery, well developed under their Ghaznawid predecessors and in the various regions that they had subsequently conquered. According to some studies, this mamlūk corps numbered between ten thousand and fifteen thousand men[53] and was chosen from among Turkish youths from tribes still living as nomads on the steppes close to the Islamic countries, or perhaps among the Turcoman tribesmen. Interesting testimony is provided by Niẓām al-Mulk, the Seljuq wazir (head administrator) and the author of the Persian work in the "mirror for princes" genre, *Siyāsat-nāmah* (*The Book of Statecraft*): military slaves (*ghulāmān*, the Persian plural of *ghulām*) were to be taken from the Turcomans, and they "should be enrolled and maintained in the same way as military slaves of the palace. When they are in continuous employment they will learn the use of arms and become trained in service. Then they will settle down with other people and with growing devotion serve as military slaves, and cease to feel that aversion [to settled life] with which they are naturally imbued."[54]

The relatively small size of the mamlūk corps, considering the vast expanse of the Seljuq Empire, may have been a result of the expenses incurred in establishing and maintaining this type of formation. In order to finance this system, the Seljuq state, under the tutelage of administrators such as Niẓām al-Mulk, adopted the *iqṭāʿ* system, which had its origins in Iraq in the late ninth century. The iqṭāʿ scheme was the allocation of lands to officers, who had the right to collect tax revenues for themselves, instead of having state officials do it and then pass the revenues on to the military class. With these revenues the officer was to support himself and his household, including his own retinue of troops, which meant their purchase, training, and upkeep. Unlike feudalism, this system did not usually entail administration of the territory in question. The possessor of the iqṭāʿ (known as a *muqṭaʿ*) could not pass the allocation on to his sons; rather, it returned to the state upon his death or when he was no longer able to serve. In addition, iqṭāʿ holders generally lived in the cities and not in their alloted area in the countryside, as did their European counterparts. Finally, the *iqṭāʿ* system did not have the trappings of the homage and contractual relations that characterized European feudal relations. Under the Seljuqs the iqṭāʿ system spread throughout the eastern Islamic world and became the predominant form of payment to the military elite in the succeeding centuries.[55]

The finest hour of the Seljuq mamlūk corps was its effort against the Byzantines at the battle of Manzikert (Turkish: Malazgird) in eastern Anatolia in August 1071. According to one Arabic source, a contingent of about four thousand mamlūks (here referred to as *ghilmān*, the plural of *ghulām*) stuck with the sultan, Alp Arslan, when most of the army had deserted him.[56] Their steadfastness ultimately led to complete victory, including the capture of the Byzantine emperor, and the subsequent breakdown of the Byzantine frontier system. This development in turn resulted in the permanent occupation of Anatolia by Turcomen tribes, the subsequent establishment of Seljuq rule, and eventual turkification of Asia Minor, in essence the birth of Turkey. The important role of the mamlūk corps had vast long-range effects.[57]

Mamlūks in the Period of the Crusades

The united Seljuq Empire was only to last until the 1090s. Subsequently, Seljuq power retreated to Iran, although a cadet branch of the Seljuq family was to rule Anatolia until 1243 (and thereafter as Mongol vassals until the early fourteenth century). The following discussion focuses on developments in the region stretching from Egypt to southeastern Turkey and northern Iraq today. It is here that we see the next important stage in the development of the mamlūk institution, the background for which was the arrival of the crusaders in 1097, their subsequent conquests, and the establishment of the Frankish states along the Syrian and Palestinian coast, as well as farther inland, including most of Palestine, a large chunk of trans-Jordan, and the area around Edessa east of the Euphrates. In Syria and the Jazīra (northern Mesopotamia, today divided among Turkey, Syria, and Iraq), political power remained mostly in the hands of various Turkish princes and officers, almost all derived in some form from the Seljuq state, often at war among themselves. In addition, they were invariably at odds with the Shiʿi Fāṭimid state in Egypt, for political and religious reasons. This disunity and infighting permitted the crusaders' conquests — the height being the taking of Jerusalem in 1099 — and the establishment of their kingdom.[58]

Over the course of the next half-century two trends emerged: the growing expression of an anticrusader, *jihād*-inspired ideology and the gradual coalescing of political unity.[59] An important milestone was the unification of Mosul and Aleppo by Zengi in the late 1120s. Zengi, whose father had been an important mamlūk officer of the Seljuqs, had started off as an *atabeg* (a guardian of a Seljuq prince) in Mosul before becoming the de facto ruler of northern Syria and much of the Jazīra. His apotheosis as a great jihadi warrior took place after he took Edessa from its Frankish ruler in 1144. After his death in 1146, Zengi was succeeded by his son Nūr al-Dīn Maḥmūd. The latter scored few significant achievements against the crusaders, but he did bring about the unification of Muslim Syria, gaining control of large revenues that could be devoted to the building of a large military force.[60] Although both these rulers employed tribal forces such as Turcomans and Kurds, the mainstay of their armies consisted of Turkish mamlūk units. Such units probably made up the bulk of the expeditionary forces sent to Egypt three times in the 1160s, led by the Kurdish general Sirkūh, who was accompanied by his nephew Ṣalāḥ al-Dīn, usually known in the West as Saladin. During more than two decades of intensive political and military activity — which included Saladin's rise to power in Egypt, his eradication of the Fāṭimid regime, the long campaign to gain control over Muslim Syria and the Jazīra, and his wars with the crusaders, culminating in the great victory of Ḥaṭṭīn in northern Palestine in 1187 and the subsequent capture of Jerusalem, followed by the need to deal with the challenge presented by the Third Crusade — Saladin's forces were composed to a large degree of professional cavalrymen, most of whom were Turkish mamlūks of sundry origin.[61] There is no reason to assume that this situation changed during the half-century or so after Saladin's death (1193), when his various direct descendants, and, more important, those of his brother al-Malik al-ʿĀdil, collectively known as the Ayyūbids, ruled a vast federation stretching from southern Egypt and Yemen to eastern Anatolia. The Arabic sources are replete with mention of mamlūks, either as individuals or as groups.

The significance of Turkish slave soldiers was to become even more pronounced during the reign of Saladin's great-nephew al-Malik al-Ṣāliḥ Ayyūb, who first gained control of Damascus in 1238. In the following year, he lost the throne when he was defeated in a battle with a coalition of his relatives, fellow princes in Egypt and Syria. Although al-Ṣāliḥ spent some time in prison (1239–40), he soon returned to power, this time to become ruler over Egypt as well as most of Syria and beyond the Euphrates. The state that he established was much more centralized than that of his predecessors, and he also intro-duced an element of political cruelty that had been previously lacking. One of the bulwarks of his regime was a relatively large and disciplined mamlūk unit known as the Ṣāliḥiyya (after his royal title) or, more famously, the Baḥriyya.[62]

The reasons for his defeat in 1239 and the conclusions that he drew in its aftermath are nicely put by the fifteenth-century historian al-Maqrīzī:

> Al-Malik al-Ṣāliḥ [Ayyūb] is he who established the Baḥrī Mamluks [*al-mamālīk al-baḥriyya*] in Egypt. It was thus: It happened to him what has been mentioned before, during the night when he lost his rule, with the abandon-ment of him by the Kurds and others of his army; no one remained with him except for his mamlūks. He was grateful to them for this. When he gained control over the province of Egypt, he bought many mamlūks, and made them the mainstay of his army.[63] He arrested the officers who had belonged to his father and brother, imprisoned them, and confiscated their land alloca-tions. He gave officer-commissions to his mamlūks, and they became his inner entourage and encircled him in his pavilion. He called them al-Baḥriyya, because of their residence with him on the fortress of al-Rawda, on the Nile River [*baḥr al-nīl*, literally "the sea of the Nile"].[64]

Although al-Ṣāliḥ was building on a long-standing tradition of military slavery, its importance was brought home to him by the experience just cited. An additional factor was the relative abundance (and thus low price) of boys and young men hailing from the Turkish tribes known as the Qipchaqs,[65] who lived as nomads in the steppes north of the Black Sea and who filled the slave markets ca. 1240. As the early fourteenth-century Egyptian writer al-Nuwayrī writes: "The [Mongols] fell upon [the Qipchaqs] and brought upon most of them death, slavery and captivity. At this time, merchants bought [these cap-tives] and brought them to the [various] countries and cities. The first who demanded many of them, and made them lofty and advanced them in the army was al-Malik al-Ṣāliḥ Najm al-Dīn Ayyūb."[66] There was a certain irony here: the Mongols had inadvertently contributed to the formation of a military unit that was to play an important role in defeating them and holding them at bay from 1260 onward.

The first great moment for the Baḥriyya was their role in repulsing the crusade led by Louis IX of France in 1249–1250. Several months after land-ing in Damiette on the Egyptian coast, the crusaders started moving down through the Delta toward Cairo. Meanwhile, the Egyptian army, led by the dying al- Ṣāliḥ Ayyūb, moved north, taking up a position at the fortified town of al-Manṣūra in the eastern Delta. For several weeks there was a standoff, with the two armies facing each other across a canal. It was at this time that the sultan passed away. A junta was formed to run affairs until the sultan's son,

Tūrānshāh, could arrive from the Jazīra (northern Mesopotamia). In the meanwhile, one morning at dawn, the Franks launched a surprise attack, leading to a Muslim rout. It was at this time that the Baḥriyya appeared and saved the day. Ibn al-Furāt (d. 1405) describes the resulting melee:

> Things were near to a total defeat involving the complete destruction of Islam, but Almighty God sent salvation. The damned King of France (*al-malik ray-dāfrans < roi de France*) reached the door of the palace of the Sultan al-Malik al-Ṣāliḥ and matters were at the most critical and difficult state. But then the Turkish Baḥrī squadron and the Jamdārīs,[67] mamluks of the Sultan, amongst them the commander Rukn al-Dīn Baybars al-Bunduqdārī al-Ṣāliḥī al-Najmī,[68] showed their superiority and launched a great attack on the Franks which shook them and demolished their formations. . . . this was the first encounter in which the polytheist dogs were defeated by means of the Turkish lions (*wa-kānat hādhahi al-waqʿa awwal wāqiʿa untuṣira fīḥā bi-usūd al-turk ʿalā kilāb al-shirk*).[69]

Soon the Franks took the decision to retreat. They were subsequently surrounded and were then forced to surrender together with King Louis. The role of the mamlūks in general, and the Baḥriyya in particular, is indisputable.[70]

The Establishment of the Mamlūk Sultanate

While the Baḥriyya were still basking in the glory of their victory, Tūrānshāh arrived at the scene. He soon made a number of political errors, chief among them not giving the Baḥriyya and other military elements the credit that they thought they deserved and also advancing his own men, including mamlūks, to positions of influence. Feeling both slighted and endangered, the Baḥriyya struck first. A group of them, including the future sultan Baybars, fell upon Tūrānshāh and assassinated him. The murder of a problematic ruler, particularly a politically inept son of the previous one, was not an unknown phenomenon in the Muslim world. Invariably, the next step was to find another member of the royal family to sit on the throne, generally a youngster who would be amenable to the control of the senior officers. For reasons that are not completely clear, this time the decision was different: the senior officers, including those of the Baḥriyya (one faction, albeit an important one, in the army), chose to shunt the Ayyūbid family aside and to run the state themselves.[71] There was, of course, no ideology of "mamlūk liberation" at play, or any previously conceived plan for running the country. In fact, it would be ten years, before the nascent state began to assume some semblance of order, and then only in the face of the Mongol threat. In the interim, the regime was characterized by internal strife and ongoing struggles with the Ayyūbid princes of Syria.[72] Shajar al-Durr, al-Ṣāliḥ Ayyūb's beloved wife, also of Qipchaq Turkish origin, played a key role in the events that followed his death until her death in 1257. She even sat briefly on the throne in 1250, but Islamic political culture was not ready to have an official woman ruler, and she was removed. She married Aybeg, the new strongman of the emerging regime, but still remained a power to be reckoned with.[73] During these years the Baḥriyya fell out with much of the remainder of the military elite. Matters reached a head in 1254, when their leader, Aqtay, was murdered, and many were imprisoned. About seven hundred of the Baḥrīs fled to Syria under their new leader, Baybars, and were to serve as mercenaries to various Ayyūbid princes until the arrival of the Mongols in early 1260, when they returned to Egypt.[74]

At the other end of the Islamic world, a similar development had taken place not long before this one. In northern India another group of mamlūks had seized power and created the so-called Sultanate of Dehli, which ruled from 1211 until the sixteenth century. Here, too, we have a parallel to Shajar al-Durr, one who enjoyed a greater degree of success. This was Raḍiyya, who ruled the sultanate from 1236 to 1240.[75] The establishment of two somewhat similar regimes based on slave soldiers at more or less the same time warrants a comment. Although the possibility of a coincidence cannot be ruled out, it may be that a larger development in Eurasia — the Mongol expansion — had its effect. Perhaps the highly unsettled conditions on the steppe that resulted from Mongol conquests led to the flooding of the slave markets with "raw material" for mamlūk units in the Islamic world, and thus the mamlūk institution became even more significant than in the past. It is difficult, however, to prove such a supposition, beyond the account by al-Nuwayrī quoted above. The parallel phenomenon of female "sultans" can also be noted. Neither was a long-term success, if by *success* one means "staying in power," but each was an unusual occurrence in pre-modern Islamic history. As has been suggested,[76] it may be that the relatively high status ascribed to women in the Turco-Mongolian tribal society in the Eurasian steppe may be an explanation, albeit a partial one, for this development. In any event, although Turkish elements had now decisively become the political elites in these two areas, bringing with them new norms of gender relations, they were not able to overturn well-established perceptions and expectations of women's role in political affairs.[77]

As interesting as are developments in the Indian subcontinent, our main thread of inquiry concerns Egypt and the Levant, where we find one of the great achievements of slave soldiers in the Islamic countries. In the 1250s the Mongols, led by Chinggis Khan's grandson Hülegü, renewed their offensive in the Islamic world. Taking Baghdad in early 1258 and then ending the caliphate, they entered Syria about two years later. In the first months of 1260 the

Ayyūbid regime in Syria collapsed. One side effect of this development was the return of Baybars to Egypt with his following of Baḥrī mamlūks. The Franks on the coast were not of one mind: those in Antioch threw in their lot with the Mongols, like the Armenians of Cilicia, while those centered in Acre adopted a more restrained attitude because of their apprehension.[78] A division of the Mongol army commanded by Kitbuqa was sent south from Aleppo and took Damascus, which surrendered without resistance. Advanced Mongol forces raided and reconnoitered as far south as Gaza and Jerusalem in Palestine, and to the north of Karak in trans-Jordan.[79] A contemporary observer would not have been thought unreasonable if he or she had predicted the permanent occupation of Syria by Mongols and their successful advance into Egypt.

Matters, however, were to turn out differently. Under the mamlūk ruler Quṭuz, who had risen to power at the end of 1259, preparations were being made to meet the Mongols in Syria. Perhaps the most important reason for this decision was the news that Hülegü had withdrawn with the vast majority of his troops, taking up a position in Azerbaijan. He had left only Ketbuqa and his division in Syria, with instructions to keep an eye on the Franks and on the rulers of Egypt.[80] Reinforced by Baybars and his supporters, as well as by Ayyūbid soldiers who had fled to Egypt, the mamlūk army set out for Syria in mid-July. An advance Mongol force at Gaza was thrown back, and the Egyptian army advanced up the coast to Acre. Receiving supplies from the Franks and an agreement guaranteeing their neutrality, the mamlūks moved into the Jezreel Valley. They soon encountered the Mongols under Ketbuqa at their position near ʿAyn Jālūt ("The Well of Goliath"), below the northern slopes of the Gilboa hills. The armies met on the morning of 3 September 1260. The fighting was touch and go for some time, but after several hours of battle, the mamlūks were finally victorious, putting to flight the Mongols, who subsequently abandoned Syria.[81]

A number of reasons offer themselves for the mamlūks' victory: their determination and leadership, their slight numerical advantage, the fleeing of Syrian Muslim troops enrolled in the Mongol army against their will, and just plain luck (the death in battle of the Mongol commander). Perhaps, however, the most decisive reason was the similarity of fighting methods of the mamlūks and the Mongols, due to their common origins in the steppes of Eurasia. This similarity and its results were well expressed by a contemporary Syrian writer, Abū Shāma (d. 1267), who wrote about this battle in his chronicle: "Among the amazing things is that the Tartars [=Mongols] were defeated and annihilated by members of their own race from among the Turks" (*min abnāʿ jinshim al-turk*). To this assessment the author adds a short poem of his own composition: "The Mongols conquered the land and there came to them / From Egypt a Turk, who sacrificed his life. / In Syria he destroyed and scattered them. / To everything there is a pest of its own kind (*jins*)."[82] This resemblance in fighting methods put the Mongols and the mamlūks on the same plane, so to speak, and enabled the other reasons suggested above to come into play and decide the battle.[83]

The impact of the battle was multifold: first, it ended Mongol rule in Syria and contributed to puncturing the myth of their invincibility. Second, it provided crucial legitimacy to the fledgling mamlūk regime, which still suffered from the way it had obtained power and the infighting that accompanied its first decade in power in Egypt. Finally, with the collapse of Ayyūbid rule in Syria and the expulsion of the Mongols from the country, the mamlūks took control, soon turning this land into an integral province of a highly centralized state based in Cairo. The mamlūk leadership was aware that the Mongol danger had not disappeared, and many of the activities and policies of the next few decades should be understood in this context.

A Quarter of a Millennium of Mamlūk Rule

The mamlūk sultanate of Egypt and Syria crystallized in the midst of a long-term war against the Mongols on one hand and the crusaders on the other. It was a military state par excellence, much of whose ostensible raison d'être was to defend Islam from these enemies.[84] The political elite was unabashedly military, and in fact over the course of the next half-century a number of important positions in the bureaucracy (such as that of the wazir, with general responsibility for financial administration) were increasingly filled by representatives of the military, thereby weakening the traditional bureaucratic class.[85] The sultan was generally a member of the mamlūk military elite, although often as a stopgap measure a son of a sultan was appointed as ruler until one of the important *amīrs* (officers) triumphed over his opponents to gain the throne.[86] No less important, the vast majority of the revenues of the state, and in general the lion's share of the agricultural surplus, were destined for the mamlūk class, particularly the sultan and the senior amirs. The mechanism for the transfer of these revenues was the *iqṭāʿ* system, which had been brought to Egypt by the Ayyūbids but had been further systemized under the mamlūks. The military class remained urban: generally only at the time of collecting the revenues did the mamlūks and their officials venture out into the countryside.[87]

The 270-year periods of mamlūk rule over Egypt and Syria have much in common; contemporaries saw them as a unity, which they referred to as *dawlat al-turk* (or *al-atrāk*), the "dynasty of the Turks."[88] We can, therefore, speak with confidence of the Mamlūk Period. At the same time, we should be aware that the Mamlūk Period was also many subperiods, each with its own peculiar characteristics. Already in the time of the sultanate, contemporary historians were aware of a general distinction between two eras. The first, stretching from 1250 to 1282, was the "Turkish" or "Qipchaq Period," called by some modern historians the "Baḥrī Period," because of the important role of this unit and its graduates in the early sultanate. The proper name for the second should be the "Circassian Period," since Mamlūks of Circassian origin made up the dominant element in the military elite; in fact, the mamlūk sources refer to this time as *dawlat al-jarākis* (the "Circassian dynasty"). This era, however, is still referred to by the modern misnomer "the Burjī dynasty," a usage that should be eschewed by careful scholars and students.[89] In any event, the second half of the history of the mamlūk state is indeed a discrete block of time, distinct in many ways from the earlier sultanate.

In fact, the history of the sultanate can be further broken down into smaller subperiods. After the "turbulent decade" of 1250–1260, described above, one can speak of a "heroic period," lasting from 1260 to 1293. This was a period of intensive warfare against both the Mongols and the Franks, when the army was strengthened in numbers and quality, and along with it, the state in general went through a process of institutionalization. The dominant personality for this subperiod was the sultan Baybars, who reigned from 1260 to 1277, having murdered Quṭuz soon after the victory at ʿAyn Jālūt. In many ways one can see this fascinating but cruel personality as the real founder of the Sultanate; besides laying down the foundations of the sultanate's institutions, he was frequently campaigning in Syria against its enemies. After a two-year hiatus in which his two sons briefly ruled, he was succeeded by his comrade from the Baḥriyya, Qalawun, who continued his policies until his death in 1290. The latter was succeeded by his own son, al-Malik al-Ashraf Khalīl, who completed the work of his two illustrious predecessors by conquering Acre in 1291, thus bringing the crusading kingdom to an end. In spite of his obvious abilities, let alone his militancy toward the enemies of the sultanate, Mongols as well as crusaders, al-Ashraf was assassinated in 1293 by a group of his father's mamlūks who were unhappy with his policies. In his place they set on the throne his younger brother, al-Malik al-Nāṣir Muḥammad, then nine years old.[90] This was the typical succession paradigm repeating itself: the mamlūks of the previous sultan could not abide the existence of a strong successor and so eliminated him, replacing him with a boy-sultan who could be easily manipulated until such time as one of the senior mamlūk officers could take control in name as well as in fact.

The next seventeen years formed an interesting interregnum, which Robert

Irwin has referred to as the "operation of faction." Twice, al-Nāṣir Muḥammad sat on the throne in name only (1293–1294 and 1298–1309), increasingly chafing under the tutelage of the senior officers. From 1294 to 1299, two
of these commanders took the sultanate, and again in 1309–1310 there was
another short-term sultan. None of these rulers, however, were able to rule
with any success, particularly given the opposition of a large section of the
officer class.[91] Finally, in 1310, al-Nāṣir Muḥammad was able to stage a come-
back from his exile in Karak in trans-Jordan. He then ruled with a heavy hand,
having learnt the lessons of his youth: during the first years of his reign, he
succeeded in eliminating the large group of officers who had been mamlūks of
his father, Qalawun.[92] His thirty-year reign is fascinating for several reasons,
among them the end of the Mamlūk-Ilkhanid war, ca. 1320,[93] and the boom in
construction, urban and rural. It was, so it would seem, a period of peace and
unbridled prosperity. Some scholars, however, have noted that in many ways it
was at this time that the seeds for the subsequent decline were sown.[94] This is a
topic that goes beyond the confines of the present chapter, so I will limit myself
to one aspect: the way the mamlūk system was deliberately changed at this
time. Al-Maqrīzī writes:

> Al-Nāṣir imported many mamlūks and slave-girls. He called the merchants
> [to come] to him, and paid them money, describing to them the beauty of
> mamlūks and slave-girls [that he desired]. He sent them off to the country of
> Özbeg (i.e., the Mongol Golden Horde), to Tabriz, Anatolia, Baghdad and
> elsewhere. When a merchant brought him a batch of mamlūks, he gave him a
> large sum for them. From the beginning, he bestowed upon the mamlūks
> splendid clothes, golden belts, horses and gifts in order to impress them. This
> was not the custom of those kings before him. When a mamlūk was brought
> to them, they ascertained his ethnic group, then they handed him over to
> the commanding eunuch, and attached him to [the members of] his ethnic
> group. He was educated with a *faqīh* (legal scholar), who taught him man-
> ners, proper behaviour and respect. He was trained in using the bow and
> arrow, lance-play, riding the horse and types of horsemanship. His costume
> was from Baalbeki cotton cloth, and medium weight flax cloth. The mamlūk's
> pay was increased from three dinars to five to seven to ten. When he joined the
> ranks, he held an appropriate position or positions, learning there what was
> necessary from proper behaviour when he was young. Then the mamlūk was
> gradually promoted. When the mamlūk reached an important position and a
> high rank, he knew its value.[95]

We first learn from this passage important information about the traditional
method of educating young mamlūks and what was expected of them when
they finished the military school and were enrolled in regular units. Although

perhaps the author may be accused of exaggeration, for which he has a certain penchant, it is clear that some basic tinkering with the way mamlūks were educated had now taken place. In the earlier period, the education of the mamlūk was centered on inculcating frugality and slow promotion based mainly on the systematic acquisition of skills and proven ability. The education of the young mamlūk trainee was a combination of religious and military training. Loyalty toward the patron (*ustādh*) and other mamlūks of the same patron (*khushdāsh*, plural *khushdāshiyya*) was inculcated. Even after official manumission at around the age of twenty or younger, at the ceremony known as *kharj*, where the trainees received a certificate of release (*ʿitāqa*), the soldiers still proudly regarded themselves as mamlūks, jealously guarding their status and maintaining — at least theoretically — their group solidarity and loyalty to their patron.[96]

But under al-Nāṣir Muḥammad — it is claimed — the young mamlūk had all kinds of luxuries showered upon him, and favorites enjoyed rapid advancement up the ranks to the highest positions. It is unclear, however, how deep this change went, and what all of its long-term implications were. One thing is obvious, though: with the end of the sixty-year war with the Mongols (thirty years after the expulsion of the crusaders), the leadership of the sultanate could now indulge with relative impunity in experiments with the system that had served it well in the past. The political troubles of the subsequent decades may be explained in part by this changing educational policy and the effect it had on discipline of the troops.

The forty-one-year period after the death of al-Nāṣir Muḥammad was one of general political anarchy and economic crisis, both exacerbated by the outbreak of bubonic plague in 1348 in Egypt and Syria. A series of twelve sultans, sons and grandsons (and one great grandson) of the great sultan, was placed on the throne and then removed when it suited the grandees. The one exception was al-Nāṣir Ḥasan, who reigned twice (1347–1351, 1354–1358); he made an attempt to assert his authority vis-à-vis the officers and suffered deposition and death as a result.[97]

Stability was reestablished with the accession of Barquq, an officer of Circassian origin, in 1382. From this time the Circassians became the dominant element in the military society, although not necessarily because they enjoyed a numerical majority. In fact, Qipchaq Turkish remained the lingua franca of the mamlūks, and paradoxically it was during the second half of the Mamlūk Sultanate that most works in this language were composed.[98] Barquq's rise was accompanied by the strengthening of the Circassians in the mid-fourteenth century; the combination of the growing Islamization of the Turkish population of the Qipchaq steppe north of the Black Sea, a possible reduction of the population available for export as military slaves, and general disorders in the Golden Horde appears to have led to the growing interest of the Circassians, a warlike mountain people from the northern Caucasus region.[99] There had been Circassian mamlūks from the inception of the sultanate, and under Qalawun they had already reached a certain prominence with the formation of the Burjiyya regiment, numbering several thousand. One of their number, Baybars al-Jāshnakīr, even reigned from 1309–1310, after a decade as one of the two strongmen of the regime.[100]

The Circassian Period is generally seen as one of economic decline, political instability, and military weakness. There is much to commend this view, although modern historians have been perhaps overinfluenced by the contemporary authors, who frequently compare their own time unfavorably to a somewhat mythical golden age. Revisionism, however, can also be exaggerated: the armies of the sultans were smaller and generally less efficient, and the state suffered chronic shortages of revenue. This may have prompted one sultan in particular, Barsbay (1422–1438), to establish state monopolies of various branches of the economy, particularly foreign trade, with long-term negative effects.[101] An ongoing problem was the discipline of the young mamlūks, who frequently rioted in the streets when their salaries were in arrears. It was often difficult to get the royal mamlūks to go out on campaigns, although this may have been an excuse to get problematic officers or mamlūks of the former sultans out of the capital and perhaps to put them in harm's way.

The combination of endemic monetary crisis brought on by the prodigious spending of al-Nāṣir Muḥammad's reign, the Black Death, and the expensive nature of the mamlūk institution resulted in a decline in military power. Financial constraints led to smaller armies, and mamlūks tended to be imported at an older age, meaning that they received a shorter and inferior military education.[102] This reduced period of training also resulted in a decline of discipline, which brought about a further weakening of the army's prowess, on one hand, and constant economic demands (often expressed in rioting), on the other. Given this somewhat sorry state, it is surprising that the mamlūk state lasted as long as it did. Two explanations for this longevity, in spite of increasing problems, present themselves: there was no local element that seriously endangered mamlūk rule,[103] and until the end of the fifteenth century, no foreign power, except for the short-term invasion of Tamerlane,[104] significantly threatened the sultanate from the outside.

The last two important sultans tried to deal with this decline in different ways. The crisis took on a new slant with the rise of the Ottomans, who were steadily encroaching on the mamlūk sphere of influence in southeastern Anatolia. The first approach was one of entrenchment by Qaitbay (1468–1496), a powerful but deeply conservative ruler. His answer to the dangers facing the sultanate and the mamlūk class was a return to older virtues of training and discipline. Horsemanship and the use of the bow and arrow were stressed. There was little room for the new gunpowder weapons. His policy seemed to be vindicated with the mamlūk victory over the Ottomans at Kayseri in 1490, as in other warfare in the frontier region against this enemy. It should be borne in mind, however, that the mamlūk victory was the result of an all-out effort on their part, while facing them was only a part of Ottoman might.[105]

Qansuh al-Ghawrī (1491–1516) appears to have taken a somewhat different tack: while not neglecting traditional mamlūk methods, he permitted a bit more experimentation with gunpowder weapons, both artillery and handguns. The former may have been a result of the appearance of the Portuguese in the Indian Ocean and the threat to mamlūk commercial interests in the region. There was even some cooperation with the Ottomans on this front. In any event, there was no major breakthrough in this area: the development of gunpowder weapons still had not become a major priority of the mamlūk elite. Perhaps no less important, although possibly not clear to most contemporaries, Qansuh spent much of his energy putting together a private fisc based on an enormous *waqf* (endowment) that he assembled through various legal machinations. This appears to have been a way to circumvent the traditional iqṭāʿ system, thus weakening the various mamlūk grandees. It is a speculative suggestion, but perhaps he pondered a way to reduce or at least supplement the mamlūk units, using this private fisc as a financial basis.[106]

Whatever Qansuh's long-term plans, they were cut short by his defeat by the Ottoman sultan Selim I at the battle of Marj Dābiq in northern Syria in 1516. A number of factors combined to bring this result, first of which was the larger and better-disciplined Ottoman army. Treachery in the mamlūk ranks played its part, too. An additional factor whose exact importance is difficult to gauge was the mamlūks' lack of gunpowder weapons, be they field artillery or handguns; the Ottomans used these to some effect. The refusal or perhaps inability of the mamlūks to modernize their army was to have disastrous effects. Yet this policy is understandable in the context of this military society. One might speak of a general tendency discernable among horsemen to disregard or disparage technological changes (this, of course, is a statement that needs proof, but the story of the Polish cavalry at the commencement of World War II comes to mind), but more concrete reasons can be suggested: the handguns of the time would have required those who used them to dismount. From the point of view of members of the mamlūk class, this completely negated their self-perceived raison d'être: anyone could use a handgun, but only a mamlūk could properly ride and use a bow and arrow. The mamlūks understood that by adopting handguns at that time they would have lost their military monopoly and by extension their right to rule. In other words, what made sense perhaps from a military perspective negated the political logic of the Mamlūk Sultanate. They had no choice, or so they believed, but to maintain the "good old ways" and to hope for the best.[107]

The mamlūk system, based on the import of excellent raw material for military purposes and training the recruits in horsemanship and archery, had been the answer par excellence to the dangers posed by the crusaders and the Mongols to much of the Islamic world in the thirteenth century. A quarter of a millennium later, they were technologically out of date and unable to do much about it. The defeat of the mamlūks by the Ottomans at Cairo in 1517, in spite of the frantic efforts made to acquire artillery, was merely the coup de grâce to a system that had long since lost its efficiency and was no longer able to defend itself.

Vestigial Remnants and Variants of the Mamlūk System

Two important variants of military slavery were to outlive the demise of the Mamlūk Sultanate. The first was in Egypt and Syria. After the battle, the Ottomans left senior mamlūk officers in place as governors in Syria and Egypt, supported by surviving mamlūks. This experiment was short-lived in Syria because the mamlūks there revolted in 1520, in the aftermath of Selim's death. The revolt was soon put down and the mamlūks eradicated there. In Egypt, mamlūks remained an important component of the local elite, although their prominence gradually declined. The eighteenth century saw a resurgence of the power of mamlūk households, and they became dominant in the country, albeit still accepting Ottoman suzerainty. This later phase has been called the neo-mamlūk system, because it is somewhat different from the prototype of the sultanate: sons of mamlūks joined the military elite, as did other non-mamlūk household members. In addition, the mamlūks had finally adopted handguns. Technological advances had produced the carbine and the pistol, which could be wielded on horseback. This Indian Summer of mamlūkdom, however, was ended at the beginning of the nineteenth century by the all-but-independent Ottoman governor of Egypt, Muḥammad ʿAlī, who brutally suppressed the mamlūk grandees.[108]

The second variant, preceding the demise of the sultanate, was the so-called janissary (< *Yeni Cheri*, "new army") system of the Ottoman Empire. The origins of this institution are somewhat obscure, but in the late fourteenth and early fifteenth centuries, units of slave soldiers emerged as an integral, perhaps a primary, part of the conquering Ottoman army. The janissaries were different from the regular mamlūk model for two reasons: first, they fought as infantrymen, and second, instead of being taken from pagan Turkish or Caucasian tribes, they were mainly drafted from the Christian population of the Balkans. That the elite corps of the Ottoman army consisted of infantry who first fought as foot archers made the transition to handguns relatively easy: it did not require a major conceptual shift to put down the bow and pick up a predecessor of the musket, as unwieldy as it might be. The history of the janissaries is beyond the scope of the present chapter, but their role in Ottoman expansion, in Europe and in the Middle East (and in later Ottoman history up to their final disbandment in 1833), was significant. It was a version of the mamlūk system that had been adopted to the changing circumstances of warfare.[109]

What can be termed vestigial examples of military slavery are found in different parts of the Islamic world in the eighteenth, nineteenth, and twentieth centuries. In Morocco, for example, black military slavery had become significant after the expansion to the south at the end of the seventeenth century, and a large corps was organized and maintained until the mid-eighteenth century.[110] At around the same time, units of black slave soldiers were organized in what today is Sudan and the surrounding countries, taking advantage of the availability of slaves in the region (building on a thousand-year tradition of the slave trade from this area to the north). These formations played an important role in the Egyptian wars of expansion into the region as well as the Mahdist resistance. Descendants of these military slaves made up a considerable component of the military in East Africa during much of the twentieth century.[111]

The Importance of the Mamlūk System

The mamlūk institution provided a bulwark of the Islamic word against invaders and, at the same time, contributed to Islamic expansion. It harnessed the military capabilities of the steppe peoples and their neighbors, mainly the Turks, for generations, constantly bringing in fresh recruits and preventing the loss of military capabilities due to exposure to civilized life. The system of military slavery in the Islamic world, particularly as it reached its apotheosis in the Mamlūk Sultanate, enabled the ongoing exploitation of the military advantages of the peoples of the Eurasian steppe even after the debilitating effects of long-term exposure to sedentary culture. A clear statement of this was expressed by the great North African historian and thinker Ibn Khaldūn (d. 1406), who spent the last years of his life in the Mamlūk Sultanate and could see its workings at first hand. In a concise *tour d'horizon* of the history of the institution of military slavery in Islam he writes:

When the ['Abbāsid] state was drowned in decadence and luxury and donned the garments of calamity and impotence and was overthrown by the heathen Mongols, who abolished the seat of the Caliphate and obliterated the splendor of the lands and made unbelief prevail in place of belief, because the people of the faith, sunk in self-indulgence, preoccupied with pleasure and abandoned to luxury, had become deficient in energy and courage and the emblem of manhood — then, it was God's benevolence that He rescued the faith by reviving its dying breath and restoring the unity of the Muslim in Egypt, preserving the order and defending the walls of Islam. He did this by sending to the Muslims, from this Turkish nation and from among its great and numerous tribes, rulers to defend them and utterly loyal helpers, who were brought from the House of War (i.e., the non-Muslim world) to the House of Islam (i.e., the Muslim countries) under the rule of slavery, which hides in itself a divine blessing, and is exposed to divine providence; cured by slavery, they enter the Muslim religion with the firm resolve of true believers and yet with nomadic virtues unsullied by debased nature, unadulterated with the filth of pleasure, undefiled by the ways of civilized living, and with their ardor unbroken by the profusion of luxury. The slave merchants bring them to Egypt in batches, like sand-grouse to the watering places, and government buyers have them displayed for inspection and bid for them, raising the price above their value. They do this not in order to subjugate them, but because it intensifies loyalty, increases power, and is conducive to ardent zeal. They choose from each group, according to what they observe of the characteristics of the race and the tribes. Then they place them in government barracks where they give good and fair treatment, educate them, have them taught the Qur'ān and kept at their religious studies until they have a firm grasp of this. Then they train them in archery and fencing, in horsemanship, in hippodromes, and in thrusting with the lance and striking with the sword until their arms grow strong and their skills become firmly rooted. When the masters know that they have reached the point when they are ready to defend them, even to die for them, they double their pay and increase their grants (iqṭā'), and impose on them the duty to improve themselves in the use of weapons and in horsemanship, and so also to increase the number of men of their own race in the service for that purpose. Often they use them in the service of the state, appoint them to high state offices, and some of them are chosen to sit on the throne of the sultans and direct the affairs of the Muslims, in accordance with divine providence and with the mercy of God to His creatures. Thus, one intake comes after another and generation follows generation, and Islam rejoices in the benefit which it gains through them, and the branches of the kingdom flourish with the freshness of youth.[112]

This unequivocal passage by a perspicacious Muslim thinker indicates that a positive view toward the phenomenon of military slavery was not unknown in the medieval Islamic world. It also suggests that mamlūks — at least during the time of the Mamlūk Sultanate — were held in high esteem, in spite of their humble origins and slave status during their youth. This would appear to belie somewhat the suggestion of Orlando Patterson that "social death" was also the status of the military slave of the Islamic world.[113] Granted, and perhaps tellingly, most of Patterson's discussion deals with the early period of the *ghilmān*, with some reference to the Ottoman *devshirme*. There is no discussion of the sultanate. For the earlier period, he suggests that it was the lack of honor, prestige, or position (in other words, "social death") that prompted the caliphs to prefer Turkish mamlūks to free aliens or to fellow Arabs. The low prestige of the slave was indeed a factor, although others have been adduced above. In any event, over the centuries, at least some Muslim military slaves evolved into a military and social elite, jealous of their privileges vis-à-vis the general population and even their own progeny. Their self-image is clearly perceived by anyone who walks the streets of old Cairo, Damascus, Aleppo, and even Jerusalem and sees the monumental schools, mosques, sufi lodges, and caravansarais, let alone fortifications that were constructed under their patronage. Whatever the exact plans of the initiator of this institution in the early ninth century, by the late middle ages, Turkish officers of slave origin saw themselves as the legitimate Muslim rulers, and the local population had no choice but to acquiesce. We see little sign of abasement and should therefore be wary of applying in a blanket way the insights derived from slavery in general to this particular variant.

Notes

1. There are excellent surveys by D. Sourdel, C. E. Bosworth, P. Hardy, and I. Inalcik on the *ghulām* (military slave) in the caliphate, Persia, India, and the Ottoman Empire in *The Encyclopaedia of Islam,* 2nd ed. (Leiden, 1160–2002), 2:1079–91, as well as D. Ayalon's article "Mamlūk," in ibid., 6:314–321. The term *mamlūk* (plural *mamālīk*) literally means "owned" or "purchased" but is used almost exclusively to mean a white military slave, although on occasion it is used by a writer to describe himself, i.e., to indicate how humble he is by calling himself a slave. The use in this chapter of *mamlūk* to describe military slaves at this early stage is somewhat anachronistic, since the usual term for this category in the first centuries is *ghulām* (plural *ghilmān*), which literally means "youth" (cf. the Hebrew ʿ*elem*).

2. For first attempts at evaluating Ayalon's mamlūk project, see R. Amitai, "The Rise and Fall of the Mamlūk Institution: A Summary of David Ayalon's Works," in Moshe Sharon (ed.), *Studies in Islamic History and Civilization in Honour of Professor David Ayalon* (Jerusalem, 1986), 19–30; Amitai, "David Ayalon, 1914–1998," *Mamluk Studies Review* 3 (1999): 1–4.

3. Jürgen Paul, "The State and the Military: The Samanid Case," *Papers on Inner Asia,* no. 26 (Bloomington, 1994), 4–5.

4. David Turley, *Slavery* (Oxford, 2000); M. L. Bush (ed.), *Serfdom and Slavery: Studies in Legal Bondage* (London, 1996) writes on p. 5: "Certain Islamic societies, notably the Ottoman Turks, operated a system of state slavery whereby the ruler's army was manned by men legally defined as slaves." This is true, but of course it ignores the major role of military slaves before the Ottomans. Orlando Patterson, *Slavery and Social Death: A Comparative Study* (Cambridge, MA, 1982), 308–314, has some interesting insights into the "Islamic Ghilmān," to which I return below.

5. On legal and social aspects of slavery in Islam, see R. Brunschvig, "'Abd," in *Encyclopaedia of Islam,* 1:24–40. See the larger discussion in B. Lewis, *Race and Slavery in the Middle East: An Historical Enquiry* (New York, 1990); in chapter 9 ("Slaves in Arms") there is a useful overview of military slavery in Islamic history.

6. The view expressed here is at variance with those presented by Patricia Crone (*Slaves on Horses: The Evolution of the Islamic Polity* [Cambridge, UK, 1980]) and Daniel Pipes (*Slave Soldiers and Islam: The Genesis of a Military System* [New Haven, 1981]), which attribute much importance to the retreat from political affairs by Muslim elites in early Islamic society, thereby leaving the arena open to various military types. Muslim elites did not voluntarily withdraw from affairs because of a distaste for political reality but rather were shunted aside from military activity, often forcibly, by the ruling circles, who replaced them with troops from the periphery, including eventually Turkish slave troops. It appears to me that no one bothered to ask the traditional religious and social elites whether they wanted to be part of the new scheme of things.

7. For the early Islamic armies, see Claude Cahen, "Djaysh, I. Classical," *Encyclopaedia of Islam,* 2:504–505; G. P. Hawting, *The First Dynasty of Islam: The Unmayyad Caliphate, A.D. 661–750* (London, 1986); Hugh Kennedy, *The Armies of the Caliphs* (London, 2000), 1–58; C. E. Bosworth, "Armies of the Prophet: Strategy, Tactics and Weapons," in Bernard Lewis (ed.), *The World of Islam: Faith, People, Culture* (London, 1976), 201–204.

8. This important area in medieval Islamic history includes modern-day Turkmenistan, northeastern Iran, and northern Afghanistan.

9. Moshe Sharon, *Black Banners from the East: The Establishment of the 'Abbasid State — Incubation of a Revolt* (Jerusalem, 1983), 49–71; Sharon, *Revolt: The Social and Military Aspects of the 'Abbasid Revolution* (Jerusalem, 1990), 297.

10. Moshe Sharon, "The Military Reforms of Abū Muslim, Their Background and Consequences," in M. Sharon (ed.), *Studies in Islamic History and Civilization in Honour of Prof. David Ayalon* (Jerusalem, 1986), 117–121.

11. For the Abnā', see Hugh Kennedy, *The Prophet and the Age of the Caliphates: The Islamic Near East from the Sixth to the Eleventh Century* (London, 1986), 135, 143–52; Matthew S. Gordon, *The Breaking of a Thousand Swords: A History of the Turkish Military of Samarra, A.H. 200–275/815–889 CE* (Albany, 2001), passim. An extremely important study of the Abnā' is the unpublished Ph.D. dissertation by Amikam Elad, "Characteristics of the Development of the 'Abbāsid Army (especially Ahl Khurāsān and al-Abnā' Units), with Emphasis on the Reign of al-Amīn and al-Ma'mūn" (Hebrew

University of Jerusalem, 1986). Unfortunately, this work, with the exception of an abstract, remains in Hebrew and is thus inaccessible to most scholars.

12. David Ayalon, "The Military Reforms of Caliph al-Muʿtasim: Their Background and Consequences," in D. Ayalon, *Islam and the Abode of War* (Aldershot, 1994), art. I.

13. David Ayalon, "Preliminary Remarks on the Mamluk Military Institution in Islam," in V. J. Perry and M. E. Yapp (eds.), *War, Technology and Society in the Middle East* (London, 1975), 48 (reprinted in D. Ayalon, *The Mamluk Military Society: Collected Studies* [London, 1979], art. IX).

14. On mawālī, mostly in the general sense of "a convert to Islam," see Patricia Crone, "Mawlā," *Encyclopaedia of Islam,* 6:874–882. For the restricted sense of "imported mawālī," see David Ayalon, *Eunuchs, Caliphs and Sultans: A Study of Power Relationships* (Jerusalem, 1999), 24–34.

15. Ayalon, "Preliminary Remarks," 50. I might note that Patterson, *Slavery and Social Death,* 309–311, lumps imported mawālī together with military slaves. Granted, the line between them appears at times to be blurred at this stage (the early ʿAbbāsid period), but on the whole the first group appears to have been composed of former prisoners of war and freedmen of sundry origin, and as an institution it appears distinct from the full-blown military slavery discernable from ca. 810 onward.

16. Abū Jaʿfar Muḥammad b. Jarīr al-Ṭabarī, *Taʾrīkh al-rusūl waʾl-mulūk,* ed. M. J. de Goeje et al. (Leiden, 1871–1901), 3:853–854; translation from Ayalon, "Preliminary Remarks," 49; see also *The History of al-Tabarī,* vol. 31; *The War Between Brothers,* tr. Michael Fishbein (Albany, 1992), 116–117.

17. A detailed rendition of the formation of al-Muʿtasim's slave regiment is found in Gordon, *Breaking of a Thousand Swords,* 1–50; see also the brief account in Hugh Kennedy, *The Early Abbasid Caliphate: A Political History* (London, 1981), 167.

18. See the article by Brunshvig, note 5 above.

19. Kennedy, *Prophet and the Age of the Caliphates,* 159–60.

20. See note 1 for discussion of the term *mamlūk.*

21. The slave status of these Turkish guard-soldiers is dealt with in detail in the introduction and first chapter of Gordon, *Breaking of a Thousand Swords,* esp. 34–26.

22. On the earlier history of the Turks and first encounters with the Muslims, see Peter B. Golden, *An Introduction to the History of the Turkic Peoples: Ethnogenesis and State-formation in Medieval and Early Modern Eurasia and the Middle East* (Wiesbaden, 1992), chaps. 1–6, 8. For a suggestion of an earlier and more massive presence in what became the eastern Islamic world, see Richard N. Frye and Aydin M. Sayili, "Turks in the Middle East Before the Saljuqs," *Journal of the American Oriental Society* 63 (1943): 194–207.

23. Ayalon, "Preliminary Remarks," 47, citing Aḥmad b. Yaḥyā al-Balādhurī, *Futūḥ al-buldān (=Liber Expugnationis Regionum),* ed. M. J. de Goeje (Leiden, 1863–66), 376, 410–441. In D. Ayalon, "Aspects of the Mamluk Phenomenon: The Importance of the Mamluk Institution," *Der Islam* 56 (1976): 205 (reprinted in D. Ayalon, *The Mamluk Military Society* [London 1979], art. Xa), we are provided with some early uses of the term *mamlūk,* even in the Umayyad period, but it is far from clear to my mind whether they are Turks and what exactly is meant by the term in these contexts.

24. "People of the Book" (*ahl al-kitāb*), i.e., Jews, Christians, and Zoroastrians, could only be enslaved under certain conditions.

25. This is a point made by Ayalon ("Aspects of the Mamluk Phenomenon," 203), although perhaps an overstated one. Nomadic populations by nature live in a somewhat dispersed state. In any case, the number of male slaves that were available appears to have been fairly high. See below for discussion of poverty as a factor in the selling of offspring in the steppe.

26. For the military abilities of the Eurasian nomads in general and the Turks in particular, see the important recent article by Peter B. Golden, "War and Warfare in the Pre-Cinggisid Western Steppes of Eurasia," in Nicola Di Cosmo (ed.), *Warfare in Inner Asian History, 500–1800* (Leiden, 2002), 105–172, as well as the editor's comments in the introduction, pp. 1–12. For relations between the nomads and the sedentary states surrounding them, see A. M. Khazanov, *Nomads and the Outside World,* 2nd ed. (Madison, 1994).

27. Abū Isḥāq Ibrāhīm b. Muḥammad al-Iṣṭakhrī, *al-Masālik wa'l-mamālik* (Leiden, 1927), 291; translation in D. Ayalon, "The Mamlūks of the Seljuks: Islam's Military Might at the Crossroads," *Journal of the Royal Asiatic Society,* 3rd ser., 6 (1996): 311.

28. Al-Jāḥiẓ (Abū ʿUthmān ʿAmr b. Bahr), *Manāqib al-atrāq,* in *Tria Opuscula Auctore,* ed. G. van Vloten (Leiden, 1903), 49; translation in Ayalon, "Mamlūks of the Seljuks," 311.

29. Abū al-Qāsim Ibn Ḥawqal al-Naṣībī, *Kitāb ṣūrat al-arḍ,* ed. J. H. Kramers (Leiden, 1938–39), 452; translation in Ayalon, "Mamlūks of the Seljuks," 312.

30. See David Ayalon, *L'esclavage du mamelouk* (Jerusalem, 1951). Gordon, *Breaking of a Thousand Swords,* 21–23, comments on the lack of information on the education of the Turkish guardsmen. See below on the training of mounted archers.

31. M. A. Shaban, *Islamic History: A New Interpretation* (Cambridge, UK, 1976), 63–65.

32. Christopher I. Beckwith, "Aspects of the Early History of the Central Asian Guard Corps in Islam," *Archivum Eurasiae Medii Aevi* 4 (1984): 29–43.

33. Gordon, *Breaking of a Thousand Swords,* 8. Gordon's book is the first monograph in English that deals in detail with the formation and early history of the Turkish guard corps composed of military slaves, putting the study of the subject on a very sound footing.

34. Ibid., 47–74.

35. John M. Smith Jr., "Archeology and Mounted Archery: Scythian and Sassanian Shots, and the Samarra 'Racetrack,'" paper delivered at the International Conference on Military Archaeology: Weaponry and Warfare in Historical and Social Perspective, at the State Hermitage and the Institute of the History of Material Culture of the Russian Academy of Sciences in St. Petersburg in 1998. This important paper will perhaps see the light of day in the near future, in a volume on military archeology that has been announced. I am grateful to Prof. Smith for providing me with a draft of this paper.

36. Ayalon, *Eunuchs, Caliphs and Sultans.* For the matter of homosexuality among the military slaves, see the comment by C. E. Bosworth, "Ghulām," *Encyclopaedia of Islam,* 2:1082.

37. Yāqūt al-Rūmī al-Ḥamawī, *Mu ʿjam al-buldān* (=*Jacut's geographiches Wörter-buch*), ed. F. Wüstenfeld (Leipzig, 1866), 1:839. The translation is taken with slight changes from D. Ayalon, "The Mamlūk Novice (on His Youthfulness and on His Original Religion)," *Revue des études islamiques* 54 (1986), 2–3 (reprinted in D. Ayalon, *Islam and the Abode of War* [Aldershot, 1994], art. VI).

38. Al-Yaʿqūbī (Aḥmad b. Abī Yaʿ qūb), *Kitāb al-Buldān*, ed. M. J. de Goeje (Leiden, 1892), 258–259; translation in D. Ayalon, "The Muslim City and the Mamluk Military Aristocracy," *Proceedings of the Israeli Academy of Sciences* 2 (1968), 317–318 (reprinted in D. Ayalon, *Studies on the Mamlūks of Egypt, 1250–1517* [London, 1977], art. VII). See also Gordon, *Breaking of a Thousand Swords*, 58, 62–63.

39. ʿAbd al-Raḥmān b. Muḥammad Ibn Khaldūn, *Kitāb al-ʿIbar* (Bulaq, 1284/1867), 5:371; translation from B. Lewis (ed. and tr.), *Islam from the Prophet Muhammad to the Capture of Constantinople* (New York, 1974), 1:98–99.

40. Later, in the Mamlūk Sultanate of Egypt and Syria, the sons of mamlūks were known as *awlād al-nās* ("sons of the people [who count]"). For more on them, see D. Ayalon, "Awlād al-Nās," *Encyclopaedia of Islam*, 1:765.

41. On this individual and the "state" that he built, see T. Bianquis, "Autonomous Egypt from Ibu Ṭūlūn to Kāfūr, 868–969," in C. Petry (ed.), *The Cambridge History of Egypt*, vol. 1, *Islamic Egypt, 640–1517* (Cambridge, UK, 1998), 86–108; Gordon, *Breaking of a Thousand Swords*, passim.

42. Most of our information about this factional conflict, or rather the conflict between units of former rulers and the latest successor, who may have been a descendant of one of the previous rulers, is taken from the time of the mamlūk sultanate. See the studies of D. Ayalon, "Studies on the Structure of the Mamluk Army," *Bulletin of the School of Oriental and African Studies* 15 (1953), 208–210, 218–220; R. Irwin, "Factions in Medieval Egypt," *Journal of the Royal Asiatic Society,* 1986, 228–246. It appears that a similar dynamic occurred in mid-ninth-century Baghdad also. See below.

43. For these events, see Kennedy, *Prophet and the Age of the Caliphates,* 166–171; Gordon, *Breaking of a Thousand Swords*, 75–90.

44. The best survey in English of this eighty-year period of instability is Kennedy, *Prophet and the Age of the Caliphates,* 171–199; on pp. 206–208 there is a discussion of these mamlūk-freebooter units. As far as I am aware there is no monograph devoted to this interesting and important "middle" ʿAbbāsid period.

45. Kennedy, *Armies of the Caliphs,* 120–121.

46. Paul, "State and the Military," 10–33.

47. See the general discussion in C. E. Bosworth, *The Ghaznavids: Their Empire in Afghanistan and Eastern Iran, 994–1040* (Edinburgh, 1963).

48. The literal meaning of the name *Turcoman* (< Ar. Turkmān < Tu. Türkmen) is unclear, but its intention leaves no questions: they were members of Turkish tribal groups (mostly of the Oghuz peoples) who entered the Islamic world, were Muslims, and maintained their nomadic, pastoral way of life. For a short discussion of the etymology of the name, see P. Golden, *An Introduction to the History of the Turkic Peoples,* 212–213.

49. The whole matter of the conversion of the Turkish tribes in the part of the Eurasian steppes that was near the Islamic world remains cloudy; see ibid., 211–213.

50. For the early history of the Seljuqs, see D. O. Morgan, *Medieval Persia, 1040–*

1796 (London, 1988), 25–40; C. E. Bosworth, "The Political and Dynastic History of the Iranian World," in *Cambridge History of Iran,* ed. J. A. Boyle (Cambridge, UK, 1968), 5:1–102.

51. In the Middle Ages, this term referred to much of the area south of the Caucasus Mountains, including a chunk of modern-day eastern Turkey, and northwestern Iran; in any event, it is a much larger region than indicated by the modern state of Azerbaijan.

52. Besides the studies cited in note 50, see C. Cahen, *Pre-Ottoman Turkey,* tr. J. Jones-Williams (London, 1968), 19–40, 66–72.

53. See Morgan, *Medieval Persia,* 29; A. K. S. Lambton, "The Internal Structure of the Saljuq Empire," in *Cambridge History of Iran,* ed. J. A. Boyle (Cambridge, UK, 1968), 5:229–230. Even these figures may be inflated. See the evidence presented below for the figures presented regarding the numbers of mamlūk soldiers at the battle of Manzikert.

54. Niẓām al-Mulk (Abū ʿAlī b. Ḥasan Ṭūsī), *Siyar al-mulūk (=Siyāsat-nāmah),* ed. H. Darke (Tehran, 1962), 131; translation taken, with some changes, from H. Darke, *The Book of Government, or Rules for Kings,* 2nd ed. (London, 1978), 102. Darke mistranslates the term *ghulām* as "page," when it clearly meant "military slave," i.e., mamlūk. Niẓām al-Mulk himself was probably mistaken when he stated that the mamlūks were taken from among the Turcoman tribes; this point is worth pursuing in future research.

55. C. Cahen, "Ikṭā," *Encyclopaedia of Islam,* 3:1088–1091; Cahen, "L'évolution de l'iqṭāʿ du IXe au XIIIe siècle: Contribution à une histoire comparée des sociétés médiévales," *Annales: Economies, Sociétés, Civilisations* 8 (1953): 25–52. For the antecedents of this system, see Gordon, *Breaking of a Thousand Swords,* 118–127. See also my "Turko-Mongolian Nomads and the Iqṭāʿ System in the Islamic Middle East (ca. 1000–1500)," in A. M. Khazanov and A. Wink, *Nomads in the Sedentary World* (London, 2001), 151–171.

56. Sibt ibn al-Jawzī, *Mirʾāt al-zamān* (Ankara, 1968), 147–152, cited in D. Ayalon, "From Ayyūbids to Mamlūks," *Revue des études islamiques* 49 (1981): 44 (reprinted in D. Ayalon, *Islam and the Abode of War* [Aldershot, 1994], art. III).

57. C. Hillenbrand, "Malāzgird. 2. The Battle." *Encyclopaedia of Islam,* 6:243–244; R. Amitai-Preiss, "Manzikert," in J. B. Friedman and K. Mossler Figg (eds.), *Trade, Travel, and Exploration in the Middle Ages: An Encyclopedia* (New York, 2000), 362–363; Cahen, *Pre-Ottoman Turkey,* 26–30.

58. There is, of course, a large literature on the Crusades. For some relatively recent research on the so-called first crusade, see J. Phillips (ed.), *The First Crusade: Origins and Impact* (Manchester, UK, 1997).

59. On these matters see E. Sivan, *L'Islam et la Croisade: Idéologie et propagande dans les reactions musulmanes aux Croisades* (Paris, 1968).

60. These events are well surveyed by P. M. Holt, *The Age of the Crusades: The Near East from the Eleventh Century to 1517* (London, 1986), 38–45.

61. For a survey of events, see ibid., 46–59. For the importance of Turks, mainly mamlūks, in the early Ayyūbid army, see D. Ayalon, "Aspects of the Mamlūk Phenomenon. B. Ayyūbids, Kurds and Turks," *Der Islam* 54 (1977): 1–32 (reprinted in D. Ayalon, *The Mamlūk Military Society* [London, 1979], art. Xb); H. A. R. Gibb, "The Armies of Saladin," in Ayalon, *Studies on the Civilization of Islam,* ed. S. J. Shaw and W. R. Polk (Boston, 1962), 74–90.

62. D. S. Richards, "al-Malik al-Ṣāliḥ Najm al-Dīn Ayyūb," *Encyclopaedia of Islam,* 8:988a–989b. Note that al-Ṣāliḥ Ayyūb's predilection for large mamlūk formations was already evident during the time of his father, al-Kāmil, and thus incurred the latter's wrath for showing too much independence.

63. Literally: "He made them the majority of his army."

64. Taqī al-Dīn Aḥmad b. 'Alīf al-Maqrīzī, *Kitāb al-sulūk li-ma'rifat duwal al-mulūk,* ed. M. M. Ziyāda et al. (Cairo, 1934–73), 1:339–340.

65. The Qipchaqs were known as Cumans and Polovtzi in the West. See G. Hazai, "Kipčak," *Encyclopaedia of Islam,* 5:125b–126b.

66. Shihāb al-Dīn Aḥmad b. 'Abd al-Wahhāb al-Nuwayrī, *Nihayat al-arab fī funūn al-adab* (Cairo, 1992), 29:417. For other sources and modern studies that discuss this matter, see R. Amitai-Preiss, *Mongols and Mamluks: The Mamluk-Īlkhānid War, 1260–1281* (Cambridge, UK, 1995), 18 and n. 63.

67. This was a smaller elite mamlūk unit, established by al-Ṣāliḥ Ayyūb. Incidentally, there is a mistake in the above rendition: the unit of knights that reached the city was led not by King Louis IX but by his brother, Robert of Artois.

68. This was, of course, the future Sultan Baybars (r. 1260–1277), with all of his pre-sultanic sobriquets.

69. Nāṣir al-Dīn 'Abd al-Raḥmān b. Muḥammad Ibn al-Furāt, *Ayyubids, Mamlukes and Crusaders: Selections from the Tārīkh al-Duwal wa 'l-Mulūk of Ibn al-Furāt,* tr. U. and M. C. Lyons; intro. and notes by J. S. C. Riley-Smith (Cambridge, UK, 1971), 1:27–28 (Arabic text), 2:22–23 (translation). The reader may note the rhyme at the end (*turk/shirk*).

70. For a good description of these events, see P. Thorau, *The Lion of Egypt: Sultan Baybars I and the Near East in the Thirteenth Century,* tr. P. M. Holt (London, 1992), 33–36.

71. Ibid., 36–40; Amalia Levanoni, "The Mamluks' Ascent to Power in Egypt," *Studia Islamica* 72 (1990): 121–144.

72. On these events see R. Irwin, *The Middle East in the Middle Ages: The Early Mamluk Sultanate, 1250–1382* (London, 1986), 21–29; R. S. Humphreys, *From Saladin to the Mongols: The Ayyubids of Damascus, 1192–1260* (Albany, 1977), 302–330.

73. See L. Ammann, "Shadjar al-Durr," *Encyclopaedia of Islam,* 2nd ed., 9:176a–b; G. Schregle, *Die Sultanin von Ägypten: Šaǧarat ad-Durr in der arabischen Geschichts-schreibung und Literatur* (Wiesbaden, 1961).

74. Thorau, *Lion of Egypt,* 43–58.

75. P. Jackson, "The *Mamlūk* Institution in Early Muslim India," *Journal of the Royal Asiatic Society* 1990, 340–358; P. Jackson, *The Dehli Sultanate: A Political and Military History* (Cambridge, UK, 1999).

76. Ammann, "Shadjar al-Durr."

77. This touches on a much larger and more complicated matter: gender relations in the mamlūk Sultanate as a whole and within the mamlūk elite in particular. See the studies by J. Berkey, H. Lutfi, and C. Petry in Nikke Keddi and Beth Baron (eds.), *Women in Middle Eastern History* (New Haven, 1991).

78. On the coming of the Mongols to the Middle East, including Chinggis Khan's first

incursion in 1219, see David Morgan, *The Mongols* (Oxford, 1986), 68–71, 145–158. For their invasion of Syria in 1260, see Amitai-Preiss, *Mongols and Mamluks,* chap. 1. For the attitudes of the crusaders toward the Mongols, see P. Jackson, "The Crisis in the Holy Land in 1260," *English Historical Review* 95 (1980): 481–513.

79. For these events, see Humphreys, *From Saladin to the Mongols,* 333–363; R. Amitai, "Mongol Raids into Palestine," *Journal of the Royal Asiatic Society,* 1986: 236–242.

80. For some possible reasons why most of the Mongol army withdrew from Syria at this time, see D. Morgan, "The Mongols in Syria, 1260–1300," in P. Edbury (ed.), *Crusade and Settlement* (Cardiff, 1985), 231–235.

81. R. Amitai-Preiss, "'Ayn Jālūt Revisited," *Tārīh* 2 (1992): 119–150.

82. Abū Shāma, *Tarājim rijāl al-qaranayn al-sādis wa 'l-sābi 'al-maʿrūf biʾl-dhayl ʿalā al-rawḍatayn,* ed. M. Kawtharī (Cairo, 1947), 208.

83. In all fairness, my view is somewhat at variance with that proposed by J. M. Smith Jr., "'Ayn Jālūt: Mamluk Success or Mongol Failure?" *Harvard Journal of Asiatic Studies* 44 (1984): 307–344, who sees significant disparity between the Mongol and the mamlūk soldiers, in spite of their similar origins; cf. Amitai-Preiss, *Mongols and Mamluks,* 214–225.

84. For the self-image of the mamlūks and their efforts to achieve legitimacy in the eyes of their subjects, see R. S. Humphreys, "The Expressive Intent of the Mamluk Architecture of Cairo: A Preliminary Essay," *Studia Islamica* 35 (1972): 69–119; I. Lapidus, *Muslim Cities in the Later Middle Ages* (Cambridge, MA, 1967), chap. 1; R. Kruk, "History and Apocalypse: Ibn al-Nafis's Justification of Mamluk Rule," *Der Islam* 72 (1995): 324–337.

85. For the institutions of the mamlūk sultanate, see Holt, *Age of the Crusades,* 138–154, esp. 143–146, for the decline of the civilian bureaucrats.

86. There is, of course, one major exception to this generalization: the third reign of al-Malik al-Nāsir Muhammad b. Qalawun (r. 1310–1340), although he was indeed a typical puppet in his first two reigns (1293–1294, 1299–1309). On the role of the sultan and the transference of power in the sultanate, see P. M. Holt, "The Position and Power of the Mamluk Sultan," *Bulletin of the School of Oriental and African Studies* 38 (1975): 237–249; D. Ayalon, "Mamlūk Military Aristocracy—A Non-Hereditary Nobility," *Jerusalem Studies in Arabic and Islam* 10 (1987): 205–210 (reprinted in D. Ayalon, *Islam and the Abode of War* [Aldershot, 1994], art. VI).

87. See the fairly technical discussion in H. Rabie, *The Financial System of Egypt, A.H. 564–741/1169–1341* (London, 1972), 26–72; Sato Tsugitaka, *State and Rural Society in Medieval Islam: Sultans, Muqtaʾs and Fallahun* (Leiden, 1997), chaps. 3–6, 8.

88. The term *dawla* today, of course, means "state," but in the later Middle Ages it still retained its earlier meaning of "dynasty." Interesting enough, the Ottoman Empire is referred to by mamlūk writers as *dawlat al-tarākima* (the "Turcoman dynasty," reflecting the origins of the Ottoman family) or even *dawlat al-rūm* (the "dynasty of Anatolia"). This was in spite of the fact that most of the late mamlūk sultans and many of the later Mamlūk elites were Circassians; see below.

89. D. Ayalon, "Bahri Mamluks, Burji Mamluks—Inadequate Names for the Two

Reigns of the Mamluk Sultanate," *Tārīḫ* 1 (1990): 3–53 (reprinted in D. Ayalon, *Islam and the Abode of War* [Aldershot, 1994], art. IV). See below for more about the mistaken use of *Burjī* to describe the second half of the sultanate.

90. For general surveys of the period, see Irwin, *Middle East in the Middle Ages,* 37–84; Holt, *Age of the Crusades,* 90–108; L. Northrup, "The Baḥrī Mamlūk Sultanate," in C. Petry (ed.), *The Cambridge History of Egypt* (Cambridge, UK, 1998), 1:242–289 (a good survey of the entire Baḥrī Period). For specific biographies of sultans, see Thorau, *Lion of Egypt;* L. Northrup, *From Slave to Sultan: The Career of al-Manṣūr Qalāwūn and the Consolidation of Mamluk Rule in Egypt and Syria, 678–689 A.H./1279–1290 A.D.* (Stuttgart, 1998).

91. See Irwin, *Middle East in the Middle Ages,* 85–104.

92. R. Amitai, "The Remaking of the Military Elite of Mamlūk Egypt by al-Nāṣir Muḥammad b. Qalāwūn," *Studia Islamica* 72 (1990): 145–163.

93. C. Melville, " 'Sometimes by the Sword, Sometimes by the Dagger': The Role of the Isma ʿilis in Mamlūk-Mongol Relations in the 8th/14th century," in F. Daftary (ed.), *Mediaeval Isma ʿili History and Thought* (Cambridge, UK, 1996), 247–263; R. Amitai, "The Resolution of the Mongol-Mamluk War," in R. Amitai and M. Biran (eds.), *Mongols, Turks and Others: Eurasian Nomads and the Sedentary World* (Leiden, 2005), 359–390.

94. The first scholar to make this important observation was D. Ayalon, whose systematic thoughts on the matter appeared in "The Expansion and Decline of Cairo Under the Mamluks and Its Background," in R. Curiel (ed.), *Itinéraires d'Orient: Hommages à Claude Cahen,* published as *Res Orientales* 6 (1994): 13–20, based on a lecture given in the early 1970s. Some earlier remarks by Ayalon on this subject were noted by R. Amitai in a review of his book *Islam and the Abode of War: Military Slaves and Islamic Adversaries* (Aldershot, 1994), which appeared in *Bulletin of the Middle East Studies Association* 29 (1995): 252. A more detailed study of the pivotal nature of the period, with many important and original observations, is A. Levanoni, *A Turning Point in Mamluk History: The Third Reign of al-Nāṣir Muḥammad ibn Qalāwūn, 1310–1341* (Leiden, 1995).

95. Maqrīzī, *Kitāb al-sulūk li-maʿrifat duwal al-mulūk,* 2:524–525; a partial translation is in Levanoni, *Turning Point,* 55. The passage continues, giving more information about how al-Nāsir Muhammad treated and pampered his mamlūks.

96. See Ayalon, *L'esclavage du mamelouk;* Ayalon, "Mamlūk," *Encyclopaedia of Islam,* 66:314–321; H. Rabie, "The Training of the Mamlūk Fāris," in V. J. Parry and M. E. Yapp (eds.), *War, Technology and Society in the Middle East* (London, 1975), 153–163.

97. Holt, *Age of the Crusades,* 121–129.

98. B. Fleming, "Literary Activities in the Mamluk Halls and Barracks," in M. Rosen-Ayalon (ed.), *Studies in Memory of Gaston Wiet* (Jerusalem, 1977), 249–260.

99. See the brief but important general comments in D. Ayalon, "Čerkes, ii. Mamlūk period," *Encyclopaedia of Islam,* 2:23–24. For the Circassian period in general, see J.-C. Garcin, "The Regime of the Circassian Mamluks," in C. Petry (ed.), *The Cambridge History of Egypt,* vol. 1, *Islamic Egypt, 640–1517* (Cambridge, UK, 1998), 290–317.

100. This is the basis for the misnomer "Burjī Period," used by some modern scholars and alluded to above, for the Circassian Period in general, as if there had been

some connection between the mamlūks of Circassian origin ca. 1300 and those of three-quarters of a century later.

101. G. Wiet, "Barsbāy," *Encyclopaedia of Islam*, 1:1053–1054; A. Darraj, *L 'Egypte sous le règne de Barsbay, 825–841/1422–1438* (Damascus, 1961). For a more positive assessment of his regime, see Garcin, "Regime of the Circassian Mamluks."

102. For two interpretations of the mamlūks' decline, see D. Ayalon, "Some Remarks on the Economic Decline of the Mamlūk Sultanate," *Jerusalem Studies in Arabic and Islam* 16 (1993): 108–124; R. Lopez, H. Miskimin, and A. Udovitch, "England to Egypt, 1350–1500: Long-Term Trends and Long-Distance Trade," in M. A. Cook (ed.), *Studies in the Economic History of the Middle East from the Rise of Islam to the Present Day* (London, 1970), 93–128 (esp. 115–128, by Udovitch).

103. There may, however, have been some signs of incipient opposition in Syria toward the end of the sultanate; see Lapidus, *Muslim Cities*, chap. 5.

104. For this affair, not one of the high points of mamlūk military prowess, see Holt, *Age of the Crusades*, 179.

105. On this campaign, see S. Harel, *The Struggle for Domination in the Middle East: The Ottoman-Mamluk War, 1485–1491* (Leiden, 1995).

106. For the two reigns of these two sultans, see the books by C. Petry, *Twilight of Majesty: The Reigns of Mamluk Sultans al-Ashraf Qaytbay and Qansuh al-Ghawri in Egypt* (Seattle, 1993), and *Protectors or Praetorians? The Last Mamluk Sultans and Egypt's Waning as a Great Power* (Albany, 1994). The matter of Qansuh's possible plans for rebuilding the military are hinted at by Petry in his article "The Military Institution and Innovation in the Late Mamluk Period," in C. Petry (ed.), *The Cambridge History of Egypt*, vol. 1, *Islamic Egypt, 640–1517* (Cambridge, UK, 1998), 478–489.

107. This is based on the argument presented in D. Ayalon, *Gunpowder and Firearms in the Mamluk Kingdom: A Challenge to a Medieval Society*, 2nd ed. (London, 1978). For a different view, see Robert Irwin's "Gunpowder and Firearms in the Mamluk Sultanate," in A. Levanoni and M. Winter (eds.), *The Mamluks in Egyptian and Syrian Politics and Society* (Leiden, 2004), 117–139, which forcefully challenges Ayalon's thesis.

108. For the events of this period, see P. M. Holt, *Egypt and the Fertile Crescent, 1516–1922* (London, 1966). For the neo-mamlūk institution, see D. Ayalon, "Studies in al-Jabartī: Notes on the Transformation of Mamluk Society in Egypt under the Ottomans," *Journal of the Economic and Social History of the Orient* 3 (1960): 148–174, 275–325. Jane Hathaway, in an important and original book (*The Politics of Households in Ottoman Egypt: The Rise of the Qazdağli* [Cambridge, UK, 1996]), has called into question much of the "mamlūkness" of this period. To my mind, her criticism of the Ayalon-Holt neo-mamlūk model is overdrawn. See my review of her book in *The Times Literary Supplement*, May 30, 1997, p. 9.

109. H. Inalcik, "Ghulām, iv. — Ottoman Empire," *Encyclopaedia of Islam*, 2:1087–1090; R. Murphey, "Yeñi Čeri," ibid., 11:322–331. For military slavery in Safawid Iran, a subject that space prevents me from exploring, see C. E. Bosworth, "Ghulām, ii. — Persia," ibid., 2:1086.

110. Lewis, *Race and Slavery in the Middle East*, 69.

111. Douglas H. Johnson, "Sudanese Military Slavery from the Eighteenth to the

Twentieth Century," in Léonie J. Archer (ed.), *Slavery and Other Forms of Unfree Labor* (London, 1988), 142–156.

112. 'Abd al-Raḥamān b. Muḥammad Ibn Khaldūn, *Kitāb al-'Ibar* (Bulaq, 1284/ 1867), 5:371; translation (with slight changes) is from B. Lewis (ed. and tr.), *Islam from the Prophet Muhammad to the Capture of Constantinople* (New York, 1974), 1:97–99. As far as I am aware, the first scholar to note this important passage was D. Ayalon, who first translated (into Hebrew) it in *Eretz-Israel* 7 (1964): 142–143; see also Ayalon, "Mamlūkiyyāt," *Jerusalem Studies in Arabic and Islam* 2 (1980): 341–346.

113. Patterson, *Slavery and Social Death*, 308–314, 331–332.

Armed Slaves and Political Authority in Africa in the Era of the Slave Trade, 1450–1800

JOHN THORNTON

No problem of power is more vexing in Africa or elsewhere than that of maintaining armed forces. Vital to any political system, both for protection from abroad and for security at home, the organization and capability of violence that makes soldiers effective also makes them a potential threat. In a search for the most loyal soldiers, African rulers sometimes opted to arm the most dependent groups in society, and indeed, the regularity with which slaves were armed in Africa suggests that fighting was as much a part of the work routine of slaves as any other labor. But by arming slaves and using them to enhance power, rulers also ran the risk of creating a cohesive group whose interests might run counter to their own, or in the worst case might lead to a military coup d'état. Furthermore, the role of slaves as private property raised the possibility that wealthy people might also recruit armies and challenge the state. As a final option, slaves might break free altogether, become corporate groups, and eventually form states in their own right.

Thinking about armed slaves in Africa is especially difficult because the continent's slavery was so elastic and ill-defined. In Africa, various institutions of dependency were widespread because, much more so than in Europe and most of Asia, dependents such as slaves played a special role as private, wealth-producing property in a legal system where land was not recognized as property. This important legal divergence explains the large numbers of

people held as slaves and the wide range of their deployment.[1] African societies are sometimes viewed as "slave societies" because of the pervasiveness
and importance of dependent institutions that can be defined as slavery, but
often slaves have rights or privileges that result in African slave-holding systems being held to be "benign."[2]

Indeed, because of the legal divergence and the wide range of employments,
as well as a lack of detailed contemporary documentation,[3] scholars have
balked at defining all the many categories of dependent groups as "slaves."
Some have opted to call them "serfs" or insisted on using terms in local languages to stress the uniqueness of their status and place them outside of comparative study.[4] To take an example in which status is detailed in contemporary documents, in Ndongo, a large kingdom in west central Africa, free
commoners were called *ana murinda* (singular *mona murinda*) or "children of
the murinda" (a term for a state), and there were at least two categories of
"slaves": *abika* (singular *mubika*), acquired largely in war and vulnerable to
sale, and *ijiko* (singular *kijiko*), perhaps originally also acquired in war, bound
to the land but not salable or transferable, except for limited circumstances, a
status that might rightly be regarded as serfdom.[5]

These definitional and related status issues make the problem of armed
slaves especially vexing for African history. For comparative purposes, I have
defined as slaves all dependent groups that originated in captivity or judicial
condemnation and bore hereditary dependent status. In many cases, however,
I have had to accept the judgment of witnesses who employed the term *slave*
(or its equivalent in languages other than English) even if an exact legal status
or origin is otherwise unknown.[6]

In addition to definitional difficulties, those who seek to understand armed
slaves as soldiers in Africa also run into serious evidentiary problems. Africa
had hundreds of distinct societies of various dimensions, and a great many of
them kept no written records or kept records that bear on these issues only
obliquely. Retrospective reconstruction from modern oral tradition and eth-
nographic analogy, once a popular way of circumventing the illiteracy of many
African societies, is increasingly seen as less effective than was once believed in
recovering institutional and social details of past times. So in examining the
question of armed slaves in Africa from the sixteenth to the eighteenth century
we are necessarily left with the uneven record of mostly outside observers.

Nevertheless, several patterns in the use of armed slaves are visible. One of
the most important was to facilitate a centralization of power. A ruler, acting
as a private citizen, often acquired slaves and used their labor to enhance his
revenue, or more important, used their potential as soldiers to create a powerful coercive force to act on his will. Using these forces, the ruler might be able

to subvert constitutional arrangements that limited his power and rule with greater efficiency and authority. The mechanisms and motivations for using armed slaves to centralize power are well illustrated by the Moroccan pashalik of Timbuktu. In 1591 Judar Pasha, a Spanish renegade operating under the auspices of the sultan of Morocco, carved this state out of the Niger Bend in modern-day Mali from lands seized from Songhay. A few years after the conquest, the troops of the pashalik, who were free and had been recruited mostly from mercenaries, were effectively independent of their Moroccan overlord.[7] Within this new state, power resided in the army, which elected its pashas in a system of rotation: each of the three divisions of the army had the option of placing their candidate before the others. If all agreed, the pasha remained in office as long as he had their support, for as soon as a major leader withdrew support, the pasha had to step down.

In this context of insecure power based on a politically engaged army, Pasha Mansur ibn Mas'ud al Za'ri turned to armed slaves to augment his standing. Elected pasha in 1712, he was deposed shortly after a humiliating military defeat caused him to lose the confidence of the army. But he was prepared to do what he had to in order to gain power, even without the army, indeed, he only reluctantly left when a senior cleric read him the law on the duties of pashas.[8] In spite of this setback, Mansur was reelected on July 5, 1716. Determined not to be deposed again, he decided to outmaneuver the formal structure of government and army and employed slaves of local (not Moroccan) origin, called *legha,* as a private military force. In order to build this body quickly he not only employed his personal slaves, who had served as a bodyguard, but increased their numbers by luring others who wished to leave their masters. In the years that followed, Mansur's slave soldiers harassed the people, redirected tax revenues due the Moroccan soldiers, and undercut their position.[9] These armed slaves also played a role in regular military expeditions.[10] His rivals quickly recognized the threat this new armed force represented to the delicate constitutional balance and challenged his position. Despite the support of a civilian crowd, however, the legha troops suppressed the rebellion.

Mansur's use of armed slaves, which drew on local and Islamic traditions, represents one pole of the use of slaves to increase power; the counterreaction it provoked reveals an equally ancient and troubling problem. Armed slaves, whether used as bodyguards for subordinate officials or perhaps as security forces for merchants, might be developed into a power base that could threaten central authority or might allow wealthier groups in the general population to demand a greater share in decision making. Therefore, just as rulers might see armed slaves as a way of developing and extending their power without having to consult others, those same others might see in their own armed slaves the means to free themselves from autocratic rulers.

If Mansur's military innovations were both promising and divisive, it did not take long for his rivals to copy his methods. In the aftermath of the rebellion, Timbuktu was sharply divided, and all of the army factions began to build up their private power, fortifying their houses and building towers from which they exchanged hostilities.[11] The religious leaders (*'ulama*) of Timbuktu led a revolt against Mansur by arming their own dependents to counter the legha.[12] A significant battle occurred in July 1719 just east of Timbuktu in which both the armed slaves of the elite of Timbuktu and the legha of Mansur played an important role.[13] Mansur's defeat in this engagement led to his downfall, which came on October 14, 1719. The legha, commanded by Shaykh Buro Kandi, were slaughtered.[14]

Mansur's rise and fall illustrate the potentials and pitfalls of arming dependents, and the lesson was not lost. Pashas who followed Mansur armed their own legha, as a part of the military establishment of the state. In 1743, for example, Pasha Sa'id marched out of Timbuktu to settle a rebellion with an army that included numbers of legha.[15] The presence of other armed slaves arrayed against the pasha's power prevented a repetition of the dramatic events of Mansur's time. For example, armed slaves reinforced the army of Sarakaina when it was attacked by the pasha's men in 1729.[16]

Mansur's attempt to expand his power through the use of armed slaves was not unique in African history; similar ploys were commonplace, particularly in times of flux when various groups competed for authority. Like Mansur, rulers of powerful states in central Africa relied on servile groups to enhance their authority and ensure the loyalty of their soldiers. Both of the two large kingdoms that dominated west central Africa in the sixteenth and seventeenth centuries, Kongo and Ndongo, used a core of highly skilled professional soldiers to fight in their wars, though countless other subjects might also be drafted for supply duties or to form a body of archers who loosed a few arrows at the start of battles but quickly retired once serious fighting began. Battles were usually resolved by the encounter of a few thousand skilled soldiers who fought hand to hand. In Kongo, these troops carried defensive arms (shields) as well as swords and thrusting lances, while in Ndongo in general they employed few or no defensive arms and used battleaxes and swords as their typical weapons. The proper and effective deployment of these weapons at close quarters required strenuous training (often encompassed in military dancing) and thus put a premium on supporting these troops for longer periods than the draftees.[17]

But the status of these professional troops diverged widely in the two countries. In Kongo they were regarded as noble and sometimes lived on stipends supplied by the state, but their status in Ndongo was more ambiguous, akin to that of slaves. Professional soldiers (*kimbari*, plural *imbari*), commanded by officers called *kilamba,* seem to have been kept in special villages for their support, but their standing lay somewhere between the two other servile classes (that is, abika and ijiko).

Events in early seventeenth-century Ndongo can illuminate the important role armed slaves played. In 1575 the Portuguese founded their colony of Angola, and a series of wars with various African powers, including Ndongo, ensued. In the 1620s, after the Portuguese had dealt a series of devastating defeats to Ndongo, its royal family fled to islands in the Kwanza River. Many of the royal dependents and slaves were captured by the Portuguese forces and placed on lands under their control. After the suicide of King Ngola Mbandi in 1624, leadership passed to his sister Ana de Sousa Njinga Mbandi, best known as Queen Njinga. From the very beginning of her reign Njinga was anxious to have "slaves" (in correspondence written in Portuguese she often used *escravo* or even *peça* to refer to such people) returned to her. Although many were ijiko, who would work fields to supply the state with its revenue, others were "war slaves." Njinga was particularly successful in persuading the kilambas to desert the Portuguese, and as the governor, Fernão de Sousa, complained, she was gaining such strength that her forces would soon surpass his, in spite of his having a number of collaborators and rivals of Njinga in his camp.[18] Ndongo's skilled soldiers were drawn from a servile class that was the mainstay of Ndongo administration, not only in the period of crisis and war against Portugal but in earlier periods as well.

Like their west central African counterparts, the rulers of late eighteenth-century Oyo sought to counterbalance powerful rural groups and court factions by recruiting slaves for their palace guard, including both infantry and cavalry. Initially, a set of professional soldiers serving under captains made up the bulk of the army, especially its highly skilled cavalry. These war leaders were appointed by the alafin, or ruler, but they recruited their own soldiers from the free population, some perhaps from slaves, according to oral evidence collected centuries later, which is admittedly vague and inconclusive. Their superior was the basorun, a powerful official who could use the power of the army to cow the ruler. Indeed, Gaha, who held the office from 1754 to 1774, became the effective ruler and killed several competitors.[19] Against the war leaders, the alafin set a corps of his own slaves that augmented the army and provided him with a force that was under his personal control.[20] Abiodun (1774–89), for example, forcibly detained a group of several thousand Popos who had come to his kingdom and joined them to his army, no doubt to bolster his own forces in the face of competition from the army.[21] In fact, the struggles over power that characterized late imperial Oyo, especially after 1830, were heightened by the increasing strength of the ruler's personal forces, which included an expanded number of slave soldiers.[22] As in Timbuktu, rival groups managed to use their own armed retainers to match the challenge posed by the state.

These examples illustrate processes taking place in larger and more powerful African political entities; much of Africa in this period, however, was dominated by considerably smaller political units. The dynamics of these small units reveal subtle differences in the ways in which armed slaves played a role in politics. The Gold Coast in the seventeenth century illustrates a pattern in which the small size of polities necessarily weakens the resources available to any person and makes developing groups of dependents particularly attractive to those seeking power. In this period, the region that is largely formed by modern southern Ghana was divided into about thirty sovereign entities, most of which did not have areas larger than about a county in the United States or populations exceeding thirty thousand. The internal constitution and hence division of authority of each one varied: some were, in the words of Willem Bosman, the Dutch factor in the last years of the seventeenth century, "republics" with a relatively weak ruler and strong subordinates and others "monarchies" where the ruler had much more sway.[23] Either way, the classification was only a tendency, for political power was often shared between a king and a group of his family members or retainers, an aristocracy that controlled offices and collected taxes, and the wealthiest of commoners, who were often enriched by trade. Such groups checked the powers of the rulers and potentially could block efforts to centralize power and decision making, thus making each polity a delicately balanced entity of opposed interests and forces, where either side might look to innovations to increase their power or defend their rights and where the smallness of scale made it possible for small groups to amass resources sufficient to alter political relationships. Therefore, considerable internal jockeying occurred between rulers holding formal power and other formal and informal groups that sought to undermine this power.

In the Gold Coast, from the sixteenth century through the late seventeenth, highly skilled and professional soldiers conducted warfare. Although many ordinary people might be recruited, the core of the fighting force was a crack unit of free professionals who fought hand to hand and who possessed specialized skills in such fighting.[24] Many Gold Coast states had professional bodies of soldiers who were attached to state service, often called *asafo*, who served as a sort of professional association and consequently seem to have had a certain amount of independent power. Certainly they refused at times to fight beyond a stipulated period, as the French visitor Jean Barbot noted in the late seventeenth century, when he said these soldiers were "under no obligation to stay abroad any longer than they think fit."[25] Not always satisfied with the demands of this professional association, and perhaps interested in extending their own decision-making power, kings employed slaves (as well as mercenaries) as special units not only to increase the size of armies but also to ensure the loyalty and service of those who fought for them. At the same time, however, the aristocrats who controlled subunits of the state and served as officers in the army had their own personal retainers and armed slaves, complicating the situation. The sum of these complexities was noted by Jean Barbot, for he observed that in dealing with the army, whether as king or aristocrat, any officer's "authority extends not beyond those who are his proper slaves."[26] Barbot's near-contemporary Willem Bosman was even more emphatic about the advantages of slave soldiers, for in his view, "only slaves could be commanded to war."[27] A French traveler, visiting the western state of Assini in the opening years of the eighteenth century, noted the importance of slaves in its armed forces, arguing that slaves were the best and most loyal soldiers in the army.[28] Thus, in these armies, free associations of professional soldiers with their own political agendas served in units where slaves, loyal either to the king or to his aristocratic officers, also served and managed to counter some of their interests.

Self-aggrandizing kings increasingly resorted to slaves or other dependents to build their armed forces. Toward the end of the seventeenth century and especially in the eighteenth, many parts of the Gold Coast witnessed the rise of new and more powerful states, characterized by a strong military and more centralization in decision making. Akwamu was among the pioneers of the new system, which rested on a strong army of slaves under the king's direct command. In enumerating the king's rights, Eric Tilleman, the Danish factor at Accra in the late seventeenth century, noted that "he has for warfare the best and most experienced slaves to be found in the entire country."[29] Others observed that the king's soldiers were all "his relatives or slaves," emphasizing the rise of new and more dependent forces. A key point was the ownership of weapons, for the free soldiers of the asafo companies owned their own materiel, while the slave and dependent soldiers had only those "that their masters gave them."[30] Perhaps, as Ray Kea, an authority on warfare in the Gold Coast, has suggested, the somewhat mysterious "Sikadinger," the "crafty young men" whom the early eighteenth-century rulers of Akwamu employed to raid their enemies and sometimes steal people as slaves, were themselves slaves of the ruler.[31]

Just as arming slaves might provide kings and aristocrats with a core of loyal soldiers and perhaps help them increase their political strength at home and abroad, so armed slaves provided some Gold Coast merchants with opportunities to set themselves up even against kings. The late seventeenth and early eighteenth centuries saw the emergence of a number of powerful merchants with varied trade connections, in both domestic and overseas trade. Many of these merchants became more or less independent of any state. For instance, John Konny, a merchant of Ahanta who had become very rich and virtually independent thanks to trade with the Europeans, set up his own stone fort with artillery mounted in the bastions. Such powerful merchants retained large groups of armed men, ranging from a few hundred to a few thousand, and engaged in some of the wars of their time. Konny, for example, was said to have "900 well-drilled soldiers" in 1711, when he defeated a Dutch force as well as creating havoc for a number of local rulers.[32] More than likely, these merchants drew their soldiers from among their own slaves.

The tendency to use slaves and dependent soldiers was probably a product of political insecurity — whether of rulers who had little faith in their political system or of merchants or subordinates who did not trust their rulers. These conditions existed until the early eighteenth century, which was the golden age of armed slaves in the Gold Coast. New polities such as Asante emerged in the mid-to-late eighteenth century, exercising greater royal power and exhibiting less need of slaves serving as soldiers than in the past. A change in weaponry may have facilitated the move away from small groups of dependent soldiers and cost the professional military companies their power. The great states of the eighteenth century used conscripted militias equipped with muskets to wage wars that focused on missile weapons requiring little skill in lieu of the professional and skilled hand-to-hand combat of earlier eras.[33]

Just as African leaders employed slaves to enhance their authority, so in Angola Europeans pursued the same tactics. When the Portuguese entered Angola they brought their own small army, which initially operated as a mercenary force under Ndongo command. After war broke out between Portugal and Ndongo in 1579, however, the Portuguese had to fight for their land on their own, and needed to increase their military strength quickly. To this end, they made alliances with dissident African nobles (*sobas*), who supplied them with troops. Sobas, however, turned out to be fickle in their loyalties, for the Portuguese found that, after a defeat in 1590, their allies abandoned them and they lost most of their military forces. From the time they entered into war in Angola, the Portuguese also began acquiring as well as selling slaves.[34] Slave-worked farms soon sprouted along the major rivers, and Portuguese planters supplied the foodstuffs that would eventually feed the slaves awaiting export in the thousands.[35] Thus Portuguese Angola became a slave colony not only for its role in the external export of people but also in its domestic economy.

Given their military weakness, the Portuguese soon made use of their own armed slaves. For instance, slaves were among the Portuguese troops that fought at the Battle of Talandongo in 1583.[36] Armed slaves continued to serve in Portuguese forces, though never as the majority of the soldiers, throughout the seventeenth century, even after the Portuguese had acquired more regular forces. In 1644, for example, in mobilizing an army to fight against Queen Njinga, the Portuguese included, among various armed groups from Portugal or the allied African rulers, slaves of the Portuguese, but they were not numerous.[37] By the late eighteenth century the army serving the Portuguese included free imbari as well as those regarded as "captive" or slaves, perhaps once simply armed slaves now settled into regular life.[38] Thus, both Portuguese and African powers in Angola employed servile dependents as soldiers, in each case using them to strengthen their hand against rival groups within their own society, and in the Portuguese case, to create a dependent group that would make them less beholden to local power holders.

In a few areas where the larger states did not emerge, the pattern of using slave soldiers survived. The mouth of the Volta River, for example, was dotted with small polities, many formed by refugee groups that had fled the regional powers farther west. Here conscripts served in the armies, to be sure, but they were still joined by a host of other groups, and the private armies of slaves raised by prosperous merchants to protect their interests in a politically insecure region still played a role. For example, in 1784 the German Isert, who worked as a Danish factor at Accra, accompanied a mixed group of allies in one war. One of the most powerful contingents raised for the war belonged to the merchant named Late Awoko, who had risen from a low estate to become prominent in Popo. Isert described his army as comprising "all his serfs," presumably his dependents and probably long-serving slaves.[39]

Although the slaves whom rulers or private citizens armed seem to have been drawn largely from among their own dependents, some systems of military recruitment can be regarded as essentially servile institutions, even though their functioning does not fully accord with the idea of slavery developed in European and colonial American contexts. For example, in the Ottoman Empire, the sultans drew the Janissary corps, an important component of their fighting forces, from a special tax levied on the Christian population of the country. This tax required Christian households to render up a child to be effectively enslaved by the state and to serve in the army for life. It is common to describe the Devshirme system, as this special taxation was called, as a special form of slavery.[40]

The Kingdom of Dahomey, located in modern Benin, where the possession of a powerful army was an important branch of royal authority, provides a good example of servile recruitment like the Devshirme. In the general military culture of the area, troops were often raised by levy by powerful local person-ages, who were styled as nobles.[41] As long as the army depended on such levies, which the crown could not control, Dahomey's centralization would not be complete. But Dahomey's rulers looked for ways to develop an army under more direct supervision. William Snelgrave, writing about the 1720s, noted that the king's army included several companies "with proper colors and officers" whose strength was maintained by acquiring young boys. The king, he noted, allows "every common soldier a boy at publick charge to be trained up, most of army consists of soldiers bred in this way."[42] These boys, according to the French observer Pruneau de Pommegorge, were raised by a levy on villages at the rate of one boy per village.[43] The basis of this interesting recruiting device may be found in further observations made by the English trader Robert Norris, who visited the Dahomey capital in 1772. He observed that some young men paid the king of Dahomey to receive wives, though he does not reveal the source of the king's possession of these wives (perhaps they were slaves). The children of these women, however, were held to belong to the king, were raised in villages remote from their birthplace, and were appro-priated by the king when they had grown and lost knowledge of the family.[44]

Arming slaves was an important tool in the arsenal of any ruler wishing to expand his power, but he might also face challenges from within the slave corps as well as from the displaced power holders or their own slave forces. The slow rise of the *ceddo,* or warrior commanders, in eighteenth-century Senegambia reveals the potential for political transformation inherent in using slaves as soldiers. Their origins lie in the turmoil of the last years of the seventeenth century, when the Kingdom of Great Jolof and the Empire of Great Fulo that absorbed it declined, giving rise to new kingdoms, especially Waalo, Kajoor, and Bawol, that sought to assert their own independent exis-tence while trying to incorporate their neighbors. At the same time, the new states often suffered internal turmoil as rivals for the throne fought each other and enlisted the aid of neighbors in their machinations. Lat Sukaabe Faal (1695–1720) sought both to consolidate his internal position and unite the two kingdoms of Kajoor and Waalo. Further inland the same sort of struggle was represented by Samba Gelaajo Jeegi (1725–31) of Futa Tooro in the middle Senegal valley, who represented the ideal of a warrior with his de-voted band of followers exploiting political weaknesses and strengthening his power.[45] These new armies and the states they created were regimes in which slaves, becoming officers and rising to commanding positions in the army, came to dominate the rulers, while all participated in constant slave raiding within and outside their domains.[46] The French governor Doumet de Siblas, in a memoir of 1769, noted that the kings of Kajoor and Waalo governed their kingdoms with a network of "captifs" who served as generals and "great men" of the country. These slave officials also commanded his only army, which was composed of his personal slaves. The remaining soldiers, raised by levy from the countryside, were free people, though they were undisciplined and of relatively little value compared to the slave soldiers of the standing army.[47] These powerful commanders exercised such influence that they had become effectively the rulers of the states where traditional leaders were powerless to make decisions without their consent. The era of the ceddo was characterized by the power of military slaves and their machinations, often criticized for their brutality and injustice by Islamic leaders and holy men. In the Bambara area, slave soldiers called *jonjon* created a new dynasty in 1776, while elsewhere they effectively ruled the country though they did not formally take power.[48]

The possibility that slaves might form corporate unions capable of overawing their rulers reveals one of the clearest dangers of using slaves to bolster power. Perhaps the most dramatic instance of slaves' becoming a power in their own right, and indeed a challenge to our understanding of the term *slave*, comes from the Imbangala of west central Africa. The origins of the Imbangala are mysterious; modern traditions of their descendents point to long migrations from deep in central Africa, which an early generation of scholars took literally but which are at best viewed as symbolic today.[49] Whatever their ultimate origin, their lifestyle was first described by Andrew Battell, an English sailor serving unwillingly with the Portuguese in Angola, who spent about seventeen months with them in 1600–1601. Based on Battell's notes, and the work of other eyewitnesses, the Imbangala appear to have been military or bandit bands (their earliest traditions traced them to officials in the central highlands of Angola). They may well have been originally army units that revolted or were set free by turbulent times in the late sixteenth century and who, like some of the freebooting armies of the Thirty Years' War in Europe, became entities unto themselves. The Imbangala were independent bands that recruited their members by capturing young boys from late childhood to young adulthood. These boys were then made to undergo a traumatic initiation that included cannibalism, perhaps intended to break their moral training and equate them with witches or other evildoers who symbolically ate their victims. Moreover, they killed any children born in their camp, so as not to be impeded in their march, and perhaps as another traumatic connection to evil. They lived by rapine, one of their distinctive habits being the destructive way that they used palm trees, which normally were grown and tapped by villagers over long periods of time. But the Imbangala way was to cut the trees down, draw out a large quantity of sap to make wine, and move on to the next region, thus devastating the economy of all areas through which they passed.[50] The palm wine, soon reinforced by European alcohol, helped to maintain control over the group. They were, in short, a band of former soldiers, ex-slaves, and slaves (their captured boys were slaves, at least for a time).

Imbangala bands entered European service in the early seventeenth century and were deployed to help Portugal break the military deadlock in their war against Ndongo. They surely did break the deadlock, although their destructive habits were so devastating that soon all parties were trying to bring them under control, while simultaneously seeking to use them as allies as they fought each other. Playing on the problems of control, one settler came up with the novel idea of importing large quantities of alcohol with which to pay them on a regular basis, perhaps to keep them from destroying loyal Portuguese areas as much as to keep them in service.[51] When the diplomatic situation in Angola and Ndongo settled down in the 1660s, a series of treaties either sought their destruction or granted bands security in one or another area where they became regional leaders, of which the model was Kasanje, a large state on the Kwango.[52]

The Imbangala method of recruitment made it possible for other leaders in central Africa to describe them as bands of slaves, as indeed Queen Njinga did in her treaty with Portugal. Fearing their power over her kingdom, when making her first set of proposals in 1655, Njinga asked the Portuguese to guarantee that they would support her "leaving my lands only to my sister and not to my slaves."[53] Clearly these were slaves unlike those employed in any previous African or European army and unlike the legha of the Middle Niger or the armed bodies of mercenaries in the service of Gold Coast merchants. Rather, they were a self-sustaining system of slavery that served only other, more highly placed slaves as masters. Paradoxically, they served no master but that of their own group, a fact that was revealed in their selection of their own leadership as late as the 1770s, even of the groups that had been integrated into the Portuguese army.[54] They were thus slaves within their group, but not slaves with regard to outside authority.

Africa thus reveals a variety of ways in which slaves were armed, serving various masters to centralize states, decentralize them, or even, in the case of the Imbangala, to destroy them altogether. The complexity of arming slaves in Africa parallels the complexity of the institution itself and challenges us to consider and reconsider our notions of the nature and meaning of slavery in the African portion of the Atlantic world. Slavery is an institution designed to provide masters with the maximum private control over their subordinates, and this two-edged sword can free them from the needs and demands of the state, but it can also subject them to the dynamics inherent in highly centralized power. When slaves are combined with armed forces, its potential to increase power or destroy it is enhanced, for as the powerful use slaves to increase their control of disciplined armed forces, they run the great risk of creating cohesive forces that can be their own undoing.

Notes

1. John Thornton, *Africa and Africans in the Making of the Atlantic World, 1400–1800,* 2nd ed. (Cambridge, 1998), 75–97.

2. For an excellent example of the problems of definition, see Joseph Inikori, "Slavery in Africa and the Transatlantic Slave Trade," in Alusine Jalloh and Stephen E. Maizlish, eds, *The African Diaspora* (College Station, TX, 1996), 39–72.

3. Reconstruction of the nature of pre-colonial slavery has often had to rely on studies conducted during the colonial period or on oral testimony about institutions that were no longer functioning. For example, a classic collection of essays on slavery in Africa, Igor Kopytoff and Suzanne Meiers, eds., *Slavery in Africa: Historical and Anthropological Perspectives* (Madison, 1977), reveals that many authors, even those who wrote historical pieces, owe a debt to anthropological research and methods.

4. This is the central contention of Inikori, "Slavery in Africa."

5. Baltasar Barreira, "Informação acerca dos escravos de Angola," 1582–83, in António Brásio (ed.), *Monumenta Missionaria Africana,* 1st ser., 15 vols. (Lisbon, 1952–88), 3: 227–28; Barreira was probably the informant for the more detailed version of Ndongo social structure (which is followed here) published by Pierre du Jarric in 1610, *Histoire des choses plvs memorables advenves tant ez Indes Orientales que autres pais de la descouuerte des Portugais* (Bordeaux, 1610), 79–80. For more documentation and modern interpretation see Beatrix Heintze, "Der Staat Ndongo im 16. Jahrhundert," in Heintze (ed.), *Studien zur Geschichte Angolas im 16. und 17. Jahrhundert: Ein Lesebuch* (Cologne, 1996), 61–92.

6. I have not been able to read the several Arabic-language sources cited below in the original language and have thus accepted translators' renderings of the texts.

7. John Ralph Willis, "The Western Sudan from the Moroccan Invasion (1591) to the Death of Al-Mukhtar al-Kunti (1811)," in J. F. A. Ajayi and Michael Crowder, eds., *History of West Africa,* 3rd ed., 1985), 1:531–76; for a more detailed history see Michel Abitbol, *Tombouctou et les Arma: De la conquête marocaine du Soudan nigerien en 1591 à l'hégémonie de l'empire peulh du Macina en 1833* (Paris, 1979). Also see his briefer statement in the context of a wider region in "The End of the Songhay Empire," in B. A. Ogot, ed., *UNESCO General History of Africa* (Los Angeles, 1992), 300–26.

8. Anonymous, *Tedzkiret en-Nisian fi Akhbar Molouk es-Soudan,* ed. and trans. O. Houdas (Paris, 1966), 26–27. This chronicle was written about 1750 by a resident of the area. It takes the form of biographies of various people arranged alphabetically, and its chronological and historical content is very diffused throughout it.

9. Ibid., 29–30.

10. Ibid., 39.

11. Ibid., 66–73.

12. These dependents might be regarded as slaves; the Arabic text calls them *hartani,* a term that is often translated as "serfs" because they were believed to be descended from ancient indigenous groups and not enslaved in war. The problem of definition need not concern us, since for our purposes a hereditary dependent class fulfills this analytical position.

13. *Tedzkiret en-Nisian,* 228–29. Another encounter involved the legha in May and June (234).

14. Ibid., 47–51, 226–27.

15. Ibid., 123, 126.

16. Ibid., 197–98.

17. John Thornton, *Warfare in Atlantic Africa, 1500–1800* (London, 1999), 99–125. See also John Thornton, "The Art of War in Angola, 1575–1680," *Comparative Studies in Society and History* 30 (1988): 360–78.

18. Fernão de Sousa to his children (c. 1632), fols. 223–23v, in Beatriz Heintze (ed.), *Fontes para a história de Angola no século XVII,* 2 vols. (Wiesbaden, 1985–88), 1:227.

19. Robin Law, *The Oyo Empire, c. 1600–c. 1836: A West African Imperialism in the Era of the Slave Trade* (Oxford, 1977), 80–81. Law relies largely on oral evidence for his reconstruction of the imperial army before 1830, much of it from Samuel Johnson's classic treatise based on oral tradition, *The History of the Yorubas* (London, 1921, but composed 1897, reprinted 1966), and in a few other cases on his own interviews or those of more recent historians.

20. Law, *Oyo Empire,* 189–92.

21. Johnson, *History,* 186–87.

22. Law, *Oyo Empire,* 189–201.

23. Willem Bosman, *Naukeurige beschryving van de Guinese Goud-, Tand- en Slave Kust* (Utrecht, 1704; 2nd ed. Amsterdam, 1709). Translated as *A New and Accurate Description of the Coast of Guinea* (London, 1705; reprint, London, 1967), 165–79.

24. This section follows Ray Kea, *Settlements, Trade, and Polities in the Seventeenth-Century Gold Coast* (Baltimore, 1982), 130–68 with regard to many aspects of military organization. See also Thornton, *Warfare,* 55–74.

25. Jean Barbot, *A Description of the Coast of North and South Guinea,* in Awnsham Churchill and John Churchill, *A Collection of Voyages and Travels* (London, 1732), 5:294. On this work, see P. E. H. Hair, Adam Jones, and Robin Law, *Barbot on Guinea: The Writings of Jan Barbot on West Africa, 1678–1712* (Oxford, 1992).

26. Barbot, *Description,* 294.

27. Bosman, *New and Accurate Description,* 180.

28. Godfrey Loyer, "Relation du voyage du royaume d'Issiny," in Paul Roussier, ed., *L'Etablissement d'Issiny, 1687–1702* (Paris, 1935), 219–20.

29. Erick Tilleman, *En Kort og Enfoldig Beretning om det Landskab Ginea og dets Beskaffenhed* (Copenhagen, 1697), 108, pagination of original marked in English translation of Selena Axelrod Winsnes, *A Short and Simple Account of the Country Guinea and Its Nature* (Madison, 1994).

30. Bosman, *New and Accurate Description,* 71, 74–75.

31. Kea, *Settlements,* 162; see the source cited by Kea, Ludewig Ferdinand Rømer, *Tilforladelig Efterretning om Negotien paa Kysten Guinea . . .* (Copenhagen, 1760),

125–26, 143–44, original pagination marked in the English translation, Selena Axelrod Wisnes, *A Reliable Account of the Coast of Guinea, 1760* (Oxford, 2000).

32. See Kwame Daaku, *Trade and Politics on the Gold Coast, 1600–1720: A Study of the African Reaction to European Trade* (Oxford, 1970), 130–31.

33. For the evolution of warfare, see Kea, *Settlements,* 158–64; Thornton, *Warfare,* 55–74.

34. For an overview, see David Brimingham, *Trade and Conflict in Angola: The Mbundu and Their Neighbours Under the Influence of the Portuguese, 1483–1790* (Oxford, 1966).

35. An early description of these slave-worked estates, called *arimos* (from the Kimbundu word *kudia,* to eat) is found in the notes of the Jesuit priest Pero Tavares, who worked among them in the 1630s. See Louis Jadin, "Pero Tavares, missionaire jésuite, ses travaux apostoliques au Congo et en Angola, 1629–35," *Bulletin, Institut historique belge de Rome* 39 (1967): 328–93.

36. Pero Rodrigues, "História da Residência dos Padres da Companhia de Jesus em Angola [1594]," Brásio, *Monumenta* 4:568.

37. António de Oliveira de Cadornega, *História geral das guerras Angolanas (1681),* ed. José Delgado and Manuel Alves da Cunha, 3 vols. (Lisbon 1940–42, reprinted in 1972), 1:347. See p. 393 for another mention of slaves or freedmen, which the Dutch lacked, in the Portuguese force in 1646.

38. Elias Alexandre da Silva Corrêa, *História de Angola* [1789], 2 vols. (Lisbon, 1937), 2:50.

39. Paul Erdmann Isert, *Reise nach Guinea und den Caribäschen Inseln in Columbia* (Copenhagen, 1788), 80–81, original pagination marked in the English translation of Selena Axelrod Wisnes, *Letters on West Africa and the Slave Trade: Paul Erdmann Isert's Journey to Guinea and the Caribbean Islands in Colombia [1788]* (Oxford, 1992).

40. See Claude Cahen, "Note sur l'esclavage musulman et le devshirme ottoman, à propos des trauvaux récents," *Journal of the Economic and Social History of the Orient* 13 (1970): 211–18, for a survey of literature.

41. Thornton, *Warfare,* 88–94.

42. William Snelgrave, *A New Account of Some Parts of Guinea and the Slave Trade* (London, 1734; facsimile, London: Cass, 1971), 77–78.

43. Pruneau de Pommegorge, *Description de la Nigritie* (Amsterdam, 1789), 164.

44. Robert Norris, *Memoirs of the Reign of Bossa Ahádee, King of Dahomey an Inland Country of Guiney* (London, 1789; reprint, London, 1968), 87–89.

45. Boubacar Barry, *Senegambia and the Atlantic Slave Trade,* trans. Ayi Kwei Armah (Cambridge, UK, 1998), 81–90.

46. See also Thornton, *Warfare,* 36–39.

47. M. Jacques Doumet de Siblas, "Mémoire historique sur les différentes parties de l'Afrique . . . 1769," mod. ed. C. Becker and V. Martin, "Mémoire inédit de Doumet [1769]," *Bulletin, Institut Foundementale de l'Afrique Noire,* ser. B, 36/1 (1974): 38–40.

48. Barry, *Senegambia,* 81–125.

49. For the best statement of the state of the research in the late 1970s, see Joseph C. Miller, *Kings and Kinsmen: The Imbangala Impact on Angola* (Oxford, 1976), which broke with an earlier interpretation that linked them to the "Jaga" who invaded Kongo in

1568. For a challenge, see John Thornton, "The Chronology and Causes of Lunda Expansion to the West, c. 1700–1852," *Zambia Journal of History* 1 (1981): 1–13. A summary of this debate is Ndaywel è Nziem, "The Poltical System of the Luba and Lunda: Its Emergence and Expansion," in UNESCO *General History of Africa,* 8 vols. (Los Angeles, 1981–93), 5:588–607.

50. "The Strange Adventures of Andrew Battell, of Leigh, in Angola . . .," first published in Samuel Purchas, *Purchas his Pilgrimmes* (London, 1625), reprint, E. G. Ravenstein, ed., *The Strange Adventures of Andrew Battell in Angola and Adjoining Lands* (London, 1901), 21–34.

51. Plan of Garcia Mendes Castelo Branco, c. January 1620, in Brásio, *Monumenta* 6:451.

52. I have covered the history of this period in Angola in Marila dos Santos Lopes (ed.), *História da expansão Portuguesa no mundo* (Lisbon, forthcoming), vol. 9.

53. Queen Njinga to Governor General of Angola, December 13, 1655, in Brásio, *Monumenta,* 12:526.

54. Silva Corrêa, *História,* 2:50.

Making the Chikunda: Military Slavery and Ethnicity in Southern Africa, 1750–1900

ALLEN ISAACMAN AND DEREK PETERSON

From the vantage point of American history, military slavery is a paradox: with rare exceptions, American slaveholders were careful to keep guns away from their slaves for fear that they would rebel. Scholars of military slavery have therefore had to explain why owners outside the American South found it desirable to arm their slaves. Among the first to propose an explanation was Max Weber. Weber argued that slaves were ideal clients of patrimonial rulers: owned by the ruler, slaves were bound to obey his commands.[1] Creating a slave army was for a patrimonial ruler a way to define a loyal, powerful constituency. Later scholars followed Weber by seeing military slavery as a strategic prop for patrimonial rulers. David Ayalon attributed the longevity of the mamlūk sultanate in medieval Egypt to its success in recruiting and training pliable young slaves. The mamlūks' Circassian slaves were enrolled in a lengthy training program that taught them to think of the sultan as their father, and themselves as his sons. Indoctrinated through their training, military slaves were loyal supporters of patrimonial mamlūk sultans.[2] Daniel Pipes offered a more specific explanation for the paradox of military slavery. Muslim citizens, argued Pipes, are inclined for religious reasons to withdraw from politics. Islamic rulers filled the political vacuum with slave soldiers recruited from outside their realms. Slave soldiers' loyalty could be secured through years of careful training, which "imbued them with lifelong attachments to the Islamic religion, their master, his dynasty, and their comrades."[3] Deracinated, isolated, and indoctrinated, slave soldiers filled the administrative, legal, and political roles left open by Muslim citizens' withdrawal from public affairs.

In summary, the scholarly consensus on military slavery has been that arming slaves was a useful political strategy for patrimonial rulers. But in their eagerness to unravel the paradox of military slavery, scholars have often ignored the lived experiences and political imaginations of slaves themselves. The focus has been on the strategies by which rulers secured slaves' loyalty, not on how enslaved men organized their daily lives and forged new social identities. Rather than treating slave soldiers as objects of rulers' indoctrination, we think it more revealing to explore slaves' own self-fashioning in relation to their rulers and to each other. It is not enough to accept at face value rulers' claims about their successes in molding slaves' political loyalties. We need also to study how slave soldiers created rituals and practices that made courage, loyalty, and military discipline seem virtuous, how, that is, they constructed a culture that idealized military service as a masculine virtue.[4]

This chapter explores how military slaves on Portuguese-run estates along the Zambesi River came to define themselves as sharers of a new social identity, Chikunda ("the conquerors"). The estates, called *prazos,* were initially granted to Portuguese settlers who, from the seventeenth century onward, moved inland from the coastal towns on the Indian Ocean to profit from the lucrative Zambesi trade. They used slaves as soldiers, equipping them with guns and spears and using them to collect taxes from peasants, patrol the borders, and police the estates. Asked to perform highly dangerous tasks in the service of their owners, slaves developed shared behaviors and beliefs, a patrilineal system of descent and inheritance, and a rich repertoire of cultural practices that celebrated their prowess as warriors and hunters and distinguished them from the indigenous peasant population. This domain of commonality, we emphasize, was never imposed on them by their owners.[5] Slaves made themselves Chikunda in order to set themselves apart from the local peasantry, gain leverage with owners, and lend meaning and prestige to their lives of danger.

The chapter begins by exploring the relation between military slavery and economic production on the prazos. Slave soldiers were also traders, hunters, policemen, and overseers. Their dangerous, demanding work enriched prazo holders. In the second section we highlight how slave soldiers, commanded to perform dangerous tasks, valorized courage and military skill. In language, songs, and ceremonies, through initiation rituals, and in clothing and in facial tattoos, slave soldiers defined themselves as Chikunda and celebrated their physical prowess. Being Chikunda, we show, was for slave soldiers a way of dignifying their work with a clear sense of vocation. In the third section we outline how, after the collapse of the prazos in the nineteenth century and the manumission of the slaves, former soldiers enlarged on their shared history and forged a Chikunda ethnic identity. This ethnic identity survives to the present day.

The Chikunda on the Prazos

The military slavery practiced on the prazos was not unique in pre-colonial African history. Slaves often served African rulers as soldiers. Their military might underpinned rulers' political power. As early as the thirteenth century, the rulers of Mali appointed slave officials and enrolled slaves in the military.[6] The eighteenth-century kingdom of Oyo similarly used slaves in administrative and military capacities. Slaves guarded Oyo's king and his family, collected taxes, and administered provincial towns. Armed with cutlasses and mounted on prized warhorses imported from the north, Oyo's slave cavalry was a terrifyingly effective military force.[7] In the nineteenth-century Sudanic state of Damagaram, slaves officered cavalry units of up to two thousand men, many of them armed with modern weapons. Slaves also occupied up to one-half of the titled positions in the state bureaucracy.[8] In northeastern Africa, Sudanese captives played a prominent role in the Turco-Egyptian army during the first half of the nineteenth century.[9] In some contexts, the unbridled power that slave soldiers exercised earned them the distrust of free citizens. In the Wolof and Sereer states of the Senegambia, seventeenth- and eighteenth-century rulers used armed slaves called *Ceddo* to conduct warfare, collect taxes, and perform other administrative tasks.[10] Their heavy drinking, bright clothing, long hair, and arrogance offended industrious Muslims.[11] For many precolonial African rulers, arming slaves was not a last resort. It was, rather, an established strategy of political consolidation, a means of controlling fractious and potentially rebellious subjects.

What makes the Chikunda case somewhat unusual in African history is the fact that the slave soldiers served individuals, not a state.[12] For the Portuguese adventurers and mercenaries who claimed vast estates along the Zambesi River in the sixteenth century, arming slaves was a means of consolidating control in a highly fluid political context (see map 1). African polities of the Zimbabwe plateau had for centuries used the Zambesi to export ivory, gold, and slaves to the coast. The Portuguese adventurers set themselves up as middlemen in this

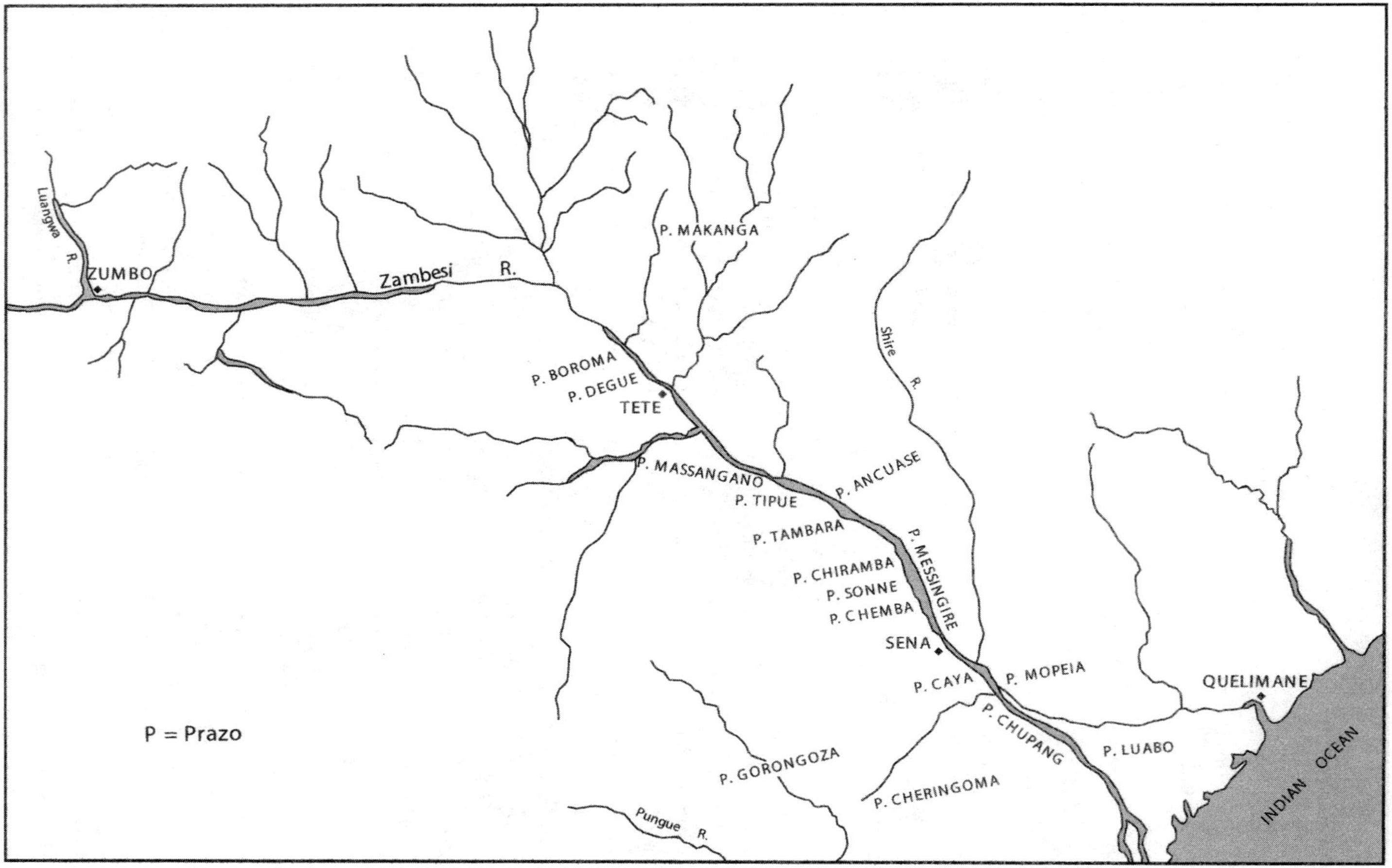

Map 1. Principal Zambezi Prazos

long-established trade, at first under the patronage of established political leaders but increasingly with the support of their own followers. These settlers became extremely powerful, forming military alliances with the rulers of the Zimbabwean plateau in exchange for economic concessions. The Portuguese Crown, eager to take advantage of local situations for its own benefit, granted powerful traders titles to massive estates, or prazos. These estate holders, called *prazeiros,* were not emissaries of Portuguese colonial authority. The prazeiros were transfrontiersmen: they crossed political and cultural boundaries and took a new way of life.[13] Over time, they intermarried with the local population. Many of them adopted the lifestyle, cosmology, and political trappings of the indigenous political authorities. Prazeiros rarely removed local chiefs or rulers living on their estates: instead, they superimposed themselves on the existing political hierarchy. Few attempted to establish commercial agriculture on their estates. Instead, they siphoned off surplus from peasant producers (*colonos*) living on the estates and accumulated additional wealth from the profitable Zambesi ivory and slave trade.

Given the exploitative economy of the prazo system, it is not surprising that the Portuguese estate holders relied on military power to support their authority. That power, however, could not come from Portugal itself. Lisbon was both unwilling and unable to station an effective colonial army in this frontier region. Throughout the eighteenth and nineteenth centuries, the number of Portuguese soldiers stationed in the Zambesi usually ranged from one hundred to three hundred. They were poorly armed, poorly organized, and poorly trained.[14] Many were debtors, vagrants, and former convicts who had been conscripted into the military. They deserted at the first opportunity. A senior official acknowledged in 1825 that the colonial army was in a complete shambles. "In all these districts," he wrote, "there are fortifications, and a garrison consisting of a company of infantrymen, roughly eighty men including officers, but rarely are more than half present, and they are badly armed and without discipline, and thus of little utility."[15]

In the absence of an effective colonial army, the prazeiros recruited and armed slaves. According to early accounts, it was not uncommon for such powerful early prazeiros as António Lobo da Silva (known by his African name, Nhema) to own upwards of five thousand slaves.[16] His contemporaries, Lourenço de Mattos (Maponda) and Sisnando Bayão (Massuampaca), also had large slave retinues. One estate owner was reputed to command an army of fifteen thousand captives.[17] With these slave armies, estimated at around fifty thousand strong in the middle of the eighteenth century,[18] the prazeiros defeated a number of Sena, Tonga, and Tawara polities located on the southern margins of the Zambesi. They also made substantial inroads north of the

Zambesi River, vanquishing several Chewa and Mang'anja polities by the end of the seventeenth century. The conquered lands and the peasants who lived on them were effectively incorporated into the prazo system.[19]

There is no seventeenth-century documentation that refers to the military slaves as Chikunda. The earliest explicit reference to the Chikunda dates from a century later. In 1752 a Portuguese priest wrote that the "respect and power of the estate holders rests on their *bazekunda* under the direction of a slave chief known as the *mukazambo* and a second in command called the *sachi-kunda*."[20] A decade later, a prominent Zambesi settler was more explicit. "The Chikunda," he wrote, "are our slaves."[21] It is difficult to be more specific. But this evidence suggests that, at least on some prazos, military slaves had forged a sense of collective identity by the middle of the eighteenth century.

The time lapse between the formation of slave military regiments and the creation of the name *Chikunda* highlights the difficulties that slave soldiers undoubtedly faced in creating a common identity among themselves, for slaves on the prazos were deeply divided by language and ancestry. Like military slave-holders in other parts of the world, the prazeiros preferred to acquire captives from distant regions rather than enslaving local peasants or acquiring captives from nearby populations. As one descendant of a prominent prazeiro family noted, "In the beginning the Chikunda were not a tribe. They were a mixture of people who came from far away."[22] A detailed list of 659 male slaves freed in the Tete area in 1856 highlights the ethnic heterogeneity of the slave population.[23] The captives came from twenty-one different ethnic groups. The overwhelming majority, 83 percent, came from well outside the prazo zone, from the matrilineal belt north of the Zambesi. The preponderance of captives from the north reflects the political chaos in that region. The decline of Undi, paramount ruler of the Chewa, set local land chiefs against one another in competition for preeminence. The prazeiros took advantage, regularly attacking the divided Chewa and Mang'anja polities during the seventeenth century.[24] These raids intensified in the first half of the nineteenth century, spurred by the dramatic increase in demand from Brazil.[25] The raids were an important source of slaves for the prazos. Other slaves came by way of purchase. Most prazeiros regularly dispatched trading caravans to areas known to have large numbers of captives available for sale. Young, easily transportable boys commanded the highest price, since it was believed that they could be easily trained in the martial arts and molded into the norms of soldierly life. After the captives arrived at the estate, they were assigned to slave soldiers' squads, made household slaves or field hands, or sold to the slave market in Quelimane.[26]

Many Africans thus became slaves involuntarily, through prazeiros' raids or through capture and purchase at the hands of African chiefs. For some, however, selling themselves into military slavery was a strategy of economic survival in dangerous times.[27] The region's low and unpredictable rainfall meant that food shortages occurred with regularity. One eighteenth-century chronicler observed that "the greatest part came to be captives from the times of famine, pestilence and locusts and because of their urgent necessity they had no alternative but to come and offer themselves as captives."[28] The actual process of self-enslavement varied. Sometimes it involved detailed negotiations in which the prazeiro pledged that the slave would never be sold outside the prazo.[29] At other times an impoverished man simply swore loyalty and accepted the conditions that his protector imposed. Entering the ranks of the Chikunda offered a number of advantages. In return for enlisting, the recruits gained highly valued imported goods including cloth, beads, and guns. Others received land, wives, and the right to hunt on the estates. To an unattached, vulnerable individual, these benefits held an obvious attraction.[30]

Divided by language and ethnicity, divided also by their experiences of enslavement, slave soldiers shared a similar mode of organization from one estate to another. They were carefully set apart from the local peasant population, settled in villages located strategically throughout the prazo. These regimental villages were called *butaka*. According to the local historian Custódio Chimalenzi, "The Chikunda lived in distinct villages, separate from the local population. They were organized into military villages. The peasants had their own villages and they never mixed."[31] Portuguese accounts from the eighteenth and nineteenth centuries confirm this spatial separation.[32] Each butaka had a clearly defined political hierarchy, with a slave chief (*mukazambo*) exercising considerable authority over his soldiers' lives.[33] With the assistance of a council of elders, the mukazambo distributed bounty received from the prazeiro, allocated land and captives, punished members of his regiment who violated local practices and laws, resolved disputes between his subordinates, and administered the poison ordeal to any Chikunda suspected of practicing witchcraft.[34] During military campaigns many slave chiefs and their subordinates were permitted to take captives of their own. Even when the action of a slave jeopardized the prazeiro's position, responsibility for disciplining the guilty party generally rested with the mukazambo. When, in 1783, a Chikunda slave fled prazo Inharuga with valuable trade goods belonging to the estate owner, it was the slave chiefs who dispatched soldiers to capture the runaway and ordered him chained and beaten.[35]

Set apart by their economic and political privileges, Chikunda soldiers were used by prazeiros as a means to control the often-restive peasant population. Such was the reputation of the Chikunda that among the settlers it was taken as fact that "twenty slaves could reduce one thousand colonos to complete and perfect obedience."[36] The prazeiros selected their most loyal slaves, called *chuanga* (plural *achuanga*), to oversee the principal villages of their estates. The achuanga were agents of the prazeiro, transmitting his orders to the land chiefs and ensuring that they were followed. They recruited peasant labor to clear roads, transport goods, and repair buildings on the estate. The chuanga personally resolved minor infractions committed by the villagers against the interests of the prazeiro. Villagers who failed to give the estate holder a proper share of meat of the animals they killed, for example, were punished by the chuanga. For more serious infractions, the chuanga referred the case to the prazeiro himself. In this way, the estate holder was informed of the activities of the peasants and could take appropriate action to contain organized opposition.

The achuanga also supervised the collection of the annual tax that all peasants were required to pay. The exact content of this tax varied substantially from prazo to prazo. One particularly knowledgeable observer noted that the tribute extracted was directly proportional to the military power the prazeiro possessed.[37] Shortly before the harvest, the slave overseers, together with the land chief and village headmen, took a census of all the households on the estate. Each household had to pay the same amount, regardless of how much it actually produced. For their loyalty, the achuanga received a portion of the taxes, as did the land chief and his assistants. The achuanga also enforced the commercial monopoly of the prazeiros, collecting sorghum, maize, and rice from peasants at harvest time. Peasants referred to this practice as *inhau-cangamiza,* or forced sale, since the prices they received for their goods from the prazeiro were well below the market rates.

Controversies frequently arose over tax and tribute collection. If an entire village failed to pay tax or refused to obey some other order of the prazeiro, the estate owner dispatched a slave squad to deal with the miscreants. Chikunda slaves publicly punished tax evaders, sometimes beating them with rhinoceros-hide whips. Other tax evaders were killed or enslaved along with their families. Indigenous authorities suspected of encouraging acts of disobedience were subject to similar punishment.[38] These harsh reprisals formed an intrinsic part of the system of domination on the prazos. They created a deep antipathy toward the alien Chikunda among the local peasant population.

Hoping to escape from the violent conditions on the prazos, many peasants ran away, seeking sanctuary from neighboring chiefs or other prazeiros. Runaways had several options. They could "jump fences" and migrate to another estate, or they could flee to a neighboring chieftaincy. Prazo holders, nervous that peasants' flight would undermine the viability of the estates, garrisoned Chikunda squads at strategic points on the frontiers in order to thwart peasants' escape. Chikunda soldiers were also used to quash peasant uprisings, which regularly occurred in the second half of the eighteenth century. According to José da Costa Xavier, great-grandson of a prominent prazeiro, "The Chikunda helped put down revolts . . . but they did very little other work."[39] Insurrections seem to have been most common on the smaller estates, where the prazeiros had only limited forces at their disposal, or on frontier estates, where neighboring chiefs would ally themselves with rebellious peasants. The Chikunda were of critical importance in suppressing these peasant uprisings.

The Chikunda were also of military importance in protecting the prazos against external threats. In the highly competitive world of the Zambezi, a strong military served as a necessary deterrent against attacks not only from adjacent African polities but also from rival prazeiros. Some of the fiercest conflicts occurred between estate holders trying to usurp the authority of their neighbors and establish themselves as the dominant economic and political power in the region. Periodic raids, full-scale battles, and prolonged wars were recurring themes in interprazo relations.

In addition to their military role, the Chikunda performed a wide range of economic activities that enhanced the wealth and power of their owners. Caravans of Chikunda traders, porters, canoe men, and soldiers, ranging in number from ten to several hundred men, traveled far into the interior exchanging imported cloth and beads for slaves, ivory, and gold. Their expeditions dealt primarily with the Chewa and Nsenga chieftaincies but went as far north as the Lunda kingdom of Kazembe. Some lasted as long as eighteen months.[40] A trusted slave official known as the *musambadzi* led the caravans, determined the itinerary, and negotiated with local rulers. Because the Zambesi Valley was a tse-tse fly–infested zone, pack animals could not be used to transport goods into the interior.[41] Slaves had to carry such heavy commodities as ivory, hippo teeth, and copper for great distances. The absence of roads made their tasks more difficult, as did the rapids and the swollen rivers that the caravans had to cross in the rainy season. Official Portuguese accounts noted the skill and daring of the canoe men "who were not intimidated by the large rocks jutting out of the Zambesi river north of Tete."[42] In addition to the natural barriers they confronted, there were the perils posed by hippopotami and crocodiles and the threats posed by marauding bands of brigands. One prazeiro lamented that "it was rare indeed when one of the musambadzi was not robbed or assassinated in the interior and the caravan returned safely."[43]

The prazeiros also profited from slave soldiers' skills as elephant hunters. Chikunda hunters armed with spears, axes, half-moon scimitars, locally made guns, and European muzzle-loaders took advantage of the large elephant herds north of the Zambesi. Oral traditions throughout the region recount the fearless way that the hunters incapacitated the elephants by cutting their hamstrings with axes and their skill as marksmen. Even those disdainful of the Chikunda because of their predatory activities acknowledged that "the Chikunda were the best hunters in the region; no one was better. In the beginning they hunted with bows and arrow and spears. Later on they began to use muskets. It was the great hunters who used muskets."[44] Although the prazeiros retained all the ivory, the hunters kept the elephant and hippo meat, which they distributed throughout the slave community and exchanged for grain with local peasants.

The multiple functions that the Chikunda performed highlight how closely military slavery, economic production, and political consolidation were linked on the prazos. In an unstable social and political context, the Chikunda were for estate holders a means of controlling the peasants living on the estates. Chikunda also produced wealth for the slave owners by means of hunting, slave raiding, and trading. Military slavery was an engine of economic production and a means of producing and solidifying prazeiros' privileged class position.

Their work demanded a rare courage and skill of slave soldiers. Asked to perform highly dangerous tasks, bound together by their common experience as skilled traders and adventurers, military slaves elaborated a culture that celebrated daring, valor, and military discipline. How and why military slaves became Chikunda is the subject of the next section.

Making the Chikunda

Uprooted from their natal linguistic and cultural communities, first-generation slave soldiers experienced a type of "social death."[45] Enslavement involved the loss of slaves' identity. Coming to think of themselves as Chikunda was probably difficult: the captives were divided by language and ancestry. Their internal divisions probably made the creation of a common identity all the more urgent. The political economy and social structure of the prazos ensured that slaves could not easily blend in to peasant communities. Their work as tax collectors, overseers, and police earned them the hostility of the peasant population.[46] And as renowned hunters and traders, the slaves had access to imported goods, which reinforced their differences with the peasantry.

But a sense of difference did not in itself create the Chikunda. Creating a common identity required intellectual and social work of slave soldiers. Over time, they created a distinctive set of rituals and practices that valorized courage and denigrated weakness and inconstancy. Making themselves Chikunda —the "conquerors"—was for slave soldiers a way to celebrate the hard work they did, making it seem honorable and socially meaningful. Crafting Chi-kunda identity was also a strategy of social differentiation, a way, that is, for proud soldiers to set themselves off from the peasants around them.

The term *Chikunda* is derived from the Shona verb *kukunda*, which signifies "to vanquish."[47] Their military work was one means by which Chikunda identified themselves. Despite the fact that most first-generation slaves came from farming communities, Chikunda regarded agricultural work with dis-dain. To farm would have reduced them to the level of a common field slave or a subjugated peasant. As one Chikunda descendant remembered, "our grand-fathers hated to work in the fields."[48] Official Portuguese accounts confirmed this aversion to farming.[49] The Chikunda had therefore to rely on the peasants living on the estates for much of the grain they ate and the beer they consumed. The slaves acquired these foodstuffs by levying taxes on peasants or by ex-changing meat for peasants' grain. The wives of the soldiers cultivated small fields, sometimes with the aid of captives, to supplement the agricultural pro-duce extracted from the local villages.[50] From the earliest days on the prazos, a clearly defined gendered division of labor marked Chikunda communities. Farming was women's work. Hunting, commerce, and warfare constituted the domain of Chikunda men.

Their disdain for agriculture — as women's work — was for male slave sol-diers a means of setting themselves off from the peasant farmers alongside whom they lived. The new gendered division of labor also reflected radical shifts within the social organization of slave soldiers' families. One of the defining features of the new Chikunda communities was the organization of slave families around a patrilineal system of descent. Most captives had origi-nally come from matrilineal peoples living north of the Zambesi. In their home villages to the north, husbands lived with their wives' relatives, maternal un-cles exercised domestic authority over a man's children, and the family's prop-erty was controlled by the wife's lineage. Men and women had taken part in farming activities. Female ancestors were central figures to northerners' re-ligious lives: the Chewa, for example, propitiated Makewana, the "Wife of the Spirit," and recognized female ancestor spirits.[51]

Slave soldiers' adoption of patrilineality was therefore a radical change from inherited practice. They probably had little choice in the matter. Living and working with their male comrades-in-arms in the prazeiros' service, slave soldiers could scarcely ask their owners for leave to live in their wives' natal homes. One elder whose ancestors lived on prazo Massangano explained the dynamics of patrilineality very simply. "The Chikunda children could not leave; they stayed and remained Chikunda."[52] Patrilineality gave permanence to new Chikunda communities. Wives were brought back to their husbands' village, creating new patrilocal residence patterns. Over time a patrilineal extended family emerged. Land, property, and familial identity were all transmitted through the male line.

If becoming Chikunda meant reworking kin relations and inheritance, it also meant rethinking the past. New patterns of ancestor veneration dignified patrilineal slave households with a local, male-centered history. The Chikunda no longer invoked the spirit of their distant ancestors but instead sought the assistance of their predecessors who had died on the prazos. They began to collectively pay homage to the local lion spirits, the *mhondoro,* who were the patrilineal spiritual guardians in the territory in which they now resided. The slaves invoked the mhondoro to insure extranatural protection during battle and before hunting dangerous animals.[53] They also propitiated the lion spirit to guarantee the fertility of their wives and their land. These religious innovations were a necessity for a people cut off from home. "The Chikunda always consulted the *mhondoro* of the area," explained Custódio Chimalizeni. "They all had to adopt the local mhondoro because they had come from a variety of people who lived far away. The Chikunda consulted the mhondoro because the mhondoro had the power to tell them where the enemy was and what dangers they faced."[54]

Bound together by a new set of ancestors, the Chikunda elaborated markers of social identity with which to distinguish themselves from peasants. In their households, communities, and military regiments the slaves spoke Chi-Chikunda. As the local historian Conrado Msussa Boroma put it, "The language of the Chikunda is a language without a land. It is a mixture of Atawara, Azimba, Makanga, Quelimane, Atonga, and Barue, each slave brought a little with him." Although a detailed historical linguistic analysis still needs to be undertaken,[55] the evidence suggests that their language was based on a substantial number of cognates introduced by slaves from the north together with Chi-Sena, Chi-Tonga, and Chi-Tawara terms borrowed from the peasants living on the prazos. The relatively large number of Portuguese greetings and expressions of deference incorporated into the language called attention to slaves' proximity to the estate owners and involvement in the larger world of the Zambesi.[56] As a "language without a land," Chi-Chikunda helped bind uprooted slaves together as members of a common cultural and intellectual community. Their speech differentiated them from the peasant population of the prazos. When Chikunda greeted each other they saluted, shuffled their feet in a differential manner and declared in their best Portuguese, "bom dia."[57] This greeting was called *kukwenga.* They made no such gestures when they encountered peasants, who, by contrast, were expected to clap their hands as a mark of deference whenever they came upon a Chikunda man.

Portuguese greetings were a mark of social superiority, a way to set soldiers off from peasants. So, too, did their bodily markings help define Chikunda identity. Men and women had a unique set of facial tattoos known as *makaju*. Makaju served as an affirmation of Chikunda superiority over the local population. As Diamond Mpande explained, "The reason that we had the makaju was to show others that we were the Chikunda. In that way we differentiated ourselves from other people."[58] But the makaju were more than social markers. They also affirmed Chikunda successes as soldiers. As one Tete elder put it, "Originally, when the Chikunda came to the prazos, they did not have makaju. The makaju developed out of warfare. It became a symbol of their position as warriors and distinguished them from the other people."[59] The Chikunda also filed their front teeth, reinforcing their menacing appearance. "Our ancestors did this," explained Diamond Mpande, "so that they looked different from the local people and so that all the other people knew that we are all Chikunda."[60] Their fierce appearance was an integral part of Chikunda identity.

Clothing was another marker of status and power on the prazos. Because of their success as ivory hunters, slave raiders, and long-distance traders, the Chikunda received bolts of calico cloth, called *kapundu,* from estate holders as a reward for their labors. Calico became their standard dress, a uniform that they flaunted. "Chikunda men wore kapundu in the old days," remembered one old man. "It was a white cloth worn over a smaller undergarment. Some also wore a sleeveless tunic."[61] Chikunda women dressed in blouses made from calico. Their attire set them apart from peasants living on the prazos. "Most peasants wore *mkuende*," explained Castro Jack. "The women removed the bark from a tree, took the fiber, washed it in water to make it soft, and made clothing called *mkuende.* Others wore *mphalame,* which were animal skins."[62]

Their clothing publicized slave soldiers' ability to negotiate the difficult work of trading. Their mythology and dances similarly celebrated Chikunda men's valor.[63] Soldiers' return from a successful military operation or hunting expedition was the occasion for great celebration. A British traveler passing through the Tete region in the middle of the nineteenth century described one such performance. "Here forms a double ring of fifty or sixty men, in each hand a bullock's horn, clashing them in unison to the stroke of one supple and lithe-limbed native, who springing into the center, leaps nearly his own height from the ground. . . . Not far from them, single dancers are weighing against each other, brandishing their weapons, muskets, assegai, battle axes, or bow and arrows, and achieving pirouettes that would open the eyes of some of our ballet dancers. In another place is a circle of women performing a more measured dance."[64] Chikunda celebrated their daring in public dances such as these. Their performance of military skills in dances publicized their courage, concretizing their military work as a virtue to be admired.

Clothing, dancing, language, and bodily markings celebrated slave soldiers' dangerous lives, joining them in the common pursuit of honor through military service. Initiation rituals were the means by which slaves learned to value military service as an honorable occupation. Boys learned from male elders, grandparents, and specialists known as *tsanculu*. They recounted the military and hunting exploits of their ancestors in evening discussions around the campfire and in Chikunda pre-puberty schools. Custódio Chimalenzi described how young captives were educated. "The original Chikunda elders formally taught the Chikunda offspring. The boys who were born into slavery had to be taught what their responsibilities were—how to make war and defend the prazos. There was a special hut in which they were taught, where they built a fire and sat around during the night discussing things. The children would sit around the fire and learn."[65] Once they finished their schooling the young men had their faces tattooed. They were then deemed ready for military service and marriage.[66]

Girls underwent a parallel process of socialization at a somewhat earlier age. Sitting under large trees in their village, they learned from elderly women, who trained them to cook, keep house, make mats and pots, and perform domestic labor. They also stressed the importance of celibacy until the girls had completed rites of initiation and became adults. One older woman described the initiation schooling: "The old woman taught the girl how to sleep with her husband, what she should do when he came to her. 'Since you are going to sleep with your husband, you must demonstrate your love for him. You must also help him to know how to make love with you. You have to gyrate your hips. Later, you must take a small cloth and wipe his penis, wash his feet, and stretch his toes and fingers. Then you rise and give thanks by clapping your hands and bending your knees up and down three times.' "[67] Once the Chikunda girls had completed initiation school, they went to the home of an elderly woman, where they pounded corn and performed other domestic chores. It was here that their faces were cut with makaju. Later, the young women returned to have additional incisions made on their necks, breasts, and thighs, which enhanced their beauty and sexuality.

The very different education that boys and girls received underscores the inextricable relation between gender and Chikunda ethnicity. Being Chikunda demanded discipline, self-sacrifice, and courage of men and domestic labor of women. This conclusion is not meant to minimize disputes within Chikunda households and communities: women may well have argued for a different division of labor. But the contrasting masculine and feminine roles taught at initiation schools does highlight how Chikunda men idealized their ethnicity by concretizing gender roles. Military men, adventurers on untamed frontiers, Chikunda men proved their virtue by their courage and daring.

Despite their success in forging a group identity and acquiring a modicum of power and wealth, one social fact remained unchanged — the Chikunda were slaves, unable to choose their own place of residence or dispose of their property. Moreover, the Chikunda lived and worked in a highly regimented and coercive labor regime. Estate owners brutally punished slaves whom they considered to be disloyal or disobedient: flogging with a hippopotamus-hide whip was common practice. Perpetrators of more serious offenses were blown out of the mouth of a cannon.[68] The well-armed Chikunda, however, were not simply pliable tools in the hands of their masters. The prazeiros were terrified that the slave soldiers would rebel. They had good reason to worry. The historical record is filled with examples of Chikunda who rebelled against estate holders either who failed to provide sufficient patronage or who excessively exploited their positions.[69] Some Chikunda were prepared to defend their privileged position on the prazos. Others, faced with a particularly rapacious or abusive master, chose to run away. By the middle of the eighteenth century the problem of slave flight was serious enough that the estate holders began a series of military campaigns to punish Chewa and Mang'anja chiefs who provided sanctuary to runaways.[70] Other runaway slaves established communities in the hinterland.[71] They posed a serious challenge to the Portuguese, both because they offered refuge to other slaves and because they had the military capacity to threaten outlying prazos. By 1806 an official census of the prazos listed almost half of the twenty thousand slaves as "missing."[72] Among those missing were Chikunda porters, traders, and elephant hunters.

The always-volatile relationship between the Chikunda and the prazeiros came to a head in the first half of the nineteenth century. Made greedy by the ever-increasing demand for slaves from Brazilian and Cuban sugar plantations, prazeiros began selling both peasants and Chikunda as slaves. Their violation of the time-honored practice forbidding prazeiros from selling the Chikunda or their family members precipitated wide-scale insurrections and flight.[73] One local functionary attributed this state of affairs to the "inability of the prazeiros to comprehend the ramifications of the slave trade."[74] This political instability, combined with recurring droughts and locust infestations, led to a dramatic decline in the agricultural production of the estates. Successive invasions by the Barue and the Nguni in the second quarter of the century sealed the fate of the prazo system. During the 1830s, invading Nguni forces occupied twenty-eight of the forty-six legally functioning prazos.[75] By the middle of the nineteenth century most of the prazos were in disarray. One official lamented that the "estates are abandoned as a result of the prazeiros' blind lust for profits."[76] The rapid disintegration of the prazos left thousands of Chikunda unattached. Lisbon's 1858 abolition decree set the remainder free over the course of the ensuing two decades.

The prazos had been the crucible of Chikunda identity. Slave soldiers became Chikunda in order to dignify their lives of danger. The collapse of the prazos compelled Chikunda, no longer legally bound as slaves, to rethink their identity. Some left their military lives behind, fleeing the prazos and returning to their homelands to become peasants. Some became freelance elephant hunters or worked in that capacity for inland Portuguese traders. Still others labored as porters and canoe men in the service of the merchant community. Most, however, were incorporated into new slave-raiding Chikunda states formed in the wake of the prazos' collapse.

Chikunda Conquest States

The nineteenth century was a time of political instability throughout eastern and southern Africa. The social unrest caused by the continuing slave trade, combined with recurring ecological crises and massive migrations of people, undermined older polities and opened up opportunities for political entrepreneurs. It was in this political context that Chikunda ex-slaves, eager to exercise the skills of hunting and fighting learned on the prazos, established slave-trading conquest states to the north of the Zambesi. José Rosário de Andrade, more commonly known by his African name, Kanyemba ("the ferocious"), was perhaps the most successful of the warlords who dominated the Zambesi interior (see map 2).[77] Son of a Tande chief and a Goan mother, Kanyemba began forming a private army in Tete in the 1870s. Many of the enlistees were Chikunda ex-slaves, some elephant hunters, all of them young and impoverished males.[78] Joining Kanyemba offered them an avenue to us their military skills for profit. Kanyemba and his followers settled in the elephant-rich region of Bawa, about two hundred kilometers east of the trading center at Tete. Over the next quarter of a century, the well-armed Chikunda ravaged a vast area of south central Africa.[79] Frederick Selous observed that Kanyemba's forces were "constantly making raids upon any people in the [interior] who have anything to be taken."[80] Elders throughout the region made a similar point: "Kanyemba never traded freely with the local peoples for slaves," remembered Sunda Mwanza. "He forced them to sell slaves. If they refused he ordered his Chikunda warriors to raid the villages, kill all the

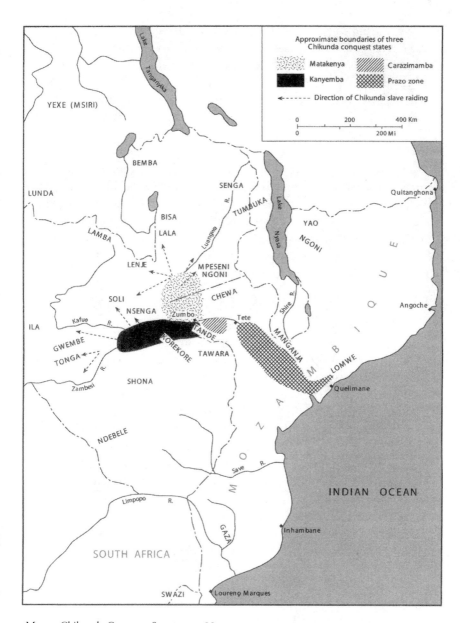

Map 2. Chikunda Conquest States, ca. 1880

elderly men and bring the young men and women back to his stockade. Because of Kanyemba's raids people on both sides [of the Zambesi River,] the Tande, Tonga and the Nsenga of Mbuluma, lived in fear."[81]

By the 1880s, the warlord had forged a powerful conquest state that was the equal of any in south central Africa. His state was modeled on the prazos, which were for Kanyemba a template of political and military organization. One observer estimated that he had ten thousand Chikunda soldiers under arms.[82] Chikunda regiments were billeted in strategic locations along the borders, near the principal population centers, and at the capital. Kanyemba's fortified village at Chipera housed several hundred Chikunda warriors, had large warehouses with arms and ammunition, and even contained a jail for slaves awaiting export to the coast.[83] Chikunda agents collected taxes from peasants, transmitted orders from Kanyemba, and enforced the warlords' monopoly on commerce. These were the same types of activities performed by the chuanga and his Chikunda regiment centuries earlier, on the prazos of the lower Zambesi.

The parallels between Kanyemba's conquest state and the prazos highlights how deeply their shared history shaped the political imagination of the Chikunda. At Bawa and in other nineteenth-century conquest states, ex-slave soldiers used the markers of communal identity forged on the prazos to found a self-reproducing Chikunda ethnicity. The core group of ex-slaves brought a shared set of practices and rituals to Bawa. These practices distinguished the Chikunda immigrants from the new recruits and the local subject population. Slaves and others who joined Kanyemba's polity adopted these markers of Chikunda identity. This process of cultural integration was easiest for the female captives whom Kanyemba distributed throughout the ranks of his military. Because most of his followers had come to Bawa without wives,[84] spouses were essential to the long-term survival of the Chikunda enclave. Whatever their origin, these women always went to live in their husband's village. If still young, they underwent Chikunda rites of initiation in which the makaju was tattooed on their faces and their front teeth were filed.[85] Cut off from their natal societies and incorporated into a new set of social networks, over time they discarded their former diverse identities and became Chikunda. Their children were always brought up as Chikunda. The offspring of free women who married Chikunda also adopted their father's ethnic identity. "My mother was Nsenga," recalled Vena Dixon, "but I am Chikunda because my father was Chikunda."[86]

Because of the patrilineal practices of the Chikunda, the assimilation of male slaves married to Chikunda women was more problematic. Many captives, especially if they were older, retained the identity they brought with them.[87]

Others, immersed in a new world, gradually became Chikunda. Emma Sin-turau described the ethnicity of her family in this way: "My father's father was a Lamba from far away. He was sold to Kanyemba's clan Abreu. I am a Chi-kunda. My grandfather was the only one who was a Lamba. He settled here and married and had children. When my grandfather came here, he stopped speak-ing his own language and started speaking Chikunda. My father was born here and became a Chikunda and so are all his children."[88] Although the details of their fathers' autobiographies varied, one social fact remained constant — the offspring of mixed marriages between strangers and Chikunda women adopted their mother's ethnic identity. That children of Chikunda mothers regularly became Chikunda — ignoring the ethnicity of the father — highlights the radically incorporative nature of Chikunda identity. Becoming Chikunda was a way that outsiders, women, and children identified themselves as loyal-ists of the warlord's conquest state. Initiation practices among the ex-slaves in Zimbabwe seem to have stressed the open quality of Chikunda ethnicity. As Willie Payson remembered: "The elders taught the children at the initiation school . . . the culture of being Chikunda, the story of how they came to be Chikunda, how the Chikunda came from the other side [Tete] and conquered the people here, and how the many tribes whom they defeated became Chi-kunda. They stressed how the Tande, Tawara, Tonga and Nsenga were initially not Chikunda, but after they were conquered they all came to call themselves Chikunda. These ideas and a sense of pride in being Chikunda were passed on from father to sons, and when the fathers died and their sons grew up, the latter passed on to their sons a pride in being Chikunda."[89]

These history lessons encouraged diverse groups of slaves, women, and children to think of themselves as Chikunda. As they learned to be Chikunda, outsiders also learned new languages. Chikunda dialect was quite different from the local Shona languages. These differences survived until the twentieth century: in 1917, one villager complained: "They were Chikunda — I knew by the way they spoke."[90] In appearance, too, Kanyemba's Chikunda were easily distinguished from both the subject populations and the recent conscripts. Whereas the latter dressed in a locally woven bark-cloth, Chikunda men were clad in imported calico cloth that they draped about their waists. Their wives also wore calico.[91] Dress marked Chikunda identity. So did the makaju, with which slaves and others who were initiated as Chikunda were tattooed. Willie Payson stressed that the makaju set boundaries between Kanyemba's partisans and Atande peasants: "What distinguished our Chikunda ancestors from the Atande was the makaju. The makaju said that a person was Chikunda. Our ancestors had three marks — one on their foreheads and one on each cheek. The makaju was like a uniform of a soldier. It signified that the person was a warrior. When Kanyemba came with his soldiers they had the makaju on their face."[92] There was more than good looks at stake. Through facial tattoos, schooling, and language instruction, ex-slaves made newcomers Chikunda. This status had once been a means by which military slaves on the prazos distinguished themselves from peasants and dignified their dangerous work. Under Kanyemba and other warlords, the marks of slaves' identity became a basis for political unification. Ex-slaves used their shared vocabulary of identity in order to incorporate strange women, men, and children. At Bawa, in other words, ex-slaves enlarged Chikunda identity in order to create and consolidate an ethnicity, a shared political community.

The final stage in the transformation of the Chikunda from descendants of slave soldiers to an ethnic group was Kanyemba's death and reinvention as a mhondoro. Mhondoro are guardians of the land, spirits in whom the lives of dead chiefs and rulers continue. When properly propitiated, they bring rain and health to their descendants. Chikunda remember that Kanyemba took special medicines to ensure that, after his death, he would be transformed into a mhondoro.[93] He died in the last years of the nineteenth century. After his death, a young boy from Chipoto named Alimação manifested Kanyemba's spirit. The young boy remained Kanyemba's medium for many years, until he was "an elderly man who used a walking stick."[94] After Alimação passed away, Kanyemba's spirit found refuge in a lion and, some time thereafter, entered the body of a woman named Joaquina. After she was recognized as Kanyemba's earthly medium, she settled in his village at Bawa and lived there at least until 1997.

With their own mhondoro, the Chikunda gained ritual security over their new homeland. As a mhondoro, Kanyemba had the power to bring the rain, ensure the fertility of the land, aid the hunters, and protect the warriors. Chikunda venerated him as a means of ensuring prosperity: "After our ancestors gathered the crops they brewed beer and brought it to him," explained Carlos Chicandari. "They then danced and thanked him for the good harvest. Before hunters [and soldiers] left they informed Kanyemba's spirit and asked Kanyemba to protect them in the bush and ensure a good hunt. If they failed to do so they would not be successful. When they returned they immediately brought meat to Kanyemba."[95]

We have argued that Chikunda identity was a historical innovation, crafted by military slaves on the prazos. In the late nineteenth century, ex-slaves expanded the markers of their identity to found a Chikunda ethnicity. For Kanyemba and his partisans this was a strategy of incorporation, a way of integrating slaves, women, and others as members of a cohesive citizenry. Imagining themselves as Chikunda, children of common ancestors and followers of shared mhon-doro, was also a way for ex-slaves to gain ritual security over the land.

Kanyemba's state did not survive colonization. In 1884–85, the Congress of Berlin decreed that European states wishing to establish colonial empires in Africa had to demonstrate effective occupation of the regions they claimed. Worried by reports that Kanyemba and other Chikunda warlords were se-cretly negotiating with the British, the Portuguese began a lengthy military campaign to subjugate them in the 1890s. Chikunda loyalists fought hard, but by 1903, the bulk of the Chikunda armies had been forced to surrender.[96]

Despite the defeat of the conquest states, Chikunda identity was preserved and reproduced in remote communities at the confluence of the Zambezi and Luangwa Rivers. There the descendants of Kanyemba and several of the other warlords became colonial chiefs, sanctioned by British and Portuguese author-ities. To this date many descendants of the ex-slaves live in Chikunda commu-nities in the backwater regions along the Mozambican-Zambian-Zimbabwe frontier. Though disarmed long ago, they still sing the praise of the great warrior hunters, recall in rich detail the exploits and abuses of their warlord chiefs, and greet each other with the traditional military salutes. They take pride in the fact that "Chikunda meant victors."

Notes

1. Max Weber, *A Theory of Social and Political Organization,* trans. A. Henderson (New York, 1947).

2. David Ayalon, *Islam and the Abode of War: Military Slaves and Islamic Adver-saries* (London, 1994). For another Weberian analysis, see Allan R. Meyers, "The Abid al-Buhari: Slave Soldiers and Statecraft in Morocco, 1672–1790" (Ph.D. diss., Cornell University, 1974).

3. Daniel Pipes, *Slave Soldiers and Islam: The Genesis of a Military Institution* (New Haven, 1981), 91.

4. For what might be done, see Dirk Kolff, *Naukar, Rajput and Sepoy: The Ethno-history of the Military Labor Market in Hindustan, 1450–1850* (Cambridge, UK, 1990). Kolff studied the *naukari* culture of military labor migrants from northern India. Through courage, discipline, and self-sacrifice, naukari songs promised, young men would earn the right to marry. Joined in the common pursuit of honor, military labor migrants created a distinct Rajput caste that celebrated physical valor, strength, and courage. The Rajputs were never slaves. But their history highlights how military service could fuel the moral and political imagination of soldiers.

5. This term is derived from Bill Bravman, *Making Ethnic Ways: Communities and Their Transformations in Taita, Kenya, 1800–1950* (Portsmouth, 1998), 5.

6. Lamin Sanneh, "Islamic Slavery in African Perspective," in *Slaves and Slavery in Muslim Africa,* ed. J. R. Willis (London, 1985).

7. Robin Law, *The Oyo Empire, c. 1600–c. 1836: A West African Imperialism in the Era of the Atlantic Slave Trade* (Oxford, 1977).

8. Roberta Ann Dunbar, "Slavery and the Evolution of Nineteenth-Century Damagaram," in *Slavery in Africa: Historical and Anthropological Perspectives*, ed. Suzanne Miers and Igor Kopytoff (Madison, 1977).

9. Ahmad Alawad Sikainga, "Comrades in Arms or Captives in Bondage: Sudanese Slaves in the Turco-Egyptian Army, 1820–1865," in *Slave Elites in the Middle East and Africa,* ed. Miura Toru and John Edward Philips (London, 2000).

10. Martin Klein, "Servitude Among the Wolof and Sereer of Senegambia," in *Slavery in Africa: Historical and Anthropological Perspectives*, ed. Suzanne Miers and Igor Kopytoff (Madison, 1977).

11. See Martin Klein, "Social and Economic Factors in the Muslim Revolutions in Senegambia," *Journal of African History* 13 (1972): 419–41.

12. Arab and Swahili planters on the East African coast did use armed slaves to oversee the captives who worked on their fields. See Frederick Cooper, *Plantation Slavery on the East Coast of Africa* (New Haven, 1977), 172.

13. Allen Isaacman and Barbara Isaacman, "The Prazeiros as Transfrontiersmen: A Study in Social and Cultural Change," *International Journal of African Historical Studies* 8 (1975): 1–39.

14. Arquivo Histórico Ultramarino [A.H.U.], Moç., Cx. 9, Marco António de Azevedo Coutinho de Montaur to Pedro de Saldanha de Albuquerque, January 20, 1763; A.H.U., Moç., Cx. 38, Luís Pinto de Souza, October 27, 1796; A.H.U., Moç., Cx. 31, Manoel Baptista Coutinho, 1795.

15. Sebastião Xavier Botelho, *Memória Estatística sobre os Domínios Portuguezes na África Oriental* (Lisbon, 1835), 50.

16. Biblioteca Pública de Ajuda [Ajuda], 51-VI-24, no. 67, fol. 290, "Tres Papeis feitos pellos Mouros em França sobre os Rios de Cuama e sobre Índia," unsigned, 1667.

17. Allen Isaacman, *Mozambique: The Africanization of a European Institution: The Zambezi Prazos, 1750–1902* (Madison, 1972), 19.

18. Miranda estimated that on forty-one of the more than ninety estates there were thirty-four thousand slaves. Arquivo Nacional de Torre de Tombo [A.N.T.T.], Ministério do Reino, Maço 604, "Memória Sobre a Costa de África," António Pinto de Miranda, undated, 36–53.

19. M. D. D. Newitt, *Portuguese Settlement on the Zambesi* (New York, 1973).

20. A.H.U., Moç., Cx. 3, Fr. Fernando Jésus, M.A., April 13, 1752.

21. A.N.T.T., Ministério do Reino, Maço 604, António Pinto de Miranda, "Memória sobre a Costa de África," 79.

22. Interview with Ricardo Ferrão et al., Tete, Mozambique, October 22, 1997.

23. Arquivo Histório de Moçambique [A.H.M.], Códice 2-1167, bk. 1, fols. 1–58, Registo dos Libertos do Distrito da Villa de Tete, unsigned, 1856.

24. See Isaacman, *Mozambique*, 95–113.

25. Ibid., 92–93.

26. A. C. Gamitto, "Escravatura na África Oriental," *Archivo Pittoresco* 2 (1859): 370.

27. Suzanne Miers and Igor Kopytoff argue that slavery was one among a variety of

options that Africans used to ameliorate difficult economic situations. See Kopytoff and Miers, "African 'Slavery' as an Institution of Marginality," in *Slavery in Africa: Historical and Anthropological Perspectives,* ed. Suzanne Miers and Igor Kopytoff (Madison, 1977).

28. A.N.T.T., Ministério do Reino, Maço 604, "Memória sobre a Costa de África," António Pinto de Miranda, n.d.

29. A. C. Gamitto, *King Kazembe* (Lisbon, 1960), 2:145.

30. José Fernandes Jr. "Narração do Distrito de Tete" (unpublished manuscript, Makanga, 1955), 3; Gamitto, "Escravatura," 399; A.H.U., Códice 1452, João Bonifácio Alves da Silva to Sebastião Xavier Botelho.

31. Interview with Custódio Luís Gonzaga Chimalizeni, Tete, Mozambique, October 10, 1997.

32. Gamitto, *King Kazembe,* 1:36.

33. A.N.T.T., Ministério do Reino, Maço 604, António Pinto de Miranda, "Memória Sobre a Costa de África," n.d., 55.

34. A.H.U., Fr. Fernando Jésus, M.A., April 13, 1752; Gamitto, "Escravatura"; interview with Chale Lupia, Massangano, Mozambique, September 28, 1968.

35. A.H.U., Cx. 20, Jozé Manuel Pinteira, January 20, 1783.

36. A.H.U., Moç., Cx. 3, unsigned, undated.

37. A. C. Gamitto, "Prazos da Coroa em Rios de Sena," *Archivo Pittoresco* 1 (1857): 62.

38. A.H.U., Moç., Cx. 34, Francisco José Lacerda e Almeida, March 22, 1798; A.H.M., Fundo do Século XIX, Quelimane, Códice 2-266, Fd. 3, fols. 17–19, João de Souza Machado et al., "Acta da Sessão do Concelho do Governo," May 30, 1842; A.H.U., Códice 1758, fol. 156, Custódio José da Silva to José Maria Pereira, July 24, 1859; interview with José António, Cheringoma, Mozambique, September 7, 1968; interview with Sete Marqueza, Gente Renço, and Quembo Pangacha, Caia, Mozambique, September 4, 1968.

39. Interview with José da Costa Xavier, Tete, Mozambique, July 22, 1968.

40. Francisco de Mello de Castro, *Descrição dos Rios de Senna, Anno de 1751* (Lisbon, 1861), 21; Manuel Galvão da Silva, "Diário ou Relação das Viagens Filosóficas, nos Terras da Jurisdição de Tete e Algumas dos Maraves," in *Anais de Junta de Investigações do Ultramar* 9, tomo 1 (Lisbon, 1954), 317–19; A.N.T.T., Maço 604, Luís António de Figuerido, "Notícias do Continente de Moçambique Abbreviada Relação do Seu Commércio," December 1, 1788.

41. Biblioteca Pública de Ajuda [Ajuda] 52-x-2, no. 3, José Francisco Alves Barbosa, "Analise Estatística," December 30, 1821.

42. Ibid.

43. A.N.T.T., Ministério do Reino, Maço 604, Diego Guerreiro de Aboime, August 27, 1779.

44. Interview with Castro Amoda Jack et al., Tete, Mozambique, October 21, 1997.

45. See Orlando Patterson, *Slavery and Social Death* (Cambridge, MA, 1982).

46. Newitt, *Portuguese Settlement,* 187–203; Isaacman, *Mozambique,* 32–42.

47. Interview with João Alfai, Chioco, Mozambique, July 26, 1968; interview with Sete Marqueza, Degue, Mozambique, July 27, 1968.

48. Interview with Kapurika, Guta, Zimbabwe, January 10, 1973.

49. A.H.U., Cx. 28, Luís de Souza Ferrez de Moura, August 2, 1794; A. N. de B. Truão, *Estatísticas da Capitania dos Rios de Sena no Anno de 1806* (Lisbon, 1889), 12.

50. Gamitto, "Escravatura," 399; interview with Castro Amada Jack; interview with Ricardo António Ferrão et al.

51. See Matthew Schoffeleers, "The History and Political Role of the M'Bona Cult Among the Mang'anja," in *The Historical Study of African Religion,* ed. Terrence Ranger and I. Kimambo (Berkeley, 1972).

52. Interview with Chale Lupia.

53. Interview with Custódio Luís Gonzaga Chimalizeni; interview with Castro Amoda Jack et al.; interview with Ricardo António Ferrão et al.

54. Interview with Custódio Luís Gonzaga Chimalizeni.

55. Interview with Conrado Msussa Boroma, Mozambique, July 28, 1968. For a preliminary discussion, see J. R. dos Santos Jr., *Contribuição para o Estudo da Antropologia de Moçambique* (Lisbon, 1944), 2:247–78.

56. António Rita Ferreira, *Estudos, Ensaios e Documentos* (Lisbon, 1958), 52.

57. Isaacman, *Mozambique,* 66; interview with Amissi Sokire et al., Nhaufa, Malawi, October 21, 1997.

58. Interview with Diamond Mpande, Bawa, Mozambique, September 24, 1997.

59. Interview with Custódio Luís Gonzaga Chimalizeni.

60. Interview with Diamond Mpande.

61. Interview with Amissi Sokire et al.

62. Interview with Castro Amoda Jack et al.

63. Interview with Tiyago Matega, Chausa, Zambia, February 18, 1974.

64. E. C. Tabler, ed., *Baines on the Zambezi, 1858 to 1859* (Johannesburg, 1982), 214.

65. Interview with Custódio Luís Gonzaga Chimalizeni.

66. Interview with Chale Lupia.

67. Interview with Vena Dixon et al., Bawa, Mozambique, September 20, 1997.

68. Newitt, *Portuguese Settlement,* 190.

69. A.H.U., Moç., Cx. 3, Fr. Fernando Jesús, M.A., April 1, 1752; Cx. 16, D. Diego António de Barros Sotto Mayor, August 1, 1780; A.H.U., Moç., Cx. 31, Manuel Ribeira de Sousa, January 7, 1795; A.H.U., Moç., Cx. 42, João Felipe de Carvalho, May 28, 1803; A.H.U., Moç., Códice 1452, João Bonifácio Alves da Sa to Francisco Henrique Ferrão, January 10, 1827.

70. A.H.U., Moç., Cx. 5, António Martins, undated; A.H.U., Moç., Cx. 5, António Gomes Machão, December 1, 1756; A.H.U., Moç., Códice 1314, fol. 34, D. Manoel António de Almeida to Francisco de Mello de Castro, July 9, 1757; Newitt, *Portuguese Settlement,* 201.

71. National Archives of Zimbabwe (N.A.Z.), LI1/1/1, David Livingstone to Secretary of State for Foreign Affairs, September 9, 1858; Francisco Raimundo Moraes Pereira, *Journey Made Overland from Quelimane to Angoche in 1752,* trans. and ed. M. D. D. Newitt (Salisbury, 1965), 27.

72. Truão, *Estatísticas,* 10; Botelho, *Memória,* 266; Livingstone, *Expedition,* 37; F. C. de Lacerda e Almeida, *Travessia de África* (Lisbon, 1938), 106.

73. A.H.U., Moç., Maço 10, Manoel Joaquim Mendes de Vasconcelos e Cirne to Conde de Brito, December 7, 1827; A.H.U., Códice 1315, Manoel Joaquim Mendes de Vasconcellos e Cirne, 1830; David Livingstone, *Missionary Travels* (New York, 1858), 630–31.

74. Isaacman, *Mozambique,* 116, n. 9.

75. A.H.U., Códice 1315, fol. 37, Francisco Henriques Ferrão to Comandante de Tete, December 10, 1829; A.H.U. Moç., Maço 8, Jozé Miguel de Brito, July 18, 1830.

76. Isaacman, *Mozambique,* 116, n. 7.

77. For a discussion of these warlords see Newitt, *Portuguese Settlement,* 295–311.

78. Interview with Mafioso Sejunga, Bawa, Mozambique, September 21, 1997.

79. A.H.M., Fundo do Seculo XIX, Distrito de Zumbo, Capitania Mōr de Zumbo, Cx. 8-3 M1 (28), Agostinho de Oliveira Bareto and Joaquim de Mendonça to Capitão Mōr das Terras de Zumbo, November 15, 1887; A.H.M., SEAV 1, no. 44 (a–c), Padre Dialer S. J. Luís Gonzaga, "Costumes e História do Zumbo e Miruru," 1909; F. Selous, *A Hunter's Wandering in Africa* (Bulawayo, 1970), 295–317; C. Weise, *Expedition in East Central Africa, 1888–1891,* ed. H. W. Langworthy (Norman, 1983), 121, 190.

80. Selous, *Hunter's Wandering,* 298.

81. Interview with Sunda Mwanza, Feira, Zambia, August 2, 1974.

82. W. Montagu-Kerr, *The Far Interior* (Boston, 1886), 46.

83. Interview with Tiyago Matega; A.H.M., Fundo do Século XIX, Governo Geral, Cx. 11, Theodório Francisco Diaz to Governador de Tete, undated.

84. Interview with Vena Dixon et al.; inteview with Carlos Chicandari, Bawa, Mozambique, September 22, 1977.

85. Interview with Mafioso Sejunga; interview with Vena Dixon et al.

86. Interview with Vena Dixon et al.

87. Interview with Carlos Chicandari.

88. Interview with Emma Sinturau, Bawa, Mozambique, September 23, 1997.

89. Interview with Willie Payson et al., Bawa, Mozambique, September 27, 1997.

90. N.A.Z., A3/18/38/1-4, "Statement of Gomo," witnessed by C. F. Molyneux, October 16, 1917.

91. Interview with Diamond Mpande.

92. Interview with Willie Payson et al.

93. Interview with Diamond Mpande; interview with Willie Payson; interview with Carlos Chicandari; interview with Mafioso Sejunga; interview with António Gregódio, Cambera Island, Mozambique, September 22, 1997.

94. Interview with Carlos Chicandari.

95. Ibid.

96. See A. Isaacman and Anton Rosenthal, "Slaves, Soldiers, and Police: Power and Dependency among the Chikunda of Mozambique, ca. 1825–1920," in *The End of Slavery in Africa,* ed. S. Miers and R. Roberts (Madison, 1988).

Transforming Bondsmen into Vassals: Arming Slaves in Colonial Spanish America

JANE LANDERS

Several key factors, including legal and cultural precedents, demographic imperatives, and the need to defend a vast and contested empire, led Spain, more than any other European nation, to depend on the military employment of slaves. Castilian slave law, codified in the thirteenth-century *Siete Partidas* and later transplanted to the Americas, was not exclusively based on race, and Africans joined slaves of other races and ethnicities who had been captured in "just wars," been condemned, or had sold themselves into slavery.[1] Considering slavery an unnatural condition, the *Siete Partidas* acknowledged a slave's moral personality, defined the slave's rights and obligations, and established mechanisms by which slaves might transform themselves from bondsmen into free vassals. One route to freedom was via meritorious service to the state, and this came to include armed military service in defense of the Spanish Crown.[2]

The early modern Spanish army was reputed to be the best in the world, and it was remarkably heterogeneous, incorporating volunteers and mercenaries from a wide variety of nationalities in forces commanded by Spanish officers.[3] The diversity of Spain's armed forces, moreover, reflected that of the larger society. Along with *conversos* (converted Jews), *moriscos* (subject Muslims), and gypsies, free and enslaved Africans formed sizeable populations in southern cities such as Seville, which one scholar described as a chessboard with equal numbers of black and white pieces.⁴ Given long-standing legal and cultural precedents and the limited number of regular forces available for duty, it should come as no surprise that once Spain acquired a vast American empire, the armies it deployed there should be equally diverse. In Europe Spain had filled its armies with Germans, Italians, Irish, and other foreigners who fought alongside Spanish peasants. In the Americas Spain depended instead on indigenous allies and on men of African descent, enslaved and free, to accomplish its early conquests.

Slave Auxiliaries in the Conquest

Spain's military campaigns against indigenous populations all included small numbers of free and enslaved men of African descent.⁵ Together, Spaniards and the Africans among them formed a specialized and limited pool of experienced expeditionaries circulating throughout the circum-Caribbean on exploratory treks, slaving voyages, and full-blown wars of conquest.⁶ Black slaves were present at every major Spanish "discovery" and risked their lives repeatedly for the Spanish Crown despite their bondage. Once the Indian wars on Hispaniola waned and settlement was well under way, a small group of battle-tested Africans joined in new circum-Caribbean campaigns, in explorations of southeastern North America, and in the epic conquest of the Aztec Empire.⁷ Others joined military expeditions into the southwestern deserts of what is today the United States, southward into Central America, and on to South America.⁸ Free and enslaved Africans participated in significant numbers in the conquest of the great Inca Empire of Peru and in the subsequent Indian and civil wars that wracked the region. Blacks deployed in small mobile units struck terror through the Peruvian hinterlands and seemed to the indigenous populations they dominated to be as ruthless as the Spaniards.⁹ Then, with promises of freedom, the rebel Francisco Hernández Girón raised an army of several hundred slaves for his unsuccessful bid to wrest Peru from Spain in 1554.¹⁰ The risk of arming such a large number of slaves was great, and little is known about how Hernández Girón utilized and controlled his slave army, but the rich kingdom he was gambling for must have seemed worth any danger. Ultimately royal interests prevailed, and although the fate of those slave rebels is unknown, it is probable that they were reincorporated into royalist forces, given that the Incas were still in revolt and that Spain needed every hand. Some of the pardoned may have been among the slaves who marched southward with Spanish military expeditions into Chile and into more warfare against the Araucanian Indians. For his valor in those wars one black slave, Juan Valiente (whose long military career extended from

1536 to his death in battle in 1553) received an estate near Santiago and later a grant of commended Indians. This unusual privilege meant status as well as income, but Valiente died a slave whose legal owner was still attempting to recover him.[11]

Slaves in the Early Defense of the Caribbean

As enslaved blacks continued to explore and expand Spanish frontiers throughout the Americas, other slaves of African descent helped Spaniards "hold the fort" in the circum-Caribbean, where the catastrophic decline of native populations was noted earliest.[12] Drawing on old Spanish patterns, in 1540 the Crown ordered residents of the Spanish-American colonies to form local self-defense groups and, soon thereafter, chronically short-handed Spanish officials began to include enslaved Africans in these forces.[13] It was common for a few slaves to appear on militia rolls as drummers, fifers, and flag bearers in their owners' units.[14] Other enslaved Africans served as interpreters and as ad hoc defense forces on rural plantations and ranches and sailed on locally organized patrol boats throughout the circum-Caribbean.[15]

When French pirates attacked Havana in 1555, however, Spanish officials were forced to arm large numbers of slaves in order to try to save their city. Havana's small garrison numbered only forty regular Spanish troops, and officials scrambled to supplement this force with about one hundred blacks and an equal number of Indians. Presumably most of the blacks were slaves, although some may have been free. When, despite their efforts, the city fell, Havana's governor hastily raised an additional force of more than two hundred black slaves from the countryside.[16] In this critical moment slaves greatly outnumbered regular white soldiers, and most were field hands. Had they chosen to, they could have handed the city over to the French. Instead they fought with the Spaniards.

Although Spaniards were forced to depend on slaves to maintain a tenuous control over thinly populated and greatly dispersed colonies under almost constant foreign attack and encroachment, they also worried about a rapidly growing racial imbalance in the circum-Caribbean. Only six years after the French pirate attack, the captain general and governor of Cuba and Florida, Pedro Menéndez de Avilés, informed King Philip II that Hispaniola was populated by thirty thousand blacks and fewer than two thousand Spaniards, while Puerto Rico held fifteen thousand blacks and only five hundred Spaniards. Menéndez claimed that the same racial disparity held true in Cuba, Veracruz, Puerto Cavallos in Honduras, Cartagena, and Venezuela and warned that, because neither England nor France then allowed slavery, any corsair might, with a few thousand men, take over all Spain's possessions by freeing and arming the grateful slaves, who, he alleged, would then slay their Spanish masters.[17]

This is an early articulation of Spain's imperial dilemma. When African slaves in the circum-Caribbean were few in number, medieval precedents could accommodate their transition to freedom and even their military deployment in times of crisis. When slaves came to outnumber Spaniards and incidences of marronage and rebellion increased, however, Spanish officials began to fear that the slaves might violently seize their freedom rather than follow the system for obtaining it.

The Crown responded to Menéndez's alarms by establishing government subsidies and posting regular troops to defend the Caribbean ports through which its American trade and treasure passed. Of these, Havana was the most significant as the rendezvous for the treasure fleets, and patterns established in Cuba were often emulated elsewhere in the circum-Caribbean. Enslaved blacks helped defend Puerto Rico in 1557, Cartagena in 1560 and 1572, and Santo Domingo in 1583.[18] Cartagena's officials reported that they had two hundred to three hundred slaves whom they could arm for service, and Santo Domingo's officials estimated an available slave force of about four hundred to five hundred.[19]

At this time Spain still held slaves of diverse ethnicities and races, most of whom were captured or condemned slaves, called *esclavos forzados*. Some were sentenced to perpetual slavery, while others served lengthy but delimited periods of enslavement. The Crown often assigned such condemned slaves to its floating prisons as rowers or employed them in public works such as the construction of fortifications. In April 1568 a Spanish court condemned Corporal Alonso Escudero, a Spaniard from Almonte, to perpetual slavery in the Cuban galleys for murdering his wife. Ten years later Escudero surfaced again on a list of king's slaves working as a sawyer.[20] The multiracial and multiethnic character of Spanish slavery was still evident many years later. In 1595 officials listed 149 forzados assigned to military service in the Havana galleys. Most of the condemned were Spanish-born, but forty-five were identified as Muslim slaves from Tunis, Algiers, Morocco, Fez, Rhodes, Anatolia, and other Mediterranean locations. Still others were Canary Islanders, Greeks, Portuguese, Mexicans, French, and Genoese, and several men were identified as gypsies. Only 3 of the 149 Cuban galley slaves were identified as black or mulatto.[21] An even later report showed 34 Spanish, French, and Flemish forzados working alongside 163 black slaves on the Morro Castle.[22] After more than a century of colonization in the Americas, Spanish slavery had not yet assumed the racial character it later would. Moreover, although Cuba's officials regularly armed and deployed their own black slaves in times of crisis, they seem not to have incorporated esclavos forzados into their military forces, suggesting that they may have trusted their slaves more than forzados.

Slaves Against Maroons

Spaniards often trusted their bondsmen enough to deploy them against escaped slaves. Not uncommonly, black ranch hands participated in military expeditions against maroon communities. In 1609 the rancher Pedro González de Herrera received a royal commission to attack maroon encampments led by the famed Yanga outside Veracruz. For the task Captain González recruited a multiracial force that included 150 Indian archers, 100 royal soldiers, some Spanish mercenaries, and black, mulatto, and mestizo cowboys. For almost a decade such troops fought long and difficult battles against Yanga's maroons, but Yanga finally made a truce with the Spaniards in 1618. With that, maroons who had cost the Crown fortunes and many lives were transformed into black militiamen who loyally defended the coast against Spain's enemies and even tracked and returned for ransom other escaped slaves.[23] Spain "reduced" other maroons it could not defeat militarily, creating legitimate and loyal free black towns in New Granada, Hispaniola, and Florida. Thereafter, their male residents formed militias to defend their new towns and the interests of Spain.[24]

The Creation of Free Black Militias

By the seventeenth century, Spain was battling not only French but also Dutch and English challengers in "the Spanish Lake" and, faced with losing all, it marshaled a mixed labor force of forzados, African slaves, and occasionally subjected Indians to erect great stone forts at Havana, Santo Domingo, San Juan, Cartagena, Portobelo, Acapulco, and St. Augustine, as well as many minor constructions in lesser ports along its threatened coasts. Spain also maintained naval squadrons and small army garrisons in the region, most of which were chronically undermanned.[25] But arming slaves and ex-slaves was what enabled Spain to hold the circum-Caribbean for more than three centuries.

Realizing that ad hoc forces such as those raised in 1555 could not meet the ever-growing threats against shipping and settlements around the Caribbean, Cuban officials began organizing more formal militias of free men of color. By 1600 Cuba's free mulatto company numbered one hundred men.[26] The Spanish governors of Jamaica and Puebla, Mexico, also organized companies of free mulattoes, and this strategy may indicate an early attempt to restrict formal military service to free persons having at least some white ancestry.[27] But necessity trumped racial and legal exclusivity when Spain began losing both treasure fleets and territory. Repeated assaults on the coastal settlements of New Granada left settlers haunted by fear of invasion throughout the colonial period, according to one historian.[28] The Dutch seized Curaçao in 1634; by mid-century French smugglers and buccaneers had converted the western portion of Hispaniola into a French colony and also occupied Tortuga; and in 1655 the English took Jamaica, despite the best efforts of Spanish slaves.

Spain's enemies now held economic and military bases from which to attack Spanish fleets and settlements.[29] Recognizing that Spain could not respond quickly enough with metropolitan troops to any foreign attacks, the king instructed the viceroy of New Spain to evaluate the formation of more free black companies. His royal order noted that the mulattoes and blacks who defended his circum-Caribbean realms were "persons of valor" who fought with "vigor and reputation."[30] By mid-century, then, the Spanish Crown had fully accepted that free men of color could be brave and honorable, and this important metropolitan acknowledgment apparently encouraged enlistments. A Central American roster from 1673 listed almost two thousand *pardos* (usually meaning mulattoes, but sometimes referring to non-Europeans of mixed ancestry) serving in infantry units throughout the isthmus.[31] Similar units of free black, or *moreno,* men were organized in Hispaniola, Veracruz, Campeche, Puerto Rico, Panama, Caracas, Cartagena, and Florida.[32]

Slave Volunteers

More significant, the Spanish Crown came to recognize that slaves might also perform valuable military service. Captain Diego Martín, alias Diego el Mulato, began life as a slave in Havana, but as a young man he took to piracy. His colorful career as a corsair for the West Indies Company included many prizes and prisoners taken from Campeche to Veracruz. Eventually, as English pirates were also doing, Captain Diego decided to "go straight." In a letter delivered to Spanish officials in Havana in 1638, Martín expressed his great desire to serve as a "valiant soldier of the king, our lord," making appropriate references to the king's championship of the Catholic faith. He promised to prevent Dutch or other enemy ships from stopping along Cuba's coasts and declared, "[E]specially knowing that I am here very few would dare pass on to the Indies, for they certainly fear me." Martín's boast must have been well-founded, for Havana officials sent the offer to Spain with a recommendation of royal pardon and a salary equivalent to that of an admiral, making no derogatory mention of his color or class.[33] Spanish officials once again demonstrated their racial pragmatism in the face of necessity.

As the slave Diego transformed himself by deeds and words, so, too, did the royal slaves who worked the copper mines at Santiago de Cuba. In the 1670s, their spokesperson, Captain Juan Moreno, reminded the king of their many previous military services on his behalf. Moreno referred specifically to tracking fugitive slaves and to having helped defend the port of Guaycabón when English forces attacked from Jamaica. On that occasion, seventy-three slave miners had volunteered and served. The slave captain assured the Crown of his fellow slaves' "ardent zeal" and promised future "great actions" even if these went unrewarded. Contemporary Spanish sources support a tradition of slave service in Santiago, which they considered a frontier because of its southern coastal location and thin population, as well as its aggressive English neighbors.[34]

At this very moment, on the northern frontier of the Caribbean, slaves escaping from the newly settled English colony of Carolina asked for and received religious sanctuary in Spanish Florida. After they converted to Catholicism and swore fealty, Spanish officials armed the "new Christians" and sent them northward on guerrilla raids against the fledgling plantations of the enemy. Arming these slaves and subsequent refugees from English slavery helped Spain to hold the Florida frontier against English raids in 1728 and a major land and naval assault in 1740, but when Spain finally ceded Florida to the English in 1763, the former slaves sailed to Cuba with the Spaniards who freed them rather than await the English, who might reenslave them.[35]

Bourbon Reform of the Black Militias

In 1700, after more than two centuries of black military service in the Caribbean, French Bourbons assumed the Spanish throne and instituted reforms in order to more effectively control the empire and its resources. In place of the existing black militias they created new "disciplined" militias of pardos (mulattoes) and morenos (blacks). To encourage enlistment they exempted recruits from tribute payments. These levies were a mark of conquest and subjugation deeply resented and protested by black militiamen. In fact, tribute payments from freed blacks had rarely been collected, so this reform cost the Crown little and gained it the goodwill of the militiamen. The Bourbon reforms also formalized the practice of allowing blacks to elect their own officers, and most important, extended the *fuero militar* to pardo and moreno units. The fuero was a corporate charter with important implications, for it exempted black militiamen from prosecution in civilian courts and put them on equal juridical status with white militiamen. The fuero also granted blacks who served in the military hospitalization, retirement, and death benefits, as well as the right to wear uniforms and bear arms. White soldiers in New Spain protested these changes and the resulting blurring of racial boundaries and sought to abridge the benefits of their fuero, generally limiting its enjoyment to officers in active service.[36] Old racial hierarchies were difficult to change in the heart of the viceroyalty, but welcome change did come in the Caribbean periphery, where the juridical and social benefits of militia membership were clearly appreciated and men of African descent developed traditions of family service.[37] In Cartagena so many blacks enlisted that they soon matched the numbers of whites.[38] In Peru more than fourteen hundred pardos and morenos enlisted in new infantry units, and several hundred more served in cavalry units.[39] By 1770 more than three thousand men of color had joined Cuba's militia, forming themselves into three battalions and sixteen additional companies which constituted more than one-fourth of the island's armed forces. The *Reglamento para las milicias de infantería y caballería de la Isla de Cuba* governed military reorganizations not only in Cuba but also in Florida, Puerto Rico, Louisiana, and Panama, where blacks also enlisted in large numbers.[40]

Slave Soldiers in Eighteenth-Century Cuba

One interesting feature of the Cuban Reglamento was the organization in Havana of an artillery company of one hundred royal slaves. Officials responsible for that unit registered the name, age, physical description (including scarification patterns), and ethnicity of each. They also gave information about their wives and children. This detailed registration and other features of the code suggest that the slave artillery company was composed largely of *bozales,* or unacculturated African-born slaves. Regulations required the commander of the slave artillery company to see to its members' religious instruction and marriage. Drawing on patterns as old as the fifteenth century, the Crown hoped to see these bozales transformed into Christian family men, and so slave wives and children were to live within the garrison with the slave artillerymen. The women would perform domestic chores such as cooking and laundry for the garrison's soldiers, but with their husband's permission they could also find work in the city. The womens' wages, or *jornales,* were to be pooled and placed in the traditional chest with three keys that the royal treasurers and religious brotherhoods also used. This communal fund of earnings would be used to pay for midwives and for other needs such as clothing for their children.[41]

Cuba's slave artillery company saw bloody battle when the British captured

Havana in 1762. English accounts of the siege document heavy casualties suffered by the Cuban defenders and distinguish "militia-natives" (presumably black militias in their uniforms) from slaves, whom they commonly described as "mulatos and negros." These English sources claimed that the latter died by the hundreds.[42] Cuba's disciplined black militia units also fought bravely to defend their homeland, and the British gave no quarter to any black men they captured. Despite that knowledge, a group of twenty Cuban slaves, armed only with machetes and acting totally independently, launched their own offensive against a superior English force at Cuba's great Morro Castle, killing some of the English enemy and capturing seven more. Some of them may have been members of the slave artillery company. The "ladies of Havana" described the slaves' heroism in a letter to the king, who freed them and awarded their leader, Andrés Gutiérrez, the title of captain. The compensation claims of their owners document other slaves who died fighting the British.[43]

Spain's Black Militias in the Era of Revolutions

The exigencies of the eighteenth century led Spain to post many of Cuba's black militiamen to the frontiers of Louisiana, Florida, the Yucatán, and Mexico, and some spent as many as twenty years abroad before returning to their homes. Others never saw Cuba again.[44] Despite the hardships of their service and lingering discrimination, black militiamen from Cuba, Florida, and Louisiana served with distinction during the American Revolution. Spain's black troops fought bravely in the Gulf campaigns at Mobile and Pensacola and in the Mississippi River campaigns at Manchac and Baton Rouge. Governor Bernardo de Gálvez nominated a number of the black men who served in the Mississippi River campaign for royal commendations, and the Crown acknowledged the importance of their contribution with silver medals and promotions. Black militiamen from Cuba and Florida later joined an expedition against the English in the Bahamas.[45]

At the end of the American Revolution, Spain regained Florida from the British and blacks resumed a long tradition of military service in that colony. Some of Spain's most effective soldiers were slaves escaped from Loyalist owners during the colonial transfer to whom Florida's governors granted religious sanctuary. The Loyalist brothers Major Henry Williams and William Williams tried for many years to reclaim three runaway slaves who escaped from them on the day after Christmas 1784, as the brothers prepared to evacuate them to New Providence in the Bahamas. The brothers' 1785 advertisement described "Reynor [Reyna], wife to Hector, and Sam, for they both have her to wife."[46] In 1788 the trio of runaways presented themselves to

Spanish authorities and disputed their purported masters' account. Hector stated that they had accompanied Major William Williams to East Florida in Hector's own boat and that they had all lived as free persons as a consequence of the men's military service. Sam's statement confirmed their free status and military service, adding the information that he had once belonged to Henry Alexander of South Carolina and that Hector and Reyna had belonged to Diego Devaux.[47] Governor Zéspedes upheld the freed slaves' claims to freedom despite numerous appeals by the Williams brothers.[48]

Men like Hector and Sam had ample opportunity to demonstrate their loyalty and military skills in the following decades. Florida's aggressive neighbors to the north bitterly contested Spain's fugitive slave policy, its use of armed blacks in military service, and its alliance with the Seminole and Creek nations, whose lands they coveted.[49] Well aware of the colony's vulnerable position, Florida's governors complained incessantly to Spain about crumbling defenses, irregular receipt of the government subsidy, and the poor quality of regular troops.[50] Even if the men had been of the best caliber, however, there were too few of them to adequately patrol Florida's great expanse. Long stretches of coastline lay beyond the control of the government located in St. Augustine, and even the sparsely populated areas surrounding the capital were laced with waterways that provided easy access into the province by assorted "banditti" and invaders. Florida's settlers and their haciendas, harvests, and slaves were always at risk.

Given the proximity of the international border at the St. Mary's River, Spain's military debility, and the challenge of monitoring Florida's difficult geography, the free black militia proved indispensable to the colony's defense. But Florida's governors also utilized slaves in times of crisis. During the French-inspired invasion of 1795, Florida's governor called up his black militias but also required all citizens with slaves to present them for government construction projects and to serve as sailors and rowers on government boats.[51] Perhaps inspired by the Cuban model, he also created a separate unit of slaves that he assigned to the artillery and trained to man the canons and in other ways relieve the regular military. The governor donated one of his own slaves to this unit, and the commandant of the Third Cuban Battalion posted in Florida donated two, but other planters offered "only a thousand excuses."[52]

The Black Auxiliaries of Carlos IV

Ironically, Spain's dependence on former slaves reached new heights as a result of the slave revolt that erupted in Saint Domingue in 1791. Although its oldest settlements lay only across the mountains from the burning plantations and bloodshed, Spain recognized old traditions and realized that immediate necessity might permit an alliance with the risen slaves and forestall disaster in Santo Domingo.

Without any previous known military training, the creole slaves Jean-François and Georges (Jorge) Biassou had assumed command of the rebel forces of the North and managed to hold their polyglot armies together against the odds. Jean-François decorated himself with the Cross of Saint Louis, Biassou titled himself the "Viceroy of the Conquered Territories," and Toussaint Louverture became an aide and physician to Biassou's large army of forty thousand men.[53] The rebels early recognized their material limitations and attempted to secure the general amnesty promised by the French Assembly. They sued for peace in exchange for their own freedom and political rights and those of their families and officers, but the reactionary planters of Saint Domingue rudely and unwisely rejected their offer.[54] Biassou angrily ordered the execution of all his white prisoners, vowing that they would pay "for the insolence of the [Colonial] Assembly which has dared to write to me with so little respect." Toussaint stayed his superior's order, but the bloody fighting continued.[55]

After England and Spain declared war on France in the spring of 1793, both powers courted the black rebels of the North. Commissioner Léger Felicité Sonthonax took the initiative to also offer freedom and alliance in the name of the French Republic, but as Robin Blackburn and others have noted, some rebels considered this a trick and believed only a king could make and keep such a promise. Jean-François and Biassou allegedly responded, "Since the beginning of the world we have obeyed the will of a king. We have lost the king of France but we are dear to him of Spain who constantly shows us reward and assistance. We therefore cannot recognize you until you have enthroned a king."[56]

Thus, Jean-François, Biassou, and Toussaint decided to accept the Spanish offer of alliance, declaring in a rhetorical flourish that they would "rather be slaves of the Spaniards than free with the French."[57] Despite their conservative rhetoric, the slave rebels were fierce fighters and could be either formidable enemies or invaluable allies. Counting on the latter, Spain designated its new armies of rebellious slaves the Black Auxiliaries of Charles IV, a much more formal title and affiliation than earlier or later black militias ever received. The Spanish captain general and governor of Santo Domingo ceremoniously decorated Jean-François, Biassou, and Toussaint with gold medals bearing the likeness of the king and presented them with documents expressing the gratitude and confidence of the Spanish government.[58] Toussaint's followers allegedly (and prophetically) warned, "You have received commissions and you have guarantees. Guard your liveries and your parchments. One day they will serve you as the fastidious titles of our former aristocrats served them."[59]

Newly supplied and under a Spanish flag, the forces of Jean-François, Biassou, and Toussaint fought many bloody battles against the French. One of the rebels' primary supporters, Father Josef Vásquez, himself a mulatto, wrote that "if divine Providence had not favored us with the blacks [allies], we would have been victims of the fury of the savage masses." He added that although the Spaniards did not fully trust the new allies who fought back the slaves, "it is they who have taken prisoners, they who have given the King 200 slaves, and they who have fought the campaign."[60]

Vásquez was correct on all counts. Despite centuries of dependence on former slaves, none of Spain's previous military recruits were known leaders of a slave revolt of such proportions. For this reason the alliance Spain struck with these three revolutionary leaders was an uneasy one marked by distrust on both sides. Spanish officials did feel compelled in general to honor promises of freedom, relocation, and support made in the name of their king, but they also watched the former slaves with fear and suspicion and tried to isolate them and the dangerous ideas they represented. And although it is clear that Spain's black allies were often embittered by the graceless way some Spanish officials treated them and never anticipated the diaspora they would experience at the end of the war, Jean-François and Jorge Biassou did not die betrayed in jail, as did Toussaint.

When the French Assembly finally abolished slavery in May 1794, Toussaint offered his services and loyalty to the French Republic, while Jean-François and Biassou remained loyal to Spain.[61] Before long the Black Auxiliaries of Carlos IV were losing battles against Toussaint, who surprised and defeated Spanish forces at San Raphael on May 6, 1794. Two months later at Bayajá, Jean-François and Biassou led their forces in a massacre of more than one thousand French men, women, and children who had accepted Spanish offers of protection for returning from the United States.[62]

This event led to a dramatic shift in Spanish attitudes toward the black auxiliaries. Although Spaniards were also involved in the killings, the governor of Bayajá later referred to the incident as a "cruel crime" that "inspired in the sanguinary hearts and entrails [of the blacks] the reckless belief that they had reconquered the town and saved the Spanish garrison from a plot against them by the French émigrés." If the black troops actually believed that the returning French planters who had rejected their freedom plotted to overturn the Spaniards who had accepted it, then their actions become more explicable, if no less bloody. One account claims that Jean-François had spent the morning in the confessional with Father Vásquez and that it was the priest, in fact, who gave the sign to commence the slaughter. If true, the actions of Jean-François and Biassou on that horrible day may have been sanctioned by their own beloved priest and counselor.[63]

Spain and the Directory of the French Republic finally concluded a peace treaty in 1795, according to which Spain ceded western Hispaniola to the French and agreed to disband the Black Auxiliaries of Carlos IV. Bayajá's governor recommended that the Crown abolish black military employment and titles immediately. Bothered by the auxiliaries' "pretensions to superiority," he argued that he had seen evidence of their fury, and "although they paint themselves with other colors, they are the same who murdered their owners, violated their wives, and destroyed all those with property." He also warned that some of the black auxiliaries thought the abandonment of their property would excuse their crimes and be proof of fidelity but that their sacrifices were only "illusions" and were made in their own interest.[64] The governor told Jean-François, Biassou, and the other military leaders they would have to evacuate Hispaniola because the French Republic did not find their presence "compatible," but he urged the "simple soldiers" to remain because they had been offered freedom by both the French Republic and Spain. The Republic would need laborers to restore the burned plantations.

The black armies wanted, instead, to maintain their units, ranks, salaries, and rations and to embark together for some designated place where they should be given lands to cultivate and be permitted to form a town. They had not given everything in order to return to their former state. They argued that they would then constitute a ready force, able to fight for the king of Spain wherever he should care to send them. There was, in fact, royal precedent for this option; only decades before this, the militia of the town of Gracia Real de Santa Teresa de Mose in Florida, also composed of former slaves, was evacuated en masse to Cuba in 1763, granted homesteads together, and allowed to retain their militia titles and perquisites.[65]

Over the governor's supposed opposition, "a considerable number" of soldiers embarked with their leaders for Havana, where, he predicted, they would expect "the same distinctions, prerogatives, luxury, and excessive tolerance" they had had in Bayajá. He assured the captain general of Cuba that he never promised the "venomous vipers" that they would be allowed to remain in Havana.[66] The captain general of Santo Domingo had once written glowing reports about the exploits of the "valiant warriors" he decorated in the king's name, but as soon as the fighting ceased, he, too, advocated that they be shipped to Havana. He wrote Cuba's governor that the blacks were "capable of being domesticated" and that any misdeeds of theirs (presumably a reference to Bayajá) were attributable to the bad governance they had experienced

under the French.[67] In the rapid evacuation families were separated and Biassou was forced to leave behind his own mother, whom he had allegedly rescued
from slavery in the early years of the revolt.[68] The embittered black general
lodged a formal complaint against the governor and urged his dismissal.[69]

On the last day of December 1795, Spanish officials carefully recorded the
exodus of the Black Auxiliaries of Carlos IV from Bayajá who sailed away for
Havana on a small flotilla of four ships.[70] Although Havana's blacks celebrated the arrival of Jean-François and his troops, Cuba's governor–captain
general was no more anxious than were the governors of Bayajá and Santo
Domingo to have a large number of unemployed, armed, and experienced
"wolves," as they were now referred to, on his hands. He hastily convoked a
war council that decided to deport the black armies, using as its authority the
royal order forbidding the introduction of blacks from French areas.[71]

Jean-François responded immediately with a formal statement in which he
reminded the Cuban officials of the "offices, decorations, and military ap-
pointments" given the blacks by the Spanish court, which should have been
"sufficient proof of their loyalty and submission." He also reminded them of
the "personal sacrifices each auxiliary made leaving hearth and home . . .
in blind obedience" to the king's orders. He added the implied threat that
the situation in which the Black Auxiliaries found themselves (floating on
board crowded ships in Havana harbor) made them question whether they
should reconsider the "advantageous treaties proposed by agents of the British
Crown." In closing Jean-François said his troops felt betrayed, and he made
three demands of the Spaniards: that they vouch for the safety of Father
Vásquez (who had not yet arrived in Havana); that his troops be allowed to
return to Bayajá if they would not be permitted to disembark in Havana; and
that the governor tell them whether they were "prisoners of the state or vassals
of the King of Spain."[72]

Cuba's governor answered that he could not permit the blacks to await the
arrival of Father Vásquez but that he would allow the priest to join them later
should he so choose. The governor had no objections to their returning to
Bayajá (anywhere but Havana), but he bristled at Jean-François's last demand,
denouncing it as "petulant" and saying that the prisoners of state, "of which
there are many in this city," were kept in tight and secure jail cells, whereas the
blacks had been received and treated well, given all they asked, and allowed to
freely choose their destinations.[73]

In fact, however, the governors of Santo Domingo and Cuba apparently
envisioned the Isle Of Pines off Cuba's southern coast as an ideal repository
where the numerous blacks could be contained, monitored, and "civilized" for
some time. Santo Domingo's governor proposed that once they had proven

themselves capable of some useful occupation, the "good blacks" could slowly be released into the general population. Meanwhile, children born on the island and raised under Spanish laws would not bear "such a horrific aspect."[74]

In the end, Jean-François and twelve of his military subordinates, along with their extended families, totaling 790 persons, sailed away from Havana for Cádiz, Spain. Although his life there was not without conflict, Jean-François continued his military service to Spain until his death.[75] The remaining members of Jean-François's group were dispersed as follows: 115 persons to Campeche, 144 to Trinidad de Barlovento, 307 to Truxillo, and 88 to Portobelo, Panama.[76] Jorge Biassou and his dependents sailed instead for Florida. Each of the Spanish governors who received these groups recognized that they had to honor the promises of the king to support his loyal black allies. Not only was the king's honor at stake, but England had let it be known that should the Spanish blacks be discontent with their new locations, they had only to say the word and transports would relocate them to the British holding of their choice.[77]

Only three months after General Jorge Biassou's followers landed in Florida, his brother-in-law and military heir, Sergeant Juan Jorge Jacobo, married Rafaela Witten in St. Augustine's cathedral. This union had important political implications, for the bride was the daughter of Juan Bautista ("Prince") Witten. Like Biassou and Jorge Jacobo, Witten was a former slave who had become a member of Spain's free black militia and had served with distinction against the Genêt-inspired invaders of 1795. The marriage of Biassou's heir, Jorge, and Witten's daughter, Rafaela, thus united the leading families of both groups of blacks who had allied with the cause of the Spanish king against the forces of French republicanism. Subsequent marriages and baptisms added new layers of connection, and the refugees consistently used the structures of the Catholic Church to strengthen their blended community. The overlapping relationships and creation of extended fictive families among blacks can be traced until the evacuation of Florida and may well have continued thereafter in Cuba.[78] General Jorge Biassou, also referred to in the Spanish records as the Black Caudillo, blended the men of both groups into a single military unit that saw almost continuous service in Florida. Until that time, the highest rank ever achieved by a black militiaman in Florida had been sergeant, and Biassou's elevated title thus raised the status of the rest.[79]

Biassou's "proud and vain character" was evident in his dress as well as his attitude. The black general walked the streets of St. Augustine in fine clothes trimmed in gold and carried a silver-trimmed saber and a fancy ivory-and-silver dagger. The gold medal of Charles IV must also have impressed the townspeople, unaccustomed to seeing such finery on a black man.[80] The governor, who may have been projecting his own concerns, alleged, "The slave-owners have viewed his arrival with great disgust, for they fear he will set a bad example for the rest of his class."[81]

The presence of the black auxiliaries caused consternation not only among the Spanish governors who reluctantly received them but also among the Anglo planters on Florida's borders, who were already disturbed by Spain's racial policies and its reliance on black militias. At a time when slave conspiracies and rebellions, maroon settlements, and Indian wars unsettled the southeastern frontier, this new black presence seemed particularly threatening, and correspondence and newspaper editorials of the day connected Florida to Saint Domingue and to Suriname and Jamaica, where other slaves had waged effective wars of liberation. Ultimately the Spaniards' dependence on armed black forces contributed to a series of invasions sponsored by the United States and to U.S. acquisition of Florida.

After the drama of Saint Domingue, Florida must have appeared tame to Biassou and his troops. In 1799 Biassou asked to be allowed to go to Spain and fight for the king in his European wars, since he had no way to demonstrate his military services in Florida.[82] A month later he asked to be allowed to organize two separate companies of pardo and moreno militias, to be placed under his command, that would have equal footing with the white militias. The request to divide his unit along color lines may seem incongruous given Biassou's race, but disciplined units throughout the Spanish Caribbean were similarly divided, and under this proposal black skin would have trumped tan.[83]

Although Biassou's plan to reorganize Florida's black troops came to naught, his desire for military action was answered the following year when the so-called State of Muskogee declared war against Spain. After a brief expedition in pursuit of marauding Indians, Biassou died unexpectedly in 1801 and was buried in St. Augustine with full honors. After a Mass at the Cathedral that included songs, tolling bells, candles, and incense, the governor and other notables accompanied his cortege to the cemetery. Drummers and an honor guard of twenty members of the black militia completed the procession, and his men discharged a volley at Biassou's grave. The public notary attested that "every effort was made to accord him the decency due an officer Spain had recognized for military heroism."[84]

On Biassou's death, his brother-in-law Jorge Jacobo succeeded to the command of Florida's black militias, which continued to patrol the Indian frontiers. Throughout the spring and summer Jacobo and his captains, Benjamin Segui, also a veteran of Saint Domingue, and Prince Witten, the battle-tested former slave from Carolina, led the free black militia. They engaged the Indians on various occasions and once rescued a detachment of white dragoons under siege at a frontier post, successes that may have been instrumental in the Seminoles' decision to sign a peace treaty with Spain in August 1802.[85]

Although the governors of Florida attempted to enforce its borders with military patrols and to control trade and immigration with passport and customs regulations, the province was almost impossible to police, and raiding Indians and Georgians could enter almost at will. In 1812 so-called Patriots from Georgia launched an ill-fated invasion of Spanish Florida that was covertly supported by President James Madison and a unit of U.S. Marines. Against these forces Florida's governor sent his black militias, Seminole allies, and slaves. Armed slaves appear on the Florida militia rosters from April through October 1812 clearly identified as *soldados esclavos*, or slave soldiers. The governor posted some of these local slaves at the Castillo de San Marcos and outlying redoubts. Other slaves, such as Samuel Hall and Esteban Creten, joined nine free black militiamen and three black officers posted at a Seminole village.[86] The governor depended heavily on another slave, Tony Proctor, "the best translator of the Indian languages in the province," to promote the Spanish-black-Indian alliance.[87] He sent Proctor to the Seminole village of La Chua (near present-day Gainesville), where the slave recruited several hundred warriors for the Spanish side. When the Patriots recognized Proctor's utility, they captured him and tried to employ him in the same capacity. Proctor, however, was true to the Spaniards. He alerted the Seminoles that he was speaking for the rebels under duress and that all he told them was false. He later managed to escape from the Patriots and returned to St. Augustine, where the grateful governor felt "obligated to reward the service and loyalty of this miserable slave." In the name of the government he paid Proctor's owner 350 pesos and granted the translator his liberty.[88]

Other Florida slaves also gained their freedom for their military service during the Patriot invasion. About twenty-one slaves took advantage of the chaos to escape from rebel plantations and present themselves for armed service in St. Augustine.[89] Although his advisors urged the governor not to pay the new inductees, he ordered that the slaves receive the same pay as the soldiers of the Third Battalion of Cuba, "as much as for necessity as to reward their fidelity."[90]

Necessity explains Spain's centuries-long military deployment of slaves in the circum-Caribbean. Outnumbered by indigenous enemies in the initial conquests and challenged by an assortment of imperial rivals in the age of piracy, at the very time that European wars required Spain to maintain large metropolitan armies, Spain had almost no other recourse but to depend on local defense forces, which from the very beginning of settlement included slaves.

This strategy was facilitated by the fact that Spanish slavery had nonracial origins and that Spain's corporatist social structures and effective legal codes provided institutional mechanisms for erasing distinctions among slave and free soldiers. The French, the English, and the Dutch, who all followed Spain to the Americas and who lacked both the long familiarity with Africans and the legal and social frameworks for incorporating African slaves, nevertheless quickly realized the utility of the Spanish model and adapted it to their own needs throughout the Caribbean.

The fidelity slaves had repeatedly demonstrated in the Caribbean also helps explain Spain's continued dependence on them and reciprocal loyalty toward them. Having armed and been defended by even the most famed slave rebels of the hemisphere, those from Saint Domingue, Spain knew that it could rely on other slaves, even in the era of revolutions. The men Spain transformed from slaves into soldiers were among her most loyal and steadfast allies despite poor pay, great risk, and lingering racial discrimination. They understood that military service to Spain would not only free them but incorporate them and guarantee them at least some reciprocal loyalty from the Crown and its officials. Although various leaders of independence movements also courted and occasionally freed slaves, many chose instead to fight for Spain. And even as Spain's empire began to crumble, it attempted to honor its responsibility for slave soldiers by ensuring treaty rights for those left behind and evacuating and supporting those who chose to join them in still-loyal Cuba.[91]

Notes

1. José Luis Cortés López, *Los orígenes de la esclavitud negra en España* (Madrid, 1986), 23–44, 121–32; William D. Phillips Jr., *Slavery from Roman Times to the Early Transatlantic Trade* (Minneapolis, 1985), 162; Ruth Pike, *Aristocrats and Traders: Sevillian Society in the Sixteenth Century* (Ithaca, NY, 1972), 170–92. Other enslaved groups in fifteenth-century Spain included Jews, Moors, Turks (actually Egyptians, Syrians, and Lebanese), white Christians (Sardinians, Greeks, Russians, and Spaniards), and Guanches from the Canary Islands. Leslie Rout, *The African Experience in Spanish America, 1502 to the Present Day* (Cambridge, UK, 1976), 17. Even Amerindians sometimes were sold as slaves in Seville, despite royal prohibitions against their enslavement. Alfonso Franco Silva, *Regesto documental sobre la esclavitud Sevillana, 1453–1513* (Sevilla, 1979).

2. The medieval ideal of charity toward "miserable classes" also led Spanish owners to manumit favored slaves, often in their wills. Furthermore, Castillian law and custom permitted slaves to hold and transfer property and, with their *peculium*, or private property, they could purchase their freedom or that of relatives or friends. Thus, the lenient attitude toward manumission created a free black class in Spain, which filled accepted economic, social, and low-level political roles. Lyle N. McAlister, *Spain and Portugal in*

the New World, 1492–1700 (Minneapolis, 1984), 24–26; Cortés López, Los orígines de la esclavitud, 133–50.

3. J. H. Elliott, Imperial Spain, 1469–1716 (New York, 1977), 132; Antonio Domínguez Ortiz, The Golden Age of Spain, 1516–1659 (New York, 1971), 35–43; Ross Hassig, Mexico and the Spanish Conquest (New York, 1994), 9.

4. Domínguez Ortiz, Golden Age of Spain, 162–72. Notarial records from Seville (1501–25) counted 5,271 slaves, almost 4,000 of whom were listed as blacks or mulattoes. Phillips, Slavery from Roman Times, 161; Ruth Pike, "Sevillian Society in the Sixteenth Century: Slaves and Freedmen," Hispanic American Historical Review 53 (August 1967): 344–59; Pike, Aristocrats and Traders, 171–92; Antonio Domínguez Ortiz, "La esclavitud en Castilla durante la Edad Moderna," Estudios de historia social de España 2 (1952): 377–78.

5. Jane Landers, Black Society in Spanish Florida (Urbana, 1999), chap. 1; Matthew Restall, "Black Conquistadors: Armed Africans in Early Spanish America" Americas 57:2 (2000), 171–205; Rout, African Experience in Spanish America, 75–77.

6. One illustrative case is that of the West African Juan Garrido, who sailed from Seville to Hispaniola in 1496. There he and other free blacks joined the wars of "pacification" against the native populations, who were in revolt. Ricardo E. Alegría, Juan Garrido, el Conquistador Negro en Las Antillas, Florida, México y California, c. 1503–1540 (San Juan de Puerto Rico, 1990), 17, 20, 30. On the wars in Hispaniola see Samuel M. Wilson, Hispaniola: Caribbean Chiefdoms in the Age of Columbus (Tuscaloosa, AL, 1990), 74–109.

7. The Spaniards conquered Puerto Rico in 1508, Jamaica in 1509, Cuba in 1511, and Florida in 1513. Alegría, Juan Garrido, 17, 20, 30. Several Aztec codices depict Juan Garrido at Cortes' side, and the African joined his patron on one final, and unsuccessful, expedition in search of black Amazons in what came to be California. Peter Gerhard, "A Black Conquistador in Mexico," Hispanic American Historical Review 58 (1978): 451–59; Alegría, Juan Garrido, 114, 116, 119, 127–38.

8. Small numbers of black slaves fought alongside Rodrigo de Contreras in Costa Rica in 1540, and other black slaves also fought in Juan Estrada Rávago's expedition through Costa Rica in 1560. Juan Carlos Solórzano, "Campañas de exploración y conquista de Costa Rica," Serie Avances de Investigación no. 54, Centro de Investigaciones Históricas de América Central, as cited in Rina Cáceres, Negros, mulatos, esclavos y libertos en la Costa Rica del siglo XVII (Mexico City, 2000), 15.

9. Frederick P. Bowser, The African Slave in Colonial Peru, 1524–1650 (Stanford, 1974); James Lockhart, Spanish Peru, 1532–1560: A Social History (Madison, 1994), 193–94. The mestizo chronicler Guaman Poma de Ayalla commonly associates Spaniards, mestizos, and mulattoes in artistic depictions of cruelty toward the indigenous population of Peru.

10. Lockhart, Spanish Peru, 194–95. Lockhart's revision of his 1968 work still underestimates African military skills, alleging that since this was the last major civil war in Peru, "blacks never again had a chance to learn the refinements of the military art as practiced by Europeans." For a first-hand account of the rebellion see Pero Lopez, Rutas de Cartagena de Indias a Buenos Aires y sublevaciones de Pizarro, Castilla, y Hernández Girón, 1540–1570, trans. Juan Friede (Madrid, 1970), 112–20.

11. Rout, *African Experience,* 76–77; Rolando Mellafe, *La introducción de la esclavitud negra en Chile, tráfico y rutas,* 2nd ed. (Santiago, 1984), 45–49.

12. Richard W. Slatta, "Spanish Colonial Military Strategy and Ideology," in *Contested Ground: Comparative Frontiers on the Northern and Southern Edges of the Spanish Empire,* ed. Donna J. Guy and Thomas E. Sheridan (Tucson, 1998), 83–96.

13. Richard W. Slatta, "Spanish Colonial Military Strategy and Ideology," in *Contested Ground,* ed. Guy and Sheridan, 83–96.

14. Isabel Macias, *Cuba en la primera mitad del siglo XVII* (Seville, 1978), 302, 308.

15. Irene Wright, *The Early History of Cuba, 1492–1586* (New York, 1916), 315; Paul E. Hoffman, *The Spanish Crown and the Defense of the Caribbean, 1535–1585: Precedent, Patrimonialism and Royal Parsimony* (Baton Rouge, 1980), 39–51; Pedro Deschamps Chapeaux, *Los Batallones de pardos y morenos libres* (Havana, 1976), 18. For example, Captain Gutierre de Miranda's Spanish-born mulatto slave, Sebastián de Miranda, accompanied him to Santa Elena, in present-day South Carolina, where he served first as a drummer and later as a member of the crew of the patrol boat *San Juan.* Data de Sueldos, June 21, 1580, Contaduría 232, Archivo General de Indias, Seville, Spain (hereafter cited as AGI).

16. After France and Spain went to war in 1552, Spanish officials complained that Caribbean waters were "as full of French as New Rochelle." Kenneth Andrews, *The Spanish Caribbean: Trade and Plunder, 1530–1630* (New Haven, 1978), 82; Información hecha por Diego de Mazariegos sobre la toma de La Habana por Jacques de Sores, 1555, Patronato 267, AGI, cited in *Documentos para la historia colonial de Cuba: Siglos XVI, XVII, XVIII, XIX,* ed. César García del Pino and Alicia Melis Cappa (Havana, 1988), 4–40.

17. Memorial of Pedro Menéndez de Avilés, undated [1561–62], in E. Ruidíaz y Caravia, *La Florida* (Madrid, 1893), 2:322, cited in Woodbury Lowery, *The Spanish Settlements Within the Present Limits of the United States: Florida, 1562–1574* (New York, 1959), 14–15, 96. This document also appears in the collection of the St. Augustine Foundation and is identified as being from the Archivo del Instituto de Valencia de Don Juan Madrid, Envio 25-H, no. 162, Council of the Indies, n.d. (probably November 1569). Menéndez's demographic estimates appear to be reasonably accurate, for in 1542, after a tour of the island, Hispaniola's archdeacon, Alonso de Castro, estimated the black population at twenty-five thousand to thirty thousand and the white population at only twelve hundred. Castro also estimated that more than three thousand maroons lived on the island. Alonso de Castro to the Council of the Indies, March 26, 1542, cited in José Luis Saez, *La iglesia y el negro esclavo en Santo Domingo: Una historia de tres siglos* (Santo Domingo, 1994), 273–74. By the time of Menéndez's report, Spaniards had battled slaves in Hispaniola (1521), Santa Marta, Colombia (1530), Cuba (1533), Mexico City (1537, 1546), Hispaniola (1545–48), Honduras (1548), and Barquisimeto, Venezuela (1555). Rout, *African Experience in Spanish America,* 99–125.

18. Hoffman, *Spanish Crown,* 41; Kris E. Lane, *Pillaging the Empire: Piracy in the Americas, 1500–1750* (Armonk, NY, 1998), chap. 1.

19. Hoffman, *Spanish Crown,* appendix II.

20. Patronato 255, AGI, Jeanette Thurber Connor Collection, P. K. Yonge Library of Florida History, University of Florida, Gainesville (hereafter cited as PKY).

21. Relación de los esclavos forzados que quedaron de la galera San Agustín de la Havana, *Documentos para la historia colonial de Cuba*, ed. García del Pino and Cappa, 63–67. On categories and ethnicities of galley slaves see Ruth Pike, *Penal Servitude in Early Modern Spain* (Madison, 1983), 3–26. Spaniards wishing to take slaves to the Americas were required to obtain licenses for their passage, and these records also document sixteenth-century slaves of diverse ethnic and racial origins. See Peter Boyd-Bowman, *Patterns of Spanish Emigration to the New World (1493–1580)* (Buffalo, 1973).

22. Juan de Eguiluz a su Magestad, La Habana, October 24, 1604, Santo Domingo (hereafter cited as SD) 129, AGI, and Cristóbal Roda a su Magestad, La Habana, July 1, 1605, SD 129, AGI, cited in Macias, *Cuba en la primera mitad del siglo XVII*, 282–83.

23. Jane Landers, "An American Crusade: Seventeenth-Century Spanish Expeditions Against the Maroons," paper delivered at the Forum on European Expansion and Global Interaction, Huntington Library, San Marino, CA, 1998; "Relación de la misión á que fué enviado el P. Juan Laurencio, acompañando a una escuadra de soldados que salía á la reducción de negros foragidos y salteadores,"in Andrés Pérez de Ribas, *Corónica y historia religiosa de la Provincia de la Compañía de Jesus de Mexico en Nueva España*, 2 vols. (Mexico City, 1896), 282–94. Lolita Gutiérrez Brockington found that 60 to 80 percent of the permanent ranch hands on Hernando Cortés's cattle ranches were black and mulatto slaves. *The Leverage of Labor: Managing the Cortés Haciendas in Tehuantepec, 1588–1688* (Durham, NC, 1989), 126–58, 171–72.

24. Jane Landers, "Cimarrón Ethnicity and Cultural Adaptation in the Spanish Domains of the Circum-Caribbean, 1503–1763," in *Identity in the Shadow of Slavery*, ed. Paul E. Lovejoy (London, 2000), 30–54.

25. Macias, *Cuba en la primera mitad del siglo XVII*, 299–300; Lane, *Pillaging the Empire*, 18–30.

26. Herbert S. Klein, "The Colored Militia of Cuba: 1568–1868," *Caribbean Studies* 6 (July 1966): 17–27.

27. Black soldiers defended Jamaica against English and Portuguese pirates. Carey Robinson, *The Fighting Maroons of Jamaica* (Kingston, Jamaica, 1971), 14.

28. Lance Grahn, *The Political Economy of Smuggling: Regional Informal Economies in Early Bourbon New Granada* (Boulder, 1997), 17–19.

29. Violet Barbour, "Privateers and Pirates of the West Indies," *American Historical Review* 16 (April 1911): 538–39.

30. Slaves and free blacks defended Cuba, Santo Domingo, Jamaica, and the coast of Mexico against foreign attacks in these years. Lane, *Pillaging the Empire*, 103–5; Royal order to the Viceroy of New Spain, July 6, 1663, México, 1070, AGI, cited in *Colección de documentos para la historia de la formación social de hispanoamérica 1493–1810*, ed. Richard Konetzke, 3 vols. (Madrid, 1953–1962), 3:510–11.

31. Stephen Weber, "Las compañías de milicia y la defensa del istmo centroamericano en el siglo XVII: El alistamiento general de 1673," *Mesoamérica* 14 (December 1987): 511–28; Santiago Gerardo Suarez, *Las milicias: Instituciones militares hispanoamericanas* (Caracas, 1984), 90–95.

32. Klein, "Colored Militia of Cuba," 17–27; Allan J. Kuethe, "The Status of the Free Pardo in the Disciplined Militia of New Granada," *Journal of Negro History* 56 (April 1971): 105–15.

33. Macias, *Cuba en la primera mitad del siglo XVII,* 375–76; Documentos relacionado con el ofrecimiento del Capitán Diego Martín, Diego El Mulato, de pasar al servicio de España, in *Documentos para la historia colonial de Cuba,* ed. García del Pino and Cappa, 139–40. Diego was also known as Diego de los Reyes and "Diego Lucifer." David F. Marley, *Pirates and Privateers of the Americas* (Santa Barbara, CA, 1994), 170.

34. Petition of Captain Juan Moreno, Santiago del Prado, July 13, 1677, SD 1631, AGI, and Captain Juan Moreno to Judge Don Juan Antonio Ortiz de Matienzo, Santiago del Prado, November 7, 1677, ibid., cited in María Elena Díaz, *The Virgin, the King, and the Royal Slaves of El Cobre* (Stanford, 2000), 70, 89–92. Díaz traces the title *capitán* for royal slaves at the copper mines near Santiago, Cuba, to the 1620s but resists asserting that it is an actual military title.

35. Like their counterparts in New Spain, New Granada, and other circum-Caribbean locales, the escaped slaves created a legitimate Spanish town and a militia to defend it. Landers, *Black Society in Spanish Florida,* chap. 2.

36. Joseph P. Sánchez, "African Freedmen and the Fuero Militar: A Historical Overview of Pardo and Moreno Militiamen in the Late Spanish Empire," *Colonial Latin American Historical Review* 3 (1994): 165–84; Lyle N. McAlister, *El fuero militar en la Nueva España. 1764–1800* (Mexico City, 1982); Allan J. Kuethe, *Military Reform and Society in New Granada, 1773–1808* (Gainesville, FL, 1978), 8–27, 38–39; Christon I. Archer, *The Army in Bourbon Mexico, 1760–1810* (Albuquerque, 1977), 4, 224–31; Christon I. Archer, "Pardos, Indians and the Army of New Spain: Inter-Relationships and Conflicts, 1780–1810," *Journal of Latin American Studies* 6, 2 (1974): 231–55; Leon Campbell, "The Changing Racial and Administrative Structure of the Peruvian Military Under the Later Bourbons," *Americas* 32 (1975): 117–33; Margarita Gascón, "The Military of Santo Domingo, 1720–1764," *Hispanic American Historical Review* 73 (1993): 431–52; Peter M. Voelz, *Slave and Soldier: The Military Impact of Blacks in the Colonial Americas* (New York, 1993), chaps. 1, 2; Ben Vinson, *Bearing Arms for His Majesty* (Stanford, 2002), 25.

37. Klein, " Colored Militia of Cuba"; Pedro Deschamps Chapeaux, *Los Batallones de Pardos y Morenos Libres* (Havana, 1976); Landers, *Black Society,* chaps. 9, 10.

38. Cartagena had one company of quadroons, four mulatto companies, and two black companies. "Reglamento para la guarnición de la Plaza de Cartagena de Indias, 1736," in Konetzke, *Colección de documentos,* 3:220–22.

39. Leon G. Campbell, "Black Power in Colonial Peru: The 1779 Tax Rebellion of Lambayeque," *Phylon* 33 (Summer 1972): 140–52.

40. Klein, "Colored Militia of Cuba, 17–27.

41. Deschamps, *Battalones de Pardos,* 65.

42. *An Authentic Journal of the Siege of the Havana by an Officer* (London, 1762, reprint, 1898), 21, 30; Patrick Mackeller, *A Correct Journal of the Landing of His Majesty's Forces on the Island of Cuba; and of the Siege and Surrender of the Havannah, August 13, 1762* (London, 1762; reprint, Boston, 1762), 9.

43. Mackeller, *Correct Journal,* 29–30.

44. Klein, "Colored Militia of Cuba"; Landers, *Black Society,* 198–200; Kimberly S. Hanger, *Bounded Lives, Bounded Places: Free Black Society in Colonial New Orleans, 1769–1803* (Durham, NC, 1887), 109–35; Vinson, *Bearing Arms for His Majesty,* 7–8.

45. Hanger, *Bounded Lives*, 119–21.

46. Runaway notice by Henry Williams, May 5, 1785, Papers on Negro Titles and Runaways, 1784–1803, East Florida Papers (hereafter cited as EFP), microfilm reel 167, PKY.

47. Hector and Sam both identified Reyna as Hector's wife. Statements of Sam and Hector, Census Returns 1784–1814, EFP, microfilm reel 148, PKY.

48. Memorial of William Williams, March 5, 1788, Census Returns, 1784–1814, EFP, microfilm reel 148, PKY. By the time the Williams brothers initiated a suit to recover Hector, Sam, and Reyna in 1788, all three had hired themselves as free laborers to Don Francis Phelipe Fatio, whose Nueva Suiza plantation was near their former workplace. Unable to get satisfaction from the Spanish governor, Major Williams finally submitted a claim to the British government for a "Negro woman slave" valued at forty pounds sterling, and his brother William submitted a claim for Sam, a carpenter, valued at fifty pounds. Wilbur Henry Siebert, *Loyalists in East Florida, 1774 to 1785: The Most Important Documents Pertaining Thereto, Edited with an Accompanying Narrative* (Deland, FL, 1929), 2:277, 281.

49. Disputes with Georgians about contested slave property involved diplomatic negotiations of the highest order. More than 250 former slaves were freed by the Spanish before pressure from United States Secretary of State Thomas Jefferson forced Spain to abrogate the sanctuary provision in 1790. The freed slaves appear in the Census of 1784, EFP, microfilm reel 76, PKY.

50. Florida, Louisiana, and even Mexico received the dregs of the Spanish army, and assignment to Florida was often a punishment for earlier misbehavior. By all accounts even severe discipline failed to produce any significant improvement in the character of the Florida troops. Letters of Vicente Manuel de Zéspedes, included in Miró to Caballo, May 12, 1790, and cited in Derek Noel Kerr, "Petty Felony, Slave Defiance, and Frontier Villainy: Crime and Criminal Justice in Spanish Louisiana, 1770–1803," Ph.D. diss., Tulane University, 1983, p. 194.

51. Accounts of the Royal Treasury, 1784–1796, Account of 1794, SD 2635, AGI.

52. Juan Nepomuceno de Quesada to Luis de Las Casas, April 21, 1794, Cuba 1439, AGI. Recognizing the weakness of Quesada's defenses, Havana finally ordered reinforcements from the Infantry Regiment of Mexico to assist St. Augustine. The group of approximately two hundred men was commanded by Colonel Sebastián Kindelán, who later became governor of East Florida and an advocate of its black militia. Additional troops from Catalonia also added force.

53. C. L. R. James, *Black Jacobins: Toussaint L'Ouverture and the San Domingo Revolution* (New York, 1963), 103–6.

54. Jean-François and Toussaint both recognized that they were betraying their compatriots, and James called them traitors and their efforts "Judas work." James, *Black Jacobins*, 104–6.

55. Ibid.

56. Robin Blackburn, "*The Black Jacobins* and New World Slavery," in *C.L.R. James: His Intellectual Legacies*, ed. Selwyn R. Cudjoe and William E. Cain (Amherst, MA, 1995), 81–97, 86; James, *Black Jacobins*. Geggus, Blackburn, and others have contrasted

the "counterrevolutionary stance" of Jean-François and Jorge Biassou with the more truly revolutionary ideologies of Toussaint.

57. The institutional precedents that permitted Spain to treat with and enlist former slaves into military service and to incorporate them into a Spanish polity were by this time centuries old, and it may be presumed the men would have had some knowledge of them. Although all three leaders agreed to the Spanish alliance, in fact, they never intended to return to slavery under any regime and were determined to cut the best deal possible for themselves, their kin, and their troops. Captain General Joaquín García to the Duque de Alcudia, December 12, 1795, cited in Emilio Rodríguez Demorizi, *Cesión de Santo Domingo a Francia* (Trujillo Ciudad, D.R., 1958), 46–48.

58. Twelve other subchiefs received medals of silver and documents attesting to their meritorious service. Captain General Joaquín García to the Duque de la Alcudia, February 18, 1794, Estado (hereafter cited as ES) 14, doc. 86, AGI.

59. James, *Black Jacobins,* 124, 155.

60. Father Josef Vásquez to the Vicar of Santiago, December 12, 1793, ES 11, doc. 98, AGI.

61. Thomas O. Ott asserts that Toussaint's defection from the Spaniards was in part motivated by his own ambition and that he felt his advancement within the Spanish camp was blocked by Biassou and Jean-François. He describes Toussaint's "power struggle" with Biassou and Toussaint's military victories over his former superior. Ott, *The Haitian Revolution, 1789–1804* (Knoxville, TN, 1973), 83–84. Carolyn Fick agrees; see Carolyn F. Fick, *The Making of Haiti: The Saint Domingue Revolution from Below* (Knoxville, 1990), 184.

62. Spanish authorities and most historians place the blame for the Bayajá massacre on Jean-François, but he accused Biassou and his men of the atrocities. Jean-François claimed that "although General Viasou [sic] made war under the same banners as we, my conduct, the direction of my troops, their discipline, and their military operations have always been better." He argued that if "disorders" occurred after Biassou's troops arrived on the scene and he should be found culpable, Biassou should be punished as required by the law (Jean-François to Luis de Las Casas, January 12, 1796, ES 5-A, doc. 28, AGI).

63. James, *Black Jacobins,* 151. David Geggus and Julius S. Scott have examined the lightning speed with which information was circulated about the revolution and the powerful ability of rumors to trigger actions. David Patrick Geggus, *Slavery, War and Revolution: The British Occupation of Saint Domingue, 1793–1793* (Oxford, 1982); Julius S. Scott III, "The Common Wind: Currents of Afro-American Communication in the Era of the Haitian Revolution," Ph.D. diss., Duke University, 1986.

64. James, *Black Jacobins,* 123–51; Memorial of Jean-François, January 14, 1796, ES 5-A, doc. 28, AGI; The Marqués of Casa Calvo to Luis de Las Casas, December 31, 1795, ES 5-A, doc. 23, AGI.

65. Marqués de Casa Calvo to Luis de Las Casas, December 31, 1795, ES 5-A, doc. 23, AGI; Jane G. Landers, "An Eighteenth-Century Community in Exile: The Floridanos of Cuba," *New West Indian Guide* 70, nos. 1 and 2 (Spring 1996): 39–58.

66. Marqués de Casa Calvo to Luis de Las Casas, December 31, 1795, ES 5-A, doc. 23, AGI.

67. Santo Domingo's governor was already under heavy pressure from angry Spanish citizens who were also being forced to evacuate and were urging Spanish troops to mutiny and renounce the treaty. In such a volatile situation he did not even allow the black troops time to dispose of their property or settle family affairs before leaving. Joaquín García to the Duque de la Alcudia, February 18, 1794, ES 14, doc. 86, AGI; Joaquín García to Luis de Las Casas, January 25, 1796, ES 5-A, doc. 36, AGI.

68. Petition of Jorge Biassou, September 14, 1796, Cuba 1439, AGI. According to one account, during his mother's rescue from the Hospital of the Holy Fathers in Le Cap, Biassou murdered all the patients in their beds. Robert Debs Heinl Jr. and Nancy Gordon Heinl, *Written in Blood: The Story of the Haitian People, 1492–1971* (Boston, 1978), 54.

69. Complaint of Jorge Biassou, May 31, 1794, ES 13, doc. 11, AGI.

70. Jean-François led the largest group, which consisted of 70 military officials, 282 soldiers, 334 women, and 94 children. Report by Luis de las Casas, January 13, 1796, ES 5-A, doc. 28, AGI. Brigadier Narciso Gil was consulted by members of the Aponte conspiracy in Havana in 1812 and later played a role in the 1812 rebellion in Santo Domingo. Geggus, "Slavery, War, and Revolution," 15. Jorge Biassou had already departed for Havana with his wife and twenty-three dependents. Luis de Las Casas to Duque de Alcudia, January, 8, 1796, ES 5-A, doc. 24, AGI.

71. Rodríguez Demorizi, *Cesión de Santo Domingo,* 75; Luis de Las Casas to Joaquín García, January 10, 1796, ES 5-A, doc. 40, AGI.

72. Petition of Jean-François, January 12, 1796, ES 5-A, doc. 28, AGI.

73. Luis de Las Casas to Jean-François, January 15, 1796, ES 5-A, doc. 28, AGI.

74. Joaquín García to the Duque de Alcudia, February 2, 1796, ES 5-A, doc. 36, AGI.

75. One account states that Jean-François ended his days as the governor of Oran in 1820: Stéphen Alexis, *Black Liberator: The Life of Toussiant Louverture* (London, 1949), 76.

76. Borrowing García's tactic, Las Casas planned to forward the unwanted blacks to a new locale without any advance notice and hope that the next governor would receive them. Trinidad was in need of homesteaders, and Las Casas hoped its governor might grant them lands in keeping with the policy of *repoblación*. The viceroy of New Spain had allocated 124,451 pesos of Cuba's *situado* for the expenses of the Black Auxiliaries, a considerable sum, given that the Spanish governor of Florida earned 4,000 pesos that year. However, with the viceroy's approval, Cuba's governor kept 100,000 pesos to cover the expenses of the exodus and sent only 6,000 pesos each with the groups headed for Trinidad and Truxillo, "to better assure," he said, "that they would be admitted there." Presumably he planned to do the same for those of Jean-François's dependents who were headed to Campeche and Portobelo. Luis de Las Casas to Joaquín García, February 17, 1796, ES 5-A, doc. 52, AGI.

77. Brigadier General Villate, the mulatto commander of Guarico, also advised that the French would be glad to receive them if they chose to return. Marqués de Casa Calvo to Luis de Las Casas, January 12, 1796, ES 5-A, doc. 28, AGI.

78. Marriage of Jorge Jacobo and Rafaela Witten, April 12, 1796, Black Marriages, Cathedral Parish Records, Diocese of St. Augustine Catholic Center, Jacksonville, FL, microfilm reel 284 L, PKY; Black Baptisms, vol. 2, CPR, microfilm reel 284 J, entries 176, 563, 670, 799, and vol. 3, microfilm reel 284 J, entry 31, PKY.

79. In one example, correspondence to General Biassou was addressed with the honorific "Don." An unknown hand scratched out "Don" and wrote instead "Señor." Orders to General Biassou, 1801, Correspondence between the Governor and Subordinates on the St. Johns and St. Marys Rivers, EFP, microfilm reel 55, PKY.

80. Testamentary Proceedings of Jorge Biassou, July 15, 1801, EFP, microfilm reel 138, PKY. An account of Biassou's dress in the early days of the slave revolt also stressed his flamboyant style. "Biassou wore a richly embroidered orange-coloured costume and sumptuous black silk scarf, spangled with silver." Alexis, *Black Liberator*, 43.

81. Ibid.

82. The governor's cover letter assured Cuba's captain general of his good conduct and "total obedience to the government[;] although at times he has been harassed by some Frenchmen, and even by those of his own color, he has endured it without requiring any other justice than that he asked of him." Enrique White to Conde de Santa Clara, May 24, 1799, Guerra Moderna, 6921, Archivo General de Simancas, Spain.

83. Memorials of Jorge Biassou, November 2, 1799 and December 6, 1799, EFP, Letters from the Captain General, microfilm reel 2, PKY; Marques de Someruelos to Enrique White, March 15, 1800, and May 28, 1801, ibid.

84. Testamentary Proceedings of Jorge Biassou, entry 2, EFP, microfilm reel 138, PKY.

85. Orders to Jorge Jacobo, Juan Bautista Witten, and Benjamin Segui, July 19, 1812, To and From the military Commanders and Other Officers, 1784–1821, EFP, microfilm reel 68, PKY.

86. Lista de Revista y Comisaria, October 7, 1812, Cuba 356, AGI.

87. On the important role of black linguists in the Seminole Wars see George Klos, "Blacks and the Seminole Removal Debate, 1821–1835," in *The African American Heritage of Florida*, ed. David R. Colburn and Jane G. Landers (Gainesville, 1992), 128–56. Even after the Spaniards left Florida, Seminoles and blacks among them maintained trade and contacts with Spanish Cuba.

88. Edward Wanton to Sebastián Kindelán, July 3, 1812, EFP, microfilm reel 61, PKY; Sebastián Kindelán to Juan Ruíz de Apodaca, August 13, 1812, Cuba 1789, AGI. Four years later, on March 8, 1816, Governor José Coppinger also awarded Tony Proctor a military service grant of 185 acres. *Spanish Land Grants in Florida*, 5 vols. (Tallahassee, 1940–41), 4:226–27.

89. The governor assigned each slave to trusted members of the community, including the free black militiaman Sandy Embara (a.k.a. Edimboro), and these men became responsible for their good behavior. Listas de los esclavos barones y en estado de tomar las armas, July 13, 1812, Cuba 357, AGI.

90. Manuel Lopez to Governor Sebastián Kindelán, August 20, 1812, and Kindelán's response, August 30, 1812, Cuba 257, AGI.

91. Landers, *Black Society*, chaps. 3, 10.

Arming Slaves in Brazil from the Seventeenth Century to the Nineteenth Century

HENDRIK KRAAY

In the first paragraphs of his treatise on slavery, published in 1866–1867, the great Brazilian jurist Antônio Marques Perdigão Malheiro outlined the ideal legal status of slaves: They were "things, subject to the *power* and *dominion* or property of another . . . [and] deprived of *all rights*." He concluded that "such is the extent of this incapacity that, among us, slaves are not even permitted to serve as enlisted men [*com praça*] in the army and navy."[1] Not only were slaves excluded from the armed forces, but since the 1500s, a host of laws, decrees, and ordinances issued by all levels of government had barred slaves from using or carrying weapons. None of this legislation should be surprising. As Perdigão Malheiro put it, "the slave is not only reputed a *domestic enemy* but also a *public enemy*, always quick to rebel, to rise up."[2]

To arm slaves or to make provisions for their enlistment in armed forces appears to be the height of folly for slaveowners, yet Brazilian history is replete with examples of both private and public arming of slaves. An examination of the circumstances under which Brazilians armed slaves goes to the heart of the slave-master relationship and casts into sharp relief the role of the state in this slave society. Central to any consideration of armed slaves is the distinction between private arming on the part of masters and public arming carried out by authorities or the state. Masters routinely armed individual slaves (or groups of them) for protection or even in order to perpetrate crimes, but this was little more than an extension of the service that slaves already owed masters. Such slaves might also be led by their masters into serving the state in military or quasi-military capacities, without implying a change in the slaves' status. When it came to private arming, the colonial and imperial states' principal concerns were to control the diffusion of weapons among slaves, particularly those beyond masters' direct supervision, and to restrict the armed might of masters.

The direct involvement of the state in arming slaves changed matters, and the enlistment of slaves as soldiers implied that they should gain freedom. As Perdigão Malheiro makes clear, "slave" and "soldier" were fundamentally different categories. Moreover, he noted the old Roman law principle that slaves who had performed notable service for the state ought to be rewarded with freedom; monarchs and authorities in Brazil tended to adhere to this maxim.[3] But any effort to turn slaves into soldiers (free men) or to free slaves who had distinguished themselves in service to the state constituted an intrusion of state power into the domestic sphere of slave-master relations.[4] Manumission, as Perdigão Malheiro explains, "requires a voluntary act of masters," and Manuela Carneiro da Cunha has pointed out that the Brazilian state only rarely and very hesitantly intervened in this private sphere.[5] All of the cases of freeing slaves who had served as soldiers (or were to do so) raised complex questions of property rights, compensation, and masters' prerogatives; ultimately, the state could not grant freedom in return for military service. Rather, manumission came from owners who either freed slaves willingly or did so under moral pressure or in response to fiscal incentives. Three republican rebellions against the Brazilian state in the first half of the nineteenth century enlisted slaves much more indiscriminately, thereby posing a grave threat to the slave order (which at least some of their leaders contemplated ending) and demonstrating what was unacceptable to most Brazilian slaveowners.

For most of the history of slavery in Brazil from the 1500s to abolition in 1888, the Portuguese colonies (after 1822, the independent empire) constituted the largest slave society in the Americas, receiving about four million Africans until the close of the trade in the 1850s.[6] Brazil's slaves were concentrated on plantations, particularly those that produced sugar along the fertile coast of the Northeast. In the nineteenth century, coffee emerged as a major slave-plantation commodity in Rio de Janeiro and São Paulo. But slavery was not restricted to plantations. In the early eighteenth century, the gold- and diamond-mining boom in Minas Gerais prompted a significant shift of the slave population to this area. By the nineteenth century, coastal cities such as

Rio de Janeiro, Salvador, and Recife boasted large concentrations of slaves as well. In fact, slaves could be found throughout Brazil, and slave ownership was widely diffused among the free (and the freed) populations.[7]

At the same time that it constituted a massive slave society, Brazil boasted a growing free and freed nonwhite population; by about 1800, the number of free and freed Afro-Brazilians equalled the number of those enslaved; the 1872 census counted 5.75 million blacks and mulattoes, of whom only 1.5 million were enslaved.[8] These demographic features meant that, in Brazil, "slave" and "black" were not roughly coterminous categories as they were in the United States. Although some colonial legislation conflated free blacks and slaves in regulating access to weapons, the arming of slaves and the arming of black men were largely distinct issues, something not always perceived by historians.[9] By the eighteenth century, the Brazilian military formed a complex of racially segregated institutions. Free coloreds served in black and mulatto militia units, and the regular army consisted, in principle, of white men. Between 1817 and 1837 this racial segregation was abolished as the state sought to tap fully the free nonwhite population for military service. Ironically, however, this shift turned the military into a magnet for fugitive slaves, who were now indistinguishable from soldiers.

This chapter begins by surveying masters' arming of their slaves before exploring public arming by the state. Despite legislation that aimed to keep arms out of the slaves' hands, the private arming of slaves was fairly extensive, particularly on the disorderly mining frontier of eighteenth-century Minas Gerais. Elsewhere, it was rarer, though not unknown, and throughout Brazil, concern about private arming merged into worries about the very different practice of self-arming by slaves, usually the prelude to crimes or rebellions. The regulation of private and self-arming by slaves was, however, no easy task for authorities, for the policing of slaves encroached on masters' private power. Public arming by the state or in its name enters the discussion in the second section, which examines the arming of slaves in order to regain Portuguese control over northeastern Brazil from the Dutch in the mid-seventeenth century and the extensive proposals to employ slave manpower for colonial defense during the wars with Spain in the 1760s and 1770s. The latter were never implemented, but the Portuguese government eventually threw its weight behind the promises of freedom made to slaves in 1645 at the height of the Dutch wars.

The first decades of the nineteenth century saw an intensification of public arming and, with the abolition of racial discrimination in recruitment, significant changes in the meaning of military service. Moreover, of course, abolition became a possibility, if only a remote one; some came to see the enlistment of slaves as a step toward the ending of slavery. The third section examines the republican rebellions that recruited slaves on a significant scale but ultimately failed to respect masters' rights. The fourth section examines the Brazilian state's policy toward arming slaves after independence, a policy considerably more cautious than that of the republican rebellions. Indeed, the imperial government never set out to arm slaves during this period, but on a number of occasions it was forced to ratify slave enlistments by arranging for the freeing of the slaves in question by the payment of compensation to owners. Finally, this chapter analyzes "slave recruitment" during the Paraguayan War (1865–1870). Here the Brazilian state proceeded with deliberate caution, carefully respecting masters' property rights and insisting that all of the men who served be freed prior to enlistment. During this period, the imperial government carefully regulated slave recruitment and largely preempted the problems that it had resolved with ex post facto manumissions earlier in the century.

Weapons Legislation, Private Arming, and Self-Arming

Concern about restricting slaves' access to weapons pervaded Portuguese and Brazilian legislation from the sixteenth century onward, but no law proved satisfactory or effective. The tools of daily work were often potential offensive weapons, and masters frequently found it necessary to arm slaves for their own protection. The result was a continual struggle to reconcile competing interests as the "state" sought to restrict weaponry and to gain a monopoly of legitimate force while masters sought to preserve their private power, their control over their slaves, and their right to employ slaves as they saw fit. These questions gained particular salience in nineteenth-century cities, where substantial police apparati were established to control the lower classes, slaves included.[10]

Monarchs, colonial governors, and municipal councils repeatedly sought to keep weapons out of slaves' hands. In 1521, for example, the king of Portugal decreed that "any Moor or captive black, upon whom might be found a sword, dagger, or lance, not accompanying his master" would be fined; if the master refused to pay, the slave would be flogged. Not all of this voluminous weapons legislation was addressed solely to slaves. Eighteenth-century sumptuary laws prohibited numerous classes of men from wearing swords, including hunchbacks, sailors, and blacks (*negros*), and there were frequent bans on the carrying of concealable weapons—pistols, short swords, and pointed daggers—that applied to all people. The latter constituted the "prohibited weapons," so well-known that they were sometimes not even specified, as in a 1756 law that modified the punishment for slaves bearing "knives and other prohibited weapons." Legislation specifically addressed to slaves (and often also to free blacks) sought to prevent them from carrying sticks and clubs. The 1830 criminal code banned the possession of offensive weapons by all but left the definition of such arms, as well as any exemptions to the ban, to municipal councils. In 1880 the town of Pirassununga, São Paulo, prohibited "blunderbusses, revolvers, pistols, shotguns, and any [other] firearms; razors, pointed knives, daggers," all types of swords, "and any [other] cutting instrument" but permitted hunters to carry shotguns and artisans to keep the tools necessary to their trades. Slaves were not specifically mentioned in these articles, which applied to all.[11]

Authorities constantly tinkered with the mix of punishments for slaves caught with such weapons. A 1738 municipal ordinance from São Paulo that banned slaves from carrying clubs under their capes prescribed a twenty-day prison term to be followed by a flogging. The arresting officer would receive the cape as a reward, but the master paid a fine. A few years earlier, the governor of Minas Gerais ordered two hundred lashes and two months in jail for slave offenders. Mid-eighteenth-century innovations — notably the sentencing of slave violators to ten-year terms of galley service — were quickly dropped in favor of increasing the number of lashes (up to five hundred over the course of ten days, according to a 1756 law). In 1816 a police edict in Rio de Janeiro mandated three hundred lashes and three months of labor on public works for slaves found in possession of weapons, but this was reduced to summary floggings in 1825. Nineteenth-century municipal ordinances typically mandated fines for free offenders and floggings for slaves; thus, in 1833, the city of Salvador banned the sale of pointed knives and daggers, prescribing a 30 milréis ($22.80) fine and eight days in prison for the free but 150 lashes for slave offenders.[12]

The repetition of this legislation indicates, of course, that it was unenforceable. Too many slaves used knives and machetes in their daily labors, and too many worked beyond the direct control of an overseer. Moreover, the free (and slaves) often went about armed, at least with a knife. In the second decade of the nineteenth century, the traveler Henry Koster observed that, in Pernambuco, "a pointed knife or dirk . . . though prohibited by law, is worn by all ranks of persons," which, if we can accept iconographic evidence, included slaves: four of Johann Moritz Rugendas's well-known engravings from the 1820s show slaves openly wearing daggers, notwithstanding the police's standing orders to search and disarm slaves.[13] In Rio de Janeiro, simple weapons possession accounted for a significant proportion of slave arrests between 1810 and 1821 (5.8 percent), and when slaves arrested for other offenses but found to have weapons of some sort are added, the proportion rises to 22.4

percent of 3,682 arrests. Of course, such data are not true indications of the incidence of the practice, but police in the capital considered it a major problem until at least the mid-nineteenth century, when the proportion of slaves in the city's population began to decline. Knives, razors, and other cutting tools were, by far, the most common weapons confiscated.[14] Many of the other instruments that slaves used in the course of their daily work could be dangerous weapons: Hoes and axes could easily be turned on masters or overseers. Not surprisingly, an 1847 coffee plantation manual recommended keeping sickles both sharp and under lock and key when not in use.[15]

Moreover, excessively restrictive legislation and zealous enforcement would unduly burden masters and encroach on their private power over slaves. Imprisoning slaves deprived masters of necessary labor and introduced what was, for owners, an unwelcome state authority into their relations with their slaves. It reportedly encouraged masters to turn a blind eye to their slaves' offenses. The governor of Minas Gerais complained in 1719 that owners "cover[ed] up their [slaves'] crimes and outrages, even when they are themselves victims, so as not to lose their property."[16] Thus, it was more acceptable to commute prison terms to floggings, after which the slave could immediately return to work. Even this practice, however, could upset masters. When the governor of Rio de Janeiro sought to impose summary floggings on slaves caught with weapons in 1730, he faced vigorous opposition from owners.[17] Blanket bans on slaves' possession of actual or potential weapons encroached on masters' rights to use their slaves in whatever occupations they saw fit. Thus, much of the legislation directed at slaves with weapons exempted, as did the 1521 law, those armed with their owners' permission or accompanied by their masters. Lawmakers' principal concern was to restrict slaves' independent access to weapons; secondarily, they sought to limit the number of armed slave retainers under masters' control.[18]

As much of this legislation suggests, Brazilian masters routinely armed their slaves, especially on the lawless frontiers. The best evidence comes from eighteenth-century Minas Gerais, then a rapidly developing gold-mining region, where authorities' correspondence is replete with complaints about the practice. Given the rugged topography, dispersed nature of placer mining, and lack of effective government authority, masters such as Sebastião Pereira de Aguilar armed slaves for their own protection. In 1716 he owned a brace of pistols for himself and twenty firearms for the forty-nine slaves who mined for him. Governors struggled to restrict the number of such bodyguards that each owner could maintain, seeking both to prevent the diffusion of weapons among slaves and to control the power of the mining lords, but they also relied on the slaves of loyal masters who helped suppress the tax rebellions of 1715 and 1720. In these episodes and in the violent squabbles between established miners and newcomers to Minas Gerais (the War of the Emboabas, 1708–1710), much of the fighting on both sides was done by armed slaves.[19]

Eighteenth-century Minas Gerais appears to have been somewhat peculiar in this respect, and the deliberate arming of slaves elsewhere generally took place on a smaller scale. A remarkable illustration from 1651 shows a Dutch-controlled sugar plantation in Pernambuco being defended from Portuguese attack by its slaves (regarding the Dutch Wars, see the following section). Armed with spears and clubs, the slaves fight on their own — the artist shows no white men leading them — while their companions keep on working at the mill.[20] In the 1830s, in the remote interior, men took justice into their own hands, according to Rugendas, who claimed that slaves "readily took on the task of defending their [masters'] interests." In 1868 the commander of a press gang reported that he could impress only two "excellent recruits" on a Bahian sugar plantation before being driven off by a dozen armed men, including a mounted slave, armed with a long-handled sickle, who dextrously knocked off the recruiter's képi. Land disputes were routinely the occasion for masters to arm their slaves and to lead them in the destruction of rivals' crops and buildings; slaves of two rival sugar planters in Pernambuco, noted Koster, were "constantly at war" with each other in the first decade of the century.[21] Historians of slave crime have discovered cases in which masters incited slaves to commit offenses, including murder.[22] A few slave occupations required that their practitioners be armed with guns. According to Jean-Baptiste Debret, armed slave retainers were indispensable to travelers in the early nineteenth century, for they doubled as hunters and bodyguards. Trained for these tasks since their adolescence, these expert woodsmen were also essential to the naturalists who depended on them to stock their collections.[23] In all of these cases, slaves were led by masters or carried out their owners' will.

Although authorities constantly worried that such private arming contributed to the uncontrolled diffusion of weapons among slaves, it is difficult to determine how readily slaves obtained offensive weapons beyond tools, improvised arms such as clubs, or simple knives. Certainly a few could acquire firearms in order to commit crimes. In 1794, Manoel da Paixão, a slave tailor, was arrested while carrying a musket and a pistol with which he intended to kill the overseer of a Rio de Janeiro plantation who had beaten a female slave, presumably Manoel's lover. He was summarily sentenced to receive five hundred lashes over the course of ten days, and the weapons were confiscated. Eighty years later, in Campinas, a coffee planter's son attempted to stop one Anastácio from stealing a sack of coffee, only to be shot dead by the slave, prompting complaints that petty shopkeepers in the region not only readily bought stolen coffee but also willingly sold firearms to slaves. In 1836 the province of Rio de Janeiro had felt it necessary to require dealers in gunpowder and weapons to sign an undertaking that they would not sell them to slaves or to otherwise suspect individuals.[24] Complaints from Bahia in the 1820s suggest a wide diffusion of weapons among slaves. In 1822 the patriot government, then leading a bitter siege of Portuguese troops holed up in Salvador, felt obliged to remind sugar planters not to permit "their slaves to have in the huts where they live muskets, lances, iron spears, scythes, cutlasses, swords and knives." A few years later, the Baron of Maragogipe, a large planter and militia commander, complained that many of his neighbors "let their slaves wander on the roads and public paths armed with all sorts of offensive weapons, which the law prohibits even to free men." Maragogipe's remarks and the patriot government's advisory, with their implication that masters condoned the possession of significant weaponry by slaves, are remarkable in light of the slave rebellions that had rocked Bahia after 1807, but they may also reflect the diffusion of weapons into the civilian population as a consequence of the war for independence .[25]

The records of the suppression of slave rebellions, by contrast, provide mixed evidence about the ease with which slaves armed themselves. Runaway slave communities, the well-known *quilombos,* reportedly found it easy to trade for powder, shot, and other weapons in eighteenth-century Bahia and in nineteenth-century Maranhão; in 1838, coffee-plantation slaves plotting a revolt in the interior of Rio de Janeiro managed to acquire "a great quantity of gunpowder in barrels" with the aid of a peddler who made the purchases (notwithstanding the undertaking that he must have signed). More remarkable yet was a report from the Brazilian consul in Hamburg that "four thousand swords destined for slaves [*negros*]" were being loaded on a ship set to sail to Bahia in 1832; the minister of justice took this report seriously enough to warn the provincial government of Alagoas.[26] Nonetheless, rebel slaves were invariably outgunned by the forces of order, and no quilombo, save the exceptionally large and long-lived Palmares (c. 1600–1695), could withstand a determined onslaught (the fugitives usually retreated).[27] The lengths to which some slave rebels went to improvise weaponry suggest that it was actually quite difficult for them to acquire sufficient arms; others made do with what they had at hand. According to a denunciation received in 1814, Hausa slaves in Salvador had produced enough darts and arrowheads out of scrap iron to fill several barrels. The revolt did not materialize, but authorities failed to locate the stores. Although the 150 rebel slaves of 1838 may have had much gunpowder, they lacked sufficient firearms; they courageously faced down the National Guard force pursuing them but were dispersed by a few volleys. In 1835, when several hundred Muslim slaves rebelled in Salvador (the largest urban slave uprising in the Americas), their principal weapons were knives, swords, and clubs, the former likely tools of work and the latter easily made. They had a handful of pistols and an "arsenal" of fifteen firearms that a freed gunsmith failed to deliver on time.[28]

Writing about eighteenth-century Minas Gerais, Kathleen J. Higgins concludes that "armed slaves" were "the rule rather than the exception."[29] Elsewhere in Brazil, when conditions resembled those of Minas Gerais at that time, masters readily armed slaves. But even on the most disorderly frontier, masters were highly selective with regard to whom they armed, giving weapons only to the slaves whom they trusted. In these areas, authorities struggled to restrict the private arming of slaves, fearing that it led to self-arming by slaves. But it proved singularly difficult to define the categories of potential offensive weapons to be prohibited — many were, after all, merely tools — and colonial legislation routinely permitted slaveowners to maintain slave bodyguards even as it sought to control slaves' access to weapons outside of masters' control. As the police records from nineteenth-century Rio de Janeiro show, keeping knives (and other arms) out of slaves' hands was a major preoccupation. To be sure, such armed slaves did not pose a mortal threat to the slave regime, but they were dangerous enough that they had to be kept in check.

The Dutch Wars (1630–1654) and Colonial Defense (1600s–1810)

Portugal's Brazilian colonies faced external threats as well as internal ones. Foreign invaders and colonial defenders understood that slaves might be useful resources in the struggle for power. As early as 1618, a Dutchman concluded that "the principal local defense [forces]" of Rio de Janeiro were the indigenous slaves of the Portuguese, "so obedient that they go into battle for their masters."[30] By contrast, during the 1711 sack and ransoming of Rio de Janeiro by French privateers, observers marveled at the ignominious defeat of the Portuguese, who had failed to make use of their available slaves, estimated at eight thousand. The French, however, were relieved that the city capitulated before the governor of Minas Gerais arrived with three thousand soldiers and six hundred slaves, all with considerable combat experience from the civil war there.[31] The use of slaves in colonial defense raised issues quite different from those posed by private arming, primarily when the state requisitioned slaves or drafted them into the armed forces, and authorities had to consider property rights, the legal status of slave-soldiers, and racial questions.

These issues were first posed by the lengthy struggle against the Dutch West India Company, which captured Recife in 1630 and held it until 1654, facing almost continual armed resistance from local sugar planters. The Portuguese were initially reluctant to use slaves in anything other than support roles, but in 1633 the Portuguese commander, Matias de Albuquerque, accepted the services of a free (or possibly freed) black man, Henrique Dias, who had organized a black guerrilla force that included some runaway slaves. Albuquerque, however, stipulated that Dias henceforth accept only free or freed blacks into his forces, and he personally indemnified the owners of the slaves already serving under Dias.[32] In 1645, sugar planters who had previously accepted Dutch rule rebelled. In the proclamation that launched the War of Divine Liberty, their leaders, João Fernandes Vieira and Antônio Cavalcanti Capibaribe, pledged that "every black [negro], Arda, Mina, Angola, creole, mulatto, métis [*mameluco*], freed or slave, who does his duty in defense of divine liberty will be freed and paid for all that he may do."[33] This is a curious document in that it promises freedom to those who were already freed and makes no mention of compensation to the masters. The degree to which this measure was sanctioned by King João IV is not known, and Vieira only later claimed to have received royal orders to this effect. Moreover, the proclamation appears to be directed at slaves. His actions, however, made it clear that Vieira had no intention of letting his slaves escape his control. At a critical moment in the Battle of Monte de Tabocas (3 August 1645), he offered freedom to fifty of his Mina and Angolan slaves if they would throw themselves into the fray; contemporary accounts concur that this was the battle's turning point. Although Vieira and Capibaribe's proclamation implied that the state would free slaves, this was a private manumission, conditioned on the freedmen's serving for the duration of the war.[34]

The Tabocas freedmen joined other black men under Henrique Dias's command, but the total number of "slaves" enrolled remained small, with Dias's troop rarely numbering more than three hundred men. Slaves were simply too valuable to be removed from sugar plantations and armed on any large scale.[35] Although Vieira had conditionally freed his slaves in 1645, other owners had not. The nephew and heir of one sugar planter claimed that his uncle had merely lent Gonçalo Rebelo and several other slaves to the troops. Thirteen years later, he tried to put Rebelo back to work on the plantation, going so far as to burn the slave-soldier's service record. Unlike Vieira at Tabocas, Rebelo's master had not freed his slaves before sending them into battle. Such treatment of his soldiers prompted Dias to travel in 1657 to Lisbon, where he obtained royal sanction for the proclamations promising freedom in the monarch's name. The queen directed that the slaves in question be freed "with the permission of their owners," hoping that the rich ones would do so voluntarily and that the poor ones would be content with "moderate compensation." Furthermore, she mandated that Dias's troop be organized into a militia regiment (*terço*) into which the newly freed men would be enlisted.[36]

The 1657 royal decision (like the 1645 proclamation) is significant for what it did not do—free slaves outright. Manumission was the private prerogative of slaveowners, and slavery rested on respect for masters' private power. Thus, Portuguese monarchs could grant freedom only with owners' "permission"; in this sense, they were far from absolute rulers. These concerns about masters' property rights and their control over manumission recurred in all of the subsequent episodes of slave recruitment, and the colonial and imperial Brazilian states never willingly went further than they did in 1657, at best strongly encouraging owners to free slaves. Unfortunately, there is no indication in the existing literature of how authorities prevailed on men like Rebelo's owner to sign manumission papers, but judging by the aftermath of the war for independence in the 1820s, this was probably a difficult task for Pernambuco's governors. Enlisting those freed into a military corporation likely allayed masters' concerns about the postmanumission control of these freedmen.

The War of Divine Liberty also raised racial questions for the Luso-Brazilian patriots. A clear segregation prevailed in the patriot forces, with black, mulatto, and indigenous units operating separately from the main white forces, a pattern reiterated when Dias's troop became a separate militia regiment. By the early eighteenth century, such segregation had become firmly established in the Brazilian armed forces. In principle, the regular army's rank and file was to consist of white men, and several visitors to early nineteenth-century Brazil remarked on the advantages that free and freed black men enjoyed during impressment drives because they could not be forcibly enlisted.[37] In practice, by the end of the colonial period, it had become acceptable to enlist men of mixed race, but the exclusion of blacks from the army remained on the books until 1837 and appears to have been respected.[38] The free and freed black men excluded from the regular army were instead enlisted in segregated militia companies and battalions formed throughout Brazil; the militia was abolished in 1831, replaced by a formally color-blind National Guard.[39]

Slaves were, of course, exempt from recruitment into the regular army's rank and file and from service in the militia, but during the wars between Spain and Portugal in the 1760s and 1770s, authorities in Brazil and Portugal considered arming them. In 1762, Bahia's government instructed Salvador's city council to conduct a census of the slave population, ordering masters to arm their slaves with muskets and bayonets or spears, and authorities in Rio de Janeiro were apparently advised to do the same.[40] In the mid–1770s, another round of Luso-Spanish conflict prompted further consideration of arming slaves. The viceroy outlined a complex plan to organize Rio de Janeiro's slaves into an auxiliary force armed with "lances, spears, muskets, [or] bows and arrows." The men were to be divided into companies with slave officers. He ordered the governor of Minas Gerais to do the same, and in early 1777, local authorities there received instructions to levy half of each owner's slaves for this purpose.[41] Fearing that a Spanish naval force was headed for Bahia, the Portuguese government ordered that all of the colony's slaves be armed with spears, and the governor of Bahia complied, instructing slaveowners in the sugar-plantation hinterland to prepare to send their spearmen to Salvador, where there were already 5,510 slaves capable of bearing arms.[42] Authorities did not envisage that the slaves so mobilized would be freed, except for those who distinguished themselves in combat or volunteered to man fireships. Were owners unwilling to free these men, the treasury would pay compensation.[43]

Although most of these slave mobilizations never took place because the Spanish invasion did not materialize, they were controversial. The governor of São Paulo refused to contemplate arming slaves with guns, considering this too dangerous. Local officials in Minas Gerais reported rumors among slaves that they had been freed by these levies; others talked about deserting to the enemy as a way to win their liberty.[44] It is difficult to assess such local resistance to slave drafts, for raising the specter of slave revolt might have simply been a way for masters to protect their property. In the early 1800s, new concerns emerged when these defense plans were reevaluated. The French occupation of Portugal and the flight of the monarchy to Brazil in 1807–1808 again raised the possibility of foreign invasion, and the government of Bahia revived the proposal that, in the event of alarm, all able-bodied male slaves be armed with lances to reinforce the captaincy's troops. This context, however, was completely different from that of the 1770s, given the general fears prompted by the Haitian Revolution and the far more immediate examples of the 1807 and 1809 slave revolts in Bahia. The measure drew a stiff rebuke from Rio de Janeiro, and the inspector-general lamely defended himself by arguing that Bahia's slaves were "accustomed to the blindest obedience" and that one owner with a whip "causes the greatest terror among a hundred slaves."[45] Such obedience could no longer be taken for granted.

Late-colonial defense plans for the use of armed slaves did not, except in special circumstances, envisage that slaves be freed as a reward for their service, nor did they consider enrolling slaves in the regular army. Rather, they treated slaves as property that could be requisitioned in case of invasion. As long as discrimination in recruitment for the regulars persisted, moreover, the vast majority of slaves would be ineligible to serve as soldiers on racial grounds as well. In these respects, the eighteenth-century plans differed significantly from those for the Dutch Wars, during which the slaves became soldiers and after which the monarchy threw its moral authority and fiscal resources behind the promise to free slaves who had helped expel the invaders. Had any of the principal slave plantation or mining districts been invaded (rather than simply raided, as Rio de Janeiro was in 1710 and 1711), matters might have been different. Instead, the slave mobilizations remained largely on paper. The rejection of the Bahian defense proposal in 1810 put an end to official consideration of this form of arming slaves, but within a few years, the issue returned in very different forms.

Revolutionary and Republican Arming of Slaves, 1817–1845

Brazil was, in many ways, a latecomer to the Age of Revolution. While the tiny educated elite imbibed Enlightenment ideals and the upheavals of the American, French, and Haitian Revolutions worried colonial authorities, the arrival of the Portuguese monarchy in 1808 prevented the outbreak of large-scale revolutionary independence struggles comparable to those of Spanish America. In 1822 Brazil gained its independence from Portugal in the form of an empire as Pedro I, son of the king of Portugal, broke with a new liberal government in Lisbon, which had recalled his father and sought to reduce Brazil's political status as a part of the monarchy equal to Portugal, granted in 1815.[46] The Brazilian empire is thus often seen as a continuation of the old regime, particularly in its maintenance of slavery. Despite British pressure, the slave trade persisted until the early 1850s, and the first emancipation measure — a "free womb" law — was passed only in 1871. Such an emphasis on continuities, however, misses the significant changes that took place in the first third of the century. Some began to question the legitimacy and utility of slavery on moral, ethical, and sometimes racial grounds, arguing that Brazil would be better off with free laborers and white immigrants.[47] Formal racial discrimination against free people of color largely disappeared from the country's legislation.

Moreover, the new imperial regime was not accepted by all. Between 1817 and 1848 several major regional rebellions challenged the social and political order in the country. Led by disaffected regional elite factions, these movements were liberal and republican in orientation, drawing extensive support from the lower classes. Three of them systematically recruited slaves and left detailed records of the debate about slave recruitment within their leadership. Although generally more sympathetic to abolition than the Brazilian government, none of these movements formally ended slavery. Some of their leaders, however, saw slave recruitment as a stage in gradual emancipation. Each of these rebellions initiated slave recruitment cautiously, but military necessity eventually forced them to undertake more widespread levies of slaves that failed to respect masters' property rights. In this sense, they marked a profound challenge to the slave order; Brazilian authorities subsequently singled out the rebel slave-soldiers for especially harsh treatment.

The first and shortest of these rebellions broke out in Recife, Pernambuco, in March 1817, well before Brazil's independence. The rebels initially drew extensive support from local notables, including sugar planters, and the movement is usually interpreted as a rejection of the centralization of power in Rio de Janeiro.[48] The arming of slaves during this rebellion took place on several levels. A number of sugar planters marched to Recife at the head of groups of armed slaves and other dependents. Smaller slaveowners also armed their slaves at the start of the revolt, while one of their leaders drafted his slaves to police the city. Some of the armed slaves were highly enthusiastic supporters of the rebellion, including one who bore a sword, followed his master, and declared himself ready to serve the "fatherland," adding that he looked forward to decapitating white soldiers.[49]

This private arming of slaves and rebel ideologues' principled opposition to slavery deeply worried slaveowners, but the republican government quickly moved to reassure them in a proclamation that, as clearly as any document, reveals the issues that bedeviled so many liberals during the Age of Revolution. While proclaiming themselves to be in favor of ending slavery, the rebels declared that they would implement only a "gradual, regular, and legal" emancipation that respected property rights, "the basis of all orderly society." Louis F. Tollenare, a Frenchman who stayed in Recife during the revolt, judged that the declaration "put to rest the worries."[50] In late April, with Recife under a strict naval blockade and royalist forces (including some masters leading armed slaves) closing in by land, the republic decreed a state of emergency and called on one thousand slaves to enlist in its army, promising them "freedom and the rights of citizenship." Masters would have to content themselves with an indemnity after the war. Tollenare feared that this was the prelude to a general emancipation and argued vigorously against the proposal with a "fanatic" rebel government member.[51] Within a month of this proclamation, however, royalists were back in control of Recife, and authorities returned the slaves to their masters, but not before brutally flogging them.[52]

The Sabinada Rebellion in Bahia twenty years later shared much with the republican movement in Recife. A radical liberal reaction to a conservative turn of the imperial government, this revolt was strongly supported by Salvador's army garrison at its outbreak on November 7, 1837.[53] Its leaders sought to reassure slaveowners by declaring that they considered abolition to be "supine stupidity," but loyalist authorities coordinating the siege of Salvador by planter-led National Guardsmen worried that desperate rebels would undertake extreme measures, including freeing slaves to enlist in their army.[54] The rebel forces attracted runaway slaves, and apparently some officers welcomed these men into their ranks, despite the opposition of the rebel minister of war, who ordered them returned to their owners.[55] In early January 1838, the rebel government tried to impose order on slave recruitment by creating a special freedmen's battalion, which would enlist Brazilian-born slaves; masters were to be compensated by the payment of one-half of the slave's salary up to a price set by the Treasury.[56] This unit explicitly excluded the majority of Salvador's slaves, the African-born, who were perceived as dangerous aliens, incapable of obtaining the same status as the Brazilian-born. In late February 1838, as the siege of Salvador tightened, the rebels decreed the freedom of all creole slaves capable of taking up arms in the rebellion's defense, apparently without compensation to the masters.[57]

The Sabinada did not long survive this measure; its defenses collapsed in mid-March, amid bitter fighting in which numerous rebels were massacred, no doubt many of the armed slaves among them. A few rebel slaves are known to have been deported to Africa, but most were returned to their owners.[58] There are no indications that authorities punished slaves prior to returning them, but the massacre of Sabinada defenders may have served the same purpose as did the public floggings in Recife in 1817. No doubt masters dealt with their slaves privately; some sold rebel slaves to unsuspecting buyers in other provinces. An owner in Rio Grande do Sul reported in 1850 that his Bahian-born slave Luiz had fled to Montevideo in 1848; only after this did he learn that Luiz "had served in the ranks of the rebels of that province during Sabino's time [the Sabinada]."[59]

The issues raised by the republican revolts of 1817 and 1837–1838 recurred in the Farroupilha Rebellion (1835–1845). Led by ranchers in the southern province of Rio Grande do Sul, this was the longest regional rebellion in imperial Brazil.[60] As in the other revolts, its slaveowning leaders rejected immediate abolition, but they strongly adhered to the principle that military service in defense of the rebellion implied freedom for slaves, and some of the rebels saw slave recruitment as a step toward abolition. They quickly organized two battalions of Black Lancers, apparently under the command of white officers.[61] At their peak, the Lancers may have enrolled as many as nine hundred men, a good number of them slaves of loyalist masters who had fled to the rebels to take up their offer of freedom. Some rebel masters donated slaves to the Farroupilha revolt or brought them along with free dependents.

The rebel government, however, went further, ordering the seizure of able-bodied slaves from those unsupportive of their cause.[62] Over-eager recruiters sometimes failed to respect even rebel masters' property rights, prompting the rebels' acting war minister to order in 1841 that all slave recruits be held for sixty days prior to enlistment so that pro-Farroupilha owners could reclaim those improperly drafted. After that, they would be formally enlisted with no possibility of discharge.[63]

To their credit, most of the Farroupilha leaders staunchly defended their soldiers' freedom. In 1838, when the imperial government threatened to administer between two hundred and one thousand lashes to any captured rebel slaves, the rebel government pledged to execute one randomly selected imperial officer for each "free man of color" flogged by the Brazilian forces.[64] As the stalemate between imperial and Farroupilha forces ground on in the early 1840s, divisions in the rebel leadership manifested themselves; the so-called majority lost ground to a more conservative minority committed to negotiating a settlement with the imperial government. A major stumbling block in the parleys was the postwar status of the Lancers. The Farroupilha representatives did not want them returned to slavery (on principle and perhaps also because such veterans would have made poor slaves). Although reluctant to reward rebel slaves with liberty, the imperial government entertained this possibility in the late 1830s and early 1840s but failed to establish a satisfactory policy for dealing with such newly freed men. A conservative cabinet secretly planned to deport the most dangerous to Africa and use the rest in public works, and a subsequent liberal ministry considered drafting them into the army.[65] In secret negotiations that are still the subject of heated controversy, the imperial commander, the Baron (later Duke) of Caxias, and David Canabarro, the principal leader of the minority, arranged a massacre of black soldiers at the so-called Surprise of Porongas (November 14, 1844), in which eighty of them were killed. In the subsequent peace treaty signed at Ponche Verde (February 28, 1845), the rebels pledged to turn over the remaining Lancers to the imperial government, which undertook to respect their freedom (and intended to remove them from the province). Caxias shortly thereafter received 120 freedmen, whom he attached to one of his cavalry corps pending their transfer to Rio de Janeiro. Later that year, the imperial government established procedures for paying compensation (up to a maximum value of 400 mil-réis, or US$208) to the masters dispossessed by these terms; the former rebels were described as "individuals who, having been slaves, are now free in consequence of the events" in Rio Grande do Sul. Parliament finally allocated the necessary funds in the budget for 1849–50.[66] Unfortunately, no historian has yet succeeded in documenting the final fate of those turned over to the imperial government, but some of the Farroupilha's slave-soldiers escaped altogether by fleeing to Uruguay or Paraguay.[67]

In the 1817 rebellion and in the Farroupilha (but less so in the Sabinada), republicans favored gradual emancipation while rejecting immediate abolition, seeing the freeing of slaves as a step toward the end of slavery. In so doing, they had moved beyond employing them in military capacities but keeping them in bondage, as late colonial military plans had envisaged. Military necessity forced them to go further, and the general appeals for a thousand slaves (1817) or all creoles (1838) to take up arms as well as the Farroupilha's seizure of its enemies' slaves were particularly objectionable, for these indiscriminate measures failed to respect masters' property rights and their exclusive control over manumissions. Ultimately, Brazilian authorities perceived these rebellions as grave threats to the slave order. Hence the brutal treatment meted out to the slave-soldiers in 1817, 1838, and 1844. Not surprisingly, too, the Sabinada's leadership was charged with fomenting slave insurrection, a crime that carried the death penalty under the 1830 criminal code; relative military success and the peace treaty ensured that the Farroupilha leaders avoided all criminal charges.[68]

Ratifying Slave Enlistments: Independence and Its Aftermath

Although the rebellions in Pernambuco, Bahia, and Rio Grande do Sul went much further than the Brazilian state did at this time — and would ever do — in inviting slaves to join their forces and in seizing slaves to serve as soldiers, the Brazilian army unexpectedly found itself accepting slaves into its ranks in the 1820s. Several related developments contributed to this innovation. The gradual elimination of racial discrimination in recruitment for the regulars between 1817 and 1837 constituted part of the context. More immediately important was the local recruitment of slaves during the war for independence in Bahia, which the empire reluctantly ratified by arranging to free the slaves in 1823. By the 1840s, the army also established a policy of freeing the occasional runaway slave who had distinguished himself in the ranks, while returning most fugitives. These constituted ex post facto manumissions of enlisted slaves, and all entailed compensation to the owner.

In 1817 the colonial government created an army battalion of "freed blacks [*pretos*]," to be stationed in recently conquered Montevideo. A number of additional units of freedmen were created in subsequent years, including an artillery battalion in Rio de Janeiro.[69] By the creation of these units, the imperial government apparently sought to tap freed manpower, carefully segregating freedmen from the rest of the regular army and usually stationing them on the dangerous war-torn southern frontier. Yet recruitment orders issued during the 1820s reveal that only already free or freed black men were to be enlisted in these units.[70] No one gained his freedom through service in these units, but their creation gradually changed the army's racial composition.

Although Brazil gained independence relatively quickly and easily, significant fighting took place around the city of Salvador, Bahia, in 1822 and 1823. During this struggle, some slaves were enlisted in the patriot forces, but no promises of freedom were issued, leaving the Brazilian state with a delicate problem to resolve after the war. The origins of this military struggle lay in the defeat of local troops by Portuguese forces in early 1822. A few months later, patriot planters in the surrounding sugar-growing districts established an Interim Council of Government in the town of Cachoeira, proclaimed their loyalty to Pedro I (then moving toward his final break with Lisbon), and organized a ragtag army to besiege the city.[71] From Rio de Janeiro, Pedro sent arms, a contingent of regulars, and a French officer, Pierre Labatut, to command the patriot forces. Shortly after his arrival, Labatut requested that the council supply as many "freed mulattoes and blacks" as possible to fill a projected Emperor's Battalion of Constitutional and Independent Freedmen, a measure parallel to the Brazilian government's decision to create units of freedmen in 1817. Labatut apparently did not wait for the council to consider his proposal and began to fill the battalion with "creoles and Africans" seized from absent Portuguese planters; as a result, rumors spread that any slave who volunteered would be freed, all of which the council considered "appalling."[72]

With no end in sight to the siege of Salvador and manpower shortages looming, Labatut proposed in April 1823 that the council arrange a voluntary contribution of slaves from Bahia's planters. The council balked, calling on Labatut to exercise more caution and recommending that municipal councils be consulted first, but Labatut insisted, sending two officers from his field headquarters to Cachoeira to supervise this levy. A week later, the municipal council of Jaguaripe advised, as might be expected, that Labatut's proposal was a great error. Not only were there few surplus slaves in the municipality, but slaves lacked the honor and disinterestedness of "worthy sons of Mars"; only the opportunity to sack enemy property would motivate them to fight. More important, concluded the council, the selection of slaves for military service would have disastrous results because those not freed would join the slave-soldiers in rebellion. Nothing came of this levy, for Labatut was deposed in May 1823, but talk of it caused a great stir: "mulattoes [*pardos, cabras*] and creoles speak of nothing else," reported the council.[73]

What motivated Labatut to recruit slaves is not clear. Little is known about him save that as an unemployed Napoleonic junior officer (with a checkered career) he had found his way to Gran Colombia very early in the nineteenth century, briefly serving in Simón Bolivar's forces. There he likely witnessed Bolivar's emancipation proclamations and the large-scale enlistments of slaves into the Spanish-American patriot forces.[74] Labatut, however, acted much more cautiously than the Liberator. His "recruitment" of slaves was, above all, an ad hoc expedient, and he apparently never formally or informally called on slaves to join the Bahian patriots in return for freedom (I have located no such promise and none of his many enemies later accused him of making one). Despite his reputation for imperiousness, he actually displayed considerable respect for Brazilian masters' property rights, repeatedly consulting with the council and only enlisting slaves who belonged to absent Portuguese planters without Brazilian heirs. On this level, the conflict between Labatut and the council simply involved the disposition of valuable war booty. Of course, the issue could not be limited to debate between the two parties, for many slaves took matters into their own hands. The patriot camps attracted runaways, some of whom were put to work as orderlies and porters, while other fugitives were enlisted as free men in the patriot forces.[75]

The patriots' victory, which came after the Portuguese evacuation on July 2, 1823, thus left unresolved the status of the slaves serving in their forces. Labatut's successor recommended that these men be freed, and with remarkable rapidity, Pedro I ordered the Bahian government to arrange for this. His ruling explained that these slaves' services merited the reward of freedom and that it would be incompatible "with the principles of justice" and his own "generous and magnanimous sentiments" to leave them in bondage. As the queen had in 1657, Pedro hoped that the owners would freely manumit their slaves; if not, the government would pay compensation.[76] Many individual owners eventually accepted compensation and relinquished their property rights, and "freed soldiers" occasionally surface in later documentation, including a Nagō (or Yoruba) who testified at the trial of the 1835 slave rebels.[77] Other owners fought their slaves' claims through the imperial bureaucracy and judiciary, with some cases dragging on for years.[78] From Itaparica Island, the merchant-planter and local military governor, Lieutenant-Colonel Antōnio de Souza Lima, wrote in 1825, expressing views shared by many masters: "Here no slave served during the campaign . . . because there were no orders issued for this. Nor have I considered that this benefit [of freedom] should be extended beyond the battalion of freedmen created [by Labatut]. . . . Some slaves performed services here but they were those who fled from the city or those who, abandoned by their owners, wandered about the countryside, perpetrating robberies and disorders. They were returned to their owners as soon as they requisitioned them."[79] By minimizing slaves' services and denying their status as soldiers, the planters who had opposed slave enlistment in the first place continued the struggle to protect their property. Some officers, in turn, defended their subordinates against masters' claims as both groups argued about the demarcation between slave and soldier, a line that all agreed ought to exist and ought to be clear.[80]

It is, unfortunately, not known how many slaves gained their freedom as a result of service in the war for independence. The freedmen's battalion numbered 327 men in July 1823, but some of its soldiers had probably been freedmen before the war, and some slaves had fought in other units.[81] Those freed as a consequence of the war usually remained in Salvador's garrison as soldiers; apparently most were segregated into one battalion, "composed in its majority of freedmen and other members of the [racially] mixed classes," according to an observer. This unit mutinied in October 1824, providing a justification for the Brazilian government to remove black and freed soldiers from Salvador's garrison and to send them to the black battalions on the southern frontier.[82]

The recruitment of slaves in the struggle for independence has some similarities with that of the Dutch Wars, insofar as the free status of the slave-soldiers was definitively established only after the successful conclusion of the conflict. No promises of freedom comparable to Vieira and Capibaribe's proclamation of 1645, however, were recorded in 1822 and 1823. The 1823 decision to free slaves applied only to those who had fought as soldiers, and it was officially justified as a reward for services granted by a just and magnanimous emperor. As in 1657, the monarch could not free slaves; he could only encourage owners to do so. Of course, authorities must have also recognized that it was folly to attempt to return such soldiers to servitude (but individual owners attempted to do so, as they had in the 1650s). The next best thing was to keep them firmly under the control of the army hierarchy, and by 1825, the Bahian masters who had opposed the freeing of slaves were further reassured by the removal of the freed soldiers from the province.

The creation of black battalions after 1817 and the freeing of the slaves enlisted by Labatut gradually changed the racial composition of the regular army, which increasingly came to resemble the creole slave population.[83] So did provisions that permitted drafted militiamen to replace themselves with slaves in 1823 and 1824 and again during the Cisplatine War (1826–1828). Such substitutes were freed by their owners prior to enlistment; their numbers were not large, and the corporation only reluctantly accepted them. Officers held that the influx of these recruits ruined the army, and after the war, commanders in Rio Grande do Sul removed the remaining slave substitutes from combat units to the transport corps.[84]

All of these developments changed the meaning of military service, and for some slaves, running away to the army became a strategy to escape bondage. To forestall this response, the Brazilian government ordered in 1824 that all "men of color" prove their free status before enlistment, but until the end of slavery in 1888, hundreds of runaways were discovered in the army.[85] Most of the cases that I located for the 1820s were the consequence of the war for independence, but after the definitive lifting of the color bar to recruitment for the regulars in 1837, the flow of fugitives increased substantially. Some were inadvertently impressed by recruiters who could not (or would not) distinguish between free and slave, but others were clearly fugitives seeking to use the army as a vehicle to escape their owners.

The army's policy toward these men was in principle straightforward and in practice utterly byzantine. Slaves were ineligible to serve, so the men had to be returned to their rightful owners, in wartime and in peacetime; the army never deliberately or knowingly confiscated slaves. Discharges, however, required proof of both ownership and the identity of the man in question so as to prevent false claims of slave status (on the part of either would-be owners or unwilling soldiers) and the enslavement of free men in cases of mistaken identity. Moreover, as had been recognized after the War of Divine Liberty and the struggle for independence, slaves who performed services for the state as soldiers should not be returned to slavery. This principle was quietly extended to runaway slaves who distinguished themselves in the ranks as early as 1824, and it became standard practice in the Brazilian army by the 1840s. In these cases, the slaves were evaluated and the owners compensated. Of course, this rule was not widely advertised, for that would have been an open invitation for slaves to run away to the army. A final irony derived from the army's fiscal concerns. Although the corporation compensated the owners of the slaves that it kept as soldiers, it also demanded reimbursement for their upkeep from masters who received their property back, likely because the men were imprisoned from the moment that they were discovered (to prevent them from deserting). One case dragged on for six years, and the owner found herself owing more to the army than she would receive as compensation for freeing him!

The 277 cases of slaves reclaimed from the army include virtually every possible permutation. Some of the slaves preferred to return home and confessed their slave status at once (but a few of these confessions were spurious because they came from free men seeking to escape military service). Others were deliberately seeking to escape slavery, including one volunteer who insisted so vehemently on being assigned to an undesireable remote garrison that officers became suspicious of his motives. A few highly complex cases involved men whose status was unclear, some of whom had enlisted as an affirmation of their free status. Virtually all of the slaves involved were creoles; Africans, as aliens, could not serve in the Brazilian army.

The army's treatment of runaway slaves is consistent with Brazilian policy toward arming slaves in the first half of the nineteenth century. Slaves could not be soldiers, and after Labatut's efforts, none were knowingly enlisted in the Brazilian armed forces. The recognition of the Lancers' freedom in the peace treaty with the Farroupilha rebels was an unusual circumstance forced by the empire's inability to win a decisive victory. In 1823 and 1845, compensation to masters who manumitted the slaves who had served maintained the legal fiction of property rights. Runaways who were freed because of distinguished service in peacetime had to be freed by their owners (for only they were authorized to manumit slaves), and compensation had to be paid to ensure that the masters' property rights were fully respected. If slaves were to serve in the military, then they had to be freed by their owners (which, of course, meant that they were not slaves but freedmen on enlistment). If slaves served in the armed forces and distinguished themselves, then the state had an obligation to arrange for manumission and compensation to the owner. These principles also governed the last and greatest episode of slave recruitment in Brazilian history, that of the Paraguayan War.

The Paraguayan War Slave Recruitment, 1864–1870

The war that broke out with Paraguay over Brazilian intervention in Uruguayan affairs was Brazil's longest and bloodiest foreign conflict. After an initial wave of patriotic fervor, the conflict became increasingly unpopular, particularly because it turned into a lengthy siege of Paraguayan fortifications by Brazilian forces, aided by Argentine and Uruguayan troops. This was a costly war, with Brazil mobilizing more than one hundred thousand men.[86] Technically speaking, no slaves were knowingly recruited for the war, and all of the slave-soldiers (with the exception of fugitives) were actually men freed on the condition of serving in the army or the navy. This was true both in the first two years of the war, when the only slaves who entered the army were privately freed by their masters, and in 1867 and 1868, when the Brazilian government paid compensation to encourage owners to free slaves for military service.[87] The Paraguayan War slave recruitment was a highly successful policy, raising a significant number of soldiers and avoiding the improvisations that had characterized earlier episodes of slave recruitment.

During the first two years of the war, slaves entered the armed forces in a number of different ways, in all cases preceded by manumission. Some were, in effect, donated by private owners, freed on condition of serving in the army or the navy. The army recorded a total of 799 such donations for the war, with 630 of them coming from the city of Rio de Janeiro. Impressed men (or designated National Guardsmen) could under certain circumstances present substitutes, and nothing prevented slaveowners from freeing a slave to serve in their place or in the place of a son. A total of 948 substitutions are recorded, with the majority concentrated in Rio de Janeiro and Rio Grande do Sul. The limited number of such substitutions derives from both the poverty of most impressed men and the fact that most classes of recruits could avoid service by paying 600 mil-réis (about US$262), roughly half the value of an adult male slave at that time.[88]

In late 1866 the Brazilian government took several steps to increase the number of slave recruits. The Council of State debated the issue extensively, resolving to free and draft government-owned slaves (Emperor Pedro II insisted that these men's wives also be freed) and to encourage masters to free slaves by offering compensation. Opponents of the measure considered it impolitic and indecorous, feared that it would lead to slave unrest, and suspected that masters would take advantage of the government to rid themselves of troublesome slaves. Speaking for the majority, Councillor José Tomás Nabuco de Araújo anticipated that any measure that turned slaves into free men would be applauded by "civilized nations." The central issue in the council's discussion was the extent of masters' property rights and, at the same time that Nabuco (incorrectly) argued that the 1823 decree freeing slaves who had fought in the war for independence constituted a precedent for obliging owners to free slaves to fight,[89] he and his colleagues shied away from such a drastic step, instead carefully restricting the government to freeing its own slaves and offering compensation to masters who would free their slaves. As he explained, there was "no danger . . . in the purchase of slaves to be freed and serve in the army, for the slaves will not themselves be called up; rather the masters will be invited to sell [them] if [the masters] so desire; . . . [their rights] will not be violated."[90] The Brazilian state carefully respected property rights.

By this time, the end of slavery was inevitable, given the closing of the slave trade in the early 1850s and the inability of the Brazilian slave population to reproduce itself. But Brazilians were deeply divided regarding abolition and whether the state should have a role in regulating it. The compensated emancipations that began in early 1867 prompted fears among slaveowners that the government would go further, particularly given Pedro II's strong support for both slave recruitment and abolition.[91] The worries subsided by the middle of the year, and compensated emancipation gradually came to be seen as a suitable way of ending slavery. Rio de Janeiro's *Semana Ilustrada* carried a number of cartoons that expressed this view, one showing a thankful slave receiving freedom and a rifle from his master. Grateful and disciplined former slaves who would serve their country and their benevolent superiors were, in fact, desired by many an abolitionist, and a stint in the army, as Nabuco had noted when considering slave recruitment, might be just what was needed to discipline newly freed men.[92]

From early 1867 through 1868, the Brazilian government made compensated emancipation a priority, nominally paying a rising price and a premium of as much as 75 percent over average prices recorded in probate inventories. Much of the premium, however, reflected the discounted value of the bonds that slaveholders received.[93] The number of "slaves" recruited for this conflict remains the subject of debate, but the combined official figure for the army and the navy of 6,905 is likely quite accurate, given the legal and fiscal concerns of authorities.[94] For slaves, the compensation program offered new opportunities. Some requested that masters "sell" them to the government. Tomás de Aquino, facing a sentence of two hundred lashes for assault, petitioned to be sent to the army instead, noting that he had long "had a vocation for brawling" (his services were declined). A more subtle and determined Quinto forced his master's hand by repeatedly running away and attempting to enlist, only to be turned away by local authorities who recognized that he was a slave; when he finally prevailed on a recruiting agent to enlist him, his master gave up and requested compensation.[95]

The legacy of wartime slave recruitment is and was widely debated. For some, it contributed to abolitionist sentiment in the armed forces and destabilized slavery when the freed veterans returned home after the war.[96] But the majority of the men freed for the war did not return home in 1869 and 1870, for they had been enlisted in the army and navy for nine-year terms, and at least one who was inadvertently discharged was later arrested and returned to the army.[97] Among the returning veterans was a small but significant number of runaway slaves who had served as free men but whose slave status had not been liquidated. That owners sought to regain these men has been presented as evidence of a duplicitous master class that freed slaves to fight only to reduce them to slavery later.[98] The imperial government, however, sought to put an end to such kidnapping of ex-soldiers by ruling that they had to be treated as free men, in other words, that they had to be presumed free and could not be imprisoned on suspicion of being fugitives. At the same time, it invited owners to submit claims for compensation so that the men could be legally freed without violating property rights.[99]

The Paraguayan War was the only time that the Brazilian state, at its highest levels, deliberately resolved to enlist slaves in its armed forces. During this carefully planned recruitment, the empire avoided what its statesmen and slaveholders perceived as the excesses of slave recruitment, such as those carried out by republican rebels earlier in the century, and the problem of post-enlistment manumissions after the war of independence and the Farroupilha Rebellion. It carefully respected masters' property rights, requiring that the slaves be freed first, and managed to secure a significant influx of freed manpower for the war effort. It could be seen as a model of master-controlled emancipation. During the debate about the 1871 free womb law, Perdigão Malheiro, the jurist of slavery, held up masters' willingness to manumit slaves for the war effort as evidence of their support for emancipation, arguing that the freeing of children to be born of slave mothers threatened property rights and the "moral force" of absolute power on which masters' authority rested.[100] Of course, paying for the emancipation of 1.5 million slaves was entirely beyond Brazil's means, and the emancipation fund set up under the terms of the 1871 law freed only small numbers of slaves. Indeed, it is striking how little direct impact wartime slave recruitment had on slavery. The numbers involved were, of course, insignificant in relation to the total slave population, and any hints of large-scale expropriations prompted vigorous opposition from slaveowners. Compared to the nearly contemporaneous civil war in the United States and the struggle for independence in Cuba, abolition in Brazil was not a war aim in the way that it was for the Union or for at least some of the Cuban patriots.[101]

Over the course of three centuries, the arming of slaves was common in Brazil as in other parts of the Americas. That many, if not most, of the weapons in slaves' hands were wielded in defense of slaveowners' interests testifies to the strength, durability, and flexibility of slavery. As so much recent scholarship has stressed, slavery cannot be reduced to a simple model of repressive owners and resistant slaves but rather was characterized by much more complex negotiated social relationships.[102] The motives of armed slaves are, unfortunately, difficult to discern. Those who took up arms in their masters' private interests — or were required to do so — may have welcomed the change from their daily routine or may have hoped that such service would later be rewarded in some way. The numerous worries that private arming would lead to slave rebellion (or at least make revolts more dangerous) are readily comprehensible. But these concerns appear to have been exaggerated; after all, masters were highly selective in arming slaves. Not every slave became a bodyguard, hunter, or hit man; only a few did, no doubt enjoying numerous privileges as a result. They thus became part of the complex social hierarchy of slavery and gained an interest in preserving it, or at least their place in it.

Where it was a possibility (however remote), freedom no doubt inspired many slaves to risk their lives in armed forces, as suggested by the runaways who joined the army and the navy during Brazil's wars (or in peacetime). They too, no doubt, sought a change in routine, often also anticipating that they could distance themselves from masters by joining the military. Evidently slaves knew of the difference between private and public arming, to judge by the excitement that Labatut's enlistments caused. Others, however, were herded into the military with little choice in the matter, but in this respect, they scarcely differed from the rest of the impressed rank and file, particularly during the Paraguayan War. Ultimately, granting of freedom in exchange for military service was a problematic matter. Not only did it usually imply risking one's life in wartime, but it also typically implied that the freedman would remain under the control of a military corporation, which many of the free-born would have considered a far cry from true liberty. Keeping ex-slaves under military discipline, however, suited masters who were deeply concerned about uncontrolled liberty and the effect of such freedmen on those still enslaved.

Most impressive is the extreme caution with which the Brazilian state proceeded when it came to interfering in the private or domestic sphere of slave-master relations. Most owners saw state regulation of slave activities, the summary punishment of slave weapons offenders by police, and of course, the liberation of slaves who had served or were to serve in armed forces as unwelcome encroachments on their prerogatives. Discipline and control over manumission ought, ideally, to remain in masters' hands. To be sure, these principles could never be upheld absolutely, especially in the nineteenth century, but when compared to the other cases of public arming of slaves discussed in this book, the Brazilian case stands out, particularly in the separation of slave arming from final abolition. None of Brazil's early nineteenth-century republican rebels approached the abolitionist fervor of French revolutionary administrators such as Victor Hugues in Guadalupe during the mid–1790s.[103] Slavery was fatally weakened by slave recruitment during the wars for independence in Spanish America; the closest counterpart in Brazil—Labatut's slave recruitment in Bahia—may have shaken the planter class and the slave regime, but both recovered, and slavery expanded there for several more decades. The Paraguayan War slave recruitment was carefully regulated, and discussions of how to manage abolition were postponed until after the war, when masters and authorities could deal with it from a stronger position. In this sense, an analysis of armed slaves underscores the strength and durability of the Brazilian slave regime.

Notes

I gratefully acknowledge financial support from the Social Sciences and Humanities Research Council of Canada. Numerous colleagues have aided this research by sharing sources and discussing issues with me; I thank especially Alexandra Brown, Célia Levy, João José Reis, Hal Langfur, Maria Medianeira Padoin, Richard Graham, Roderick Barman, Roger Kittleson, Sandra Lauderdale Graham, Stuart B. Schwartz, Vitor Izeck-sohn, and Walter Fraga Filho. Jewel Spangler, Philip Morgan, and Christopher Brown provided helpful comments on earlier versions of this chapter. The following abbreviations are used in the notes: AAPEBa (*Anais do Arquivo Público do Estado da Bahia*); ABNRJ (*Anais da Biblioteca Nacional, Rio de Janeiro*); AHEx/RQ (Arquivo Histó-rico do Exército, Requerimentos); AHRGS (Arquivo Histórico do Rio Grande do Sul); AIHGB (Arquivo do Instituto Histórico e Geográfico Brasileiro); ANRJ (Arquivo Nacio-nal, Rio de Janeiro), SPE (Seção do Poder Executivo), AP (Arquivos Particulares); APA (Arquivo Público de Alagoas); APEBa/SACP (Arquivo Público do Estado da Bahia, Seção de Arquivo Colonial e Provincial); BNRJ/SM (Biblioteca Nacional, Rio de Janeiro, Seção de Manuscritos); CLB (*Coleção das Leis do Brasil*); PAEBa (*Publicações do Archivo do Estado da Bahia*); RIGHBa (*Revista do Instituto Geográfico e Histórico da Bahia*); RIHGB (*Revista do Instituto Histórico e Geográfico Brasileiro*); Rio (city of Rio de Janeiro).

1. [Antônio Marques] Perdigão Malheiro, *A escravidão no Brasil: Ensaio histórico, jurídico, social,* 3rd ed., 2 vols. (Petrópolis, Brazil, 1976), 1:35 (italics in original).

2. Ibid., 1:51 (italics in original).

3. Ibid., 1:96.

4. Many scholars have stressed the limits of state power in slave societies and the unwillingness or inability of the state to intervene in slave-master relations. See, among others, Stuart B. Schwartz, *Sugar Plantations in the Formation of Brazilian Society: Bahia, 1550–1835* (Cambridge, UK, 1985), 260–62; Ilmar Rohloff de Mattos, *O tempo saquarema* (São Paulo, 1987), 109–29.

5. Malheiro, *Escravidão,* 1:94; Manuela Carneiro da Cunha, "Silences of the Law: Customary Law and Positive Law on the Manumission of Slaves in 19th-Century Brazil," *History and Anthropology* 1:2 (1985): 427–43.

6. Herbert S. Klein, *The Atlantic Slave Trade* (Cambridge, UK, 1999), 211.

7. Standard English-language works on Brazilian slavery include Schwartz, *Sugar Plantations;* Mary C. Karasch, *Slave Life in Rio de Janeiro, 1808–1850* (Princeton, 1987); Stanley J. Stein, *Vassouras, a Brazilian Coffee County: The Roles of Planter and Slave in a Plantation Society* (Princeton, 1985); João José Reis, *Slave Rebellion in Brazil: The Muslim Uprising of 1835 in Bahia,* trans. Arthur Brakel (Baltimore, 1993); Kathleen J. Higgins, *"Licentious Liberty" in a Brazilian Gold Mining Region: Slavery, Gender, and Social Control in Eighteenth-Century Sabará, Minas Gerais* (University Park, PA, 1999).

8. Richard Graham, "Free African Brazilians and the State in Slavery Times," in *Racial Politics in Contemporary Brazil,* ed. Michael Hanchard (Durham, 1999), 31.

9. See, e.g., Peter M. Voelz, *Slave and Soldier: The Military Impact of Blacks in the Colonial Americas* (New York, 1993); Karasch, *Slave Life,* 79–81. Part of the problem

derives from the multiple meanings of the contemporary Brazilian "racial" terms *preto* (black, slave, or African) and *negro* (black or slave).

10. Urban policing has been the subject of several major studies. See Leila Mezan Algranti, *O feitor ausente: Estudos sobre a escravidão urbana no Rio de Janeiro, 1808–1822* (Petrópolis, Brazil, 1988); Thomas H. Holloway, *Policing Rio de Janeiro: Repression and Resistance in a Nineteenth-Century City* (Stanford, 1993); Alexandra Kelly Brown, "'On the Vanguard of Civilization': Slavery, the Police, and Conflicts Between Public and Private Power in Salvador da Bahia, Brazil, 1835–1888" (Ph.D. diss., University of Texas at Austin, 1998). See also the critique in Carlos Eugênio Líbano Soares, *A capoeira escrava e outras tradições rebeldes no Rio de Janeiro, 1808–1850* (Campinas, Brazil, 2001), 500–502.

11. Decree, July 8, 1521, Law, January 24, 1756, and Decree, January 9, 1732, in *Children of God's Fire: A Documentary History of Slavery in Brazil*, ed. Robert Edgar Conrad (Princeton, 1983), 246, 249, 250; Articles 297 and 299, Law, December 16, 1830 (Codigo Criminal do Imperio do Brazil), *CLB;* Articles 68–69, *Codigo de posturas da camara municipal de Pirassununga* (São Paulo, 1880), 9. See also A. J. R. Russell-Wood, "Ambivalent Authorities: The African and Afro-Brazilian Contribution to Local Governance in Colonial Brazil," *The Americas* 57:1 (July 2000): 24–25.

12. Ordinance, São Paulo, February 8, 1738, in Luiz de Aguiar Costa Pinto, *Lutas de famílias no Brasil (introdução ao seu estudo),* 2nd ed. (São Paulo, 1980), 109, n. 36; Decree, January 9, 1732, and Law, January 24, 1756, in *Children,* ed. Conrad, 249, 250; Holloway, *Policing,* 42, 47, 49; *Repertório de fontes sobre a escravidão existentes no Arquivo Municipal de Salvador: As posturas, 1631–1889* (Salvador, Brazil, 1988), 48. See also Silvia Hunold Lara, *Campos da violência: Escravos e senhores na capitania do Rio de Janeiro, 1750–1808* (Rio, 1988), 80.

13. Henry Koster, *Travels in Brazil in the Years from 1809 to 1815,* 2 vols. (Philadelphia, 1817), 1:287. See Johann Moritz Rugendas, *Viagem pitoresca através do Brasil,* trans. Sérgio Milliet (São Paulo, n.d.), plates 4/5, 4/15, 4/16, 4/18.

14. Leila Mezan Algranti, "Slave Crimes: The Use of Police Power to Control the Slave Population of Rio de Janeiro," *Luso-Brazilian Review* 25:1 (Summer 1988): 35; Karasch, *Slave Life,* 330; Holloway, *Policing,* 78, 136, 197; Soares, *Capoeira,* 104, 111, 188, 345, 444–45, 457, 481.

15. Lara, *Campos,* 291–92; Soares, *Capoeira,* 108; Francisco Peixoto de Lacerda Werneck, *Memória sobre a fundação de uma fazenda na província do Rio de Janeiro* (Rio, 1985), 65.

16. Quoted in Julio Pinto Vallejos, "Slave Control and Slave Resistance in Colonial Minas Gerais, 1700–1750," *Journal of Latin American Studies* 17:1 (May 1985): 15.

17. Soares, *Capoeira,* 439–41.

18. Russell-Wood, "Ambivalent Authorities," 25.

19. Higgins, *"Licentious Liberty,"* 38, 190–95; Vallejos, "Slave Control," 5–7, 11–13, 16, 33; Hal Lawrence Langfur, "The Forbidden Lands: Frontier, Settlers, Slaves, and Indians in Minas Gerais, Brazil, 1760–1830" (Ph.D. diss., University of Texas at Austin, 1999), 257–58; Charles R. Boxer, *The Golden Age of Brazil, 1695–1750* (Berkeley, 1962), 51, 62, 63, 79, 194–95; Donald Ramos, "O quilombo e o sistema escravista em

Minas Gerais do século XVIII," in *Liberdade por um fio: História dos quilombolas no Brasil*, ed. João José Reis and Flávio dos Santos Gomes (São Paulo, 1996), 185–86.

20. Matheus van den Broeck, *Journael, ofte historiaelse beschrijuinge . . .* (Amsterdam, 1651), plate 2.

21. Rugendas, *Viagem*, 191; João Calmon du Pin e Almeida to President of Bahia, Engenho Cavalcanti, November 20, 1868, APEBa/SACP, maço [bundle] 3491; Koster, *Travels*, 1:322; Lara, *Campos*, 169, 193–99.

22. Solimar Oliveira Lima, *Triste pampa: Resistência e punição de escravos em fontes judiciais no Rio Grande do Sul* (Porto Alegre, Brazil, 1997), 70, 72; Nancy Priscilla Naro, "Fact, Fantasy, or Folklore? A Novel Case of Retribution in Nineteenth-Century Brazil," *Luso-Brazilian Review* 33:1 (Summer 1996): 59–80; Pinto, *Lutas*, 107–8; Lara, *Campos*, 119–20, 200.

23. Jean-Baptiste Debret, *Viagem pitoresca e histórica ao Brasil*, 3 vols. in 2, trans. Sérgio Milliet (São Paulo, 1972), 1:174; see also the plate between pages 164 and 165.

24. Lara, *Campos*, 182; Denise Aparecida Soares Moura, *Saindo das sombras: Homens livres e pobres vivendo a crise do trabalho escravo, 1850–1888* (Campinas, Brazil, 1998), 251–52; José Antônio Soares de Sousa, "O efêmero quilombo do Pati do Alferes, em 1838," *RIHGB* 295 (April–June 1972), 36.

25. Ruling of Interim Council, Cachoeira, November 28, 1822, in *Children*, ed. Conrad, 255; Baron of Maragogipe to President of Bahia, Pimentel, December 1, 1827, APEBa/SACP, m. 3458. On the revolts of the early nineteenth century, see Reis, *Slave Rebellion*, 40–53.

26. Acting Governors to King, Salvador, January 14, 1764, and President of Maranhão, *Relatório* (1853), 7–8, in *Children*, ed. Conrad, 380, 387; Legion Chief to President of Rio de Janeiro, Valença, November 8, 1838, in Sousa, "Efêmero quilombo," 43; Minister of Justice to President of Alagoas, Rio, August 14, 1832, APA, L-133, E-20.

27. On quilombos, see the articles in Reis and Gomes, *Liberdade*.

28. Stuart B. Schwartz, "Cantos e quilombos numa conspiração de escravos Haussás: Bahia, 1814," in *Liberdade*, ed. Reis and Gomes, 381, 386; Sousa, "Efêmero quilombo," 50; Reis, *Slave Rebellion*, 90.

29. Higgins, *"Licentious Liberty,"* 196.

30. Dierick Ruiters, cited in *Outras visões do Rio de Janeiro colonial: Antologia de textos, 1582–1808*, ed. Jean Marcel Carvalho França (Rio, 2000), 40.

31. Jonas Finck, in *Visões do Rio de Janeiro colonial: Antologia de textos, 1531–1800*, ed. Jean Marcel Carvalho França (Rio, 1999), 70; René Duguay-Trouin, Guillaume François de Parscau, Chancel de Lagrange, and Joseph Collet, cited in *Outras visões*, 69, 121, 144, 171.

32. Evaldo Cabral de Mello, *Olinda restaurada* (Rio, 1975), 166, 177; Charles R. Boxer, *The Dutch in Brazil, 1624–1654* (Oxford, 1957), 64.

33. Proclamation, May 15, 1645, in Francisco Augusto Pereira da Costa, *Anais pernambucanas*, 11 vols., 2nd ed. (Recife, Brazil, 1983–85), 3:202.

34. E. C. Mello, *Olinda*, 177; Costa, *Anais*, 3:255–56; Boxer, *Dutch*, 169; José Antônio Gonsalves de Mello, *Henrique Dias, governador dos crioulos, negros e mulatos do Brasil* (Recife, Brazil, 1988), 35; A. J. R. Russell-Wood, *The Black Man in Slavery and Freedom in Colonial Brazil* (London, 1982), 74.

35. E. C. Mello, *Olinda*, 172, 176; Pedro Puntoni, *A mísera sorte: A escravidão africana no Brasil holandês e as guerras do tráfico no Atlântico Sul, 1621–1648* (São Paulo, 1999), 143.

36. Costa, *Anais*, 3:362; E. C. Mello, *Olinda*, 266; J. A. G. Mello, *Henrique Dias*, 50–52.

37. Koster, *Travels*, 2:184; Rugendas, *Viagem*, 127, 249; Louis F. Tollenare, *Notes dominicales prises pendant un voyage en Portugal et au Brésil en 1816, 1817 et 1818*, ed. Léon Bourdon, 3 vols. (Paris, 1971), 2:451, 484.

38. On imperial Brazilian recruitment legislation and practice, see Hendrik Kraay, *Race, State and Armed Forces in Independence-Era Brazil: Bahia, 1790s–1840s* (Stanford, 2001), 185–200.

39. Russell-Wood, *Black Man*, 84–93; Hendrik Kraay, "The Politics of Race in Independence-Era Bahia: The Black Militia Officers of Salvador, 1790–1840," in *Afro-Brazilian Culture and Politics: Bahia, 1790s–1990s*, ed. Kraay (Armonk, 1998), 30–56; Kraay, *Race*, 82–105, 218–32.

40. Acting Governors to Count of Oeiras, Salvador, April 10, 1762, *ABNRJ* 31 (1909), 491; Count of Cunha to Oeiras, Rio, June 30, 1765, *RIHGB* 254 (January–March 1962), 319.

41. Marquis of Lavradio to Dom Antônio de Noronha, Rio, June 20, 1775, and November 4, 1775, in Marquês de Lavradio, *Cartas do Rio de Janeiro, 1769–1776* (Rio, 1978), 161, 163; Langfur, "Forbidden Lands," 138.

42. Marquis of Pombal to Manoel da Cunha Menezes, Ajuda, August 3, 1776, BNRJ/SM, I-31, 30, 17, fol. 1v; Advisory to Proprietors, Salvador, October 9, 1776 (copy), ANRJ/SPE, IG1, m. 112, fol. 121v; Menezes to Pombal, Salvador, November 1, 1776, *ABNRJ* 32 (1910), 334.

43. Lavradio to Noronha, Rio, June 20, 1775, in Lavradio, *Cartas*, 161; Pombal to Menezes, Ajuda, August 3, 1776, BNRJ/SM, I-31, 30, 17, fols. 3v–4r; Dauril Alden, *Royal Government in Colonial Brazil, with Special Reference to the Administration of the Marquis of Lavradio, Viceroy, 1769–1779* (Berkeley, 1968), 215.

44. Vallejos, "Slave Control," 16; Langfur, "Forbidden Lands," 141.

45. Count of Linhares to Interim Government, Rio, February 28, 1810, APEBa/SACP, m. 110, doc. 60; João Baptista Vieira Godinho to Linhares, May 8, 1810, ANRJ/SPE/ IG1, m. 112, fols. 116r–19r. See also Russell-Wood, *Black Man*, 87; Russell-Wood, "Ambivalent Authorities," 33.

46. The best English-language overview of Brazilian independence is Roderick J. Barman, *Brazil: The Forging of a Nation, 1798–1852* (Stanford, 1988).

47. Emilia Viotti da Costa, *The Brazilian Empire: Myths and Histories*, rev. ed. (Chapel Hill, 2000), 126–28.

48. Glacyra Lazzari Leite, *Pernambuco, 1817: Estrutura e comportamentos sociais* (Recife, Brazil, 1988).

49. Marcus J. M. de Carvalho, "Revisitando uma quartelada: Os aparelhos repressivos e a questão social em 1817," *Debates de História Regional* 1 (1992): 73, 77; Amaro Quintas, *A revolução de 1817* (Rio, 1985), 118; Carlos Guilherme Mota, *Nordeste 1817: Estruturas e argumentos* (São Paulo, 1972), 99.

50. Proclamation, March 15, 1817, in Costa, *Anais*, 7:392; Tollenare, *Notes*, 2:568.

On this question more broadly, see David Brion Davis, *The Problem of Slavery in the Age of Revolution* (Ithaca, 1975), esp. chap. 6.

51. Costa, *Anais,* 7:402; Tollenare, *Notes,* 2:260; Carvalho, "Revisitando," 73–74.

52. Tollenare, *Notes,* 3:647; Costa, *Anais,* 7:423.

53. Paulo Cesar Souza, *A Sabinada: A revolta separatista da Bahia, 1837* (São Paulo, 1987); Hendrik Kraay, "'As Terrifying as Unexpected': The Bahian Sabinada, 1837–1838," *Hispanic American Historical Review* 72:4 (November 1992): 501–27.

54. Proclamation of João Carneiro da Silva Rego, November 14, 1837, *Jornal do Commercio* (Rio), November 27, 1837, p. 1; Vice-President of Bahia to Minister of Justice, Cachoeira, November 16, 1837, ANRJ/SPE, IJJ9, m. 605.

55. Daniel Gomes de Freitas, "Narrativa dos successos da Sabinada," *PAEBa* 1 (1937): 267–68, 276–77, 281; Ordem do Dia 10, *Diario da Bahia,* January 12, 1838, p. 2.

56. Proclamation of Carneiro, January 3, 1838, *PAEBa* 2 (1938): 83–84.

57. Decree, February 19, 1838, BNRJ/SM, I-31, 12, 1, fols. 404v–5r; Freitas, "Narrativa," 300. On anti-African sentiment, see Reis, *Slave Rebellion,* 203–4.

58. President of Bahia to Chief of Police, Salvador, March 31, and April 3 and 19, 1838, *PAEBa* 5 (1948): 266, 269, 281.

59. "Relação dos escravos fugidos . . . ," 1850, AHRGS, lata [box] 531, m. 1.

60. Spencer L. Leitman, *Raízes sócio-econômicas da Guerra dos Farrapos: Um capítulo da história do Brasil no século XIX* (Rio, 1979); Maria Medianeira Padoin, *Federalismo gaúcho: Fronteira platina, direito e revolução* (São Paulo, 2001).

61. Several scholars have analyzed the Farroupilha's policy toward slaves, though none provide a fully satisfactory account: Spencer L. Leitman, "The Black Ragamuffins: Racial Hypocrisy in Nineteenth-Century Southern Brazil," *The Americas* 33:3 (January 1977): 504–18; Mário Maestri, *O escravo gaúcho: Resistência e trabalho* (Porto Alegre, Brazil, 1993), 76–82; Helga I. L. Picolo, "A questão da escravidão na Revolução Farroupilha," *Anais da V Reunião da SBPH* (1986): 225–30; Claudio Moreira Bento, *O negro e descendentes na sociedade do Rio Grande do Sul, 1635–1975* (Porto Alegre, Brazil, 1976), 148–73; Margaret Marchiori Bakos, "A escravidão negra e os Farroupilhas," in *Revolução Farroupilha: História e historiografia,* ed. Décio Freitas (Porto Alegre, Brazil, 1985), 79–97; Wilson Sander et al., "A presença do negro e do índio no decênio farroupilha," *Estudos Ibero-Americanos* 9:1–2 (July–December 1983): 211–21.

62. Colonel Jacinto Guedes da Luz to Citizen General Antônio [de Souza] Netto and to Citizen Captain José do Amaral Ferrador, Paipasso, November 2, 1840, AIHGB, D.L. 845.36.

63. Acting Minister of War to Souza Netto, Piratini, February 13, 1841, AIHGB, D.L. 845.37; Ordem do Dia 37, São Gabriel, February 27, 1841, AIHGB, D.L. 127.19.

64. These decrees are analyzed by Bento, *Negro,* 157–59.

65. See the analysis of government policy by a well-connected conservative journalist, Justiniano José da Rocha, "Os soldados dos republicanos do Rio Grande," *O Brasil* (Rio), June 5, 1841.

66. Baron of Caxias to Minister of War, Bagé, March 5, 1845, in *Ofícios do Barão de Caxias, 1842–1843 . . .* (Rio, 1950), 170; Resolução, July 19, 1845, in *Consultas do Conselho de Estado relativamente a negocios do Ministério da Guerra desde o anno de 1843 a 1866 . . . ,* ed. Candido Pereira Monteiro (Rio, 1872), 24; Decree 427, July 26,

1845, *CLB;* "Instrucções para a commissão encarregada de avaliar os individuos que havendo sido escravos, se achão livres em consequencia dos acontecimentos da Provincia de São Pedro," cited in Karasch, *Slave Life,* 338, n. 8; Article 6, Paragraph 26, Law 514, October 28, 1848, *CLB.*

67. "Relação dos escravos fugidos...," 1850, AHRGS, Lata 531, m. 1. Contradictory and undocumented assertions about the Farroupilha freedmen's fate pervade the literature. Compare Bento, *Negro,* 20; Piccolo, "Questão," 230; Leitman, "Black Ragamuffins," 518.

68. Souza, *Sabinada,* 145–46.

69. Decrees, May 10, 1817 and November 12, 1822, *CLB.*

70. Decisions 57, 244, and 25, March 5 and October 22, 1825, and February 11, 1826, and Decree, July 14, 1828, *CLB.*

71. On independence in Bahia, see Kraay, *Race,* chap. 5. The slave "recruitment" in this war is treated confusingly in the literature. F. W. O. Morton denies that it took place at all in "The Conservative Revolution of Independence: Economy, Society, and Politics in Bahia" (Ph.D. diss., Oxford University, 1974), 267–68. Others note that it took place but do not investigate it fully: Braz do Amaral, *História da Independência na Bahia,* 2nd ed. (Salvador, 1957), 7, 272, 285, 291–92; Aydano do Couto Ferraz, "O escravo negro na revolução da independência da Baía," in *Revista do Arquivo Municipal* (São Paulo) 56 (1939): 195–202; João José Reis and Eduardo Silva, *Negociação e conflito: A resistência negra no Brasil escravista* (São Paulo, 1989), 90, 96–98; Ubiratan Castro de Araújo, "Sans gloire: Le soldat noire sous le drapeau brésilien, 1798–1838," in *Pour l'histoire du Brésil: Mélanges offerts à Kátia de Queirós Mattoso,* ed. François Crouzet et al. (Paris, 2000), 527–40. I have examined this episode more fully in my "'Em outra coisa não falavam os pardos, cabras e crioulos': O 'recrutamento' de escravos na guerra da independência na Bahia, 1822–1823," *Revista Brasileira de História* 22:43 (2002): 109–26.

72. Interim Council to Pierre Labatut, Cachoeira, November 22, 1822, *AAPEBa* 41 (1973), 28, and to Minister of Empire, Cachoeira, December 23, 1822, *RIGHBa* 14 (1897), 561, 563.

73. Interim Council to Labatut, Cachoeira, April 12 and 14, 1823, *AAPEBa* 41 (1973), 88, 89; Labatut to Interim Council, Cangurungú, April 16, 1823, in Silva, *Memorias,* 4:2, n. 2; "Termo de Veriação," Jaguaripe, April 23, 1823, *AAPEBa* 10 (1923), 63–65; Interim Council to Minister of Empire, Cachoeira, April 16, 1823, *RIGHBa* 17 (1898), 362–64.

74. On Labatut's background, see Affonso Ruy, *Dossier do Marechal Pedro Labatut* (Rio, 1960), chap. 3. Bolivar's slave recruitment is analyzed by Nuria Sales de Bohigas, "Esclavos y reclutas en sudamérica, 1816–1826," in *Sobre esclavos, reclutas y mercaderes de quintos* (Barcelona, 1974), 85–102.

75. Joaquim Pires de Carvalho e Albuquerque to Major Commanding, Fixed Artillery, Rio, March 16, 1825, AHEx/RQ, JJ-237-5790.

76. José Joaquim de Lima e Silva to Minister of Empire, July 16, 1823, BNRJ/SM, II-31, 35, 4; Decision 113, July 30, 1823, *CLB.*

77. Maria Inês Cortes de Oliveira, "Viver e morrer no meio dos seus: Nações e comunidades africanas na Bahia do século XIX," *Revista USP* 28 (December 1995–February 1996): 191.

78. See, e.g., Lieutenant-Colonel Commander, Fourteenth Battalion, to Governor of Arms, Salvador, March 23, 1827, APEBa/SACP, m. 3367.

79. Antonio de Souza Lima to Governor of Arms, Itaparica, July 30, 1825 (copy), APEBa, m. 3365.

80. Artillery Commander to President of Bahia, Salvador, May 9, 1825, BNRJ/SM, II-33, 31, 4, no. 5, doc. 19; Commander, Fourteenth Infantry, to Governor of Arms, Salvador, March 23, 1827, APEBa, m. 3367.

81. Silva, *Memorias*, 4:59, n. 28.

82. Ibid., 4:179. On the mutiny, see Luís Henrique Dias Tavares, *O levante dos Periquitos* (Salvador, 1990); Kraay, *Race*, 110–11; 124–25; 132–33; 138–39.

83. Few African freedmen found their way into the corporation.

84. Francisco de Paula Cidade, "O soldado de 1827 (ninharias de história, relativos aos soldados da Guerra Cisplatina)," *Revista Militar Brasileira* 17:1 (January–March 1927): 47; Maria Stella de Novaes, *A escravidão e abolição no Espírito Santo: História e folclore* (Vitória, 1963), 57; "Relação nominal dos Pretos, e Pardos que por occazião da Guerra forão offerecidos para assentarem prasa em lugar dos seus senhores," São Francisco de Paula, October 23, 1830, ANRJ/AP 31 (Gustavo Henrique Brown), doc. 213.

85. The following discussion is entirely based on my " 'The Shelter of the Uniform': The Brazilian Army and Runaway Slaves, 1800–1888," *Journal of Social History* 29:3 (Spring 1996): 637–57. Álvaro Pereira do Nascimento's study of fugitives in the imperial navy reveals similar patterns, "Do cativeiro ao mar: Escravos na Marinha de Guerra," *Estudos Afro-Asiáticos* 38 (December 2000), www.scielo.br (March 13, 2002).

86. The standard English-language work on the war, Charles J. Kolinski's *Independence or Death: The Story of the Paraguayan War* (Gainesville, 1965), is now partially superseded by Thomas L. Whigham's *The Paraguayan War: A History*, vol. 1, *Causes and Early Conduct* (Lincoln, 2002).

87. I examine this episode more fully in my "Slavery, Citizenship and Military Service in Brazil's Mobilization for the Paraguayan War," *Slavery and Abolition* 18:3 (December 1997): 228–56. For different interpretations, see Jorge Prata de Sousa, *Escravidão ou morte: Os escravos brasileiros na Guerra do Paraguai* (Rio, 1996); Ricardo Salles, *Guerra do Paraguai: Escravidão e cidadania na formação do exército* (Rio, 1990); André Amaral de Toral, "A participação dos negros escravos na Guerra do Paraguai," *Estudos Avançados* 24 (May–August 1995): 287–96.

88. Kraay, "Slavery," 232–34.

89. In this respect, he repeated an error of Perdigão Malheiro, *Escravidão*, 1:100.

90. Minutes of Council of State, November 5, 1866, Brazil, Senado Federal, *Atas do Conselho de Estado: Obra comemorativa do sesquicentenário da instituição parlamentar* (Brasília, 1973), 6:71–90.

91. Kraay, "Slavery," 236–37.

92. *Semana Illustrada* (Rio), November 11, 1866, 2469; Minutes of Council of State, November 5, 1866, Brazil, Senado Federal, *Atas*, 6:83.

93. Kraay, "Slavery," 239–44.

94. I present the evidence for the accuracy of the official total in "Slavery," 239–46; others, however, suspect undercounting. See Sousa, *Escravidao*, 82–90; Salles, *Guerra*, 63–76.

95. Petition of Thomaz de Aquino to President of Bahia, c. 1867, APEBa/SACP, m. 3671; President of Rio Grande do Sul to Chief of Police, Porto Alegre, April 8, 1867, AHRGS, Correspondência dos Governantes, m. 109.

96. Robert B. Toplin, *The Abolition of Slavery in Brazil* (New York, 1972), 219; Paulo Mercadante, *Militares e civis: A ética e o compromisso* (Rio, 1978), 107; Nelson Werneck Sodré, *História militar do Brasil* (Rio, 1965), 141–42.

97. Commander of Arms to President of Bahia, Salvador, December 29, 1873, APEBa/SACP, m. 3430.

98. Sousa, *Escravidão*, 67, 72, 102, 113.

99. Decisions 54 and 158, February 9, and June 15, 1870, *CLB*. I analyze one such case in detail in "Slavery," 247. For another, see Peter M. Beattie, *The Tribute of Blood: Army, Honor, Race, and Nation in Brazil, 1864–1945* (Durham, 2001), 52–53.

100. Speech of Antonio Marques Perdigão Malheiro, June 10, 1871, *Anais da Câmara dos Deputados* (1871), 2:52. These points are analyzed more fully by Sandra Lauderdale Graham, "Slavery's Impasse: Slave Prostitutes, Small-Time Mistresses, and the Brazilian Law of 1871," *Comparative Studies in Society and History* 33:4 (1991): 683–93; and Eduardo Spiller Pena, *Pajens da casa imperial: Jurisconsultas, escravidão e a lei de 1871* (Campinas, Brazil, 2001), chap. 3.

101. Ira Berlin et al., *Slaves No More: Three Essays on Emancipation and the Civil War* (Cambridge, UK, 1992), 187–223; Rebecca J. Scott, *Slave Emancipation in Cuba: The Transition to Free Labor, 1860–1899* (Princeton, 1985), 48–62.

102. Robert W. Slenes, *Na senzala, uma flor: Esperanças e recordações na formação da família escrava — Brasil sudoeste, século XIX* (Rio de Janeiro, 1999); Reis and Silva, *Negociação;* Lara, *Campos.*

103. Laurent Dubois, " 'The Price of Liberty': Victor Hugues and the Administration of Freedom in Guadeloupe, 1794–1798," *William and Mary Quarterly,* 3rd ser., 56:2 (April 1999): 363–92.

Arming Slaves in the American Revolution

PHILIP D. MORGAN and

ANDREW JACKSON O'SHAUGHNESSY

The American Revolution occasioned major innovations in the military use of slaves throughout the Atlantic world. The role of slaves in the Revolutionary War in North America is well known, but the tendency to treat the thirteen mainland colonies in isolation has obscured the significance of the war for the arming of slaves.[1] Only when we incorporate the other British Atlantic colonies does the scale of the practice become fully apparent. Indeed, the war had more profound consequences for arming slaves in the British Caribbean than anywhere else in the Americas. The British evacuation of slave troops in the southern states led to the establishment of the first permanent peacetime army garrisons composed of slave soldiers, called the South Carolina Pioneer Corps. It became the foundation of the West India Regiments, which formed the largest slave army of any European power between 1794 and 1833.

Powerful inducements encouraged the use of slaves as soldiers. The exigencies of war, typically shortages of manpower, made it a useful expedient. This need was especially true in the Caribbean, where warfare was perennial, slaves composed a high proportion of the population, and mortality rates were catastrophic among regular soldiers from Europe. Colonial officials and military commanders had long observed that black troops seemed more immune to tropical diseases than European troops. They crudely calculated that using black soldiers would spare the lives of white troops and cut the considerable cost of garrisons. Furthermore, slaves were familiar with local terrain, resulting in their frequent use as scouts. Some commanders regarded blacks not only as highly effective but as superior to white troops. They also appreciated the potential to divide and rule by selectively recruiting trusted slaves to encourage loyalty and to provide incentives in a system otherwise dependent primarily on coercive authority.

Another factor recommending slaves for military service was their prior experience in Africa. Rather than see slaves as dishonored captives, some whites pragmatically valued them as ex-soldiers. At no time was this recognition more explicitly stated than in 1696, when the directors of the Dutch West India Company told their representative in Curaçao to consider arming newly arrived African slaves. "Since we have been told that the Negroes shipped there [Curaçao], and in particular the Angolans, are men who have served in wars in their country, and know how to handle a gun," the Dutch officials noted, "we think that we could and should seize this opportunity to supply weapons to these Negroes, each according to his own skill, and have them exercise continually in the European fashion, along with our own militia." The governor of Curaçao seems not to have followed these directions, but that they were made at all is striking. African groups other than Angolans also gained a reputation for military prowess. In the Caribbean, many so-called Coromantees, Akan-speaking peoples from the Gold Coast, had military experience, which may well account for the familiarity with guns and even cannon that they showed in late seventeenth-century Jamaican rebellions. In 1675 a Barbadian governor described Coromantees as "warlike." A direct connection can be drawn between the leaders of the Akan state of Akwamu, captured in war between 1730 and 1732, and the slave revolt of 1733 in the Danish West Indies. In short, many slaves had served in African armies prior to their enslavement, and, as ex-soldiers and veterans of African wars, they probably needed little encouragement to serve again. Some of the tactics of maroons and other rebellious slaves — small bands, skirmishing, close combat — may owe something to homeland experiences. Military service abroad was a significant theme of the African diaspora.[2]

Although the reasons for using slaves as soldiers were compelling, their employment raised fundamental problems for the plantation system. The very conditions that made the arming of slaves necessary, in particular acute shortages of white manpower, also made it a dangerous expedient in the perception of slaveowners. Apart from that pragmatic and seemingly crucial reason for not arming slaves, other rationales were at hand. The arming of slaves contradicted the alleged inferiority of blacks and undermined the racial myths that justified slavery. Since the slave was, in theory, a socially dead person, often a captive in warfare and a defeated enemy, many planters considered it anathema to convert slaves into warriors. Soldiers supposedly possessed the qualities of honor and courage, and slaves were the dishonored par excellence. Making soldiers of slaves, then, seemed a contradiction. In the harsh, exploitative slave societies of the New World, military slavery could never be a central institution, and slaveowner opposition to the arming of slaves was always intense in the Americas.[3]

The American Revolution was, in many ways, an unpropitious moment to consider arming slaves. The size of the slave population and the proportion of slaves in the larger colonial populations were greater than at any time in the history of British America. Furthermore, planters were especially fearful of rebellion owing to the dislocation caused by the war and the revolutionary rhetoric of liberty. Some Caribbean planters blamed the spread of revolutionary ideals from America for the major slave rebellion in Jamaica in 1776. They suspected that household slaves overheard their masters debating the merits of the revolutionary cause and toasting liberty with too much fervor. The combatants on both sides risked alienating the support of whites in the southern and island colonies by using slaves as soldiers. The British use of slaves as soldiers caused many white colonists to become patriots in plantation societies such as Virginia. The regular British army garrisons and local militia in the Caribbean were insufficient to resist external attack, let alone a simultaneous large-scale internal slave revolt during the American Revolution.[4]

Yet the American Revolution was a decisive turning point in the arming of slaves in the Americas, especially in the British Caribbean. True, the arming of slaves was never part of a deliberate or concerted policy but rather was warily adopted as an urgent measure in response to a crisis. Furthermore, important precedents, outlined in the first part of this chapter, existed from the earliest times of European expansion, culminating in the Seven Years' War. To put the revolutionary experience in perspective requires a cursory overview of the colonial experience. Nevertheless, the American Revolution occasioned major innovations in the arming of slaves, in the functions they performed, and in the scale of their operations. These radical changes become particularly evident when developments in the Caribbean and North America, places that were deeply connected but often treated separately in historiographies, are linked. Events in one region had repercussions in the other. We therefore treat the two regions in turn, but always with an eye toward the intersections and connections between the two. Piers Mackesy, who wrote one of the few histories of the American War for Independence that is not exclusively centered on the North American theater, claims that "the American War had been largely fought and decided in the Caribbean." The Caribbean is vital to the Atlantic story we wish to tell.[5]

A tradition of arming slaves arose with the beginnings of settlement in the Americas, but the practice was more limited in scope and scale — indeed was often about *dis*arming — than it was during the American Revolution. Following the metropolitan example in denying guns to potentially dangerous groups, all colonial legislatures passed laws aimed at keeping most slaves unarmed. Acts that were on the books to deny arms to indentured servants (and other groups, such as Catholics) were easily modified and extended to slaves. The first law to forbid slaves in the British Atlantic world to bear arms was probably the 1661 Barbados law directing slaveowners to search the houses of slaves fortnightly for "clubs, wooden swords, or other mischievous weapons." No doubt the act enshrined customary practice, for Richard Ligon, who lived on the island between 1647 and 1650, observed that Barbadian slaves were "not suffered to touch or handle any weapons." Other island and mainland colonies followed the Barbadian example: in 1680 Virginia prohibited "Negroes" from carrying clubs, swords, guns, or other weapons of defense or offense. Both the French Code Noir of 1685 and the Spanish Code of 1680 forbade slaves to carry arms.[6]

Laws categorically denied slaves access to guns, and yet in emergencies many slave societies employed slaves as soldiers. Slave soldiers were less common in North America than in the Caribbean, but in frontier regions everywhere, at sea, and on many an individual plantation or farm, slaves often had a surprising degree of access to firearms and weapons of many sorts. It is a gross exaggeration to say, as Michael Bellesiles has done, that slaves "did not have a single gun." Perhaps precisely because whites denied guns to slaves, bondmen valued all the more their possession of such banned items. Furthermore, at least some slaves' access to guns was routine, a regular occurrence. An inherent ambiguity therefore existed in colonial society between keeping firearms out of the hands of slaves and arming them whenever it seemed necessary or useful. And some slaves plainly armed themselves, without any assistance from, or in opposition to, whites.[7]

At the same time that whites generally attempted to deny firearms to their slaves, they were always willing to make exceptions. The Spanish were pioneers in this regard, launching, for example, an attack on Providence Island in 1640 with a force that included a small group of "Mulatoes and Black creoles." The Dutch, also always lacking men, were not very far behind the Spanish in the military use of blacks. But in both cases slaves do not appear to have been greatly used as soldiers because free blacks and mulattoes were available and proved a far more palatable source of military personnel. By the mid-seventeenth century free blacks and mulattoes were serving in formally organized militias throughout the Spanish New World.[8]

In the Caribbean, a cockpit of imperial rivalry, with warfare endemic and deadly diseases frequent, the military use of slaves was nigh essential. The English pioneer was once again Barbados, where the recruiting and arming of slaves began in the 1660s, just when whites were leaving the island in droves. About a third of the men mobilized during alarms, such as an imminent-seeming French attack of 1707, appear to have been slaves. In 1702 Bermuda's militia numbered 750 whites and 600 slaves, the latter armed with lances; they marched, wheeled, and advanced in formation together. In 1742 more than one thousand "Armed Negroes" were present on Antigua. The French islands seem to have gone further than the English ones in arming slaves, probably because the French colonists were outnumbered by the English and had little military support from the metropolis, at least before 1744.[9]

Military expeditions in the Caribbean relied on slaves primarily as auxiliaries like those sent alongside fourteen thousand soldiers from Britain and North America against Spain's Central American and Caribbean empire in 1740–41. According to complaints, a few "old worn-out" blacks from Maryland were pressed to fill the ranks of the three thousand or so North American troops raised for this expedition. But so-called baggage negroes, raised in the Caribbean, were deemed vital to the success of the expedition—although there was an issue of how many could be managed. In 1741 General Wentworth and Admiral Vernon, the leaders of the expedition, rejected an offer by the Jamaican Assembly to provide five thousand slaves for the army on Cuba because they did not believe they could control that number of slaves in hostile territory. Instead, they agreed to accept only one thousand. Most worked in an unarmed capacity as pioneers or drudges rather than as "shot negroes," as they were popularly known, but at least one-third of five hundred slaves raised in Jamaica were so termed and so used. A limited precedent for arming independent ad hoc black corps for service abroad did, then, exist, early in the eighteenth-century British Caribbean.[10]

Among the British mainland colonies, greater security and insulation from foreign attack, a much healthier environment, and a larger white population than existed in the Caribbean meant that there was much less military use of slaves. One exception to the extremely limited deployment of armed slaves on the mainland was the lower South, a region that resembled the Caribbean in being more exposed to enemy incursions and having a large slave population. South Carolina experimented with the arming of slaves during Queen Ann's War and the Yamassee War, and in 1739 the threat posed by Spanish St.

Augustine led South Carolina again to empower militia captains to enlist "recommended" slaves, since some slaves had shown "faithfulness and courage." A year later, in an expedition aimed at conquering the St. Augustine garrison, General James Oglethorpe proposed extensive use of slaves as pioneers, although he did arm a few slaves and put them in companies. Thereafter, South Carolina never again publicly armed slaves during the colonial period, although in 1747 the assembly passed a law allowing the drafting of slaves during emergencies, during the Cherokee War of 1760 a motion to arm four hundred blacks lost by only one vote in the assembly, and as late as 1770 Governor William Bull estimated that the militia could be "reinforced with a number of trusty negroes (and we have many such) not exceeding one-third of the corps they are to join."[11]

If the arming of slaves occurred most significantly in emergencies and crises, routine, regular usages also took place. Armed slaves seem to have been common on slaving vessels and on the African coast. Slaves and free blacks also gained knowledge of arms by serving on privateering, naval, merchant, and even pirate vessels. Individual masters always reserved the right to arm their slaves, no matter what the public policy stated, and their actions sometimes got them into trouble. In frontier regions, where defense and game hunting were important concerns, planters generally had the right to arm their slaves. Thus in Virginia, slaves on frontier plantations could use guns, but the master was supposed to procure a permit or license for the armed slave.[12]

In short, before the American Revolution, slaves had greater access to guns than laws often suggested, although that access was always limited. One of the best insights into the surprisingly widespread availability of firearms among New World slaves is the archaeological evidence from slave sites. Almost all have produced evidence of lead shot, gunflints, and, in some cases, gun hardware. A rather remarkable example of the general distribution of arms among Chesapeake slaves was a discovery made in one county on the eve of the Revolution: a Committee of Inspection collected about "eighty Guns, some bayonets, swords, etc." from their slaves. Nevertheless, undoubtedly only a minority of slaves ever had access to guns. Only about 1 percent of runaway slaves in either Virginia or South Carolina, and only four known colonial Georgia fugitives, had weapons. When slaves rose in revolt, generally they used clubs, staves, hoes, axes, bills, or their bare hands — much in the same way that European and American rioters and rebels wielded stones, clubs, and farm implements.[13]

Whites always revealed great ambivalence about arming their slaves. To be sure, evidence accumulated that slaves could be trusted and fought well, as did the slaves who defended Providence Island against the Spanish in 1640–41 and St. Christopher and Nevis against the French in 1706. In 1740, after praising his free black militiamen for warding off an English attack, the governor of St. Augustine noted that "even among the slaves a particular steadiness has been noted, and a desire not to await the enemy within the [fort] but to go out to meet him." Other Europeans were less sure and described slave soldiers on occasion as either cowardly or insolent. Even advocates of arming slaves expressed uncertainty. When in 1734 Governor William Mathew of Antigua proposed arming one thousand slaves, he labeled the move a "dangerous experiment." Perhaps the census takers in Tobago best summarized conventional thinking when, in 1773, they distinguished 96 percent of slaves as "not to be trusted with arms." Some whites were prepared to trust a tiny minority of slaves — one in twenty-five, in this instance — with arms. Many planters were not willing to go that far[14]

The war that crystallized the ambivalence about arming slaves most acutely was the Seven Years' War, or the French and Indian War. Fred Anderson has described this war as "the most important event to occur in eighteenth-century North America." It was, of course, a world war — a great war for empire — in the limited sense applicable to eighteenth-century warfare. Viewed from places outside the thirteen mainland colonies, Anderson claims, "the Seven Years' War was far more significant than the War of American Independence." In North America, black enlistments were uncommon and slave enlistments rare. Only a handful of the twelve hundred provincial troops in Virginia in 1756 and 1757 were black or mulatto. Especially in the plantation regions of North America, white leaders were more concerned about a possible slave rebellion than about French and Indians on the frontier. In Virginia the priorities were evident in the military appropriation for 1756: more than half went to the militia, the agency for controlling slaves, and less than half to the Virginia Regiment, in charge of defending the frontier. In the same year, Charles Pinckney argued that South Carolina's militia could not be relied on to perform any duty except keeping slaves in order.[15]

In the Caribbean, the ambivalence about arming slaves was most acute because there the need for armed slaves was all the more imperative. The Seven Years' War in the Caribbean was most notable for the arming of independent ad hoc black corps for service abroad. There were precedents, as in Vernon's expeditions, but now the greater scale of the conflict necessitated a greater involvement of slaves and free blacks. Thus, slaves served under Major-General Peregrine Hopson in the conquest of French Guadeloupe in 1759 and under Major-General Robert Monckton at Martinique in 1761. The expedition against Cuba was an even more massive undertaking in which the importance attached to the black forces is captured by a remark of Commodore Augustus Keppel, second in command of the naval force employed in the attack against Havana: "The more Negroes we have the better." In Cuba after the war, the Spanish military enlarged its use of slaves and created a company of one hundred black slaves to work in the artillery, especially in the ammunition and storage sections. These experiments in free black corps and extensive use of slave enlistments would serve as precedents during the American Revolution.[16]

In summary, some colonial slaves regularly had access to guns, and many slaves, particularly in the Caribbean, frontier, and maritime settings, quite often played a secondary and subordinate role in armed warfare. To stress how much a radical departure arming slaves was from so-called civilized practice, how exceptional a measure it was, does not seem fully to describe the reality of much of slave life in the New World. Arming slaves was a dangerous expedient, but one resorted to frequently.[17]

The ambivalence about arming slaves continued and was accentuated during the American Revolution. No formal British or American policy existed concerning the wisdom of the idea, and for the most part individual commanders and leaders acted independently, depending on local circumstances. Plans to arm slaves were regularly proposed, opposed, and discarded. Yet with no consistent planning, the force of military exigency propelled the idea forward — but more in an erratic zigzag than in any linear way. Nevertheless, by the end of the war, many schemes for making soldiers of slaves had been generated and quite a few tried. That tens of thousands of slaves served as soldiers and sailors throughout North America and the Caribbean during the Revolutionary War was a catalytic event. Never before in this pan-Atlantic world had so many slaves served in such a concentrated period of time, and some were formed into independent black regiments, occasionally with their peers in charge — unprecedented events.

Why did the most ambitious schemes to arm slaves occur during the American Revolutionary War rather than the Seven Years' War? They were both global wars in which Britain faced the combined strength of France and Spain. The difference was that Britain had no foreign allies to share the burden of the war during the American Revolution. It also no longer enjoyed a friendly rapport with the mainland colonists that would allow it to obtain provisions for its army and to support the militia. The expectations of widespread internal support against the patriots proved illusory, and military commanders were slow to exploit those willing to serve in provincial corps of Loyalists. The consequence of this fatal isolation was that the navy was overstretched: the British fleet was inferior to the combined fleets of France, Spain, and Holland.

There were often fewer ships than islands in the eastern Caribbean. These islands were easy prey for the French, beginning with Dominica (1778), St. Vincent (1779), Grenada (1779), St. Kitts (1782), Montserrat (1782), and Nevis (1782). There was little choice but to deploy slaves. Furthermore, slaves necessarily became involved when the main focus of the war in the Americas switched from the North to the plantation colonies in the South and in the Caribbean after 1778.

Even before the outbreak of war, rumors that the idea of arming slaves had found favor in official political circles in England had gained currency. Thus in the fall of 1774 William Draper, who had returned to London from a tour of America, published a pamphlet arguing that the rebellion might be suppressed by proclaiming "Freedom to their Negroes." Arthur Lee, who was then living in London, thought the plan to arm slaves against their masters met "with approbation from ministerial People." By early 1775, similar information had reached America. Thus, in January a letter from England alleging that "the design of [the] administration [is] to pass an act (in case of rupture) declaring all slaves and servants free that would take up arms against the Americans" was read out in a Philadelphia coffee house. A month or so later, General Thomas Gage, then commanding troops in Massachusetts, intimated that South Carolina, with its large black population, was especially vulnerable, grimly predicting that its "rice and indigo will be brought to market by Negroes instead of white people." In March, Edmund Burke openly questioned the wisdom of arming slaves, apparently popular in governmental circles, in the House of Commons. As early as the following month, Lord John Murray Dunmore, governor of Virginia, began publicly threatening to arm slaves. In May North Carolina patriots thought that "there is much Reason to fear . . . that the Slaves may be instigated and encouraged by our inveterate Enemies to an Insurrection." In the following month, Gage contemplated arming slaves, and it took a fellow commander, Lord William Campbell, to advise him against the idea, telling him not to "fall a prey to the Negroes." At about the same time North Carolina governor Josiah Martin's statement that "nothing could justify the design falsely imputed to me of giving encouragement to the negroes, but the actual and declared rebellion of the King's subjects" was interpreted as "publicly avowing the measure of arming the slaves against their masters." In August a Philadelphian received a letter from London informing him that "the Ministry have thoughts of declaring all your negroes free, and to arm them." By the fall, debates in the House of Commons openly discussed schemes to arm slaves, and merchants in London addressed a petition to the king expressing "indignation and horror" at the reports of slaves' being incited to insurrection.[18]

As an indication of the plans that were in the air, in late 1775 Captain John Dalrymple of the Twentieth Regiment proposed a diversion in the southern colonies to aid General William Howe's operations in the North. His plan had three elements: first, an independent corps would be raised in Ireland, commanded by Protestant officers, and sent to aid Lord Dunmore; second, Dunmore himself would recruit a large body of indentured servants and convicts in and around the Chesapeake towns of Baltimore, Annapolis, Alexandria, and Fredericksburg; and, finally, "To these, He may, & indeed should, add the bravest & most ingenious of the black Slaves whom He may find all over the Bay of Chesapeake." African-born blacks, Dalrymple averred, should not be confused with "Virginia or Maryland Black[s] born in those Provinces," for the latter are "full of Intelligence, Fidelity & Courage."[19]

Thus, considered in context, Lord Dunmore's famous proclamation of November 7, 1775, represented the culmination of an existing trend rather than a dramatic departure. Furthermore, it was not a particularly radical statement. It addressed indentured servants as well as slaves, as Dalrymple had suggested, and it targeted only those who were in the hands of rebels and who were willing and able to bear arms. It also had little impact, for it was issued on board ship, and slaves had somehow to traverse land and water to reach the so-called British haven. At best, about eight hundred slaves escaped to Dunmore. Nevertheless, the dramatic symbol of putting together a regiment of escaped slaves — three hundred or so — outfitted in military garb with the inscription "Liberty to Slaves" emblazoned across the breast, was a revolutionary act, although the only action Lord Dunmore's "Ethiopian Regiment" saw was the inglorious rout at Great Bridge. The proclamation itself aroused a firestorm of protest. Contemporaries spoke of being "struck with horror" and of daggers being placed at their throats. "Hell itself could not have vomitted anything more black than this design," wrote one Philadelphian. Some of these reactions may have been exaggerated in order to whip patriots into a frenzy, but the anguish was genuine enough. The furor was of such passionate intensity as to tell British governors and commanders, if they needed telling, that the issue of arming slaves was explosive and likely to call opprobrium down on the head of any advocate.[20]

From the beginning, the Caribbean and the North American theaters were interconnected. Thus, a couple of months after Dunmore's proclamation, Archibald Campbell, lieutenant colonel of the Seventy-first regiment, serving in North America, and a veteran of three campaigns in the West Indies, suggested a more radical step than that taken by the Virginia governor. He proposed that a regiment be formed in the West Indies of fourteen hundred "stout Active Negroes" who would then suppress the revolt in America and, with "much more dreaded and . . . more fatal consequences to the Rebells than the loss of Battle," encourage the desertion of slaves. According to Campbell, the capitulation of Guadeloupe in the Seven Years' War owed more to the desertion of eight hundred French slaves in one morning than to three months of "all our Attacks." Accordingly, he continued, "many Gentleman of Large Estates & property in the different West India Islands . . . expressed their surprise" that the government did not ask them to supply slaves for military service in North America. Nothing came of Campbell's suggestion because it was too radical and it raised the specter of potential retaliation. Reports in English newspapers claimed that American emissaries were encouraging Caribbean slaves to rebel and were providing them with ammunition and guns. Indeed, Silas Deane, America's first agent in Paris, advocated American support for an uprising of the Caribs in St. Vincent and a slave revolt in Jamaica. Such rumors were not theoretical for white West Indians: they thought the great slave rebellion that engulfed Jamaica in the summer of 1776 was directly connected to events in North America. On the British and on the American patriot side, then, arming slaves was a way of undermining the others' war efforts — whether by employing West Indian slaves in North America or by encouraging West Indian slaves to rebel. In each case, the potential dangers outweighed the anticipated benefits.[21]

After Dunmore's actions, British commanders moved back and forth on the idea of arming slaves. In 1776, following his recapture of New York, General Sir William Howe offered protection to all who came within his lines. A year later, through his aide Alexander Innes, he reversed himself, ordering all "Negroes, Mollatoes, and other Improper Persons" discharged from the garrison, so as to put the provincial forces on "the most respectable footing." In 1778 in a widely publicized debate in the House of Commons, Edmund Burke offered a fiery denunciation of the policy of arming slaves, conjuring up specters of murders, rapes, and barbarities of all kinds. Such reservations were cast aside the following year in the wake of the British defeat at Saratoga (1777) and the French entry into the American Revolution (1778). Sir Henry Clinton, in his Philipsburg Proclamation (1779), ignored Burke's warning and offered freedom to rebel-owned slaves, although he resisted the temptation to follow Dunmore in establishing slave regiments. In 1780, anxious that his proclamation was encouraging too many black fugitives to flee to the British lines, Clinton began to reverse the policy. In the following year, as Cornwallis's army moved northward from Charleston to Yorktown, black foraging parties had authority to get provisions, but the British commander was sufficiently nervous about what they might do that he issued orders that they were not to carry firearms under any circumstances. British policy, insofar as there was such a thing, was an untidy sequence of advances and retreats, with no simple forward movement, with respect to the idea of arming slaves.[22]

The actions of the slaves themselves, flocking to British lines and wishing to serve, kept the pressure on the British commanders. Murphy Stiel can stand as one radical example. Having fled slavery in North Carolina in 1776, he joined the Black Pioneers under General Samuel Birch. In August 1781 Stiel, then a sergeant in the Pioneers and living in New York City, recounted how he had repeatedly heard "a Voice like a Man's (but saw no body)," telling him to inform Sir Henry Clinton, commander in chief of British forces, that Clinton and Lord Cornwallis would put an end to the rebellion, and "that the Lord would be on their Side." Stiel told Clinton that he should "Send Word to Genl Washington That he must Surrender himself and his Troops to the King's Army, and that if he did not the wrath of God would fall upon them." If Washington refused, Clinton must say that he would raise "all the Blacks in America to fight against" the Americans. Military experience and evangelical Christianity fused for Stiel to form an apocalyptic vision. What Clinton thought about such a radical proposal can only be imagined.[23]

As the war effort became more critical on the mainland, the British increasingly became willing to embody separate units composed entirely of escaped slaves and thereby to follow Dunmore's and various West Indian precedents. In 1779 the small British garrison at Savannah, under siege, formed a body of two hundred to three hundred "armed" blacks that took part in skirmishes outside British lines. After the siege was lifted, however, Savannah residents sought their disarming, because ostensibly they behaved with "great Insolence." When George Galphin's fortified plantation house, Fort Dreadnought, fell to patriot forces in 1781, the captured garrison consisted of sixty-one slaves, many of them armed, and fourteen armed boatmen. During the British occupation of Charleston in 1781–1782, cavalry units consisting entirely of fugitive slaves patrolled the countryside outside of the city. Black soldiers in South Carolina, one patriot general observed, aroused "the resentment and detestation of every American who possesses common feelings." In early 1782 Dunmore, who was then in Charleston, along with John Cruden, proposed an elaborate scheme to raise ten thousand black soldiers. Cruden reasoned that the slaves who became soldiers would be "only changing one master for another," because they would serve the king forever; also, by recruiting the "most hardy, intrepid, and determined blacks," they would keep the slaves in "good order," and their own military discipline would prevent "cabals, tumults, and even rebellion." Dunmore added that blacks were "not only better fitted for service in this warm climate than white men, but they are also better guides, may be got on much easier terms, and are perfectly attached to our sovereign."

He thought blacks were "as soon disciplined as any set of raw men that I know of," and envisaged blacks as noncommissioned officers. A few months later, an even more desperate General Alexander Leslie thought that putting arms in the hands of blacks would "soon become indispensably necessary" and began doing just that. By the spring of 1782 the British reportedly had about seven hundred African Americans under arms and in uniform, including several mounted troops.[24]

If British policy toward arming slaves meandered, though in increasingly radical directions, patriotic Americans were generally more uniform and consistent in their opposition to the idea. The reason, of course, was that many Americans had a direct stake in slavery. An occasional idealistic voice could be heard, even from the South. Thus in June 1775 a resident of Fredericksburg, Virginia, thought proclaiming freedom to slaves who would join in the defense of America a dangerous but "necessary Measure." The incompatibility of waging a "glorious struggle" for liberty while holding many in slavery was one strand of this anonymous man's argument, but warding off the promises of the British was the other. As the Continental Army took shape in the summer of 1775, opposition to arming slaves mounted. In July 1775 the adjutant general of the American army, Horatio Gates, in an action that predated Howe's order by two years, instructed recruiting officers that they should not enlist any "stroller, negro, or vagabond." And at a council of war later that year, American generals excluded free blacks and slaves from possible reenlistment. Individual states generally followed suit. Gun ownership among blacks also became a ticklish issue. One Committee of Observation in New Jersey in 1776 ordered that all blacks with guns or other weapons turn them in "until the present troubles are settled." When in August 1776 a former member of Congress from New Jersey drafted a plan for creating a battalion of slaves — arguing that "Neither the Hue of their Complexion nor the Blood of Africk have any Connection with Cowardice" but offering reassurance that he would always restrict "their Numbers, so as not to suffer them to bear any large Proportion to the whites" — John Adams responded that "Your Negro Battallion will never do. S. Carolina would run out of their Wits at the least Hint of such a Measure."[25]

Once, however, Congress began to fix troop quotas for the states, from 1777 onward, the pressure to enlist blacks mounted. Northern states with small black populations found it easier to arm slaves than did southern states. Occasional ambitious proposals surfaced, although they bore no immediate fruit. In 1777 in Philadelphia, one "Antibiastes" argued that a "general emancipation of the Slaves, enlisted in the army or the navy ought immediately to take place," with compensation for their masters. Thomas Kench, an artillery captain who in 1778 proposed a detachment of ninety-five black soldiers (eleven of whom would have specialized roles) to be overseen by five white officers, was rebuffed by the Massachusetts Legislature. Kench thought such a separate regiment would act as an incentive for blacks "to outdo the white men." Similarly, when the Rhode Island legislature debated and eventually passed a slave enlistment act, some objected to slaves' defending the liberties of America. The First Rhode Island Regiment was, in reality, composed of not only slaves but also of free blacks, mulattoes, and Narragansett Indians. A recent study has found more than 700 black Rhode Island soldiers, of whom 142 were enslaved at the time they were enlisted; most served between 1777 and 1780. As Benjamin Quarles notes, the New England states probably furnished more black soldiers than any other region. Of southern states, Maryland came closest to authorizing the arming of slaves. In 1780 the legislature seemed on the verge of passing a proposal to raise a regiment of 750 slaves. Major Edward Giles of Maryland was enthusiastic about "raising a black Regiment," believing that "the Blacks will make excellent Soldiers." Experience proved their worthiness, he said, and opponents were "forever frightening themselves with Bugbears of their own Creation." But the bill did not pass. Charles Carroll of Carrollton, who disliked it, offers insights into why it failed: he thought the compensation inadequate, spoke darkly of his fear of "bad consequences," and described it as a "harsh and violent" measure, unfair and "oppressive" because it applied only to slaveowners with six or more slaves and took away a person's property.[26] The refusal of the political leaders of the Upper South, where many did open their hearts to the idealism of the Revolution, to consider the enlistment of slaves indicates the hurdles the idea faced.

The fate of the congressional recommendation of March 1779 that South Carolina and Georgia raise three thousand slaves is even more instructive. The planters of the Lower South were horrified. Christopher Gadsden's reaction was typical: resentment and disgust ran high, he said, at this "very dangerous and impolitic Step." The South Carolina Council was so irked that it considered making the state neutral and dropping out of the war effort. John Laurens, an ardent but rather solitary proponent of arming slaves in the Lower South, railed at the "howlings of a triple-headed monster in which prejudice Avarice & pusillanimity were united." The younger Laurens's dream of black troops wearing white uniforms, faced with red, because they would "form a good Contrast with the Complexion of the Soldier" remained simply that — nothing but a dream. Furthermore, when in December 1781 General Nathanael Greene recommended that South Carolina recruit at least two thousand slaves and form four black regiments, each with a corps of Pioneers and a corps of Artificers, he encountered a frosty response — "old prejudices and the love of interest" was his indictment — even though he had "not the least doubt" that "they would make good Soldiers." As the legislature debated Greene's proposal, one South Carolinian acknowledged that he was "very much alarmed" on "the Subject of arming the Blacks" and reckoned that only about a dozen assemblymen were in favor and a hundred opposed. He hoped that its defeat would "rest for ever & a day."[27]

The onset of the American Revolutionary War in the Caribbean did not initially occasion anything as dramatic as Dunmore's proclamation, but it did create a demand for more black sailors, some use of free blacks to build fortifications, and a heightened sense of insecurity. The insecurity owed much to the famines that began sweeping the islands because of curtailed commerce and the movement of some British troops from islands to mainland, which in turn helps account for the Jamaican slave insurrection of 1776. Insecurity became panic with the entry of France and then Spain into the war in 1778–1779. The West Indian islands were imperiled by foreign invasion as never before. Once Dominica capitulated in September 1778 to a French expeditionary force, the recruitment of slaves intensified. Governor William Burt of the Leeward Islands conscripted 5 percent of the slaves of St. Kitts to build fortifications, and, in the event of an invasion, he planned to organize slaves into armed parties to act as foragers and attack the enemy at night. Also in the fall of 1778, the British abandoned Philadelphia primarily to free five thousand troops for the invasion of St. Lucia, the gateway to French Martinique, the headquarters of the French navy. Once St. Lucia fell, slaves built all the defenses that the British required. Slaves were gradually being drawn into greater involvement in the Caribbean war effort.[28]

In these early years, whites found free blacks more acceptable as soldiers than as slaves. In the fall of 1778, in response to the heightened French threat, a Jamaican creole, soon joined by others, proposed a professional regiment of free blacks and free coloreds, an extension of separate companies within the militia that had been noted for their "extraordinary alertness in Military manoeuvres." These Jamaican whites argued that a corps of native-born mulattoes would be able to withstand the labor and marching that proved so arduous for Europeans. The entry of France into the war also saw Caribbean free blacks arriving in North America. In 1779 Admiral Charles d'Estaing set sail from Saint Domingue with an expeditionary force that included 545 free black and free colored volunteers. They played a minor role — seemingly doing little more than digging trenches, although one died and seven were wounded defending their handiwork — in the failed two-month siege of Savannah. D'Estaing did learn that his "black soldiers from Saint Domingue" were abstemious, for they "would not drink the mixture of sugar, water and fermented molasses which make up the nectar the Americans call grog"; by contrast, he sadly noted, "it was wine for most of our officers and all our soldiers." One company of 62 free blacks and free coloreds escorted casualties to Charleston and was the sole French troop serving during the siege of that city in the spring of 1780.[29]

Even as insecurity heightened, opposition to the arming of slaves and free blacks was still formidable in the Caribbean, as Stephen Fuller, the agent for Jamaica, emphatically made clear when acting on behalf of the West India lobby in London. In December 1778 he rebutted the idea that "many of the Domestic Negroes by being Armed might contribute in some degree to" island defense, maintaining that "melancholy experience" had shown that "very little trust can be placed even in such of them as are considered the most confidential." The best policy, he averred, was to keep slaves "disarmed, and to remove them from every opportunity of using firearms." Arming them promised "relief for the present" but was "pregnant with future evils"; the "Hoe & the Pick-axe" were the only fit instruments for slaves. Furthermore, he argued that only nine hundred "sencible" free black men inhabited Jamaica, and dependence might be placed on at most five hundred. He warned that "the free negroes & mulattoes are not to be trusted in corps composed of themselves only, & the incorporating of them with the whites will not be endured."[30]

Continuing threats of invasion and actual invasions largely trumped the fears of Fuller and others like him. During the invasion scare of 1779, the Barbados legislature voted to arm slaves, and many, according to William Dickson, "were armed with swords and spears." The following year, Antigua armed one thousand slaves and hired the equivalent of another thousand for pioneering work. When the French invaded particular islands, the slaves often put up fierce resistance. In 1781, during the French invasion of Tobago, a corps of armed slaves served with "undaunted courage" against French regulars. In 1782 one observer on St. Kitts thought that "there were as many Frenchmen killed by negroes, only for coming onto the estates they belonged to, as were destroyed by all the troops we had to defend the Island." These slave irregulars almost managed to ambush and capture the enemy commander-in-chief, and the French threatened to lay waste to the island if their masters did not bring them to heel. In the same year, Jamaica conscripted more than five thousand slaves during the period of martial law, and the governor began compiling lists of all slaves "who have distinguished themselves for their attachment & fidelity to their masters, for their knowledge of the country, the woods, and use of arms." Nevertheless, the legislature rejected his proposal to arm trusted slaves with guns and bills as "an expedient of too dangerous a nature to adopt." Still,

Governor Campbell managed to persuade the legislature to permit the creation of two regiments of free blacks and free coloreds. Three years earlier the island had seen the temporary, ad hoc creation of a regiment of free colored people that was part of a professional force, salaried, well equipped, and under army discipline, but now the legislature agreed to fund the plan, and soon a third regiment was formed. The most novel military developments in the deployment of blacks occurred in British-occupied St. Lucia, in part because of its strategic importance overlooking Martinique, but also because the military commanders did not have to consult with planters or an elected legislature. There Brigadier General Edward Mathew gathered slaves from many places and assembled the core of the first permanent black army regiment in the British West Indies.[31]

A key reason for the novel deployment of blacks in the Caribbean was the high attrition rate of white troops. The British lost more than 5,000 troops during their brief occupation of Havana in 1762–63, exceeding their total losses in North America throughout the Seven Years' War. During the Revolutionary War, 11 percent of European soldiers died aboard troop transports en route to the Caribbean. The annual mortality rate of soldiers, once in the region, was 15 percent, compared to 6 percent of those stationed in New York and 1 percent in Canada. The losses in the West Indies accounted for about 6,000 men, more than half the deaths in North America, estimated at about 10,000. Of the 1,008 men of the Seventy-ninth Regiment stationed in Kingston, Jamaica, in 1778, "scarcely a man remained of the original number" twelve months later. The high mortality rates among white troops had strategic consequences including the British decision to abandon San Juan (seized in an expedition conducted by Governor John Dalling against Spanish Central America in the fall of 1779) only seven months after its capture, owing to the deaths of more than three-quarters of the force, caused primarily by disease. Mutinies and desertion were also more common among troops going to the West Indies than to other regions. Punishments in the West Indies exceeded all those in other postings, an indication of the greater indiscipline present among troops in the region.[32]

During the war and the early postwar period, whites drew attention to the healthiness of blacks. As John Hunter noted, "The Negroes afford a striking example of the power acquired by habit of resisting the causes of fevers; for, though they are not entirely exempted from them, they suffer infinitely less than Europeans." He pointed in particular to "the negroes who were sent along with the troops against Fort St. Juan, of whom scarcely any died, although few or none of the soldiers survived the expedition." Similarly, in 1783, Thomas Dancer noted that the three hundred to four hundred slaves brought to Jamaica by John McGillivray, a provincial colonel, from Georgia and employed on public fortifications were "in the highest state of health during the[ir] hard labour." Five years later, Hunter argued that blacks were not only useful as pioneers and servants, saving white soldiers "from certain duties of fatigue," but should be employed as soldiers, with black and European troops "intermixed," so as to "save the European troops from such parts of regimental duty as may be injurious to their health."[33]

In the Caribbean in particular in the later years of the Revolutionary War, slaves and free blacks played a major role at sea as well as on land. The desperation of the navy for manpower brought black recruits, both slave and free, onto British warships. In 1783 the Antiguan legislature complained of the "desertion of their slaves and generally their most valuable slaves who have been taken away from English Harbour in his Majesty's ships." Seamen apparently blocked planters from boarding naval vessels to recover their runaways. During the Revolutionary War, John Perkins, a colored man, rose from piloting the flagship of the Jamaica Squadron to commanding a schooner tender and then to being lieutenant in command of a man-of-war. He would command frigates in the French Revolutionary Wars and eventually die in Kingston. He was the only British naval officer to spend his entire career on one station, without ever visiting England. Privateers also increasingly employed blacks. In 1779 a Dutch sloop trading between Curaçao and Hispaniola had a number of blacks on board; when captured by an English privateer, the Dutch captain declared that the blacks were all free men, willingly acting as crew. The captain of the English privateer took a number of these same black men as crew members, promising them a share of any prize money won on the way with their help.[34]

In 1782 a United States naval vessel took a Bermudian privateer as its prize in Carolina waters. Only five members of the seventy-five-man crew were white, all officers; the sailors were all black slaves. At the ensuing vice admiralty court trial, the Massachusetts justices broke with precedent and offered the slaves their freedom rather than consider them forfeited chattel to be sold at auction. To a man, the Bermudian blacks declined the offer and asked instead to be sent to their island home on the next flag-of-truce; rather than embrace the freedom offered to them by the new republic, they chose to return to Bermuda and slavery. They chose to return to the island of their birth, their families, and, by comparison with most slaves and some freedmen, a profitable way of life to which they were accustomed. They did not go empty-handed. Sixty of them took passage on an American flag-of-truce ship bound for New York. Off Cape Cod, they shouted "Huzzah for Bermuda!" and rose up with other prisoners on board to seize the vessel. On reaching Bermuda, the ship was condemned as their prize. Such were the possibilities and ambiguities of arming slaves.[35]

The American Revolutionary War considerably expanded the opportunities for New World slaves to serve with arms on land or at sea. Britain became increasingly desperate for manpower as it faced the possibility of a defeat that might entail not only the loss of America but the entire British Empire. Its very future as a global power was at stake. Britain simultaneously faced the danger of rebellion in Ireland, the threat of a foreign invasion in the summer of 1779, and domestic revolution with the Gordon Riots in London in 1780. It became more difficult to recruit at home owing to financial constraints and to the reluctance of men to enlist. Lord George Germain, the secretary of state for America, was willing to consider almost any source of manpower including unprecedented numbers of Irish Catholics, traditionally debarred from service in the British army owing to the Test Acts, and even American prisoners of war from South Carolina.[36] Thus, not only was the geographic scope wider, but qualitatively the arming of slaves assumed new dimensions — first the raising of ad hoc, all-black regiments, then the openness to black noncommissioned officers, and finally the embryonic emergence of permanent black garrisons. Furthermore, the scale was greater than ever before. By the end of the war, some British planners envisaged recruiting as many as ten thousand black soldiers in particular places. Overall, perhaps about thirty thousand blacks, some free but most slaves, served during the American Revolutionary War, admittedly more as pioneers, auxiliaries, and domestics than in an army capacity. Still, in North America, about five thousand black Americans served in the Continental Army, another thousand or so in the navy and on privateers, and perhaps twelve thousand on land and at sea on the British side. In the Caribbean, at least twelve thousand blacks served on both land and sea.[37]

But these numbers must be put in perspective. The Revolutionary War saw a significant use of slaves as soldiers and auxiliaries, but as a proportion of the total war effort, they were always a minor component. The six thousand or so African Americans who served in the Continental Army and in the patriot forces at sea represented less than 3 percent of total patriot mobilization, including state militias, although in 1778, when it is possible to identify the black presence in individual regiments of the Continental Army, it ranged from 6 to 13 percent. About half a million Britons were under arms in the course of the conflict, representing about one in seven or eight of the 3.8 million eligible British men (this proportion was greater than in the Seven Years' War, in which the military participation rate was about one in nine or ten, but less than in the Napoleonic Wars, when it was about one in four or five). The Hessian troops numbered about thirty thousand overall and the Loyalist troops another twenty thousand or so; therefore, the roughly twenty-four thousand slaves serving on the British side represented about 4 percent of the whole British war effort. Their numbers were impressive, however, in relation to the size of the British army (including Hessians and Provincials) specifically assigned to the West Indies or to North America, which amounted to slightly more than forty-four thousand men in July 1779, together with another seventy-five hundred in Canada.[38]

The United States did not arm slaves on a similar scale until the Civil War, but the situation was radically different in the Caribbean, where the British evacuation of slave soldiers in the southern states led to the establishment of the first permanent peacetime army garrisons composed of slaves, the South Carolina Corps. They in turn formed the embryo of the largest European slave army in the Americas, the West India Regiments, which began with two regiments in 1795 and reached their full complement of twelve by 1798. Ironically, during the period 1795–1808, the British government became the biggest individual customer for African slaves, buying about one in ten of those imported into the islands to serve in its army. The successful use of slave soldiers in the American Revolution helps explain the willingness of the imperial government to repeat the experiment on a more massive scale during the French Revolutionary Wars. Of course, France's militarization of its black population was part of the inspiration, as was Britain's own Indian precedent, its native, or *sepoy*, regiments. Yet Sir John Vaughan, who championed and implemented this scheme to recruit thousands of slaves into standard regiments, was present at General Monckton's conquest of Martinique in 1761–62, in which slaves were used as auxiliaries, and, more important, he had served as commander-in-chief in the Eastern Caribbean during the American Revolution (1779–1781). He was convinced that war in the Caribbean could be prosecuted only by "opposing Blacks to Blacks."[39]

At the end of the Revolutionary War, a diaspora of black soldiers and sailors, their military experiences seared into their minds, scattered throughout the Atlantic world. Perhaps the most unlikely destination was Brunswick, Germany, which in the summer of 1783 witnessed the arrival of a "negro drum-corps brought from America by General Riedesel." After the British evacuation of Georgia, some black troops calling themselves "The King of England's soldiers" decamped to the Savannah River swamps, where they waged guerilla warfare for at least another five years against their ex-masters. In 1783 slaves armed with cutlasses, clubs, and pikes left St. Augustine, Florida, with Colonel Andrew Deveaux's band of Loyalist irregulars to wrest Nassau, Bahamas, from the Spaniards. Perhaps some of them were responsible for plundering whites on the island of Abaco "with Muskets and fix'd Bayonets" four years later. With echoes to his past, Lord Dunmore, the governor of the Bahamas, issued a proclamation of amnesty for all fugitive slaves who would surrender themselves. In 1793, in response to the French threat, a former East Florida Loyalist, Denys Rolle, argued that slaves of his in Exuma should be armed and go on patrols, since they would defend their master's land as if it were their own. Of the black exodus to Nova Scotia about a third or more had been enrolled in British armies, and many lived in towns such as Birchtown, named after their military commanders. When in 1794 Governor Zachary Macaulay reorganized the militia in Sierra Leone, a place peopled by black Nova Scotians and London's black poor, he allowed each company of thirty-five men to elect its own captain, lieutenant, and three sergeants. As a result, black officers sometimes commanded white troops, and, when some European officials protested, Macaulay pointed to their proven military experience in the American War. The black Nova Scotians named three streets in Freetown, Sierra Leone, after generals — Tarleton, Rawdon, and Howe — with whom they had served in the Revolutionary War.[40]

African Americans who had served on the patriot side during the Revolutionary War were also proud of their accomplishments. Latchom, a Virginia slave, gained his freedom for saving General John Cropper when he was stuck in a marsh and about to be bayoneted; Latchom shot Cropper's British assailant and then carried the general to safety, though he weighed about two hundred pounds. Cropper purchased Latchom's freedom. In Connecticut the Superior Court liberated Jack Arabas, who had enlisted in the army with his master's consent, served three years, found himself reclaimed by his master, and then successfully sued for his freedom. Service at sea offered greater opportunity for North American blacks than action on land. For this reason, no doubt, James Forten volunteered as a privateer, and when, in 1781, he was captured and offered English freedom rather than imprisonment on the prison hulk *Jersey,* he rejected the offer, insisting, "I have been taken prisoner for the liberties of my country, and never will prove a traitor to her interest." Applying for a Revolutionary War pension in 1836, Jehu Grant, at least eighty years of age, who escaped from a Tory master in Rhode Island and served ten months "in the American army of the Revolutionary War," spoke of "the songs of liberty that saluted my ear, [and] thrilled through my heart." Military experiences changed the lives of many individual African Americans.[41]

The use of slave troops helped undermine the slave regime in both subtle and overt ways, as many planters had feared. The British often did not make good their promises of freedom to slaves who left their patriot masters, but they were nevertheless forced to manumit many slaves, particularly those who had fought on the British side, resulting in a large rise in the number of free blacks in London, Nova Scotia, and Sierra Leone. The use of slave troops exposed the contradictions within slavery. It demonstrated that slaves were indeed capable of the courage and honor that the plantation regime sought to deny. The confidence and skills derived by the slaves is a matter of speculation, in the absence of any written accounts by veterans, but among the "trusted" slave soldiers from St. Domingue (Haiti) who served in the French siege of Savannah (1779) were many future heroes of the Haitian Revolution. Granville Sharpe also thought that stolen and reenslaved Sierra Leonians, "hardened fellows by Service on board the English Man of War; & in the British Army in America," played a major role in the St. Domingue slave revolt of 1791. Arming slaves, as Dr. George Pinckard, a regimental surgeon in Barbados, recognized, would "instruct them that they are men."[42]

Notes

We wish to thank Christopher Brown, Philip Boucher, Stephen Conway, David Eltis, Jillian Galle, Ronald Hoffman, Michael Jarvis, Wim Klooster, Paul E. Kooperman, Cassandra Pybus, and Louis Wilson for their assistance.

1. The best studies are Benjamin Quarles, *The Negro in the American Revolution* (Chapel Hill, 1961), and Sylvia Frey, *Water from the Rock: Black Resistance in a Revolutionary Age* (Princeton, N.J., 1991).

2. WIC directors to Governor Joan Doncker, November 13, 1676, Niuewe West-Indische Compagnie 467, fol. 19, Algemeen Rijksarchief, The Hague (thanks to Wim Klooster for this reference); John Thornton, "The Coromantees: An African Cultural Group in Colonial North America and the Caribbean," *Journal of Caribbean History* 32:1–2 (1998): 161–178; John K. Thornton, "War, the State, and Religious Norms in 'Coromantee' Thought: The Ideology of an African American Nation," in Robert Blair St. George, ed., *Possible Pasts: Becoming Colonial in Early America* (Ithaca, N.Y., 2000), 181–200; Monica Shuler, "Akan Slave Rebellions in the British Caribbean," *Savacou* 1 (1970): 8–31; Ray A. Kea, " 'When I die, I shall return to my own land': An 'Anima' Slave Rebellion in the Danish West Indies, 1733–1734," in John Hunwick and Nancy Lawler, eds., *The Cloth of Many Colored Silks: Papers on History and Society, Ghanaian and Islamic, in Honor of Ivor Wilks* (Evanston, 1996), 159–193. For other discussions of the slaves' African military background, see other work by John K. Thornton: "African Dimensions of the Stono Rebellion," *American Historical Review* 96 (1991): 1101–1113; *Africa and Africans in the Making of the Atlantic World, 1400–1800* (New York, 1998), 280, 293–298, 306, 309; "African Soldiers in the Haitian Revolution," *Journal of Caribbean History* 25 (1991): 58–80; "The African Experience of the '20. And Odd Negroes' Arriving in Virginia in 1619," *William and Mary Quarterly*, 3rd ser., 55 (1998): 421–434; and *Warfare in Atlantic Africa, 1500–1800* (London, 1999).

3. Quarles, *Negro in the American Revolution*, 13–14; Orlando Patterson, *Slavery and Social Death: A Comparative Study* (Cambridge, Mass., 1982), 288–293, 308–314;

David Brion Davis, *The Problem of Slavery in the Age of Revolution, 1770–1823* (Ithaca, N.Y., 1975), 73–76.

4. Andrew Jackson O'Shaughnessy, *An Empire Divided: The American Revolution and the British Caribbean* (Philadelphia, 2000), 153; Woody Holton, *Forced Founders: Indians, Debtors, Slaves, and the Making of the American Revolution in Virginia* (Chapel Hill, 1999).

5. Piers Mackesy, *The War for America, 1775–1783* (Cambridge, Mass., 1964), 518.

6. Jerome S. Handler, "Freedmen and Slaves in the Barbados Militia," *Journal of Caribbean History* 19:1 (May 1984): 7–8; Michael A. Bellesiles, *Arming America: The Origins of a National Gun Culture* (New York, 2000), 72, 75, 76; William W. Hening, *The Statutes at Large: Being a Collection of All the Laws of Virginia*, 13 vols. (Philadelphia, 1810–1823), 2:481; David Barry Gaspar, *Bondmen and Rebels: A Study of Master-Slave Relations in Antigua with Implications for Colonial British America* (Baltimore, 1985), 139; Elsa V. Goveia, *The West Indian Slave Laws of the 18th Century* (Barbados, 1970), 18, 40, 45, 46. For other laws restricting the giving of guns to slaves, see Marvin L. Michael Kay and Lorin Lee Cary, *Slavery in North Carolina, 1748–1775* (Chapel Hill, 1995), 68; Elsa V. Goveia, *Slave Society in the British Leeward Islands at the End of the Eighteenth Century* (New Haven, Conn., 1965), 156; Peter M. Voelz, *Slave and Soldier: The Military Impact of Blacks in the Colonial Americas* (New York, 1993), 353–357.

7. Bellesiles, *Arming America*, 97.

8. Karen Ordahl Kupperman, *Providence Island, 1630–1641: The Other Puritan Colony* (New York, 1993), 289 (for the quotation); Thornton, *Africa and Africans*, 279; Graham Russell Hodges, *Root and Branch: African Americans in New York and East Jersey* (Chapel Hill, N.C., 1999), 12. Also see Voelz, *Slave and Soldier*, 23; Jane Landers, *Black Society in Spanish Florida* (Urbana, Ill., 2000), 22, 29–60, 202–228; Herbert S. Klein, "The Colored Militia of Cuba: 1568–1868," *Caribbean Studies* 6 (1966): 17–27; Gerret Specht to the WIC, January 21, 1767, NWIC 318, Algemeen Rijksarchief (The Hague) (thanks to Wim Klooster, for this reference); Allison Blakely, *Blacks in the Dutch World: The Evolution of Racial Imagery in a Modern Society* (Bloomington, Ind., 1993), 237–240. For arming free blacks or coloreds, see Allan J. Keuthe, "The Status of the Free Pardo in the Disciplined Militia of New Granada," *Journal of Negro History* 56 (1971): 105–117; Jackie R. Booker, "Needed but Unwanted: Black Militiamen in Veracruz, Mexico, 1760–1810," *Historian* 55 (Winter 1993): 259–276; Joseph P. Sanchez, "African Freedmen and the Fuero Militar: A Historical Overview of Pardo and Moreno Militiamen in the Late Spanish Empire," *Colonial Latin American Historical Review* 3 (1994): 165–184; Ben Vinson III, "Free Colored Voices: Issues of Representation and Racial Identity in the Colonial Mexican Militia," *Journal of Negro History* 80 (1995): 170–182; Stewart R. King, *Blue Coat or Powdered Wig: Free People of Color in Pre-Revolutionary Saint Domingue* (Athens, Ga., 2001), esp. 52–77, 226–265; and Ben Vinson III, *Bearing Arms for His Majesty: The Free-Colored Militia in Colonial Mexico* (Stanford, 2001).

9. Handler, "Freedmen and Slaves," *Journal of Caribbean History* 19:1 (1984): 8–9, 11, 13, 17; Gaspar, *Bondmen and Rebels*, 118–122; Governor Benjamin Bennett to William Popple, January 12, 1702, and Bennett to the Council of Trade and Plantations,

August 19, 1702, *Calendar of State Papers, Colonial Series* (London 2000), vol. 20, no. 25, and vol. 21, no. 1014; Shelby T. McCloy, *The Negro in the French West Indies* (Lexington, Ky., 1966), 53, 55; Clarence J. Munford, *The Black Ordeal of Slavery and Slave Trading in the French West Indies, 1625–1715,* 3 vols. (Lewiston, N.Y., 1991), 3:752, 754.

10. Richard Harding, *Amphibious Warfare in the Eighteenth Century: The British Expedition to the West Indies, 1740–1742* (London, 1991), 74, 91, 130, 133, 143, 168–169; David Syrett, "The Raising of American Troops for Service in the West Indies During the War of Austrian Succession, 1740–1," *Bulletin of the Institute of Historical Research* 73 (2000): 20–32; Richard Pares, *War and Trade in the West Indies, 1739–1763* (Oxford, 1936), 254. See also John R. McNeill, "The Ecological Basis of Warfare in the Caribbean, 1700–1804," in Maarten Ultee, ed., *Adapting to Conditions: War and Society in the Eighteenth Century* (University, Ala., 1986), 26–42.

11. In general, see Hening, ed., *Statutes at Large,* 1:226, 251, 336, 3:251, 336, 4:119, 5:17, 6:533, 7:95; Benjamin Quarles, "The Colonial Militia and Negro Manpower," *Mississippi Valley Historical Review* 45 (1959): 643–652, esp. 644–645; William M. Wiecek, "The Statutory Law of Slavery and Race in the Thirteen Mainland Colonies of British America," *William and Mary Quarterly,* 3rd ser., 35 (1977), 258–280, esp. 268; Bellesiles, *Arming America,* 76. For the Carolinas, see Thomas Cooper and David J. McCord, eds., *The Statutes at Large of South Carolina,* 10 vols. (Columbia, S.C., 1836–41), 7:33, 347–349, 349–351, 3:108–110, 9:645–663; Peter H. Wood, *Black Majority: Negroes in Colonial South Carolina from 1670 Through the Stono Rebellion* (New York, 1974), 126–128; William L. Saunders, ed., *The Colonial Records of North Carolina,* 10 vols. (Raleigh, N.C., 1886–1890), 2:178, 254; John Tate Lanning, ed., *The St. Augustine Expedition of 1740* (Columbia, S.C., 1954), 11–12, 17, 25, 62, 72, 73, 85, 93, 96–97, 98–99, 102, 114, 126, 129–130, 132, 148, 169, 173 (the actual number of slaves used as pioneers in this expedition is never specified); Rodney E. Baine, "General James Oglethorpe and the Expedition Against St. Augustine," *Georgia Historical Quarterly* 84 (2000): 197–229 (which says little about black participation); John R. Alden, *John Stuart and the Southern Colonial Frontier: A Study of Indian Relations, War, Trade, and Land Problems in the Southern Wilderness, 1754–1775* (Ann Arbor, Mich., 1944), 113–114; William Bull to Earl of Hillsborough, November 30, 1770, in K. G. Davies, ed., *Documents of the American Revolution, 1770–1783* (Shannon, Ireland, 1972), 2:273.

12. For the slave trade and the African coast, see K. G. Davies, *The Royal African Company* (London, 1957), 227; David Eltis, *The Rise of African Slavery in the Americas* (Cambridge, U.K., 2000), 148, 226, 228–229, 231, 233, 250; Robin Law, "Warfare on the West African Slave Coast, 1650–1850," in R. Brian Ferguson and Neil L. Whitehead, eds., *War in the Tribal Zone: Expanding States and Indigenous Warfare* (Santa Fe, N.M., 1992), 103–126, esp. 109, 115–116; E. Arnot Robertson, *The Spanish Town Papers: Some Sidelights on the American War of Independence* (New York, 1959), 131. For other vessels, see Hodges, *Root and Branch,* 6–7; Landers, *Black Society in Spanish Florida,* 21; W. Jeffrey Bolster, *Black Jacks: African American Seamen in the Age of Sail* (Cambridge, Mass., 1997), 13–15; Peter Linebaugh and Marcus Rediker, *The Many-Headed Hydra: Sailors, Slaves, Commoners, and the Hidden History of the Revolutionary Atlantic* (Boston, 2000), 166; David J. Starkey, *British Privateering Enterprise in the Eighteenth*

Century (Exeter, Eng., 1990), esp. 262; Carl E. Swanson, *Predators and Prizes: American Privateering and Imperial Warfare, 1739–1748* (Columbia, S.C., 1991), 127; N. A. M. Rodger, *The Wooden World: An Anatomy of the Georgian Navy* (London, 1986), 159–160; Nicholas Rogers, "Archipelagic Encounters: War, Race, and Labour Along the Caribbean Frontier, 1740–1750" (unpublished paper). For individual masters, see Philip D. Morgan, *Slave Counterpoint: Black Culture in the Eighteenth-Century Chesapeake and Lowcountry* (Chapel Hill, N.C., 1998), 390–391; Betty Wood, *Slavery in Colonial Georgia, 1730–1775* (Athens, Ga., 1984), 123; Handler, "Freedmen and Slaves," 15; Holton, *Forced Founders*, xiii–xv; B. W. Higman, *Montpelier, Jamaica: A Plantation Community in Slavery and Freedom, 1739–1912* (Mona, Jamaica, 1998), 101–102; Kay and Cary, *Slavery in North Carolina*, 329–330 n. 58. For frontier regions, see Hening, *Statutes at Large*, 3:459; 4:131; 12:182; Quarles, "Colonial Militia," *Mississippi Valley Historical Review* 45 (1959): 648; Wood, *Slavery in Colonial Georgia*, 117; O. Nigel Bolland, *The Formation of a Colonial Society: Belize, from Conquest to Crown Colony* (Baltimore, 1977), 30, 73–77, 84; Carl J. Ekberg, *Colonial Ste. Genevieve: An Adventure on the Mississippi Frontier* (Tucson, 1996), 348–349; Edward Rutledge Jr. to John Rutledge, April 8, 1788, Rutledge Papers, University of North Carolina at Chapel Hill; Douglas V. Armstrong, *The Old Village and the Great House: An Archaeological and Historical Examination of Drax Hall Plantation, St. Ann's Bay, Jamaica* (Urbana, Ill., 1990), 177.

13. Morgan, *Slave Counterpoint*, 139, 330, 390–391; Wood, *Slavery in Colonial Georgia*, 185; Higman, *Montpelier*, 216; Armstrong, *Old Village*, 175; Betty Wood, *Women's Work, Men's Work: The Informal Slave Economies of Lowcountry Georgia* (Athens, 1995), 45. We are grateful to Jillian Galle of the Thomas Jefferson Memorial Foundation, who, along with Fraser Neiman, is coordinating a major comparative study of slave sites in Virginia and who provided detailed information about five sites where there is evidence of much lead shot (eighty-seven pieces at one dwelling on Mulberry Row, Monticello, for instance), gunflints, gun barrel parts, gunlock parts, trigger guards, pistol barrels, and so on. For example, at the Clifts plantation, 1720–1735, forty-seven pieces of shot, one gunflint, ninety-six flint debitages, one trigger guard, one pistol barrel, and one cock were found.

14. Kupperman, *Providence Island*, 170 n. 72, 291, 338; Richard S. Dunn, *Sugar and Slaves: The Rise of the Planter Class in the English West Indies, 1624–1713* (Chapel Hill, N.C., 1972), 144, 259; Landers, *Black Society in Spanish Florida*, 38; Gaspar, *Bondmen and Rebels*, 119; Pares, *War and Trade*, 253, 255; State of the Island of Tobago, June 24 to May 1, 1773, CO 101/17, folio 181, Public Record Office, London.

15. Fred Anderson, *Crucible of War: The Seven Years' War and the Fate of Empire in British North America, 1754–1766* (New York, 2000), xv, 160; James Titus, *The Old Dominion at War: Society, Politics, and Warfare in Late Colonial Virginia* (Columbia, S.C., 1991), 78–88; John Ferling, "Soldiers for Virginia: Who Served in the French and Indian War?" *Virginia Magazine of History and Biography* 94 (1986): 307–328; Bellesiles, *Arming America*, 151. For other colonies' practices, see Walter Clark, ed., *State Records of North Carolina*, 26 vols. (Winston, N.C., 1895–1914), 22:370–380; New York Historical Society, *Collections* 24 (1892), 61, 71, 73, 183, 287, 365, 385, 387, 399, 403, 407, 419, 421, 427, 429, 441, 443; Connecticut Historical Society, *Collections* 9

(1903), 15, 37, 38, 53, 101, 103, 123, 141, 160, 169, 170, 172, 182, 211, 215, 226; and Harold E. Selesky, *War and Society in Colonial Connecticut* (New Haven, 1990), 168, 174, 175.

16. Marshall Smelser, *The Campaign for the Sugar Islands, 1759: A Study of Amphibious Warfare* (Chapel Hill, N.C., 1955), 37, 52, 98 (Moore's proposal); David Syrett, *The Siege and Capture of Havana, 1762* (London, 1970), xiv, xviii, 21–22 (Egremont), 38, 94, 100, 107, 137, 195 (Keppel), 210, 259, 324; Daniel E. Walker, "Colony versus Crown: Raising Black Troops for the British Siege on Havana, 1762," *Journal of Caribbean History* 33:1–2 (1999): 74–83; Klein, "Colored Militia of Cuba," 20.

17. Frey, *Water from the Rock*, 70.

18. William Draper, *The Thoughts of a Traveller upon Our American Disputes* (London, 1774), 21; Arthur Lee to Richard Henry Lee, December 6, 1774, Lee Family Papers, as cited in Holton, *Forced Founders*, 140. See also Charles W. Carey Jr., " 'These Black Rascals': The Origins of Lord Dunmore's Ethiopian Regiment," *Virginia Social Science Journal* 31 (1996): 65–77; William Bradford to James Madison, Jan. 4, 1775, in William T. Hutchinson and William M. E. Rachal, eds., *The Papers of James Madison* (Chicago, 1962), 1:132 (also see Madison to Bradford, November 1774, in ibid., 1:129–130 and June 1775, 1:153); Alden, *John Stuart and the Southern Colonial Frontier*, 171n (Gage letter, c. February 1775); Edmund Burke, *Speeches and Letters on American Affairs* (London, 1908), 102; Jon Sensbach, *A Separate Canaan: The Making of an Afro-Moravian World in North Carolina, 1763–1840* (Chapel Hill, N.C., 1998), 88; Quarles, *Negro in the American Revolution*, 21 (Dunmore), 111 (Gage and Campbell); Peter Force, ed., *American Archives*, 4th ser., 3:8 (Martin), 256 (Philadelphian), 1010–1011 (petition), 6:18–30 (debate). See also ibid., 2:42.

19. Captain John Dalrymple, "Project for Strengthening General Howe's Operations in the North by a Diversion in the South without taking off the Troops," 1775?, George Germain Papers, vol. 4, William L. Clements Library, University of Michigan (the proposal is in the 1775 volume and may date to October, when Howe succeeded Gage as the British commander-in-chief). See also Frey, *Water from the Rock*, 68.

20. Still the best study of Dunmore's proclamation is Quarles, *Negro in the American Revolution*, 19–32, but also see Carey, " 'These Black Rascals' "; Holton, *Forced Founders*, 133–163; John E. Selby, *Dunmore* (Williamsburg, 1977), 36–44.

21. Archibald Campbell to George Germain, January 16, 1776, Germain Papers, vol. 4, Clements Library; O'Shaughnessy, *Empire Divided*, 151–153 (Jamaican rebellion), 152 (for newspaper and Deane); Frey, *Water from the Rock*, 69 (Campbell), 71 (Deane), 71–72 (Jamaican rebellion).

22. General Howe's Proclamations, August 23, 1776 and November 30, 1776, 30/55/37, ff. 254 and 334, Public Record Office, Kew, England, as cited in Ellen Gibson Wilson, *The Loyal Blacks* (New York, 1976), 29. For more on the situation in New York, see Graham Russell Hodges, "Black Revolt in New York City and the Neutral Zone: 1775–83," in Paul A. Gilje and William Pencak, eds., *New York in the Age of the Constitution, 1775–1780* (Cranbury, N.J., 1992), 20–47; Hodges, *Root and Branch*, 139–161. The later Clinton reference comes from the King's American Department Orderly Book, Orderly Book Collection, Clements Library (courtesy of Christopher Brown); also see Alexander Innes to Sir Henry Clinton, November 9, 1779, in Alfred E. Jones, ed., "A

Letter Regarding the Queen's Rangers," *Virginia Magazine of History and Biography* 30 (1922): 368–372; William Cobbett and T. C. Hansard, eds., *The Parliamentary History of England from the Earliest Period to the Year 1803,* 36 vols. (London, 1806–1820), 19:694n., 698, as cited in Frey, *Water from the Rock,* 76 (Burke), 113–114 (Clinton proclamation), 119 (Clinton's reversal), 164 (Cornwallis directive); Quarles, *Negro in the American Revolution,* 113–114 (Clinton proclamation), 140–141 (Cornwallis directive). For a letter that may have helped Clinton shift strategy, see Randall M. Miller, ed., "A Backcountry Loyalist Plan to Retake Georgia and the Carolinas, 1778," *South Carolina Historical Magazine* 75 (1974): 207–214.

23. Murphy Stiel to General Henry Clinton, August 16, 1781, Clinton Papers, vol. 170, no. 27, Clements Library. See also Hodges, *Root and Branch,* 160 and Todd W. Braisted, "The Black Pioneers and Others: The Military Role of Black Loyalists in the American War for Independence," in John W. Pulis, ed., *Moving On: Black Loyalists in the Afro-Atlantic World* (New York, 1999), 3–37, esp. 17.

24. Quarles, *Negro in the American Revolution,* 148–151; Frey, *Water from the Rock,* 97–98, 100–102, 137–140; Dennis M. Conrad et al., eds., *The Papers of General Nathanael Greene,* vols. 8 (Chapel Hill, 1995), 294; 9 (Chapel Hill, 1997), 650–651; 10 (Chapel Hill, 1998), 19; 11 (Chapel Hill, 2000), 64–66. The most interesting documents are John Cruden's sketch Embodying Ten Thousand Black Troops in the Province of South Carolina, January 5, 1782, CO 5/175 ff. 411–413 and Dunmore to Clinton, February 2, 1782, CO 5/175 ff. 407–410, 415–417, PRO; both are reproduced in George Livermore, *An Historical Research respecting the Opinions of the Founders of the Republic on Negroes as Slaves, as Citizens, and as Soldiers* (Boston, 1862), 182–189.

25. Unknown to John Adams, June 9, 1775, in Robert J. Taylor et al., eds., *Papers of John Adams* (Cambridge, Mass., 1979), 3:18–20; Quarles, *Negro in the American Revolution,* 15–17 (Gates, council of war, and NJ committee); Jonathan Dickinson Sergeant to Adams, August 13, 1776 and Adams to Sergeant, August 17, 1776, in Taylor et al., *Adams Papers,* 4:453–455, 469.

26. "Antibiastes," *Observations on the Slaves, and Indented Servants in the Army, and in the Navy of the United States* (Philadelphia, 1777); Thomas Kench proposal, Revolutionary Rolls, CXCIX, no. 80, Mass. Arch., as cited in Quarles, *Negro in the American Revolution,* 54–55, and reproduced in Livermore, *An Historical Research,* 160–161; Paul F. Dearden, *The Rhode Island Campaign of 1778: Inauspicious Dawn of Alliance* (Providence, 1980), xiii; Louis Wilson, "Rhode Island's First Rhode Island Regiment — The "Black Regiment" 1777–1780" (unpublished paper); thanks to Ronald Hoffman for providing a copy of the Charles Carroll letter of June 4, 1781, and accompanying documentation, which essentially confirms Quarles, *Negro in the American Revolution,* 56–57.

27. The best studies of this subject are Gregory D. Massey, "The Limits of Antislavery Thought in the Revolutionary Lower South: John Laurens and Henry Laurens," *Journal of Southern History* 63 (1997): 495–530 (quotations on 512–513); Conrad et al., *Nathanael Greene Papers,* 10:22, 74, 228–229, 304, 472, 506–508, 11:35, 115, 307–309, 504.

28. Richard B. Sheridan, "The Jamaican Slave Insurrection Scare of 1776 and the

American Revolution," *Journal of Negro History* 61 (1976): 290–309; O'Shaughnessy, *Empire Divided*, 175.

29. Petition of William Henry Ricketts to the Assembly of Jamaica, October 30, 1778, CO 140/60, and companion memorials of 1780 and 1782, PRO; John D. Garrigus, "Catalyst or Catastrophe? Saint-Domingue's Free Men of Color and the Battle of Savannah, 1779–1782," *Revista/Review Interamericana* 22 (Spring–Summer 1992): 109–125; *The Siege of Savannah in 1779 as Described in Two Contemporaneous Journals of French Officers in the Fleet of Count D'Estaing* (Albany, N.Y., 1874), 20, 39, 40, 59; Benjamin Kennedy, ed. and trans., *Muskets, Cannon Balls and Bombs: Nine Narratives of the Siege of Savannah in 1779* (Savannah, 1974), 52 (quotation); Alexander Lawrence, *Storm Over Savannah: The Story of Count d'Estaing and the Siege of the Town in 1779* (Athens, 1951); George P. Clark, "The Role of the Haitian Volunteers at Savannah in 1779: An Attempt at an Objective View," *Phylon* 41 (1980): 356–366.

30. Fuller to Germain, December 23–24, 1778, Fuller MSS 256 ff. 110, 113, 133, Nicholas M. Williams Ethnological Collection, Boston College; O'Shaughnessy, *Empire Divided*, 177, 181.

31. O'Shaughnessy, *Empire Divided*, 178–179, 180–181 (quotation); *Annual Register*, 1781, 112–113, as cited in George F. Tyson Jr., "The Carolina Black Corps: Legacy of Revolution (1782–1798)," *Revista/Review Interamericana* 5 (Winter 1976): 652.

32. Paul E. Kopperman, "The British Army in North America and the West Indies, 1755/83: A Medical Perspective," in Geoffrey Hudson, ed., *War, Medicine and Britain, 1600–1815* (London, forthcoming); Sylvia Frey, *The British Soldier in America* (Austin, Tex., 1981), 37; David Patrick Geggus, *Slavery, War, and Revolution: The British Occupation of Saint Domingue, 1793–1798* (Oxford, 1982), 363; John Hunter, *Observations on the Diseases of the Army in Jamaica, and on the Best Means of Preserving the Health of Europeans in That Climate* (1788; reprint, London, 1808), 11, 37, 47, 58, 60; Andrew O'Shaughnessy, "Redcoats and Slaves in the British Caribbean," in Robert L. Paquette and Stanley L. Engerman, eds., *The Lesser Antilles in the Age of European Expansion* (Gainesville, 1996), 105–127; Roger Norman Buckley, *The British Army in the West Indies: Society and the Military in the Revolutionary Age* (Gainesville, 1998), 60, 104, 210, 218, 219, 229, 237.

33. Hunter, *Observations on the Diseases of the Army*, 20, 270–273; Thomas Dancer, M.D., *The Medical Assistant, or Jamaica Practice of Physic. Designed Chiefly for the Use of Families and Plantations* (St. Jago De La Vega, 1809), 180.

34. O'Shaughnessy, *Empire Divided*, 179–181; Robertson, *Spanish Town Papers*, 137 (see also 138–140 for accounts of free blacks who were probably enslaved). See also Alan G. Jamieson, "American Privateers in the Leeward Islands, 1776–1778," *American Neptune* 43 (1983): 20–30.

35. Michael J. Jarvis, "Maritime Masters and Seafaring Slaves in Bermuda, 1680–1783," *William and Mary Quarterly*, 3rd ser., 59 (2002): 585–586.

36. Stephen Conway, *The British Isles and the War of American Independence* (Oxford, 2000), 189; Germain to Campbell, 7 September, 1781, CO 137/80 f. 290, PRO. Stephen Conway has mentioned to us that various offers to raise Catholics in the American War exist; see also Arhele Margon, "A Weapon of War Yet Untried: Irish Catholics

and the Armed Forces of the Crown, 1760–1830," in T. G. Fraser and Keith Jeffrey, eds., *Men, Women and War* (Dublin, 1993), 66–85.

37. Quarles, *Negro in the American Revolution,* 73; the British figures are compiled from previously cited material, for the most part, and involve a fair amount of guesswork and extrapolation.

38. Continental army and state militia numbers are reported in Robert Middlekauf, *The Glorious Cause: The American Revolution, 1763–1789* (New York, 1982), 547, and Charles Patrick Neimeyer, *America Goes to War: A Social History of the Continental Army* (New York, 1996), 82–85. The numbers concerning British mobilization, which include army, navy, and home militia, are from Conway, *British Isles,* 11–44, esp. 28–29; see also his earlier "British Mobilization in the War of American Independence," *Bulletin of Historical Research* 72:177 (1999): 58–76. The numbers of Hessians come from Rodney Atwood, *The Hessians: Mercenaries from Hessen-Kassel in the American Revolution* (Cambridge, U.K., 1980), 52, 153, 157, 233, 254–257. Numbers of Loyalists are from Paul Smith, "The American Loyalists: Notes on Their Organization and Numerical Strength," *William and Mary Quarterly,* 3rd ser., 25 (1968): 259–267. For the numbers for July 1779, see Mackesy, *War for America,* 524–525.

39. The standard account of the West India regiments is Roger Norman Buckley, *Slaves in Red Coats: The British West India Regiments, 1795–1815* (New Haven, 1979), which can usefully be supplemented by Voelz, *Slave and Soldier,* 181–212, 224, Buckley, *British Army in the West Indies,* 117–124, 137–138, 186–201, and Bryan Dyde, *The Empty Sleeve: The Story of the West India Regiments in the British Army* (Antigua, 1997). Tyson, "Carolina Black Corps," makes explicit the continuity between the American Revolution and the French Revolutionary Wars.

40. "The Brunswick Contingent in America, 1776–1783," *Pennsylvania Magazine of History and Biography* 15 (1891): 224; Quarles, *Negro in the American Revolution,* 174; Frey, *Water from the Rock,* 226–227; Michael Craton and Gail Saunders, *Islanders in the Stream: A History of the Bahamian People,* vol. 1, *From Aboriginal Times to the End of Slavery* (Athens, 1992), 170, 187, 200, 207; Wilson, *Loyal Blacks,* 34–35, 81; James W. St. G. Walker, *The Black Loyalists: The Search for a Promised Land in Nova Scotia and Sierra Leone, 1783–1870* (New York, 1976), 6, 22, 192; Pulis, *Moving On,* esp. 59–60, 123; Christopher Fyfe, *A History of Sierra Leone* (Oxford, 1962), 73, 99.

41. Quarles, *Negro in the American Revolution,* 184, 198; Gary B. Nash, *Race and Revolution* (Madison, 1990), 63–64; Julie Winch, *A Gentleman of Color: The Life of James Forten* (New York, 2002), 46; John C. Dann, ed., *The Revolution Remembered: Eyewitness Accounts of the War of Independence* (Chicago, 1977), 26–28.

42. Granville Sharp to his brother, January 14, 1792, Sharp Papers, Hardwicke Court, as cited in Wilson, *Loyal Blacks,* 166; Pinckard, *Notes on the West Indies,* 3:194–195, as quoted in Buckley, *Slaves in Red Coats,* 34.

The Arming of Slaves in the Haitian Revolution

DAVID GEGGUS

The Haitian, or Saint Domingue, Revolution of 1789–1803 took place in one of the largest and most productive slave societies of the eighteenth century. The major supplier of sugar and coffee to the Atlantic market, Saint Domingue was in 1791 home to about a half-million slaves, thirty thousand whites, and a similar number of free people of color when it was transformed by simultaneous uprisings among the slave and free colored populations. Twelve years of internal strife and foreign invasion led to the ending of slavery and, eventually, of French colonial rule. Although the conflict brought more than eighty thousand European troops to the colony, slaves and former slaves constituted a large proportion of combatants on all sides. The extent to which defenders of slavery armed slaves in the Haitian Revolution was without precedent in the Caribbean, and it had few counterparts in Latin American history until the military manumissions of the nineteenth century. It was both the product of unique circumstances and a continuation of trends long under way in America's plantation societies.

Prerevolutionary Developments

The arming of slaves in the American tropics was a response to the small size of white populations, the vulnerability of European troops to the disease environment, and their poor performance in thickly forested and mountainous terrain. As long as conflicts in the region primarily pitted European soldiers from different countries against each other, and as long as warfare centered on seaborne landings, pitched battles, and sieges of towns, interest in forming a black military remained limited. It was presumably restrained by the security risk and encroachment on private property that such measures involved, and by differences between African and European styles of warfare. When regimes faced an enemy drawn from the majority black population, however, which enjoyed significant immunity to local diseases and proved adept at fighting in jungles and mountains, the advantages in arming black slaves greatly increased.

By the eighteenth century, colonizers of all national backgrounds in the Caribbean and Latin America were familiar with black soldiery, but those soldiers generally were drawn from the free population. Nonwhite militias grew rapidly in size during the century, and the later large-scale use of slave soldiers doubtless owed something to this precedent. By the time of the Haitian Revolution, free men of color made up about half of the militia in Saint Domingue. To assuage white colonists' unease with this development, the administration imposed white officers on free black and mulatto units after the 1760s, which was typical of the British but not the Iberian and Dutch colonies. Another relevant and more controversial trend was the increasing tendency of colonial regimes to come to terms with certain indomitable maroon communities by recognizing them as free and enlisting them as bounty hunters against fugitive slaves and as potential defenders against foreign enemies. Panama (1579), Mexico (1609), New Granada (1686), Jamaica (1739, 1740), and Surinam (1760, 1762, 1767) provide the best-known cases. In 1784 the French and Spanish administrations that shared Hispaniola also signed such a treaty, with the Maniel maroons of southeastern Santo Domingo. This proved extremely unpopular among French colonists and was not ratified by the French government. Nonetheless, such "treaty maroons," like the nonwhite militias, generally became effective defenders of the slaveholding regimes. Despite creating alarm, their example thus presumably reduced resistance to the arming of slaves.

As Peter Voelz's encyclopedic study shows, the use of black slaves as soldiers in the Americas began with the conquest itself and was remarkably widespread and varied, but it tended to be sporadic and temporary. When slaves were drafted, it was usually during wartime emergencies or for overseas expeditions. They most often served as support personnel, building defenses, foraging, and carrying baggage, although Pernambuco in the 1640s and early South Carolina provide important exceptions. If slaves were armed, it was not usually with firearms. (For those who routinely worked with machetes, the change thus did not have the implications of distributing knives in a state penitentiary.) And when their service was over, it seems the great majority returned to their former labors. A significant development for the Caribbean came in the Jamaican Maroon War of the 1730s with the formation of units of "Confidential Black Shot." These were homogeneous combat units that seem to have enjoyed some longevity. The three hundred Black Rangers raised in Surinam in 1772 represented a further advance in that they were recruited with promises of freedom and the corps became permanent. Both of these corps were explicit responses to the difficulties of fighting maroons in tropical forest environments. The formation of slave corps by the British during the American Revolution evinced perhaps a different type of motivation: the desire to undermine (economically and psychologically) a slaveowning enemy. Given the numbers involved and the survival of at least the Carolina Corps, transferred in 1783 to the West Indies, they constitute another step forward in the developing use of slaves as soldiers.[1]

The French Caribbean saw nothing quite so dramatic but nonetheless witnessed similar developments in the military use of slaves. From at least the late seventeenth century, bodies of slaves sometimes were armed in defense of their colonies, and some participated in overseas expeditions. At first, only individuals of exceptional valor gained their freedom, but during the Seven Years' War a group of sixty slave defenders on Guadeloupe were manumitted (on condition that they leave the island), as was another group on Martinique. In Saint Domingue, whose slave population grew rapidly while its military garrison did not, the government sought to boost recruitment to the free colored mounted police (*maréchaussée*) and to two short-lived free colored battalions during the American Revolutionary War by offering tax-free manumissions to the few masters who would provide slaves to "serve for their freedom" in these units. After the war, the colonial ministry apparently discussed plans for using black soldiers, but a proposal in 1789 to emancipate slaves in return for only six years' maréchaussée service was decried as dangerous by the local administration.[2]

Armed blacks were therefore an increasing presence in eighteenth-century colonies, and a sporadic tendency toward arming slaves was discernible. Such developments remained rare, however, and for colonists and administrators, highly controversial. In Saint Domingue, the presence of a relatively large free colored population perhaps reduced the incentive to arm slaves. Not only did the colony that produced the Americas' greatest slave insurrection have a very limited prior history of violent rebellion, but its extensive use of slave soldiers to combat that insurrection also had little local precedent to follow.

The Haitian Revolution

The first two years of the Saint Domingue Revolution that began in 1789 consisted largely of white factions competing with one another and with the free population of color. Although some scholars have recently claimed that both sides armed slaves from early in the conflict, it was not until the great slave uprising of August 1791 in the colony's northern plain and the simultaneous uprising of free people of color in western and southern Saint Domingue that the phenomenon first really emerges. The arming of slaves by free persons postdated the slave revolution and was in no sense a cause of it.[3]

During the two years following the uprising, as the slave revolution spread and the free coloreds achieved rapid victory in their struggle for racial equality, the military use of slaves developed in a number of formats. Four types might be identified: plantation guards, irregular corps raised by colonists, alliances with insurgents, and formal corps formed by states.

PLANTATION GUARDS

The performance of guard duty by slaves on their own estates represented the most basic type of militarization. It might involve the distribution of firearms to a select few, the improvisation of lances, or merely the carrying of machetes and axes. Information is sparse about the identity of guards, but slave drivers and artisans were evidently involved and presumably so were slaves who already carried weapons, such as hunters and watchmen. The phenomenon was found in all parts of the colony after 1791 and lasted as long as slavery survived. Protection of plantations usually involved joint operations in which slaves cooperated with white employees and owners; where whites had abandoned the countryside, it was sometimes initiated and perpetuated by the slaves themselves.

The first signs of this perhaps surprising behavior were seen in the early days of the slave insurrection in the northern plain, when some workforces, headed by conservative drivers, tried to fight off incursions by the insurgents. Resembling village headmen caught up in twentieth-century guerrilla conflicts, such slave drivers became prime targets for assassination. The revolt in the north proved so devastating that within weeks little remained to defend in much of the plain, but on a few abandoned estates close to the city of Cap Français groups of sixty or more male slaves remained through the insurrection as autonomous armed guards resisting attacks, capturing insurgents, and putting out fires. Some were freed by the Colonial Assembly in 1792.[4]

Armed guards, protecting estates, were far more typical of plantations in the northwest region and west and south provinces of Saint Domingue, where slave rebellion developed more slowly and on a smaller scale amid a civil war fought between different white factions and free people of color. Although work regimes progressively broke down in these areas, most estates were still substantially intact when slavery was abolished in August 1793, and in much of the region slavery would be maintained by British invaders until 1798. In the wake of the uprising in the north, planters and estate managers in the Cul de Sac plain behind Port au Prince armed slaves whom they trusted at the same time as they established night patrols and added extra white guards, if they could find men willing to reside in the plain. Nearly seven years later, in the last days of the doomed British occupation, some enslaved men continued to shoulder muskets alongside white plantation staff, while the black republican army liberated the last slaves in the colony.

On the absentee-owned Marin plantation, slaves in 1791 and 1792 spontaneously took on the role of defenders. They limited damage to the estate by raiders, made the plantation attorney leave for town at a dangerous moment, and hid in the canes and reedbeds to avoid forced recruitment in a conflict they evidently did not see as their own. Ten years later, 92 of the 155 original slaves were still there, and supposedly no more than 10 had joined the insurgents. In the attorney's words, they were "attached to a soil they saw as belonging to them." They told him they were preventing pillage of "the plantation, the big house, and our chickens and pigs." Since the slaves were rather less zealous about maintaining the production of sugar, it seems they identified with the plantation as the site of their provision grounds and "proto-peasant" activity. Their behavior bears comparison with that of workforces before the revolution who sometimes would capture or go in pursuit of fugitive slaves, in part because they threatened their provision grounds. That insurgents sometimes sought to burn slave quarters as a recruitment tactic sheds further light on slaves' interest in being plantation guards. As elsewhere, the role of the driver was central; the Marin slave driver dictated letters to the owner in France throughout the revolution.[5]

Further insight into slaves' willingness to defend the plantations on which they lived comes from Bernard Foubert's massive study of the Laborde plantations in the southern plain of Les Cayes. When local free nonwhites rebelled late in 1791, they recruited plantation slaves, supposedly promising them freedom, and terrorized workforces that did not join them by burning slave quarters and killing slave drivers. Most of those who left to join, first, the free coloreds and, later, independent slave rebels, were recently arrived Africans, young men without local roots. The armed guards who served alongside whites were drawn from the plantations' creole (that is, locally born) elite, generally married men with families, those who might most reasonably expect

manumission for their loyalty. Once again, slave drivers proved to be key figures. In the south, as in the north, however, the leaders of the slave insurgents
were frequently also creole slave drivers. In fact, a wider study of western and
southern plantations shows that, although young Africans and field slaves
proportionately were most likely to become insurgents, slave drivers were
almost equally represented among those who rebelled and those who remained on their plantations. Social structure thus helps explain behavior during the revolution, but only up to a certain point.[6]

IRREGULAR CORPS

The Swiss. "Les Suisses" were the first corps of armed slaves raised in
the revolution. They were used as auxiliaries during the period September–
October 1791 by the free colored insurgents in the Port au Prince region, who
demanded an end to racial discrimination but not to slavery. The origins of the
Swiss have long been controversial. White contemporaries claimed that the
free coloreds recruited them on white colonists' plantations with promises of
freedom or at least a reduced work schedule. The free coloreds and their subsequent defenders offered two alternative versions. One is that white colonists
first mobilized slaves, especially their own domestics, but that these slaves
deserted to the free coloreds when the latter decisively repulsed the white
forces that marched against them. The other version holds that the Swiss consisted of existing fugitives, rebels who had burned plantations in the mountains, and others who spontaneously abandoned their estates to join the victorious free colored army. All three versions were self-serving but have some
grounding in fact. The number of Swiss fluctuated between two hundred and
about two thousand but was generally between three hundred and six hundred. The initial group formed at the end of August in the mountains above
Port au Prince and then was swollen by massive desertions from lowland sugar
estates following the battle of Pernier, fought a few days later at the edge of the
Cul de Sac plain. The free colored leaders persuaded most of these slaves to
return to their plantations, but they kept and armed several hundred and
drilled them daily. For a very tense two months, the free colored army then
negotiated with the whites controlling the capital city the issues of racial
equality and what was to be done with the slaves in arms.[7]

The Swiss were valuable to the free coloreds for political rather than military reasons. The several thousand freemen of color enjoyed a considerable
edge as soldiers over their white opponents. Their black auxiliaries served as
an unstated threat that, if the whites did not grant racial equality, the free
nonwhites might raise the slaves en masse. The free coloreds' ability to control
the countryside in the south and west provinces, where they were most nu-

merous, is the main, though little understood, reason those regions did not experience a slave uprising like that in the north. In their negotiations with their opponents, the free nonwhite leaders represented the Swiss as a threat to the propertied classes with whom the free coloreds, as essential intermediaries, were diplomatically struggling to deal.

The question of the Swiss brought into conflict the class interests and racial sensibilities of the free coloreds, and it is especially interesting, because it casts a spotlight on free coloreds' attitudes toward slavery at a moment when the balance of power between whites, blacks, and coloreds was about to careen out of control. Because of its tragic ending, the story has become emblematic of the relations between slaves and freemen and between their respective descendants in independent Haiti.

With the slave revolution raging in the north, a few free coloreds in the west suggested that a controlled and compensated end to slavery might be a prudent policy. Many more favored emancipating several hundred of the Swiss. Apart from considerations of justice, they saw that ingratitude to their allies might poison future relations between slaves and free people of color, precisely what their white opponents hoped to achieve. But slaves who had borne arms in rebellion were usually executed. White planters in the plain of Cul de Sac proved willing to compromise and adopted a proposal to free the Swiss after eight years' service in the rural police, a prerevolutionary manumission procedure. These planters, who reluctantly accepted the free coloreds as essential allies in preserving slavery, thought driving the Swiss back into slavery would be too dangerous. Yet the urban radicals of Port au Prince wanted to punish the black soldiers and insisted that rewarding them would encourage further rebellion. A stalemate ensued.

On September 22 the free colored leader, Bauvais, reported that angry Swiss being returned to their owners had rioted in his camp and nearly killed a white colonist; he had opened fire on them, but some had fled with their weapons. He asked Port au Prince urgently to send field cannon and guns. Probably suspecting a ruse, the whites did nothing. Meanwhile, the free coloreds divided violently for and against their auxiliary troops. The younger men tended to take their side, whereas the most senior figures favored acquiescing to white demands. At stake was the free coloreds' moral authority to speak for all the colony's nonwhites.[8]

Matters came to a head when a treaty was signed in late October ending racial discrimination. The free colored army triumphantly marched into Port au Prince, accompanied by more than two hundred Swiss. They were variously described as the "most alert" or the guiltiest of the slaves, mainly artisans and slave drivers. About a tenth were of mixed racial descent. "Impudently," a contemporary wrote, the Swiss walked the streets "with the assurance of free men." But the triumph was short-lived. White politicians denounced a dangerous "excitement" among urban slave artisans and domestics caused by the presence of the armed blacks, who reportedly told them, "If you had done like us, the country would be ours!" According to a colonist, who called the Swiss "tigers": "Every good citizen was seized with panic; each feared for his property and his life." Some suggested that the black soldiers be sold in South America or thrown into the sea.[9]

The free colored leaders, anxious to preserve their own political gains, finally bowed before white pressure and accepted a plan to deport the Swiss and settle them on the Mosquito Coast of Nicaragua. Although the free nonwhite poor demonstrated in their support, about 215 Swiss were forced at gunpoint onto a ship and put in chains. Then began an odyssey that few of them would survive. After the ship's captain tried to sell the men to the lumberjacks of Belize, they were abandoned on a desert island, shipped to Jamaica and then back to Saint Domingue, to the remote port of Môle Saint Nicolas. There many were murdered by white paramilitary ruffians, and the rest spent a year chained in a ship's hold. A handful, at most, eventually returned to Port au Prince.[10]

The Swiss were unfortunate pioneers. Just as slaveowners in the north province vehemently refused any meaningful negotiation with the slaves in insurrection, those in the west were not ready to accept a corps of armed slaves associated with rebellion. Times were changing, however. The free coloreds' successful control of the Swiss encouraged others to experiment further with using slave auxiliaries. There was no shortage of slaves willing to seize the opportunity. On the other hand, the messages the most militant of them must have drawn from the story of the Swiss were that collaboration would bring betrayal and that slaves had to fight for themselves. Local rebellions began to multiply in the south and west provinces.

The Company of Africans. Having driven a wedge between free coloreds and slaves, the Port au Prince radicals (who included seamen, shopkeepers, artisans, and some merchants) soon renewed their fight against the free coloreds. Appreciating their need for black troops, the radicals made an unsuccessful and bizarre request to the governor of Jamaica to send them Blue Mountain Maroons, and in December 1791 or a little later they raised a new corps among the urban slaves of Port au Prince. The corps was known as the Compagnie des Africains and probably consisted of unemployed waterfront workers. Confusingly, they were sometimes called "Swiss." (Just as the term *Suisse* had the generic meaning of "guard," *Africains* acquired at this time the connotation of "black corps.") The men, who were not freed, carried sabers or the wooden clubs favored by slaves for stick-fighting. The corps had a white commander, Breton de la Villandry (an estate attorney), and another leader called Philibert or Caïman, who was a young black slave owned by a merchant. The person responsible for forming the unit was the radical leader and millionaire planter Jean-Baptiste de Caradeux, who had already armed slaves on his plantations against his enemies in the surrounding plain. In 1793 the unit grew to be twelve hundred strong.[11]

The Africains conducted night raids into the Cul de Sac plain and were paid a bounty for the heads of mulattoes that they brought back. This grisly ritual perhaps reflects the influence of Jean-Baptiste de Caradeux, who had a penchant for decapitation, and also of African religious beliefs concerning protection against the vengeance of the deceased, but in any event, headhunting would be widely practiced in the revolution, by European as well as local soldiers. In March 1792 the corps formed part of an expedition of troops and urban whites that traversed the plain pillaging plantations, forcibly recruiting slaves, and stealing the slaves' pigs and chickens. This set off a massive uprising in which thousands of crudely armed rural slaves joined the free coloreds in driving the Port au Prince army back to the capital. The expedition's losses were heavy but would have been greater had not the African Company fought so well and had its spies not learned of the attack in advance. Out of this conflict a new black corps was formed.[12]

Hyacinthe's Gendarmerie. After unleashing the power of the slaves, the free coloreds, as men of property, now wished to get the insurgents back to work on the estates. They also needed a counterweight to the Company of Africans and assistance in facing down new autonomous bands of slaves that were appearing in the plain and the surrounding mountains. With their white planter allies, they therefore formed a mounted police force of forty *gendarmes,* which grew to one hundred, whose members were promised their freedom. It was headed by a young vodou priest named Hyacinthe from the Ducoudray sugar estate, who was probably a household domestic. He had led the Cul de Sac slaves' headlong attack on the Port au Prince expedition waving a bull's tail and crying out that the soldiers' bullets were water. Estimates of the slaves' casualties ranged between five hundred and three thousand killed, so his influence over his followers was clearly considerable.[13]

Probably because of his religious role, Hyacinthe achieved a notable ascendancy over the slave drivers of the plain, and with uneven success he helped reestablish sugar production with a reduced workweek. This required a good deal of violence and some bribery on the part of plantation managers. When one workforce refused to cut cane and opened fire on his men, Hyacinthe charged at them impetuously and killed ten. Later in the year, he administered one hundred lashes to a slave accused of theft. Yet according to plantation attorney Charles Malenfant, Hyacinthe kept the respect of the Cul de Sac slaves. When one of his gendarmes was arrested in Port au Prince, he was able to mobilize several thousand plantation workers to march on the capital to get him released. In February 1793 he marched into the camp of the rebel leader Mamzelle and hanged several of his men in reprisal for their recent attack on the free coloreds. He was reputedly paid nearly a thousand livres coloniales (about US$120) per month.[14]

Hyacinthe is a difficult figure to assess. A political player in his own right, he maneuvered through the tortuous politics of the unfolding revolution with much sleight of hand, playing one faction against another. Yet it seems that, as the free coloreds moved closer to the urban radicals after the abolition of racial discrimination, Hyacinthe's primary alliance remained with the conservative white planters of the plain. Their leader, Hanus de Jumécourt, was reputedly initiated into vodou and known to slaves as "the white who knows everything." Like the planters, Hyacinthe flirted with the Spanish of neighboring Santo Domingo after the French Republic went to war in the spring of 1793, and like them he allied with the British when the latter occupied Port au Prince in June 1794. He was assassinated shortly afterwards in the camp of an independent black leader when making overtures on behalf of the British-planter alliance.[15]

Jean Kina's Corps. As the civil war between whites and free coloreds spread into Saint Domingue's south province in late 1791, so did the use of armed slaves by both parties and autonomous rebellions by the slaves themselves. The central part of the south peninsula soon became a free colored stronghold and remained so for the rest of the decade, but in the southeastern frontier district of Saltrou the slaves of white planters defended their estates against the free coloreds for two years, and in the Grande Anse at the western end of the peninsula both slavery and a white supremacist regime remained largely intact until 1798. At the beginning of the conflict, the free men of color incorporated their own slaves into their armies and raiding parties, but little is known of their organization. In response to their attacks, planters in the Cayemittes district of the Grande Anse in early December 1791 became the first whites to arm their slaves. Their counterparts in the plain of Les Cayes, on the south coast, briefly armed 10 percent of their slaves the same month and later attached to their camp a body of armed slaves led by an African named Couacou. The Colonial Assembly had by then already ordered the manumission of several of these slave defenders in the southeast and southwest and sent details of their proceedings to the National Assembly in France. As libertarian ideology gained ground, such defenders had a propaganda value for slaveowners as well as a military one.[16]

Easily the best known was Jean Kina. He was a slave craftsman from a cotton plantation in the parish of Tiburon, the front line of the Grande Anse. Still one of the most isolated places in Haiti and far from any town, Tiburon was a district of small estates with resident owners and relatively high ratios of whites to nonwhites and free persons to slaves. Along this exposed coast, planters had customarily armed their slaves in wartime. "These brave colonists," wrote an observer in 1788, "are almost all artillerymen and their slaves are soldiers . . . experience shows that till now this has produced nothing but good effects." It was in this region that there appeared, when the French Revolution shook Saint Domingue, the planters' ideal *bon nègre,* a fearless defender of royalty, slavery, and white supremacy.[17]

Jean Kina first emerges from the anonymity of the plantation at the beginning of 1792 maneuvering through mountain forests of the Grande Anse commanding a group of sixty slaves. In newspapers and memoirs, colonists praised him extravagantly for his cool head, bravery, and military sense, and for his devotion to the cause of the white planter class. Apart from his martial skills, he made the slaves work, and he had a certain symbolic value as well. "This negro," one of them wrote, "is absolutely feared by all the brigands and non-brigands, mulattoes and slaves; they tremble at his appearance." A man of fierce temper, he appears to have shared in the mentality, found among whites and slaves, that classed the free coloreds as objects of envy but not respect — paradoxically, for Kina was now officially a freedman himself. He was manumitted first by the Tiburon commune, with his master's consent, and then by the governor and the Colonial Assembly. Yet for at least a year he made a show of refusing this change of status; this was to set an example for his fellow slaves, he said. In July 1792 the Colonial Assembly awarded him a medal and a small pension. Slave or free, he was determined to live well. Within a year, his family's food bill, paid at public expense, had to be cut back to 50 livres (about $60) per month.[18]

The size of Jean Kina's corps soon grew to consist of a nucleus of 170 slaves, probably Africans, who by mid–1793 also had gained their freedom. The corps may have been reinforced on occasion with levies from the plantations to reach as many as five hundred. In January 1793 Kina took part in a successful attack on the rebel slave stronghold of les Platons, which in August had heavily defeated an expedition led by the governor. This time, however, the insurgents were driven from their mountain fastness, largely thanks to Jean Kina. Although the attackers numbered more than nineteen hundred, including more than three hundred troops of the line, all agreed that it was his ragged and barefoot troop that won the day. They were described months later by a British captain as follows: "[They have] a bush fighting warfare peculiar to themselves. . . . Their appearance was . . . very grotesque — instead of the drum and fife, they used the Banger and Coromantee flute, the musical instruments of their native country. Some had firearms; others, bill hooks fastened to long poles and plantation watchmen's hangers, and were in general wretchedly attired in their osnaburgh frocks."[19]

Like Hyacinthe, Jean Kina joined the white planters in allying with the British forces that occupied parts of western and southern Saint Domingue in the period 1793–98. Conscious of their tenuous hold on the colony, successive British commanders were careful to award Kina marks of respect. He was made a colonel and received several swords, gifts of cash, a high collar, and a portrait of George III. His men received British pay and uniforms. Several more times the corps distinguished itself in combat. Once the British began to raise full-scale regiments of chasseurs, however, its role was diminished. It also changed in composition. To replace battle casualties, Kina had to recruit prisoners of war, usually republican free coloreds deported to Jamaica. In the summer of 1796 he was allowed to tap a new source that anticipated by several months the method that would be used by the British West India Regiments. This was the purchase from slaveships of Africans "accustomed to a state of warfare in their own countries." In all, he seems to have bought about forty. Their wages were paid to him, and no provision was made for their eventual emancipation. The ex-slave was now a slaveowner on a large scale, and his "Chasseurs de Georges III" became a curiously hybrid unit, divided into one company of chasseurs and one company of free coloreds. Because losses among the Africans to death and desertion were heavy, the corps consisted mainly of freedmen at the end of the British occupation in September 1798.

Kina's subsequent career reads like something from a picaresque novel. It took him to Jamaica, England, and Martinique, where he led a bloodless rebellion in defense of the rights of local free people of color. After a spell in Newgate prison in London, he moved to France, where he was promptly jailed again and put in the Fort de Joux (in a cell above that of Toussaint Louverture), from which he was eventually released to join the Napoleonic army in Italy.

ALLIANCES WITH INSURGENTS

In the preceding cases, men were generally recruited from a state of slavery, usually with a promise of eventual freedom. A different type of recruitment emerged in the first half of 1793, when France went to war with Spain and Britain, and the contest for Saint Domingue became more desperate. This new type of recruitment involved appeals to groups of insurgent or maroon slaves, people who had effectively already freed themselves. This was considerably more unpopular with slaveowners, who tended to regard it as rewarding rebellion and involving alliance with men they perceived not merely as their own property but as murderers, rapists, and agents of their ruin. The relations of power in such arrangements were also radically different. During the spring of 1793 a contest developed between French republican officials in Saint Domingue and the royalist Spanish administration in Santo Domingo to win over the different bands of insurgents in revolt in the north and the west. This development may have saved the slave revolution that, at the beginning of the year, had been in full retreat before the finally united forces of whites and free coloreds.[20] The Spanish essentially won this contest when, in the course of May and June 1793, they contracted an alliance with the armies of the principal rebel leaders, Jean-François, Georges Biassou, and Toussaint (soon to be called Louverture).

Since the beginning of the slave uprising in 1791, Spanish colonists and soldiers in Santo Domingo had traded across the frontier with the insurgents, and local officials applied Spain's official policy of neutrality in the conflict with a good deal of anti-French bias. It remains uncertain, however, whether the administration itself actively favored the rebel slaves prior to the outbreak of war (as many contemporaries and historians have alleged). Only when war in Europe seemed certain did Madrid make the extraordinary decision to recruit as "auxiliary troops" the men who had devastated Saint Domingue's northern plain eighteen months earlier. They were to be offered freedom for themselves and their families, "exemptions, favors and privileges," and land in the French or Spanish part of the island or elsewhere.[21]

Spain's decision to restore slavery with an army of revolted slaves grew out of long Hispanic traditions of arming blacks and encouraging the resettlement of fugitive slaves. Even in the context of the international and local trends sketched above, however, it represents a daring experiment. The decision reflected the high stakes for which the colonial powers were playing, and on the part of Spain, a desire to recover from the French what had been part of its first American colony. Intense conservative antipathy for the French Revolution and for the type of secular, individualist society exemplified by Saint Domingue perhaps also formed part of the equation, along with the low moral profile and financial problems of the Godoy government, which had recently come to power. Not least was the adroit diplomacy of the insurgents themselves, who from the start of the uprising had assiduously cultivated contacts with the Spanish, presenting themselves as defenders of church and king.

The alliance was initially successful. By the early months of 1794, insurgent leaders had occupied most of the northern half of Saint Domingue in the name of the king of Spain. About five thousand Spanish troops had been sent to the colony but, with the significant exception of taking the city of Fort Dauphin, they were mainly used to guard the frontier, and their heavy losses in fever epidemics suggest the wisdom of this limitation on the use of European soldiers. The number of black auxiliaries recruited is impossible to ascertain, but in mid–1793 Jean-François claimed to command 6,647 men (6,522 slaves, 67 free mulattoes, and 58 free blacks). Biassou claimed a slightly smaller number that included forces under Toussaint Louverture. Later estimates were usually smaller; Jean-François's army was estimated at 3,000 men in late 1794 and at 1,000 in February 1795, although the Spanish also supplied other insurgents. The rank-and-file soldiers received no pay, and the Spanish were very slow in supplying uniforms and very cautious in supplying weapons. To begin with, the policy was relatively cheap; the first four months cost about $40,000. Eighteen months later, however, Jean-François's army alone reputedly was costing $12,000 per month; some said that Spanish officials pocketed half the sum budgeted. The monthly salary of Jean-François and Biassou was fixed at $250 (and the former received a $100 supplement). Colonels, who were numerous, received $20 to $30, and captains $15.[22]

The main problem for the Spanish was that they found they had little control over their allies, who proved maddeningly independent. The Spanish had no say in the organization of their *tropas auxiliares*, particularly in the distribution of ranks. Jean-François called himself Grand Admiral; Biassou adopted various titles. The black soldiers seemed to fight among themselves almost as much as against the French. Appreciating how much the Spanish depended on them, they needed to be cajoled, flattered, and bribed. Biassou established himself in a Spanish frontier town and called himself its governor, running up large bills for food and drink. In the tradition of Spanish missionizing, priests were used as key intermediaries. This aggravated Spanish military officers, who complained that they were fighting "a war of Pater Noster and Ave Maria." The archbishop of Santo Domingo complained that the military were disdainful of their black allies and ignored their requests. In return, black officers sometimes demanded precedence over Spanish counterparts or refused to obey local commanders. The inability of the Spanish to control the situation became spectacularly evident in July 1794, when Jean François's men massacred in one day about seven hundred French colonists under the eyes of an immobile Spanish garrison in the town of Fort Dauphin.[23]

In the spring of 1794 the general Toussaint Louverture switched allegiance from Spain to the French Republic, so ending any chance of Spanish success. Historians have long disputed the degree to which Toussaint's volte-face resulted from the French decision to abolish slavery (taken locally in August 1793 and ratified in Paris the following February). Certainly Toussaint was not the only officer in the tropas auxiliares to feel conflicted in fighting to restore slavery once the French had abolished it. He was not the first to switch sides. Yet one cannot conclude that emancipation introduced a fatal flaw into Spanish policy, since the major black leaders remained loyal to Spain and continued to sell black captives. And Toussaint's motives were undoubtedly complex.[24]

This continued loyalty of the majority of the auxiliaries presented Spanish officials with a dilemma when Spain abandoned its oldest colony in 1795 and surrendered Santo Domingo to France. What should be done with the auxiliary troops? Many of the soldiers, and the French, thought it would be dangerous for them to remain on the island. They would not, however, be welcome in another slave society. Turned away from Cuba and Trinidad, an irreducible group of about 650, including family members, was finally distributed among several destinations in Florida, Mexico, Central America, and Spain. There they lived as pensioned exiles, very assertive of their rights as former soldiers of the king.[25]

FORMAL CORPS

La Légion de l'Egalité. Soon after the outbreak of war became known in Saint Domingue in mid-April 1793, the republican commissioners there, Sonthonax and Polverel, formed the Legion of Equality. At first, the nascent regiment acted as their personal bodyguard, and in the second half of the year it became three separate corps stationed in each of the colony's provinces. The commissioners had been sent from France to enforce racial equality in the colony and to defeat the slave insurrection. In early 1793 they had come close to doing so. This probably ran contrary to the aspirations of Sonthonax, who had an abolitionist past. The Legion of Equality is therefore particularly interesting because of the way it served the radical commissioners as a stepping stone to the dramatic abolition of slavery that they would announce at the end of August. The legion was recruited by assembling at Port au Prince and manumitting various bodies of slaves who already had been armed by the colonists. "Men who have been armed by their master and fought for him can no longer be treated nor considered as slaves," they declared. After defending his life and property, adopting his quarrels, and carrying out his vengeance, they could not be returned to work as docile slaves. Any crimes committed by the slave were the responsibility of the master. Sonthonax and Polverel thus undermined their planter enemies and blamed them for this new breach in the slave system.[26]

In late 1792 Sonthonax, with the interim governor, Rochambeau, had already added armed slaves to some National Guard units and *compagnies franches* to fight insurgents. Now he combined a miscellany of small units from around the west and south provinces. The commissioners exempted the remnants of the Swiss at Cap Français and the Africains at Port au Prince in order to avoid accusations that they were encouraging slave rebellion. Those men were declared free in mid-May and placed as crew on board two French warships. Jean Kina and Hyacinthe also avoided drafting into the new corps, which came to include 20 slaves from Grands Bois serving five years for their liberty in a local police force, 70 infantry and cavalry sent from the Artibonite plain, 33 from the Cul de Sac, 108 Jacmel "Hussars," and others who were serving in military camps. They were to be freed immediately and serve under the same conditions as line troops; officers and noncommissioned officers would be transferred from European regiments. Slaves of mixed racial descent were especially prominent in the corps. It had 366 men by mid-June and was projected to have 1,200 men and 600 horses.[27]

Faced with Spanish and British invasion and a coup by the colonial governor, the civil commissioners were soon forced to adopt more desperate measures. On June 20 they offered freedom to any insurgents in arms who would defend the French Republic, and to expel the governor, they had to allow the sack of the colony's main city, Cap Français. Failing to control their new allies, they modified their offer on July 2, specifying that it would apply only to those who joined the new Legions of Equality. The offer was expanded to soldiers and their families, but this was no more than the Spanish were already offering. More slaves were recruited in the south, and then, on August 29, Sonthonax declared the slave regime abolished. This was the beginning of the black republican army that, after another decade of almost uninterrupted warfare, would make Haiti independent in 1804. Because of the emancipation that emerged from the military crisis of 1793, however, that army was henceforth recruited not among slaves but among former slaves.

The British Chasseurs. Colonists were usually hostile to large formal corps, which in their view "corrupted" slaves. To the extent that they accepted the arming of slaves, colonists preferred to arm their own, to lead them into battle and then back to work, as one put it. This was the Grande Anse model, at least in idealized form. It is noteworthy, therefore, to find the colonist who, in 1791, had done the most to combat the northern insurgents advocating in August 1793 an ambitious new development. Lenoir de Rouvray, an eccentric conservative, proposed (to the Spanish) that all the colonial powers combine forces and offer freedom to the rebel slaves. Those who accepted should be formed by French officers into twelve regiments of one thousand men each, which, when the war was over, would be deported to another colony. Although such a scheme was never realized, the British, who were about to intervene in Saint

Domingue, would expand the use of slave soldiery to its greatest extent in the Haitian Revolution.[28]

Under the British occupation of 1793–98, the military use of slaves continued in different formats, but the development of formal corps was the key trend. After the capture of Port au Prince in June 1794, the British commander negotiated with the insurgent leader Dieudonné, who led several thousand men in the mountains above the city. Dieudonné agreed to serve under white officers, if necessary, but insisted on freedom for all his men. Because the British governor was not empowered to dispose of planters' property, he replied that he would need royal permission to do so, and could offer only British pay and freedom from vexation by former masters. The negotiations failed. Necessity soon overcame the scruples about private property, but the British had only slightly more success in negotiating with members of Jean-François's army at the time of the Spanish withdrawal in 1795–97. It was in recruiting corps among plantation slaves that the main developments occurred.[29]

In the summer of 1794 the small British garrison was decimated by fever epidemics, as its French and Spanish predecessors had been. To supplement their dwindling numbers, local commanders (one British, one French colonial) drafted several hundred slaves in the plains of Cul de Sac and the Artibonite, where there were many abandoned plantations. Following a model already used in some rural police units, the British promised the slaves freedom after five years' service. In September the British position became more critical following the revolt of their free colored allies, and in the ensuing fighting, the black troops' talent for a war of patrols and ambushes was particularly evident. In November 1794 a regiment of eight hundred chasseurs began recruiting in the Cul de Sac.

Most planters opposed this development. "If you train them to arms," one said of the slaves, "to that pride, that equality, and familiarity necessary in the military life, the entire colonial system is lost." Only colonists hoping to use the chasseurs as instruments of vengeance against the free coloreds were said to welcome the new corps. At first recruiting was limited to slaves volunteered by ruined or public-spirited planters and those taken from absentee or forfeited estates. Then in June 1795 a levy of one in fifteen slaves was made compulsory, and regiments were raised in all parts of the occupied zone. The institution, strongly favored by military men, was thus able to prove itself gradually. London's refusal to allow manumission after five years' service was simply ignored. Governor Adam Williamson suggested helpfully that perhaps not many recruits would live that long, or they would want to reenlist.

By the end of 1796, the black corps in the British occupied zone numbered about sixty-seven hundred men, of whom a little more than five thousand were slaves. In July 1798 there were perhaps six thousand. All officers were white, but freedmen could serve as sergeants and occasionally as sergeant-majors. The rank and file carried a musket and a machete, wore a red jacket and a round hat, and received British pay and rations. Almost all the slaves were Africans; owners and estate managers tended to pick their least wanted workers or, later in the occupation, to purchase imported slaves to supply their quota. By March 1796, however, it was said that half of the chasseurs were former rebels who had changed sides, attracted by the terms of service.

Money, a full stomach, and a prestigious uniform: the attractions were, up to a point, those that caused young males in any poor and oppressed group to become soldiers. For field slaves at the bottom of the plantation hierarchy, men who worked half-naked six days a week and who prided themselves on their Sunday dress, the appeal must have been especially great. The scarlet tunic, moreover, was not just a flamboyant item of clothing but, as Jean-François said, *l'habit du Roi*. Each black corps had a chaplain who was instructed to end public prayers with three shouts of "Vive le Roi!" and each service with "God Save the King." Because most Africans came from monarchical societies, they would have found such rituals, decked out with the usual trappings of flags, medals, and ceremonies, at least comprehensible and perhaps appealing. As for the regimentation, discipline, and flogging, these were nothing new. Slaves adapted well to military life. In some units, an intense esprit de corps seems to have evolved. Until the final campaign of the occupation, desertion from the black corps was less than that among the white troops. And during the final campaign some chasseur units fought with a suicidal bravery few colonists were willing to show.

During the British evacuation in 1798, thousands of chasseurs were refused entry to Jamaica, and most were sent back to Saint Domingue, where they were returned to plantation work by Toussaint Louverture, no longer soldiers but no longer slaves.

Conclusion

As David Brion Davis underlined a quarter-century ago, opportunities for slave emancipation opened up in both war and revolution, but particularly in revolutionary wars. This chapter surveys four formats in which slaves were armed during the Haitian Revolution that mark a trend toward an increase in scale, formal organization, and offers of freedom in exchange for military service. The first two types of militarization, the use of plantation guards and informal corps, emerged in the period 1791–92; alliances with slave insurgents and the formation of formal corps began in 1793. The outbreak of the war between France, Spain, and England in the spring of 1793 constituted, then, a critical turning point in the use of slaves.[30]

A change in the identity of armed slaves also occurred over time. Those initially armed by slaveowners tended to be trusted members of the slave elite, usually locally born, and (though the evidence is sparse) not infrequently of mixed racial descent. Among the insurgent-allies and in most of the impersonally raised formal corps, Africans greatly predominated — an evolution that would be matched in that of the British West Indian Regiments, which began recruiting in 1795. In addition, the cases studied exhibit a wide variety in the degree of autonomy these slave soldiers enjoyed, although it varied within as much as between categories. Plantation guards might work side by side with white personnel or have the run of abandoned estates. Of the heads of informal corps, Hyacinthe was more a political than a military leader, and clearly more independent than Jean Kina, Caïman, or the leaderless Swiss. Polar types in this respect were the chasseurs, in which a slave could not even be a noncommissioned officer, and the Tropas Auxiliares de Carlos IV, which were totally autonomous.

For enslaved men, the chief attractions of military service seem to have been liberty, prestige, and material gain. Bearing arms brought immediate freedom from plantation labor, and increasingly, the prospect of the status of freedman, poignantly symbolized in the formal corps by the transition from bare feet to shoes. Material rewards varied enormously between different types of organization and between leaders and followers. Jean Kina and Jean-François's officers became men of considerable property, although they lost much of it when forced to migrate. Uniforms were guaranteed only to the British chasseurs. The Spanish auxiliaries for a long time cut a very ragged appearance, but their officers prized their uniforms, fitted with extra gold braid, and some still had them twenty years later.[31]

The long-term consequences of enlistment varied greatly, too, between the select few and the mass of soldiers. Escape from Saint Domingue proved difficult for the Swiss, the British chasseurs, and most of the Spanish auxiliaries. Only a few hundred made new lives elsewhere. Some of the chasseurs sent to Trinidad after being turned away from Jamaica were captured at sea by the French and incorporated into the predominantly black army of Guadeloupe. Some of the auxiliaries disbanded by the Spanish joined the British occupation forces and fought against the republicans until 1798. Others preferred to live in Santo Domingo, which they defended against Toussaint Louverture's invasion in 1801 and Dessalines's in 1805, thus preserving their military identity. The chasseurs and auxiliaries who remained in Saint Domingue were probably forced back into plantation work, but not slavery. Because they had fought on the wrong side, their military service was not the springboard to social mobility it was for those in the republican army. On the other hand, they probably escaped enlistment in the bitterly destructive War of the South (1799–1800) between Toussaint and André Rigaud and the apocalyptic War of Independence (1802–03).

The arming of slaves was always controversial and generally opposed by slaveowners when they did not personally control the process (rather like manumission). Certain cases responded to political needs: the Swiss served the free coloreds as a bargaining chip and threat; Kina had symbolic value for proslavery ideologists. The arming of slaves, however, primarily resulted from the slaveowners' need to combat an enemy who was adapted to the Caribbean disease environment, climate, and terrain. From the first months of the slave uprising, colonists crowded together in the towns or, performing military service in the countryside, suffered escalating death rates from disease. By 1793 a yellow fever pandemic had taken hold in the Caribbean that would be fed throughout the decade by the massive influx of nonimmune European troops. French, British, and to a lesser extent Spanish regiments commonly lost half of their complement in less than one year. Alternative military units (white militia and troupes soldées; free colored militia and gendarmeries) also had notable defects (indiscipline, desertion, expense, and poor health).[32]

Black soldiers, too, fell sick, of course (12 percent of chasseurs were regularly hospitalized), but the contrast was very real. They proved themselves far more resistant to fatigue than ineptly dressed white soldiers, and able to survive on much less. They marched long distances under a vertical sun and scaled precipitous slopes at speed. In addition, they proved adept at tracking and at ambushes in forested terrain. Their chief defect, the French and the British found, was that they lacked the European soldier's training to stand bolt upright when being shot at. "They are not accustomed to our way of holding firm when fighting," wrote commissioner Polverel to an irritated general, "yet do not think them bad soldiers; they don't fear death more than we do, and soon will get used to our ways." It is not clear how much fighting styles changed with regimentation, but evidence suggests that black soldiers in uniform continued to scatter to exploit terrain and to fire in a prone position.[33]

Although it has never been fully elucidated, the experience of the British in Saint Domingue probably played a major role in preparing the way for the twelve British West India Regiments launched in 1795 and perhaps also their reliance on newly arrived Africans. How much the successful use of slave soldiers in the Haitian Revolution more generally enhanced European opinions of blacks is uncertain. Admirers of black troops tended to dwell on biological factors and so emphasized racial difference. Tactical sense was rendered as "cunning," bravery as "boldness" or "indifference to life." Loyalty and physical endurance were both military virtues and slavish qualities.[34]

Armed slaves generally proved effective defenders of slavery. In the Haitian Revolution, however, the policy of arming slaves probably ensured slavery's destruction. Although it is possible that the slave revolution was unstoppable by early 1793, it is also possible that the outbreak of war between the colonial powers and their rush to acquire black allies rescued the insurgents from defeat and drove the French to abolish slavery. Thereafter, the international conflict continued to remove young men from the plantations and promote the formation of a black military that would defeat attempts to restore slavery and finally would take the colony to independence.

Notes

1. Peter M. Voelz, *Slave and Soldier: The Military Impact of Blacks in the Colonial Americas* (New York, 1993), 131–32, 138–40, 181–84; John Gabriel Stedman, *Narrative of a Five Years Expedition Against the Revolted Negroes of Surinam,* ed. R. Price and S. Price (Baltimore, 1988), lxxxv; Ira Berlin, *Many Thousands Gone: The First Two Centuries of Slavery in North America* (Cambridge, 1998), 230, 257–58.

2. Shelby T. McCloy, *The Negro in the French West Indies* (Lexington, 1966), chap. 4; Lucien Peytraud, *L'esclavage aux Antilles françaises avant 1789: D'après des documents inédits des archives coloniales* (Paris, 1897), 479–80; Stewart R. King, *Blue Coat or Powdered Wig? Free People of Color in Pre-Revolutionary Saint-Domingue* (Athens, 2001), 56; Centre des Archives d'Outre-Mer, Aix-en-Provence (hereafter CAOM), F3/91, 1785 draft budget; CAOM, F3/150, letter of July 28, 1789. Slaves who served in the Chasseurs Volontaires that went to Savannah were still awaiting manumission in 1789: Jean Philippe Garran Coulon, *Rapport sur les troubles de Saint-Domingue,* 4 vols. (Paris, 1797–99), 2:8.

3. "Finally, in August 1791, after fighting for nearly two years on one or another side of free persons who claimed they were fighting for liberty, the slaves of the Plain du Nord [sic] applied their fighting to their own cause": Franklin W. Knight, "The Haitian Revolution," *American Historical Review* 105 (2000): 111–12. A few persecuted colored landowners very briefly "fortified" their plantations early in 1790, but these were ephemeral incidents that took place in remote parts of the west province. The government certainly did not arm three thousand slaves to crush the small free colored rebellion of October 1790, as stated in Michel-Rolph Trouillot, *Ti dife boule sou istoua Ayiti* (New York, 1977), 67.

4. Archives Nationales, Paris (hereafter AN), Dxxv/78/772, document AA 148; CAOM, F3/141, ff. 231–32, 338–41; Marc Favre, "Le début de la révolte de Saint-Domingue dans la Plaine du Cap," *Généalogie et Histoire de la Caraïbe* 48 (1993): 777, 782; AN, Dxxv/64/654, declaration of April 8, 1792; Samuel G. Perkins, *"On the Margin of Vesuvius"—Sketches of St. Domingo, 1785–1793* (Lawrence, 1995), 19; *Moniteur Général de la Partie Françoise de Saint-Domingue* 86 (1792). I am not including here

the St. Michel estate adjoining Cap Français, which was close by a military camp and which remained largely intact until slavery ended: David Geggus, "Une Famille de La Rochelle et ses plantations de Saint-Domingue," in *France in the New World,* ed. D. Buisseret (East Lansing, 1998), 119–36.

5. Archives Départementales, Bouches-du-Rhône, Marseille, 1Mi 34/26 (hereafter Marin Papers), letters of October 8 and 28, 1791, March 31, and April 3, 1792, April 29, 1793; Archives Départementales, Vendée, La Roche-sur-Yon, 1Mi 102/2, letter of September 2, 1791; David Geggus, *Slavery, War and Revolution: The British Occupation of Saint Domingue, 1793–1798* (Oxford, 1982), 310–14. On his frontline plantations in the northwest, the merchant François Lavaud organized night patrols of one hundred slaves. They promised to defend "your property which is also ours." See AN, CC9A/8, Lavaud to Lavaux.

6. Bernard Foubert, *Les habitations Laborde à Saint-Domingue dans la seconde moitié du XVIIIe siècle* (Lille, 1990), chap. 10; David Geggus, "The Slaves of British-Occupied Saint Domingue: An Analysis of the Workforces of 197 Absentee Plantations, 1796/97," *Caribbean Studies* 18 (1978): 36–40.

7. David Geggus, "The 'Swiss,' and the Problem of Slave/Free Colored Cooperation," in *Haitian Revolutionary Studies,* ed. D. Geggus (Bloomington, 2002), 99–118.

8. Georgia Historical Society, Savannah, Caradeuc Papers, doc. 3/19.

9. Archivo General de Indias, Seville, Audiencia de Santo Domingo (hereafter AGI, SD) 955, García to Bajamar, February 27, 1792; AN, Dxxv/78/773, anonymous letters, October 27 and 31, 1791; *Production historique des faits qui se sont passés dans la partie de l'Ouest* (Port au Prince, 1792), 14–15.

10. See above, note 7.

11. CAOM, CC9A/5, letter to Pinchinat, November 9, 1791; AN, Dxxv/61/611, letter by P. J. Raboteau, November 20, "1792" [1791]; Commission des Colonies, *Débats entre les accusateurs et les accusés dans l'affaire des colonies* (Paris, 1795), 3:187, 7:206; AN, Dxxv/46/439, Jumécourt to Pinchinat, October 13, 1791; Jamaica Archives, Spanish Town, Council Minutes, deposition by Félix Ouvière, March 14, 1793. On the magical properties attributed to wooden clubs, see David Geggus, "Haitian Voodoo in the Eighteenth Century: Language, Culture, Resistance," *Jahrbuch für Geschichte von Staat, Wirtschaft und Gesellschaft Lateinamerikas* 28 (1991): 33–34.

12. Henri de Grimouärd, *L'Amiral de Grimouärd au Port-au-Prince* (Paris, 1937), 67; Thomas Madiou, *Histoire d'Haïti,* 8 vols. (1847–48; Port au Prince, 1989), 1:129, 167, 171; David Geggus, "The Caradeux and Colonial Memory," in *The Impact of the Haitian Revolution in the Atlantic World,* ed. D. Geggus (Columbia, 2001), 238; Stedman, *Narrative,* 638; Marin Papers, April 3, 1792; Charles Malenfant, *Des colonies et particulièrement de celle de Saint-Domingue* (Paris, 1814), 17. The corps also fought well as part of a similar expedition one year later. Madiou evidently thought Caïman and Philibert to be the same person. Others have argued that Philibert was white or free colored. When the free coloreds and radical whites made peace in mid–1792, the unit was disbanded and its members were sent back to their owners. Philibert, however, became head of the *maréchaussée* of the south coast city of Jacmel. He later returned to the capital, where he repeatedly provoked conflicts with free coloreds. The unit was reestablished in late 1792 and remained a tool of the radicals. See Beaubrun Ardouin, *Études sur l'histoire d'Haïti,*

11 vols. in 1, ed. François Dalencour (1853–60; Port au Prince, 1958), 1:58; Commission des Colonies, *Débats*, 7:206; A. Corre, *Les papiers du Général A.-N. de La Salle (Saint-Domingue, 1792–1793)* (Quimper, 1897), 38.

13. Malenfant, *Des colonies*, 18–20, 27, 75; Madiou, *Histoire d'Haïti*, 1:131–32; Ardouin, *Etudes sur l'histoire d'Haïti*, 1:70; Corre, *Papiers du Général de La Salle*, 36–37. The slaves' owners were each paid 50 *portugaises* ($400) in compensation; only three of them, who wanted to execute their slaves, objected. One source claims that this corps was already in existence, raised either by white or free colored planters in the mountains of Port au Prince in late December 1791: Bibliothèque Nationale, Paris, Manuscrits (hereafter BN), NAF 14878, f. 96.

14. University of North Carolina, Chapel Hill, Southern Historical Collection, Caradeuc Papers, Boissonière Desuré to Caradeux, September 21, and November 13, 1792; Malenfant, *Des colonies*, 18–20, 34, 44; AGI, SD 955, García to Acuña, November 25, 1792; CAOM, F3/141, f. 393 and F3/267, f. 397–98; Archivo General de Simancas, Guerra Moderna (hereafter AGS, GM) 7157, Aybar to Portillo, June 24, 1793.

15. AGS, GM 7157, letters of Bobadilla and Portillo, June–August 1793; Geggus, *Slavery, War and Revolution*, 105, 130, 312; Madiou, *Histoire d'Haïti*, 1:237, 249–50.

16. Petit Séminaire Saint-Martial, Port au Prince, Manuscrits, declaration of Lascaves, 3 Jan. 1792; Commission des Colonies, *Débats*, 3:183–84; Foubert, "Les habitations Laborde," 786; *Procès-Verbaux de l'Assembléé Générale* (1791), 350–51; *Mémoires du général Bigarré* (Paris, 1893), 28. Bigarré recalled that Couacou led six hundred men. This is most unlikely; he led only fifty-seven in January 1793. See Bernard Foubert, "Les volontaires nationaux de l'Aube et de la Seine Inférieure à Saint Domingue," *Bulletin de la Société d'Histoire de la Guadeloupe* 51 (1982): 38.

17. David Geggus, "Slave, Soldier, Rebel: The Strange Career of Jean Kina," *Jamaican Historical Review* 12 (1980): 33–51.

18. Letter of March 24, 1792, in *Moniteur Général de la Partie Françoise de Saint-Domingue* 155 (1793); AN, Dxxv/20/206, f. 1–3; CAOM, F3/141, f. 370, 400–401; Foubert, "Les volontaires nationaux," 37.

19. Captain Colville's notebook (unpaginated), property of Lord Colville of Culross.

20. Geggus, *Slavery, War and Revolution*, 100–104, 389.

21. David Geggus, "The Great Powers and the Haitian Revolution," in *Tordesillas y sus consecuencias: La política de las grandes potencias europeas respecto a América latina (1494–1898)*, ed. Berndt Schröter and Karin Schüller (Madrid, 1995), 115–21; AGS, GM 7161, Acuña to García, February 22 and March 26, 1793.

22. AGI, SD 1031, García to Llaguno, June 11, 1793, SD 956, Bellair to García, September 16, 1793, and Estado, 1/3, expediente 10, enclosure 8; Bibliothèque Municipale, Rouen, Ms. Leber 5847, f. 60.

23. Public Record Office, London, WO 1/59, f. 229–99; AGS, Estado 8150.

24. David Geggus, "From His Most Catholic Majesty to the Godless République: The Volte Face of Toussaint Louverture," *Revue Française d'Histoire d'Outre-Mer* 65 (1978): 481–99.

25. Jane Landers, "Rebellion and Royalism in Spanish Florida: The French Revolution on Spain's Northern Colonial Frontier," in *A Turbulent Time: The French Revolution and the Greater Caribbean*, ed. D. B. Gaspar and D. P. Geggus (Bloomington, 1997),

156–77; David Geggus, "The Slave Leaders in Exile: Spain's Resettlement of Its Black Auxiliary Troops," in Geggus, *Haitian Revolutionary Studies*, 179–203.

26. AN, Dxxv/7/62, f. 12, and Dxxv/7/61, f. 26.

27. Baillio, aîné [Sr.], *Mémoire pour les citoyens Verneuil, Baillio jeune, Fournier, et Gervais, déportés de Saint-Domingue* (Paris, 1794), 9; CAOM, CC9A/9, Gasnier to Navy Minister, March 18, 1793; AN, Dxxv/7/61, f. 49, 60, 67; BN, NAF 14878, f. 104; AN, Dxxv/20/208, f. 11.

28. Service Historique de l'Armée de Terre, Vincennes, Ms. 590 (unpaginated), memoir by Charles DeronoNcourt, September 1794; AGI, SD 1031, memoir dated August 25, 1793.

29. This section is drawn from Geggus, *Slavery, War and Revolution*, 315–25.

30. David Brion Davis, *The Problem of Slavery in the Age of Revolution, 1770–1823* (Ithaca, 1975), 72–82.

31. AGS, GM 7157, García to Acuña, July 3, 1793, and GM 7159, García to Gardoqui, April 10, 1794; José Luciano Franco, *Las conspiraciones de 1810 y 1812* (Havana, 1977), 95.

32. On gendarmeries, see AN, Dxxv/31/315; on the militia, see New York Public Library, West Indian Collection, Santo Domingo, De Cressac Papers; *Moniteur Général de la Partie Françoise de Saint-Domingue* 68 (1792). The governor wrote that the militia were good for a coup de main but hopeless for anything longer, because "the whites cannot stand any sort of fatigue or discomfort; they have to have wine, liquor, fresh meat, stews, and servants. It's quite pitiful, and an incredible to-do just to move them." See AN, Dxxv/46/433, letter of November 16, 1791.

33. AN, Dxxv/12/116, letter of August 3, 1793 (quotation).

34. Geggus, *Slavery, War and Revolution*, 287–89. On the British West India regiments, see Roger N. Buckley, *Slaves in Red Coats: The British West India Regiments* (New Haven, 1979), and Michael Duffy, *Soldiers, Sugar, and Seapower: The British Expeditions to the West Indies and the War Against Revolutionary France* (Oxford, 1987).

Citizen Soldiers: Emancipation and Military Service in the Revolutionary French Caribbean

LAURENT DUBOIS

In 1794 a British troop attacked Pointe-à-Pitre, the economic capital of the island of Guadeloupe, in a failed attempt to wrest it from the control of French republican troops. As he led his troops into the city, a captain was severely wounded by the explosion of an ammunition depot. His burning clothes were pulled off by some of his "brother officers," but his "face and hands were rendered entirely black by the explosion." In the confusion, a group of his own grenadiers, "taking him for one of the French blacks, attacked him with charged bayonets, and wounded him in three places before he could make himself known to them." At the time of this incident, emancipation had only recently been decreed, and the British in the Eastern Caribbean had not been confronting republican troops comprised of a majority of ex-slaves for very long. Yet "blackness" had already become a kind of military uniform of the French, a military "color" that could incite immediate attack.[1]

A few years earlier it would probably have been difficult for anyone, white or black, to imagine that black soldiers—many of them ex-slaves—would soon be the backbone of the French army in the Caribbean. When, in the wake of the 1791 insurrection in Saint-Domingue, there were reports that among the slave insurgents were whites who "were leading them with blackened faces, who were discovered by their hair," the idea that whites and blacks were joined in rebellion was stunning and execrable to most observers. But by 1794, insurrection had been transformed into military assimilation as part of the Republic's war, and the idea of whites, blacks, and *gens de couleur* joined together in a struggle for liberty was the foundation of France's colonial policy. In an engraving celebrating the "liberty of the colonies," two black figures dressed in what was intended to be African costume were shown under the heading "Rights of Man." One of the black figures had his arm around a uniformed white soldier, while a white woman held out a similar uniform to another slave. Despite the racist intimations of its portrait of African "primitivism" being concealed by republican "civilization," the engraving was an acknowledgment of the radical implications of the incorporation of ex-slaves into the military units of the Republic.[2]

During the 1790s the Caribbean region became a major theater in the global conflict that raged between France and Britain. As the war between the two nations exploded in 1793, the British took advantage of the conflicts within the French colonies and achieved a rapid series of victories. They invaded Saint-Domingue in September 1793 and within a few months were firmly established in the rich western province of the colony. Soon afterwards, they overran Guadeloupe and Martinique, the two major French possessions in the Eastern Caribbean. In all these attacks, they profited from the support of local French royalists. In Saint-Domingue, the republican commissioners Sonthonax and Polverel were in the midst of consolidating their regime of emancipation when the British invaded, and they used ex-slaves in their defense of the colony, but they only managed to stop, and not reverse, the British advance.[3]

The decree of emancipation passed by the National Convention in Paris in February 1794 transformed the imperial conflict in the Caribbean into a war over the existence of slavery itself. French military fortunes soon began to change, at least for a while. In June 1794, Toussaint Louverture rallied to the French Republic, bringing a sizable army with him, and soon carried out a series of brilliant victories against both the Spanish (whom he had previously been serving) and the British. In the Eastern Caribbean, a small troop of French soldiers took back Guadeloupe by recruiting the slaves they liberated into the army. From Guadeloupe, republican troops supported pro-French rebels in Grenada, St. Vincent, and St. Lucia, in the latter case capturing the island for the British. Ultimately, the large British expeditions that were mounted to counter the French advances drained resources and men — by the end of the 1790s an estimated sixty thousand British soldiers had lost their lives — playing a crucial though often unacknowledged role in the global Franco-British conflict.[4]

The mobilization of armies of citizen-soldiers was a major part of the political transformations brought about by the French Revolution on the European

continent. Military service provided many men with unprecedented opportunities for social mobility based on merit rather than background, and service
in the military was frequently presented as the ultimate expression of republican citizenship. In the French Caribbean, the recruitment of gens de couleur
(free coloreds) and ex-slaves into the armies of the Republic also had a major
impact on social structure and politics. Before emancipation, it was through
military action that slave insurgents most clearly expressed their demands for
citizenship. Indeed, it was the transformation of insurgents into defenders of
the Republic in Saint-Domingue in 1793 that propelled the abolition of slavery
by the National Convention the following year. In the wake of this decision,
as administrators in the French Caribbean struggled to contain and channel
emancipation, military service became a way for male ex-slaves to demonstrate
and perform their attachment to republican France, and the courage of slaves
turned citizen-soldiers was touted as proof of their capacity for citizenship. It
was in the military arena that the principles of racial equality announced by the
abolition of slavery were applied to their fullest extent.[5]

For gens de couleur, service in the republican army was in many ways the
continuation of pre-revolutionary service in militias and the *maréchaussée*
(police), although the new order provided more opportunities for promotion
than the old. For ex-slaves, however, military service represented an even more
radical transformation from a plantation or domestic laborer to a soldier with
a salary, a gun, and new mobility and social standing. For both these groups,
being part of a racially integrated republican army created important new opportunities. It is not surprising, therefore, that attacks against the racial egali-
tarianism of this army during the late 1790s and early 1800s were a crucial part
of turning many of these citizen-soldiers against French administrators.[6]

The history of the military in revolutionary Saint-Domingue has been fairly
well documented, notably in the biographies of figures such as Louverture,
Jean-Jacques Dessalines, and Henri Christophe, but less attention has been
paid to the armies of the French colonies of the Eastern Caribbean during this
period. This chapter focuses on the lives of the soldiers and sailors from Guadeloupe (and, to a lesser extent, Martinique), which provide us with insight
into the political meaning and social impact military service had in this region. Although the general processes of recruitment in both areas were similar,
there were significant differences between the two theaters of war. Whereas
the campaigns in Saint-Domingue were primarily confrontations between
land armies, the campaigns in the Eastern Caribbean involved attacks that
fanned out from Guadeloupe to several other islands and unorthodox alliances between arriving troops and slaves in the British colonies. And whereas
the black officer Toussaint Louverture was in military and political control of

much of Saint-Domingue by the late 1790s, in Guadeloupe military and administrative control remained in the hands of white men sent from the metropole, at least until a revolt broke out on the island in 1802. The fate of the ex-slaves and gens de couleur of the two colonies was also sharply distinct: in Saint-Domingue, the armies forged by Louverture and his generals ultimately won a dramatic victory against the French troops sent to crush them; in Guadeloupe they were decimated in an equally dramatic defeat that was followed by the reenslavement of most of the population.

Slaves into Soldiers

On February 5, 1794 — one day after the abolition of slavery in all the French colonies was decreed across the Atlantic by the National Convention — the citoyen Lacharrière-Larery mounted the stand of a Jacobin club in Guadeloupe's capital, Basse-Terre. He was an *homme de couleur,* one among many who during the preceding year had become active participants in the political life of the island. His speech, however, was aimed at integrating another group into the political life of the colony: the slaves. Lacharrière-Larery argued in favor of a project to arm slaves to protect Guadeloupe from internal and external enemies of the Republic. "Let us create new defenders of liberty," he commanded, dismissing those who feared that "as soon as they are released from slavery," these armed men would attack their fellow soldiers rather than the enemy. Service to the nation, he argued, would transform worthy slaves into valuable citizens: "We cannot give political rights to people who have done nothing to deserve it, it will be said; perhaps not, but we can show them what is expected and give them the means to achieve it. May he who can show three wounds be freed immediately . . . may he who has saved the life of a citizen, be immediately declared a citizen himself. The recompense for actions and virtues will awaken honor in the souls of these new men, and will prepare them by degrees to be admitted into the class of free men. . . . [T]o make war you need two things, men and money; men we can make." These arguments were seconded at the same club four days later by Joseph Hays, another free colored citizen of Basse-Terre. Hays called on all to unite behind the Republic and support the arming of the slaves. Having heard this speech, the Jacobin Club voted enthusiastically to publish it with the signatures of all its members, along with the signatures of those who had been in the galleries during the speech.[7]

Although on the surface Lacharrière-Larery's proposal was fairly timid — it was consistent with a long tradition of freeing slaves for heroic military service, and few slaves would have fulfilled the conditions he set for the boon of freedom — it had radical implications in the particular context in which it was presented. A little less than a year earlier, in April 1793, the deadliest slave revolt in the history of the island had taken place in the nearby town of Trois-Rivières, during which many of the resident whites had been killed. The insurgents spared only one plantation, and its owner, one of the few pro-republican planters in the town. They did not loot the plantations or burn the cane. Instead, they followed their insurrection with an orderly march toward the capital of Basse-Terre, and when they met the white troops sent to put down the revolt, the slave participants presented themselves as "citizens and friends" and explained that they had risen up to defend the Republic against their royalist masters. The whites of the island essentially accepted this version of the events and pursued — to a large extent based on the testimony of the slave insurgents themselves — the various groups of whites the slaves had attacked. The slaves, then, had given palpable proof of their potential power, and some republican whites on the island, chafing from various defeats they had suffered at the hand of the royalists on the island, openly declared that the slave insurgents had saved the colony.[8]

The actions of the insurgents of Trois-Rivières and of their leader Jean-Baptiste had both provided an example of and created the conditions for the arguments made in favor of the arming of slaves by administrators and political activists in the colony in early 1794. Jean-Baptiste had in fact been held in custody in Basse-Terre during the previous year, although he had the right to circulate as he pleased. He might well have discussed the question of the arming of slaves with individuals such as Hays and Lacharrière-Larery. Indeed, among the names signed to the speech supporting Hays's call for the creation of slave troops was one "Jean-Baptiste" — perhaps the insurgent leader, or perhaps a free individual with the same name. In the end, however, the attempt to arm slaves in defense of Guadeloupe was too little, too late. The governor of the island did raise a battalion of three hundred *chasseurs noirs,* recruited from among the plantation slaves, to fight for the Republic. The reward for their service was to be "indefinite liberty." The presence of this small unit did little to save the deeply divided colony against the large British expedition that invaded Guadeloupe in late March 1794. As the British troops, having taken over Pointe-à-Pitre, advanced toward Basse-Terre, the "Bataillon d'Esclaves" — "Slave Battalion" — apparently abandoned its post above the town. Many royalist whites, meanwhile, actively collaborated with the British occupiers. A group of republicans who fought the invasion and were deported from the island eventually brought the story of the Trois-Rivières insurrection to France, describing how the republicans of Guadeloupe had been saved from a royalist conspiracy when "some of the negroes who had been armed to carry it out turned the weapons against the conspirators, crying that they were Republicans," and in so doing "pulled the patriots out of their lethargy" — only to see the incompetence of the governor and the hostility of the planters to the idea of arming slaves pave the way for a British takeover.[9]

The situation took a very different course in Saint-Domingue. There, the republican commissioner, Légér Félicité Sonthonax, faced some of the same problems as his comrades in Guadeloupe: royalist whites were in open sedition against the Republic, and some were actively courting the British, who they hoped would invade and preserve slavery and racial hierarchy in the colony. But Sonthonax also faced an imposing military force of slave insurgents who, since the mass uprising of August 1791, had consolidated their forces and established themselves in camps throughout the northern province of the colony, in the process effectively smashing plantation slavery in much of the region. Although Guadeloupe's republicans had found slave allies during the Trois-Rivières revolt, the military power of the insurgents there paled in comparison to that of those in Saint-Domingue. While the republicans of Guadeloupe discussed recruiting slaves to form a pro-republican military force, Sonthonax made an alliance with a military force that had already proved its power and effectiveness. In 1793, when an uprising broke out against Sonthonax in Le Cap, he turned to the insurgent slaves, offering them liberty and citizenship if they came to his assistance. This first act spiraled into a broader offer of freedom to all slaves who joined the Republic and ultimately into a general emancipation in Saint-Domingue. For the slaves of Guadeloupe, this abolition in their sister colony would ultimately bring them freedom as well, for in February 1794 the emancipation proclaimed by Sonthonax in Saint-Domingue was ratified and extended to all the French colonies.[10]

In June 1794 a flotilla of republican troops arrived from France, led by a man named Victor Hugues. He had been given the mission of bringing the decree of emancipation voted in Paris to the Eastern Caribbean. Hugues faced a well-fortified island manned by the British troops who had occupied the island with the help of royalist French. Nevertheless, in a military action that was touted by avid republicans in France as an example of the almost superhuman qualities of the *sans-culottes* who fought for universal liberty, the French soldiers — joined by the slaves they freed — managed to rout the British forces and take back Grande-Terre. In celebrating the initial victory two months later, Hugues compared the military feat of the republicans in Guadeloupe to the military accomplishments of the Roman legions and praised the population of the colony, including the "*Citoyens noirs* who, thankful for the blessings granted them by the French nation, have shared in our victories by fighting for Liberty."[11]

Writing a few years later, the historian Bryan Edwards pointed to the recruitment of "blacks and mulattoes" by Hugues as one of the reasons for the French victory: "Observing how severely his own troops, as well as ours, suffered from the climate, [Hugues] conceived the project of arming in his service, as many blacks and mulattoes as he could collect. These men, inured to the climate, and having nothing to lose, flocked to his standard in great numbers, and were soon brought into some degree of order and discipline." We have few details about how the recruitment worked during the days after the French expedition arrived, but after the taking of Pointe-à-Pitre, the commissioners made a haphazard policy official, calling on "citizens of all colors" to join in the fight against the British, who had made the citizens of Guadeloupe "without distinction" into a "people of slaves." In a report he wrote a few weeks later, Hugues said of the new recruits: "Many have taken up arms and shown themselves worthy of the fight for Liberty." His decision to create battalions composed of sans-culottes of all colors, he wrote, was a success. It was, indeed, a quite remarkable early experiment in the formation of interracial military units, one in which the equality of soldiers was—at least officially—complete. "This mix has had the best possible effect on the former slaves. I have granted them the same pay as the troops from France. They exercise twice a day and are flattered to be treated like our brothers the *sans-culottes,* who, thanks to my constant fraternal exhortations, respect the former slaves as much as is possible." Hugues praised these new soldiers' behavior in battle: "the Black Citizens, our new brothers, have shown on this occasion what the spirit of Liberty can accomplish; out of men previously brutalized by slavery, she made heroes." His opinion of the slaves was seconded by the naval officer Pierre Villegegu, who wrote: "In all our diverse attacks the *Citoyens nègres* behaved themselves well and we can praise them for their courage." Hugues, however, also tempered his praise by adding that "the blacks alone, without Europeans, will never fight well." The integration of army units, then, was for Hugues as much a way of making sure "Europeans" were always alongside the black troops as it was an expression of a desire for equality. Nevertheless, the creation of such units, and the granting of equal pay to ex-slaves and Europeans, was a remarkable step for the time.[12]

In the next few years, ex-slaves became the backbone of the republican army of Guadeloupe. In 1796 Hugues boasted that blacks made up "7/8ths of the army soldiers, sergeants and corporals" and "a third of the officers" in his army. "We have nothing but praise for their wisdom," he continued; their presence and their discipline are "the despair of our enemies." The first Bataillon des Sans-Culottes he had formed in 1794 had been followed by several others. In 1795 and 1796 there were at least four other battalions on the island, including the second and third Bataillions des Sans-Culottes and the

Bataillion des Antilles. By 1796, of the approximately forty-six hundred soldiers in the garrison of Guadeloupe, only 20 percent had arrived from France, and more than 50 percent were ex-slaves. The following year it was estimated that there were about thirty-six hundred soldiers, with similar proportions of Europeans and ex-slaves; thus about 5 percent of the freed men in the colony were serving in the army. But these numbers did not include the substantial number of soldiers, from Guadeloupe and Martinique as well as from the British islands, who fought in the service of the French Republic elsewhere in the region, for instance, in a unit called the Bataillion de Sainte-Lucie. There may have been as many as eleven thousand such soldiers at the height of the campaigns, during 1795 and 1796, when for a moment it seemed as if the French Republic was on the verge of gaining control of the some of the most valuable British colonies in the Eastern Caribbean.[13]

The Contagious Republic

The recruitment of ex-slaves into the army of Guadeloupe starting in 1794 set the stage for a military campaign against three British colonies in the Eastern Caribbean: St. Lucia, Grenada, and St. Vincent. These colonies, originally settled by French inhabitants, were ceded to the Great Britain at the end of the Seven Years' War. The many French settlers who stayed lived in an uneasy peace with the arriving British settlers and administrators, who were often suspicious of their loyalty. (In St. Vincent the political conflict between British and French inhabitants was made more complicated by the presence of the "Black Caribs," a group descended from the mixture of Caribs and African maroons and who had long had a close relationship with the French.) After 1789, many French settlers responded enthusiastically to the news of the Revolution, especially free people of color who drew inspiration from the ultimately successful struggle for racial equality in the French Empire. Repressive policies implemented against free coloreds by the British administrators, meant in principle to avoid political tumult, instead encouraged many French residents to turn against British administrators, particularly in St. Lucia. These conflicts set the stage for the warfare of the mid–1790s, when large numbers of slaves took up arms against the British on several islands.[14]

The 1794 decree of emancipation and its effective application by Hugues in Guadeloupe sent ripples of revolt and fear through the Eastern Caribbean. Lieutenant General Sir Charles Grey wrote in September 1794 that the British were "ever apprehensive of an Insurrection among the Negroes, in consequence of the Note of Emancipation of the French Government." Hugues understood that the promise of liberty offered to British slaves could be an extremely potent weapon, and he sent envoys to support and stir up local insurrections and ultimately sent black troops from his base in Guadeloupe to fight with local rebels to take over the islands for the French.[15]

In March 1795 an insurrection broke out among the slaves and gens de couleur in Grenada. Led by Julian Fedon, an homme de couleur of French ancestry, it quickly engulfed the island. Doubting the loyalty of the free coloreds and French whites who composed more than half of the militia on the island, British officials withheld arms from them, and in so doing seriously undermined their ability to respond to the revolt. The insurgents killed whites and took the British governor prisoner, demanding the surrender of the island's forts and ordering all residents to rally to the French flag. Hugues declared his support for the insurgents and sent an agent to the island. Fedon, meanwhile, gathered together a substantial fighting force of several thousand men that far outnumbered the British troops on the island. When the British attacked, he defeated them and executed his British prisoners, including the governor. The British retreated to the capital of St. George, while Fedon's army pillaged and destroyed the abandoned plantations on the rest of the island. They could do little against the massive and growing army of slaves determined to gain their freedom by means of a French takeover of the island.[16]

The British responded to Fedon by arming slaves to fight him. They created a corps of Black Rangers, recruiting slaves and promising them individual freedom in return for their service. Officials in St. Vincent, who were battling an uprising among Black Caribs and slaves on the island, also formed such a corps. Although members of the Rangers sometimes defected to the other side, attracted perhaps by the French promise of universal emancipation, most of these slave troops served loyally. Indeed, they played a crucial role in sparing the British a total defeat in St. Vincent and Grenada. Although republicans managed to keep control over much of the territory of these two islands until the middle of 1796, they never managed to take over the islands.[17]

In St. Lucia, however, the French and their slave allies delivered a total defeat to the British. Since the early 1790s, the island had harbored a particularly bold French republican contingent. They managed to depose the British governor in 1792 and took effective control of the island. In early 1794, however, the same expedition that conquered Guadeloupe reestablished British control in St. Lucia. Many of the French retreated to the interior of the island and continued to harass the British. Lieutenant General Sir John Vaughan, then commanding in St. Lucia, suggested in January 1795 that the British "arm and train a regiment of negroes, obtaining men either from the various islands, if the local government would grant them, or if that were not practicable, to import them" to fight the republicans. Though this policy was not implemented, Vaughan did deploy the Black Carolina Corps, a unit composed of former slaves and free blacks who had fought with the British during the American War of Independence, to fight the French "brigands."[18]

In February 1795 Hugues sent an envoy from Guadeloupe to make contact with the French republicans. His name was Jean-Joseph Lambert, and he was an homme de couleur who had lived in St. Lucia and fought with the republicans in the early 1790s; he had escaped to Guadeloupe after Hugues' arrival. Lambert carried a declaration to all the people of St. Lucia, calling on them to join the French forces. His visit helped inspire slaves to leave their plantations and join the rebels in the mountains. In April Hugues sent another agent, Commissioner Goyrand, to the island, this time with soldiers and weapons. Guided by a St. Lucian slave named Eustache, Goyrand joined with the insurgents on the island, and together they managed to secure republican control over most of the territory outside the capital.[19]

A series of British counterattacks made little progress against the insurgents, who rarely committed themselves to large battles and instead continued low-level harassment from posts scattered throughout the interior of the island. Meanwhile the ranks of the republican forces were swelled by the slaves who had deserted their plantations. In June a small group of republicans, crying "Vive la République," managed to send the British in a disorderly retreat from their last stronghold on the island. It was an impressive victory that echoed Hugues' success in Guadeloupe, for, as Goyrand described it, three hundred volunteers from the island, armed with guns, along with three hundred pike-toting slaves, had defeated twenty-four hundred British soldiers. The event was "one of the most disgraceful events that ever happened," according to one British witness, "for we had more Regular troops in Garrison there, than the whole Brigand army, and which mostly consisted of Color'd People," and yet the British had retreated precipitously without a shot fired. Saint Lucia was in the hands of the French Republic. "We have shattered the chains of the Africans in two beautiful colonies, Guadeloupe and St. Lucia," wrote Goyrand. It was a victory for the slaves who had risen up in St. Lucia and for those who had come to fight with them from Guadeloupe. The French policy of emancipation had proved itself a potent weapon of war.[20]

Soldiers as Citizens

Military service transformed the identities of the gens de couleur and ex-slaves who became part of the republican forces, providing them with new political, social, and economic power. Like the army that had been defending France at the time Victor Hugues left for Guadeloupe, the republican army of the Caribbean was notable for the possibilities for rapid promotion it provided soldiers of all social classes. Indeed, military service in the Caribbean opened up social mobility to an extent that surpassed that available in metropolitan France, since slaves who had always stood outside the legal order had now found a place as primary defenders of a new legal order.

Although documentation about the army units set up by Hugues is fragmentary, it is possible to piece together a few details about their structure and the ways they influenced the lives of those of African descent who served in them. In Bataillon des Sans-Culottes, the first unit created by Hugues after his arrival in 1794, there came to be a number of officers of African descent, such as Noël Corbet and Pierre Gédéon, who were probably free before 1794, as well as a leper named Jean-Baptiste Vulcain, who was likely an ex-slave. Vulcain had become an officer thanks to a provision by which any man who brought more than twenty recruits to join the army would automatically be named a sergeant. Within a few months he had already risen to the rank of captain and commanded both gens de couleur and ex-slaves. Ex-slave soldiers were a presence in the new units that quickly multiplied on the island. The second battalion, for instance, included many ex-slaves, some of them African-born, who served in infantry as well as artillery companies. Service in this integrated army unit seems to have created new networks that brought together ex-slaves and metropolitan whites. For example, when ex-slave soldiers from this unit were married, as several were in 1795 and 1796, the witnesses usually included officers of African descent as well as European soldiers serving in the same unit as the groom. The Bataillon des Sans-Culottes and the relationships that grew out if it therefore represented potent enaction of the possibilities for social integration embodied in the republican decree of emancipation.[21]

The weddings of ex-slave soldiers also give us some insight into the new social and legal opportunities opened up by military service. With emancipation, all ex-slaves gained the legal rights that had always been denied them, including the right to be legally married. A significant majority of the ex-slaves who appear in the registers taking advantage of this new right, however, were soldiers, probably because their integration into the bureaucratic structures and social networks of the military facilitated and encouraged their participation. Some soldiers were garrisoned close to their families, such as the former slave Charles, who served in Basse-Terre close to his companion Léonide and his newborn son Désir, who still lived on the nearby Bisdary plantation, where they had all once been slaves. But many soldiers, and often their partners and wives, moved away from their plantations and to the towns when they served in the military, in the process encountering new challenges and opportunities. Military service also created contexts for sustained involvement with the republican symbols and ideologies. The influences are difficult to uncover, although occasional evocative traces remain, as in the ex-slave Eugenie, who gave her newborn child the name "Sans-Culottes," perhaps as a way of honoring the father, Pierre, who served in an artillery unit.[22]

The republican armies that served in Guadeloupe and in the campaigns of the Eastern Caribbean also brought together men from a wide range of Caribbean islands. The French colony of Martinique, like Guadeloupe taken over in 1794, remained under British control throughout the 1790s. But many soldiers from Martinique ended up in Guadeloupe nevertheless. Some — like the thirteen-year-old Alou and the thirty-two-year-old Romain — had likely escaped from British domination, and continued slavery, in Martinique. Others, like the Martinican gens de couleur Louis Delgrès and Magloire Pélage, had been soldiers fighting for the Republic in 1794 when they were captured by the British. Sent to Europe, they eventually made their way back to the Caribbean to serve the Republic once again. As they fought alongside one another, Martinicans and Guadeloupeans also came in contact with individuals in the British colonies they were invading, notably the free coloreds and slaves who were battling with them. In St. Lucia and Grenada many ex-slaves became part of the republican army. In St. Vincent the ten-year-old ex-slave Augustin Miston fought with the French. Louis Jason, who was sixty-two years old in 1794, had escaped from the British island of Dominica to join the republicans. Among the recruits from all these islands, furthermore, were many who had actually been born in Africa. As they encountered one another, these men from various islands probably confronted their differences but also had the opportunity to create and imagine new kinds of connections and alliances. Most of the soldiers who fought against the British were eventually captured and sent as prisoners to Europe, where they ended up in metropolitan France through prisoner exchanges. This transatlantic experience also certainly gave them new perspectives on the Caribbean societies in which they had lived. Officers such as Delgrès and Pélage would draw on these experiences when they became political leaders in the early 1800s.[23]

The unconventional warfare practiced by the French republicans in Grenada, St. Vincent, and particularly St. Lucia, in which battlefield promotion took on a particular importance, opened up opportunities for such new recruits to rise through the ranks of the army. After his victory against the British, Commissioner Goyrand promoted many officers, notably Delgrès and Pélage, who became one of the highest-ranking officers in St. Lucia. Among the officers Goyrand promoted in 1795 and 1796 were a number of men who could not read or write and who may have been former slaves. Goyrand also selected two men who had been leaders of the republican insurgents before his arrival to lead troops he sent to St. Vincent. One of them, Marin Pèdre, was a native of St. Lucia who was either a free colored or a slave before joining the French, and his seventeen-year-old son also joined the republican army. Once in St. Vincent, Marin Pèdre, like other agents appointed by Goyrand and Hugues, also promoted officers. Having been chosen and promoted, officers of African descent gained the power to make their own determinations about who should become an officer. As the ranks of the army became integrated, so did the structure of promotion, and along with it the form and meaning of the hierarchies and networks within the military.[24]

Of course, military service could carry with it serious costs, and it left many recruits from the Antilles permanently crippled. Among a group of black and gens de couleur veterans gathered together on an island off the coast of France in 1798, for instance, was Guenette, whose left leg had been fractured by bullets, leaving it shorter than the right. A soldier named Guillaume had his left leg destroyed by an exploding cannon ball. Narcisse's wrist had been destroyed by a bullet, Coffie and Coquille had been shot in the arm, and Jean-Baptiste had lost several fingers to gunfire; all of them were incapable of handling a weapon. Another soldier named Jean-Baptiste had been shot repeatedly through the torso, leaving him with a hernia. Fréderic had lost an eye. Marc and Crepein Laporte had each had one of their legs amputated, while Celestin and François Eglise had lost both of theirs. In a group of seventy-one wounded soldiers from the Caribbean at the Ile d'Aix, thirty-three had been crippled during imprisonment or battle in Europe during the winter, having lost toes, sometimes all of them, to the frost. In addition to all those who were wounded were those who died in battle or from disease, such as Claude Theodore, an ex-slave of Basse-Terre, who was twenty-two when he was emancipated in 1794 and, after fighting and being captured by the British, died at the age of twenty-seven in a hospital off the coast of France.[25]

Soldiers who faced such dangers were justifiably proud of their service to the Republic and were ready to defend the rights they believed such service granted them. One of the benefits of such service was, of course, the salaries granted to soldiers and officers, which especially for ex-slaves provided newfound economic power. Their salaries enabled them to take advantage of the opportunities for consumption in the towns and certainly changed their daily lives and their relationships with family and friends. This economic power could be defended, in turn, by the social power these individuals had as soldiers. In 1801, when a number of soldiers in Basse-Terre felt that they were being overcharged by local merchants, several of them openly confronted the injustice. Though the values of the various forms of currency used in Guadeloupe during this period were in principle fixed, merchants in the town often granted less than the official amount. Soldiers demanded the full value of their currency from merchants; when shop owners refused, some soldiers simply took what they thought they were entitled to for the money they had paid. Not surprisingly, soldiers and merchants often ended up fighting in shops and in the streets. Sometimes the fights were about something else: the lack of respect shown by white merchants to black soldiers. After the grenadier Michel fought with the merchant Descombes in the streets of Basse-Terre, officials declared that Descombes had started the fight by saying "things that were infuriating to this grenadier." Perhaps to still the anger of Michel and other black soldiers who were increasingly angry with the officials of the island, Descombes was sentenced to eight days' imprisonment in the Fort St. Charles. Whatever it was he said to "infuriate" Michel — a racial slur, perhaps — he learned that it was dangerous to disrespect a soldier.[26]

The Republican Corsairs

Military service in the army coexisted with another form of potentially lucrative military service: that of the sailors who manned the republican corsairs. These small, speedy vessels were specially equipped and manned to capture enemy or neutral ships going to foreign islands and bring their confiscated cargo into the nearest French port. Beginning in January 1793, when the National Convention passed a decree inviting citizens to arm corsairs to attack enemy shipping, many French merchants and sailors participated in privateering in the Atlantic, attacking ships coming and going from British ports. Victor Hugues began arming corsairs soon after his arrival in 1794, and by the end of the year thirty were roving the local waters. By 1798 an estimated sixty to eighty larger ships (with crews of several dozen sailors) and probably a number of smaller ones with smaller crews were operating out of Guadeloupe. Between 1796 and 1798 alone, cases involving the capture of seven hundred ships were heard in the court on the island. The island corsairs were different in one crucial respect from those outfitted in the metropolitan ports: their crews included many ex-slaves freed by the 1794 emancipation decree. The exact proportions are difficult to determine, but on many ships sailors of African descent were apparently a majority. In 1797 one British officer noted that the corsair crews were "chiefly Blacks and Mulattoes," and one historian has estimated that during Hugues' regime an estimated thirty-five hundred ex-slaves were employed as sailors on corsairs. Such sailors faced a unique danger, for when the British managed to capture corsairs, they often sold captured blacks into slavery rather than treating them as prisoners of war.[27]

Sailors who served on corsairs were compensated by receiving a portion of the captured loot. Although sometimes these shares could be quite large, sailors often came home with little or nothing to show for their efforts. A rare document drawn up in 1800 by the local tribunal in Cayenne, which shows the division of the loot from the capture of a ship from Massachusetts, suggests how meager the profits for sailors could be even when their corsair was successful. A third of the total sum garnered from the sale of the vessel and its cargo was set aside for the crew members, who were rewarded according to their rank. The basic crew members, the *matelots,* received a portion worth about 340 francs; the captain received five times this amount, and the lowest-ranked *mousses,* such as "Simon, noir" received a half portion. What they owed from the voyage was assiduously subtracted from these carefully calculated sums; Simon may well have wondered whether the 63 francs he finally received for his efforts had been worthwhile. Comparatively, Simon was lucky, since in another case where the *Bergère* participated with two other vessels in a capture, *mousses* such as Augustin received only about 20 francs, before subtractions, for their efforts. The tribunal of Cayenne set aside the portions of those who were "dead or absent," in addition to receiving claims from various parties who were owed money by sailors on the corsairs; Pistache, Magloire, and Izidor, for instance, all owed the Citoyenne Gaulthier of Cayenne for shirts she had made for them.[28]

Still, sailors who were lucky might amass enough over the course of a few years to live fairly well and even to invest in land on their islands. In 1799, for instance, it was possible to buy a small piece of property in the heart of Guadeloupe's capital of Basse-Terre for twenty-five hundred francs and plots of land in the country or in smaller towns for substantially less. The sailors on the corsairs were not the only ones who might profit from the loot they gained. Since sailors often left before they could receive their portion of their ship's latest captures, they named citizens of the port towns (often women) to take charge, in their absence, of collecting the amounts due to them. If the sailors did not return, these individuals would inherit their portions. Although sailors did not have the comfort of the consistent salaries soldiers received, the opportunity to serve on corsairs raised the possibility of an economic windfall that might transform their lives. Like other black sailors in the Atlantic world, they gained new perspectives on themselves and the broader world in which they lived through their contacts with other sailors and their wide-ranging journeys in the Caribbean.[29]

The Danger of Soldiers

In 1796 a Guadeloupean planter complained: "The blacks compose almost all of the army, and they take advantage of the rarity of whites, although most of them, or nearly all of them, preserve a certain respect for whites which is a good sign." The next year, he noted that the multiple mutinies that had occurred among the troops were the result of having only a "small number of whites" in an army "almost completely composed of blacks." The emergence of a new group of soldiers and officers of African descent in the Caribbean alarmed white planters for obvious reasons. Military service drew men away from the plantations, and it encouraged them to see themselves as equals to whites and as full members of a Republic they had defended with their lives. Black troops were the vanguard of the broad social transformation in French colonial society, and during the latter half of the 1790s they came to be a symbol for many whites of the dangers of the emerging order.[30]

The military achievements of the black troops of the French Caribbean in the years following the emancipation decree of 1794 were enormous. In Saint-Domingue, Toussaint Louverture had led his majority black troops in the defeat of a large British invasion. In the Eastern Caribbean similar troops had sometimes trounced and regularly harassed France's enemy. By 1796, however, the tide was turning against the French advances in the lesser Antilles. A large military expedition sent from Great Britain in early 1796 had managed to land in St. Lucia, although the republicans once again regrouped in the middle of the island and continued to fight. These reinforcements set in motion the defeat of the French-supported insurrections in Grenada and in St. Vincent, where the entire population of Black Caribs was deported in 1797. In 1798, Victor Hugues was removed from his position in Guadeloupe to be replaced by more moderate administrators, while the French began tempering their use of privateering. The period of French military expansion — and the concomitant expansion of possibilities for ex-slaves — was coming to an end. As it did, the racially integrated army this period had produced also came under attack from certain quarters.

In May 1798, the Minister of the Colonies, a planter from Saint-Domingue named Baron de Bruix, called for the creation of a segregated military unit that would regroup all of the "black or colored" soldiers in metropolitan France. Most of these soldiers had arrived in France after having been captured in the Caribbean during the British campaigns of 1796 and 1797, and then exchanged for British prisoners held in France. Once in France, some had been incorporated into other units and fought in different parts of Europe. The 1798 order required them to leave these units and to travel to an island off the coast of France, the Ile d'Aix, where they would be regrouped into the new unit. Once they arrived, many of those who had been officers were demoted with the justification that their promotions on the field of battle in the Caribbean were not legitimate — despite the fact that the homme de couleur captain of the new company, Marin Pèdre, had in fact promoted many of them himself when he led the republican mission in St. Vincent and was willing to vouch for them. Some voted with their feet — the day after he was demoted from the rank of sergeant to that of a common soldier, Peper Sejourna deserted with another soldier from his hometown of St. Pierre, Martinique. But others sought redress from the Republic they had served loyally during the previous years, writing to a deputy named Etienne Mentor — an homme de couleur from Martinique who represented Saint-Domingue in the Parliament at the time. They asked him to intervene on their behalf to end "their humiliating separation from the whites" and request that they be employed "without distinction, like their comrades-at-arms, in the armies of the Republic." Mentor took up their case in Parliament, sharply attacking the formation of the battalion, arguing that it set up a situation in which these soldiers were "isolated from their European comrades, so that it seems that they are being punished for having supported, in the New World, the principles of the Republic." How could governors dare "to re-establish such insulting distinctions"? "These courageous soldiers wish only to die fighting for the French Republic," he declared. Mentor's proposition to retract the order was "unanimously adopted." Soon afterwards, Bruix was relieved of his functions.[31]

Although this attempt to institute racial segregation in the military failed, the broader political movement of which it was a part only grew stronger in the following years. Planters and merchants who argued that emancipation was an economic and social disaster gained an increasing hearing within government circles in Paris. Although at first few advocated a return to slavery, many did suggest the need to return to some of the old forms of coercion and racial hierarchy. White administrators wanted to make sure that the plantations would continue to be worked by individuals who, if they were no longer enslaved, were still unremittingly submissive, and many saw the presence of black troops and officers as incompatible with this goal. The movement to turn back the changes brought on by emancipation won a victory in 1801 when Napoleon Bonaparte declared he would apply a set of "particular laws" to the colonies. Representing a break from the previous policy of political integration between the French metropole and its colonies, it meant that there would no longer be colonial representatives in Paris to stand up for the people of the Caribbean as Etienne Mentor had in 1798. Having become a major force in the changed societies of the French Caribbean, black soldiers understood that such attempts to reverse these changes had dangerous implications for them and their communities. In Saint-Domingue, Toussaint Louverture had made himself the de facto leader of the colony. The army, which served to discipline plantation laborers as well as protect the colony from invaders, was almost entirely under the command of black generals. Louverture boldly responded to Bonaparte's 1801 decision by creating his own constitution for Saint-Domingue, which made him its governor.[32]

In Guadeloupe, however, white officers and administrators were still in control. Late in 1801, the officer Magloire Pélage — the Martinican homme de couleur and high-ranking veteran of the campaigns in St. Lucia — was passed over for promotion by a metropolitan administrator who named himself general of the army in his place. Black troops on the island rebelled and expelled the administrator from the island, and Pélage formed a provisional government to rule Guadeloupe. The insurgents appealed to the metropole, expressing their loyalty to France even as they argued for their right to full access to military and political rights. By then, however, Bonaparte — well on his way to signing a peace treaty with the British — had sent expeditions to the Caribbean to crush the power of the black leaders in both Saint-Domingue and Guadeloupe and prepare for a return to the old order of plantation slavery and racial hierarchy. The French troops encountered resistance in Saint-Domingue, but within a few months they won what seemed like a final victory, capturing Toussaint Louverture and winning over most of the black troops and officers. They did so in part by denying that they had the intention of reestablishing slavery in the colony and playing on the loyalty to France of many of the black veterans on the island. An expedition led by General Richepance did the same thing in Guadeloupe, where it encountered resistance led by the homme de couleur officer Louis Delgrès. Helped by allies among the black troops, notably Magloire Pélage, they managed to defeat the rebels. Plantation workers also joined in the fighting in Guadeloupe, often spurning the more traditional tactics of the soldiers in favor of burning plantations and attacking white civilians. And after the mass of the insurgents had been defeated, small bands, including one led by a veteran of the invasion of St. Lucia, continued to fight the French.[33]

Having defeated most of the resistance in Guadeloupe, the island's new administrators executed thousands of insurgents and deported many more, giving some captains orders to drop them off on abandoned coasts in the United States and sending hundreds to Europe, where they ended up in Corsica. General Richepance was convinced that the preservation of the colony depended on the elimination of all former slaves or gens de couleur who had served the army. "Let us not fall into the error of believing that we can arm blacks and use them in our army," he wrote to the minister. Accordingly, he had more than a thousand hommes de couleur and noirs who had been "part of the armed forces" and were "recognized in the colony as dangerous men" deported. Even Magloire Pélage and other officers who had fought with the French in Guadeloupe suffered the same fate; the Minister of the Colonies made it clear that, notwithstanding their previous military positions, they were to be treated as enemies of the Republic because of the "unsurpassed" crimes that had "bloodied the American colonies." Apparently, rebellion was contagious; a group of French officers whose only crime had been to be held prisoner briefly by Delgrès and his troops in the Fort St. Charles were also imprisoned and deported by Richepance.[34]

The repression of the revolt was the first step in the reestablishment of slavery in the colony, which was carried out successfully in the following months by a new colonial administration. At one point the ranking general suggested that in order to wipe out the last vestiges of resistance it might be useful to recruit plantation laborers to fight against them. The idea gave the prefect of the island, the one-time abolitionist Daniel Lescallier, a bout of insomnia. "I barely slept last night," he wrote. "Once they are free," he wondered, "what will we do with them? They will be vagabonds who from then on will disdain cultivation and will become dangerous to society because of that, and from the habit of carrying guns." Lescallier believed that the practice of granting freedom for military service, which had helped shatter slavery a few years earlier and had become one of the key symbols of republican emancipation, could ultimately have no place in a coercive colonial order.[35]

He was probably wrong. Louverture's regime in Saint-Domingue had in fact created an order in which plantation labor was effectively overseen by black troops, and plantations were distributed to trusted officers who took on the roles that had once been occupied by white slave owners. Perhaps racial equality and the sharing of power with individuals of African descent could have guaranteed the preservation of a plantation system in France's most valuable colony and kept sugar flowing across the Atlantic to its ports for decades to come. Ultimately, though, the threat of black military power drove France's leaders into an unreasoned, brutal, and disastrous attempt to destroy the armies that once had saved their colonies. When news of what had happened in Guadeloupe filtered into Saint-Domingue, the ex-slaves who made up the army of the Republic began deserting and transformed themselves into an army of national liberation. The mass of soldiers, and the plantation laborers who joined them, understood that defeat would mean reenslavement. Only their own Republic, with their own army, could guarantee that the freedom they had won would be theirs for good.[36]

Notes

I thank Christopher Brown, David Geggus, Jane Landers, Andrew O'Shaughnessy, and Philip Morgan, whose comments shaped the final version of this chapter. The chapter draws on and condenses material presented in various parts of my *A Colony of Citizens: Revolution and Slave Emancipation in the French Caribbean, 1787–1804* (Chapel Hill, 2004).

1. Cooper Williams, *An Account of the Campaign in the West Indies in the Year 1794* (London, 1796; reprint, Basse-Terre, 1990), 125.

2. For the white insurgents in blackface, see *Philadelphia General Advertiser* 321 (October 10, 1791); on the engraving—which is generally dated 1791 but which was probably printed in 1794—see Helen Weston, "Representing the Right to Represent: The Portrait of Citizen Belley, Ex-Representative of the Colonies, by A.L. Girodet," *Res* 26 (Autumn 1994): 83–109, 89.

3. On the British campaigns in Saint-Domingue and the eastern Caribbean see David Geggus, *Slavery, War and Revolution* (Oxford, 1982). See also Michael Duffy, *Soldiers, Sugar and Seapower: The British Expeditions to the West Indies and the War Against Revolutionary France* (Oxford, 1987).

4. Louverture's military victories are described in C. L. R. James, *The Black Jacobins* (New York, 1963). An overview of the events in Grenada, St. Vincent, and St. Lucia is provided in Michael Craton, *Testing the Chains: Resistance to Slavery in the British West Indies* (Ithaca, 1982), chaps. 15 and 16; see also Duffy, *Soldiers, Sugar and Seapower.*

5. On Saint-Domingue see Carolyn Fick, *The Making of Haiti: The Saint Domingue Revolution from Below* (Knoxville, 1990). The classic study of the French Revolutionary army is Richard Cobb, *The People's Armies* (New Haven, 1987).

6. On free-colored service in the militias see John Garrigus, "Catalyst or Catastrophe? Saint-Domingue's Free Men of Color and the Battle of Savannah, 1779–1782," *Revista Interamericana* 22:1–2 (Spring 1992): 109–124; and Stewart King, *Blue Coat or Powdered Wig? Free People of Color in Pre-Revolutionary Saint Domingue* (Athens, 2001), chap. 4.

7. "Extrait des régistres . . . Société de Amis de la République française," 17 Pluviôse An 2 (February 5, 1794) and 21 Pluviôse An 2 (February 9, 1794), Archives Nationales, Paris (hereafter AN), AD VII 21C, nos. 45 and 46.

8. I describe this event in detail in *Colony of Citizens,* pt. 1.

9. On the formation of the battalion of *chasseurs noirs,* see Anne Pérotin-Dumon, *Etre patriote sous les tropiques: La Guadeloupe et la Révolution française* (Basse-Terre, 1984), 217; on the attack of Guadeloupe see Duffy, *Soldiers, Sugar and Seapower,* chaps. 2–6, particularly 93–97; on the "Slave Battalion," see the declaration of Michel Gaudin in the first "Cahiers de Déclarations" of Guadeloupean deportees, p. 66, in AN DXXV 123, dossier 976, no. 1; "Les Patriotes déportés de la Guadeloupe par les Anglais aux membres de la Convention Nationale composant la Commission des Colonies," 20 Brumaire An 3 (November 10, 1796), AN AD VII 21C, no. 44.

10. On these events in Saint-Domingue see Fick, *Making of Haiti,* 157–160; Robert Louis Stein, *Léger Félicité Sonthonax: The Lost Sentinel of the Republic* (London, 1985), chaps. 4, 5.

11. On Hugues's regime see Dubois, *Colony of Citizens,* pt. 2; for the reports on the taking of Guadeloupe see "Les Commissaires Délégués aux Iles du Vent par la Convention Nationale aux représentants du peuple composant le Comité de Salut Public," 18 Prairial An 2 (June 6, 1794), Archives Nationales—Section Outre-Mer, Aix-en-Provence (hereafter ANSOM), C7A 47, 5–6; "Le Commissaire délégué . . . aux Républicains des armées de terre et de mer de la République, actuellement à la Guadeloupe," 1 Thermidor An 2 (July 19, 1794), ANSOM C7A 47, 18.

12. Bryan Edwards, *The History, Civil and Commercial, of the British Colonies in the West Indies* (London, 1801), 3:470; "Les Commissaires délégués . . . à tous les citoyens de la Pointe-à-Pitre," 20 Prairial An 2 (June 8, 1794), ANSOM C7A 47, 9; Hugues to the Comité de Salut Public, 4 Thermidor An 2 (July 22, 1794), ANSOM C7A 47, 20–25.

13. "Les Commissaire délegués au Ministre de la Marine et des Colonies," 22 Thermidor An 4 (August 9, 1796), ANSOM C7A 49, 43–45. Names of different battalions appear in numerous état civil acts from these years; see, e.g., ANSOM EC Basseterre 6, nos. 5, 13, 33, 41, and EC Basseterre 7, no. 92; for the Bataillon de Sainte-Lucie see EC Basseterre 9, nos. 9, 28. The estimates of numbers of soldiers are from Jacques Adélaïde-Merlande, *Delgrès: La Guadeloupe en 1802* (Paris, 1986), 37–48, and Louis-François Tigrane, "Histoire méconnue, histoire oubliée que celle de la Guadeloupe et son armée pendant la période révolutionnaire," *Revue Historique* 571 (July–September 1989): 167–186.

14. See Edward Cox, *Free Coloreds in the Slave Societies of St. Kitt's and Grenada, 1763–1833* (Knoxville, 1984). On the Black Caribs see Philip Boucher, *Cannibal Encounters: Europeans and Island Caribs, 1492–1763* (Baltimore, 1992); Peter Hulme, *Colonial Encounters: Europe and the Native Caribbean, 1492–1797* (London, 1986).

15. David Barry Gaspar, "La Guerre des Bois: Revolution, War and Slavery in Saint Lucia, 1793–1838," in *A Turbulent Time: The French Revolution in the Greater Caribbean,* ed. David Barry Gaspar and David Geggus (Bloomington, 1997), 105.

16. Edward Cox, "Fedon's Rebellion 1795–1796: Causes and Consequences," *Journal of Negro History* 67:1 (Spring 1982): 7–19; Gordon Turnbull, *A Narrative of the Revolt and Insurrection in the Island of Grenada* (London, 1796).

17. Cox, "Fedon's Rebellion," 8, 13; "Les Commissaire délégués . . . Arrêté," 11 Germinal An 3 (31 March 1795), ANSOM C7A 48, 10; Charles Shephard, *An Historical Account of the Island of St. Vincent* (London, 1831; reprint, London, 1971), 149–175.

18. Gaspar, "La Guerre des Bois" (quotation is at 107); Duffy, *Soldiers,* 89–91.

19. "Mémoire de Jean-Joseph Lambert," AN ADVII 34A, no. 13; Goyrand, "Dépêche du Commissaire de la Convention Nationale," 16 Vendémiaire An 4 (8 October 1795), ANSOM C7A 49, 110; "Compte rendu par le Sr. Goyrand," 6 Thermidor An 7 (24 July 1799), ANSOM C7A 49, 67–109, 73–80.

20. Gaspar, "La Guerre des Bois," 104–109; Duffy, *Soldiers,* 142.

21. ANSOM EC Basse-Terre 6, nos. 4, 5, 6, 13, 14, 16, 50. On Vulcain see also Auguste Lacour, *Histoire de la Guadeloupe* (Basse-Terre, 1858), 2:314. See ANSOM EC Basseterre 6, nos. 36, 42, 45; EC Basseterre 9, no. 136; EC Basseterre 10. nos. 40, 69.

22. ANSOM EC Basseterre 7, no. -#146, EC Basseterre 10, no. 107.

23. I draw the information about the troops who served in St. Lucia and St. Vincent from the two "Etats des Mouvements," in Archives Historiques de l'Armée de Terre, Vincennes (hereafter AHAT), Xi, carton 80.

24. "Formation de la Compagnie des hommes de couleur," "Etat des officiers des différents grades," "Etat des sous officiers à la suite," AHAT Xi, carton 80; for Séraphin see ANSOM EC Basse-Terre 6, no. 66.

25. "Etat des hommes blessés" and, for Claude Thedore, "Etat des mouvements," AHAT Xi, carton 80.

26. Lacour, *Histoire,* 3:231–232; arrest of Descombes, 8 Messidor An 9 (27 June 1801), in ANSOM C7A 55, 62.

27. H. J. K. Jenkins, "Guadeloupe's Commerce Raiding, 1796–98: Perspectives and Contexts," *Mariner's Mirror* 83:3 (August 1997): 303–309, 305; Jenkins, "Slavery and French Privateering in the 1790s," *Mariner's Mirror* 72:3 (1986), 359–360; Jenkins, "The Heydey of French Privateering from Guadeloupe, 1796–1798," *Mariner's Mirror* 64:3 (August 1978), 245–250, 249. See also the register of captures in ANSOM, C7A 48, 158–212. For the numbers of ex-slaves on the corsairs, see Tigrane, "Histoire méconnue," 180–181. The only corsair crew lists I have found are for ships outfitted in 1800 in Cayenne, French Guiana. Of the sixty-five sailors on an 1800 crew list for the corsair *Importun*, twenty-one were listed with only one name and were likely ex-slaves, but Cayenne had a smaller proportion of slaves in its population than Guadeloupe; "Repartition des prises," 9 Brumaire An 8, Archives Départementales de la Guyane, Cayenne (hereafter ADGn) X, 16.

28. "Répartition des prises," 15 Messidor AN 8 and 1 Thermidor An 9. in ADGn X, 16.

29. For examples of distribution of loot from the corsairs by women see ADG Vauchelet 2E2/164, 7 Nivôse An 6 (27 December 1797) and 2E2/165, 12 Ventôse An 6 (1 March 1798); ADG Bonnet 2E2/41, 11 Messidor An 6 (29 June 1798), 30 Prairial An 6 (18 June 1798), 11 Thermidor An 6 (29 July 1798); for the cost of the house in Basse-Terre see the purchase by the mason Augustin in ANSOM Dupuch 2E2/24, 13 Messidor An 7 (1 July 1799).

30. Thouluyre Mahé to the Minister, 2 Ventôse An 4 (21 February 1796), and "Coup d'oeil," ANSOM C7A 49, 133, 138–143.

31. See the law, from 3 Prairial An 6 (22 May 1798), in AN ADVII 20B; for the soldiers at the Ile d'Aix, see the "Formation de la Compagnie des hommes de couleur," the "Etat des sous-officiers," the "Etat des officiers des différents grades," the "Contrôles des femmes et enfants," and the "Etat des mouvements," AHAT Xi, carton 80; on the letters sent by the soldiers, see Mentor's angry letter to the Baron de Bruix of 21 Ventôse An 7 (10 March 1799), reprinted in Marcel Dorigny and Bernard Gainot, *La Société des Amis des Noirs, 1788–1799: Contribution à l'histoire de l'abolition de l'esclavage* (Paris, 1998), 385–392; for Mentor's speech see "Motion d'ordre faite par Mentor," AN ADVII 21A, no. 52.

32. See Yves Benot, *La demence coloniale sous Napoléon* (Paris, 1991).

33. For more details see my *Colony of Citizens*, pt. 3.

34. Richepance to Minister, 11 Prairial An 10 (31 May 1802), ANSOM C7A 57, 1; Lacrosse to Minister, 1 Vendémiaire An 11 (23 September 1802), ANSOM C7A 56, 157–158. On Pélage's deportation, see the "Etat nominatif" and the "Acte d'accusation" in ANSOM C7A 56, 278–288; for the white officers, see their declaration of 18 Germinal An 11 (8 April 1803), in AHAT B9, 2.

35. Ménard, Arrêté, 23 Vendémiaire An 11 (15 October 1802), ANSOM C7A 57, 202–203; Lescallier to Lacrosse, 30 Vendémiaire An 11 (22 October 1802), ANSOM C7A 57, 204.

36. See Mats Lundahl, "Toussaint L'Ouverture and the War Economy of Saint-Domingue, 1796–1802," *Slavery and Abolition* 6:2 (September 1985): 122–138.

The Slave Soldiers of Spanish South America: From Independence to Abolition

PETER BLANCHARD

The long and bitter warfare that destroyed Spain's colonial empire in South America in the early nineteenth century provided the area's slaves with an unprecedented opportunity to engage in military activity and simultaneously to undermine the institution that kept them in chains. The wars prompted both patriot and royalist recruiters to tap a variety of sources to meet their military needs, including professionals from Spain and the colonies, foreign mercenaries, local militiamen, draftees and volunteers from the colonial population, vagabonds, criminals, and slaves. The recruitment of slaves indicated the gravity of the situation, reversing as it did longstanding prohibitions against arming this sector of the population. Thousands were officially recruited, and countless others managed to serve by fleeing their owners and enlisting as freemen. Slaves consequently came to play a prominent role in the colonial struggles, fighting to preserve the imperial tie as well as to destroy it. With personal freedom the usual reward, their service also helped to weaken slavery, both by reducing the number of slaves and by raising the hopes of those left in bondage. Their struggle continued after the wars ended, because almost everywhere slavery managed to survive the long period of disruption. That struggle frequently took place in the context of warfare as new conflicts erupted, leading to renewed recruiting, with freedom once more the reward. The freeing of slaves along with the termination of the slave trade and the aging of the slave population helped undermine slavery further, rendering it less and less viable. In response, countries began introducing abolition legislation, until by the 1860s this relic of the colonial past had all but disappeared from Spain's former mainland colonies.

African slaves had a long history of military service in Spanish America. During the Spanish conquest of the early sixteenth century, some slaves belonging to conquistadors fought as soldiers, and subsequently they were on occasion used for military or security purposes, for example, serving on royal ships and hunting down runaway slaves. The creation of militia units for local defense obviated the need to arm slaves except in extreme circumstances, but some of their descendants continued to play a military role with the incorporation of free blacks and mulattos (or *pardos*) into these units. The number of militiamen increased in the late colonial period as the Crown, fearing foreign attack, introduced a series of reforms that bolstered local military units. Consequently, the sight of blacks in uniform and bearing arms was not uncommon in cities such as Buenos Aires, Caracas, Cartagena, Lima, Montevideo, and Panamá. There were black noncommissioned officers and even some black officers, although whites were always in command. A few slaves may also have been found in these units, in the person of runaways who had managed to convince the authorities that they were free. In general, however, slaves were excluded from the military, because those in positions of authority voiced numerous objections. They pointed to the sanctity of property rights, the high cost of compensation, and the slaves' importance to economic activities; they raised questions about slave loyalty; and they shared the widely held fear of arming slaves. Moreover, alternative recruits were available from the free population, whether white, Indian, black, or of mixed blood.[1]

Opposition to slave recruiting intensified in the late colonial period in response to an increase in slave numbers and growing fears of that expanding population. Spanish reforms in the eighteenth century included loosening controls on the African slave trade, resulting in an influx of African slaves. In Buenos Aires, for example, about 45,000 were imported between 1740 and 1810, and 15,000 passed through Montevideo in the final fifty years of colonial rule. Consequently, on the eve of the struggles for independence, slaves numbered around 30,000 in the Viceroyalty of Rio de la Plata, 78,000 in New Granada (modern Colombia), more than 64,500 in Venezuela, and 40,000 in Peru. Nowhere did they exceed more than 10 percent of the total population, but they tended to be concentrated in certain regions, such as the gold-mining area of Colombia and the coastal valleys of Peru, adding weight to their numbers.[2]

Opposition to arming slaves was also a response to the flurry of slave unrest that marked the late eighteenth century. Most threatening was the St. Domingue revolution, which eventually ended slavery in the French colony and established the black republic of Haiti. Uprisings in neighboring regions, particularly Venezuela, aroused fears that French and Haitian revolutionary ideas were spreading and led to increased attention to the slave population. In Venezuela, for example, slave imports from Africa were curtailed, and in Montevideo an 1803 order prohibited slaves as well as free blacks from carrying any type of weapon.[3]

Arming slaves was thus a contentious issue, but necessity could overcome even the strongest opposition, as the British invasions of the Viceroyalty of Rio de la Plata in 1806 and 1807 plainly revealed. A footnote to the Napoleonic Wars, the invasions were attempts to liberate a colony of France's ally, Spain. They proved to be a humiliating disaster for the British as the local population rallied twice to defend the area and to expel the invaders. Among those recruited to confront the British were almost seven hundred local slaves who served with a "loyalty and courage which surprised those who had hesitated about arming them."[4] The reward for their service was personal freedom that, though not respected in every case, set a precedent for what was soon to follow.[5]

The struggle for independence was a far more extreme circumstance than the British incursions and created an immeasurably greater need for soldiers. The fighting lasted from 1810 to 1826 and spread throughout the continent, forcing recruiters to look beyond the pool of professionals, militiamen, and volunteers to consider nontraditional sectors. At first, in areas with a large black population, continuing concerns about arming slaves and violating owners' property rights dictated policy, so that while free black units proliferated, slaves remained largely untouched. Some owners donated a slave or two as a gesture of support for self-rule or loyalty to the Crown, but the total numbers were small. Other slaves ran away and joined on their own. Before long, however, recruiters began to target slaves specifically, in response to military demands and the realization that slaves possessed attributes that seemed to make them ideal soldiers. Most notably, there were large numbers of them and they were accustomed to discipline. In addition, those recently arrived from Africa were primarily young men who were believed — rightly or wrongly — to possess both previous military experience and a propensity to savagery. Although recruiters expressed no preference as to creole or African-born slaves, they made the case that those who had been recently enslaved probably remembered what it was like to be free, so that offering them freedom was likely to win their loyalty and at the same time impose a degree of control over them.[6]

Slaves were responsive to the offer, although in the majority of cases they probably had no real choice. Most were donated or sold to the military. Others were press-ganged by one army or another that apprehended unclaimed or vagabond blacks, trolled jails, and confiscated the property of slave-owners who were considered enemies. Frequently, however, slaves took the initiative, expressing their wish to serve or pressuring their owners to donate them. In Buenos Aires one slave paid his owner to do so. Many more indicated their desires by running away to join. They had numerous reasons to enlist. Loyalty to king, homeland, or a local leader was frequently mentioned. Many saw military service as an escape from the rigors of slave life and considered it no more dangerous than their existing work. They may also have viewed it as an opportunity to demonstrate that they were human beings and not simply another person's property. Similarly, they may have wanted to challenge the existing stereotype of slave docility; military service provided an environment where they could be as bloodthirsty as they wished without fear of retribution. They could earn money and perhaps a degree of respect, for they were joining an increasingly important and influential institution. The arms and the uniforms were also lures, as was the possibility for social mobility through military promotion, because many former slaves became noncommissioned officers. Some even managed to rise to the lower ranks of the officer grades.[7]

All these attractions, however, paled beside the principal reason for the slaves' decision, which was to obtain their freedom. Manumission, especially for young males, had been a scarce commodity before independence — as it remained afterwards — so that being offered freedom in return for military service proved a powerful incentive. This was apparent from the comments of runaways who enlisted, men such as Alejandro Campusano, an Ecuadorian slave, who recalled that "the sweet voice of the *patria* came to my ears, and desiring to be one of its soldiers, as much to shake off the yoke of general oppression as to free myself from the slavery in which I existed, I ran swiftly to present myself to the liberating troops of Quito."[8] Runaways such as Alejandro believed that freedom was virtually assured because armies were offering it as a reward for service. Those beliefs were reinforced by military officers and civilian courts, which, when called on to consider the issue of returning runaways with military experience to their owners, denounced such treatment as iniquitous and urged instead that the owner be compensated. Their public declarations and decisions gave a clear signal that military service could lead to freedom, providing a further impetus to run away and enlist.[9]

Slave recruiting was most successful in the southern Viceroyalty of Rio de la Plata. Concentrated in the coastal urban centers, slaves were not vital to the viceroyalty's major economic activities, a fact that may have facilitated acceptance of them as soldiers. Following the May Revolution of 1810, when

American-born creoles took control of the government in Buenos Aires, some slaveowners demonstrated their loyalty to the cause by donating slaves to the army. Formal recruiting began in 1811, when an invading army from Buenos Aires challenged the royalist government operating out of Montevideo. The Argentine commander forcibly recruited the slaves of Spaniards, aiming both to reinforce his army and to deprive the royalists of possible soldiers. He also offered freedom to any slave living in the Uruguayan capital who enrolled in his army. Perhaps as many as a thousand men, women, and children responded to the patriot offer, indicating their desire for freedom. Three hundred and forty joined the Argentine army. Most accompanied the army when it withdrew to Buenos Aires later in the year, but others continued to serve in Uruguay under several patriot commanders, most notably the Uruguayan nationalist José Gervasio Artigas. They so impressed him with their military skills that he became increasingly reliant on them as he fought for the liberation of his country. A second invasion by Argentine forces in 1812 produced a new outpouring of slave support as the invaders again offered freedom in return for military service. The recruits had to serve four years, during which time they remained *libertos* (freedmen) of the state.[10]

The experiences in Uruguay set the stage for slave recruiting in Buenos Aires and the other Argentine provinces. The creoles who led the May Revolution may have expressed liberal ideas, with slavery among their targets for reform, but they were also pragmatists who wanted to avoid racial unrest, obtain soldiers, and deprive the royalists of black support. As a result, beginning in February 1812 they issued a series of antislavery laws that included ending the African slave trade and freeing the newborn children of slaves. Simultaneously, local slave recruiting began. In July 1812 the government purchased thirty-nine slaves for a new corps of libertos, offering freedom as well as a uniform and a small daily wage in return for six years of "good service." In May 1813 the first recruiting law was issued; its intent was to create a Regiment of Libertos. The law was called a *rescate,* or "rescue," imbuing it with moral force. It compelled owners to sell a certain number of their slaves, aged thirteen to sixty. The slave's occupation affected the chances of his selection, with domestic slaves most likely to be recruited and rural slaves the least likely. To ensure that property rights were recognized and protected, the value of the chosen slave was determined and compensation offered. The recruits were given their freedom when they enrolled, but they had to complete the designated term of five years, leaving them in a somewhat ambiguous legal situation. Eight hundred were enrolled pursuant to the initial law, but further military demands produced new decrees in December 1813 and February 1814 that added to the numbers. In January 1815, following rumors of the imminent landing of a Spanish expeditionary force, the government targeted the slaves belonging to Spaniards. Later in the year the same source was compelled to provide another four hundred slaves. Further laws in 1818 and 1819 considered using slaves for patrolling the frontier and filling the ranks of the militia. Freedom was no longer offered to the recruits, however, indicating the growing conservatism of Argentina's rulers.[11]

The more than two thousand slaves enlisted following passage of these laws represented the wide spectrum of slaves who lived in the area. They were drawn from Buenos Aires and the surrounding provinces; they were single and married, urban and rural. Many came originally from Africa, listing themselves as natives of the Congo, Mozambique, Benguela, and other nations. Some had indicated to their owners that they wanted to serve. In the words of one owner, his slave Antonio was "set on serving with the troops of the *patria* and I cannot deny him his wish." Whether such wishes were ever really uttered is open to question, and there is ample evidence that owners used the opportunity of the recruiting laws to unload problem slaves. The authorities were expecting this, however, and insisted that every recruit had to be fit and capable of performing military duties. To this end a surgeon checked them and returned the unfit to their owners, who had to supply a replacement. The recruits were assigned primarily to the infantry and artillery companies of newly formed black regiments, but they could also find themselves in one of the integrated regiments of the line, the navy, the cavalry, or local militia units. They fought on various fronts and in numerous battles, defending the country from royalist invasions in the north, participating in unsuccessful invasions of Upper Peru, and lending their strength to the continuing struggles in Uruguay.[12] In the process they established a reputation as dependable and effective soldiers.

One commander who was particularly impressed was the Argentine José de San Martín. More than once he noted that although whites were "the best" for the cavalry, "slaves make the best troops of the line, as a result of their undeniable subordination and natural readiness for hard work."[13] Preparing an army in the western Argentine city of Mendoza to invade Chile and eventually to attack the royalist stronghold of Peru, he hoped to obtain as many as ten thousand slave recruits. Political problems, competing demands, and slaveholder resistance forced him to revise his figure downwards, yet he managed to secure almost sixteen hundred from the nearby provinces and other parts of the country. They made up at least 40 percent of his army when it crossed the Andes early in 1817 in a brilliant and unexpected campaign that caught the royalist forces in Chile completely by surprise.[14]

San Martín invaded a country where the military contribution of slaves was less prominent than in his homeland, largely because of their small numbers — only six thousand — as well as the nature of the local struggles for independence. Some were prepared to serve: a group of three hundred slaves took to the streets of Santiago in 1811, a year after local creoles assumed control of the government, demanding that they be given their freedom and an opportunity to defend the new system. Subsequently laws were passed to permit slaves to enlist in two new regiments; however, only a few seem to have responded. Equally unsuccessful was a recruiting law issued in 1814 in response to a royalist invasion from Peru. Runaways were willing to join, but their numbers were too small to hold back the royalist advance and prevent the fall of the creole government later in the year. With San Martín's invasion and his victories at the battles of Chacabuco in February 1817 and Maipó the following year, recruiting of slaves was tried once again and this time attracted greater support. Patriotic owners were now willing to donate their property, and other sources such as jails provided further recruits. Some had fought already. Luciano, a donated slave, had accompanied his master in the fight against the royalists starting in 1813, displaying "a heroic valor" in several battles. The recruiting intensified as San Martín prepared his army to move north into Peru, producing an invasion force with a significant black component. According to one source, almost half the soldiers of the liberating army were manumitted slaves.[15]

Slaves thus played a significant role in the southern struggle for independence. Elsewhere, however, although they participated as extensively, they tended to be part of the resistance to independence, not its proponent. This was particularly true of the Viceroyalty of New Granada, where for many years slaves actively opposed the republicans and threw their support behind the royalist cause, largely because it seemed to offer a better route to personal freedom. In contrast to areas to the south, in New Granada slavery was central to economic activity, providing workers for the gold mines of Colombia and the plantations of Venezuela and Ecuador. It was not a benign system, for it provoked numerous instances of flight and rebellion in the late colonial period that, together with the proximity of Haiti, produced a profound fear of the black population among the colonial elites. That fear was evident when radical creoles took over the government in Caracas in 1810 and declared Venezuela's independence the following year. Social equality was not part of their program; they were willing to end the African slave trade, but they were not prepared to abolish slavery or grant full citizenship to free pardos. More confrontational was their creation of a National Guard to apprehend runaways, maintain law and order in the countryside, and compel slaves to work. The black community responded by rebelling. Promoted by royalist agents and churchmen, the racial unrest spread throughout the viceroyalty but was especially bloody in Venezuela and soon developed a momentum of its own. Republican landholders were especially targeted and massacred in large numbers. At the same time, forces loyal to the Crown began mobilizing slaves and free blacks to wrest political control out of the hands of the patriots under Francisco de Miranda, offering personal freedom as an inducement. Miranda responded with a similar offer to those who volunteered for his armies, but he demanded ten years of service. His offer attracted few takers, and it alienated creole planters, who demonstrated their hostility by withdrawing their support. As a result, the republic fell in July 1812 to a royalist army that was composed "almost totally of *pardos* and men of the other castes," including freed slaves.[16]

Loyalty to the Crown remained strong among the slave population. When the revolutionaries, now under the charismatic Venezuelan Simón Bolívar, regained political control of Caracas in August 1813 and declared the second republic, many slaves once again threw their support behind royalist leaders. They were particularly drawn to José Tomás Boves, a Spaniard who turned the multiracial inhabitants of Venezuela's interior plains into an effective guerrilla force. Slaves, with their owners and on their own, joined his army, attracted by the offer of a uniform, the prospect of loot, which often took the form of the property of whites, and the possibility of social improvement, because blacks were promoted ahead of lighter-skinned individuals. Marching into battle shouting "Death to the whites!" they killed hundreds as they retook patriot-held territory. Many subsequently asked for and received their freedom, citing in their requests their loyalty to the Crown. One was Ramón Piñero, who declared, "I have served my King with much love and faithfulness, and have no desire to lose the favor that your sovereign mercy has conceded to those like myself who have defended your rights with weapons in hand."[17]

Bolívar did little to win them over. A slaveholder himself, he described the rebelling slaves as an "inhuman and atrocious people, nourishing themselves on the blood and possessions of the patriots."[18] He and other independence leaders managed to draw some into their armies, including runaways, donated slaves, and those compelled to accompany their owners, but many soon deserted, suggesting that they had different feelings of loyalty than their owners and a better appreciation of the realities of the military situation. They switched to the royalist cause after weighing the options and deciding that it was a more likely route to personal freedom. Bolívar's defeat, largely at the hands of black royalist forces, and the fall of the second republic in 1814 proved the astuteness of their choice.[19]

What was occurring in Venezuela had a profound impact on neighboring

Colombia. Some of the regional creole governments that took over after 1810 made gestures in the slaves' direction, the most liberal being the gold-mining province of Antioquia, whose leaders called for gradual abolition. These abolitionist moves, however, had all ended by 1816 with the defeat of the various independence movements. Owners, dependent on slave labor and fearful of slave unrest, generally opposed slave recruiting, and commanders hesitated to arm them. Campaigning in the south in 1813, the independence leader Antonio Nariño was prepared to use hacienda slaves, and offered them their freedom if they served him "with honour," but they were to serve as laborers, not soldiers. In this role, they provided invaluable support when royalist forces defeated his army, for it was the slaves who managed to save the muskets, powder, and cartridges that permitted an orderly retreat. "Without this help we certainly would have surrendered and perished," a participant observed. But it was not sufficient to prevent Nariño from being captured and imprisoned and this initial attempt at independence from being crushed.[20]

The arrival of Pablo Morillo in 1815 with a Spanish army of more than ten thousand men altered the pattern of royalist recruiting in the viceroyalty. The presence of the Spanish veterans seemed to limit the need for locally recruited soldiers, and the recruiting of slaves was specifically halted in an attempt to end the continuing racial unrest. The royalists tried to maintain black support by abolishing the slave trade, introducing a gradual emancipation scheme, and granting freedom to those of Boves' troops who had been slaves, but his army was disarmed and dispersed. (Boves was no longer a factor, having died in battle in 1814.) Although the manner of the disbanding and the anticolonial attitudes of Morillo's forces prompted a number of Boves' veterans to switch allegiance to the patriots, most remained committed to the royalist cause and were prepared to serve if given the chance. The door was not completely closed to their participation because some slaves, such as those who had fought for the insurgents, were welcomed into the royalist army and given their freedom when they enlisted. Runaways also continued to join. Morillo was prepared to accept them, but, like Nariño, he seemed interested primarily in using them as laborers — for carrying and moving equipment such as artillery — not as combatants.[21]

While the royalists reduced their black contingent, the patriots began making renewed efforts to attract slave support. Bolívar remained suspicious of their loyalty, but military exigencies and his passionate desire to free his homeland forced him gradually to change his attitude. He came to the realization that military victory was impossible if the black population continued to oppose him. As a result, in exchange for essential supplies, he promised the Haitian president, Alexandre Pétion, that he would free all the slaves in the lands that he liberated, and in June 1816 he offered freedom to slaves aged fourteen to sixty who joined his army. But there was an iron fist beneath the offer: those who refused to serve faced the prospect of perpetual servitude, not only for themselves but also for their families and parents. At the time, the offer had little impact because the patriots' limited political control placed few slaves under their jurisdiction. Nonetheless, the cause of independence had improved somewhat. Boves' death had both removed an effective enemy commander and shifted the loyalties of some blacks, largely because the new leader of the interior guerrillas was José Antonio Páez, a supporter of independence. Slave unrest continued, but it no longer focused on patriot creoles with the fierce hostility that it had in the past. In 1817 Bolívar sought to prevent racial divisions in his own forces by ordering the execution of Manuel Piar, a mulatto commander who was suspected of plotting an antiwhite movement. The Liberator's fear of the black population had obviously not diminished, and he frequently criticized slaves for their lack of support. Yet by 1818 he and other patriot leaders were beginning to attract them in sufficient numbers to cause Morillo to comment that in some areas "all the slaves remain at the disposition of the rebels who enlist many of them."[22] The royalist commander had also begun recruiting plantation slaves, in part to prevent the enemy from using them, in part because disease and desertion were ravaging his Spanish army, and in part because his attitude toward slaves had changed since his arrival in Venezuela. He now considered them "excellent soldiers," noting their discipline and their ability to cope with the climate. In 1818 he claimed that two thousand were serving him, and he was keen to draft more because slaves remained largely committed to the royalist cause. Loyalty to the king was much more tangible than loyalty to concepts as vague as independence and the patria. Moreover, Bolívar had still to prove that he could defeat the royalists.[23]

In order to achieve that victory, the Venezuelan decided to take a radical step where slavery was concerned. Despite his continuing reservations about the black population and his continuing ownership of slaves — both of which raise questions about the sincerity of his words — the Liberator became an open and vocal foe of slavery. At the Congress of Angostura, convened in February 1819 to draft a constitution for his planned northern republic, he called for the complete abolition of slavery. His reasoning was summed up in his oft-cited comment to his vice president, Francisco de Paula Santander: "It seems to me madness that a revolution for freedom expects to maintain slavery."[24] But slaves had to risk their lives to obtain their freedom. Following the battle of Boyacá in August 1819, which secured Colombia's independence, he asked Santander to supply two or three thousand slaves who would serve for two or three years. "We need robust and vigorous men, men accustomed to harshness and fatigue, men who embrace the cause and the career with enthusiasm, men who identify their interest with the public interest and for whom the price of death is little different from that of life," he wrote.[25] He preferred bachelors and residents of lowland Colombia who would be able to cope with the heat of Venezuela. Santander's efforts provided some recruits, but Bolívar's wishes conflicted with the economic demands of the region. The slaves themselves also remained less than wholly convinced, so that although the number of recruits grew, including deserters from the royalist forces, they were still prepared to switch sides if the patriots faltered. Fortunately for Bolívar, divisions within the royalist ranks resulting from political chaos in Spain and the declaration of a truce in the colonies gave him an opportunity to launch a new offensive in Venezuela. His victory at the battle of Carabobo in June 1821 sealed the fate of the north. His appeal for slave support had obviously paid dividends, for according to one observer the majority of both the patriot and the royalist forces at Carabobo had been composed of black soldiers. Bolívar sought to expand this support by implementing his plans to abolish slavery in the new nation of Gran Colombia, created from the old viceroyalty. Less liberal congressional representatives, however, frustrated his wishes. Nevertheless, he managed to ensure that the African slave trade was abolished and that a free womb law was in place. He also established a manumission fund to purchase slaves' freedom, giving priority to those who enlisted. Some of these, along with volunteers and draftees, joined his victorious army as it moved southward, mopping up the royalist forces in Ecuador and preparing to advance on Peru, the last bastion of royalist power.[26]

Peru, like New Granada, boasted a substantial number of slaves, but they played a minor role in the struggles before San Martín's invasion in 1820. Royalist recruiters had largely ignored them because the existing military forces had proved adequate not only to control the area but also to suppress separatist movements in Chile and Ecuador and to prevent Argentine armies from invading through Bolivia. Nevertheless, a few slaves, runaways and volunteers, had joined the royalist forces. One was Pedro Rosas, whose 1798 marriage certificate described him as a slave of the Congo caste. He had subsequently obtained his freedom and in 1811 offered his services to the royalist forces, fighting in several campaigns in Bolivia until his death in battle in 1814.[27]

Extensive slave recruiting began in the area with the arrival of the patriot forces. The commander of the Chilean navy, Admiral Thomas Cochrane, took the first "recruits," slaves who were abducted to supplement the crews of ships that were patrolling the Peruvian coast. With San Martín's invasion, Cochrane returned to his earlier landings and used his recruits to win over relatives and friends to the patriot side. In the following months San Martín's recruiting efforts, as well as his antislavery reputation, attracted large numbers, so that by January 1822 the majority of his army of forty-eight hundred men was said to be composed of slaves. Indeed, at least one observer believed that his entire army was composed of slaves.[28] Serving as soldiers, sailors, artillerymen, guides, and spies, they were confronted by other slaves who wore the uniforms of royalist units, enlisted at the behest of the Peruvian viceroy. He wanted fifteen hundred recruits, men who were "agile, robust, and of a middling age," men who would be freed at the end of the war and their owners compensated.[29] San Martín's previous efforts, however, limited the numbers available to the royalists. Moreover, many of the royalist recruits soon deserted and joined the enemy, indicating their views as to the more dominant side and forcing the viceroy to turn to Andean Indians to meet his needs. San Martín's appeal lay in cultivating slave support following the Argentine pattern. He introduced legislation freeing the newborn children of slaves and abolishing the African slave trade. In response to threatened royalist attacks and military requirements, he specifically called up slaves and freed some as a reward. He recruited the slaves of royalists who had left Peru and ordered that all slaves receive militia training. Many of these laws were soon revoked in the face of slaveholder opposition and San Martín's wish not to alienate masters and disrupt the economy, yet his army continued to enroll donated slaves, deserters, and runaways. At one point it was reported to have almost two thousand new slave recruits in training.[30]

These Peruvian recruits were among the soldiers who fought in the deciding battles that brought an end to Spanish rule in Peru and on the continent as a whole. In addition to the local slaves were the survivors of those brought from Argentina and Chile as well as the black soldiers from Gran Colombia who were part of the army that Bolívar led into Peru following San Martín's resignation and the Venezuelan's assumption of command in 1823. Facing them were other slaves fighting under the royalist banners. They were part of the multinational and multiethnic armies that fought at the battles of Junín and Ayacucho in highland Peru in 1824. Victorious, the patriots could finally and confidently declare all of Spanish South America free, even if the last royalist forces would not withdraw until 1826.

Slaves had served militarily in much of the continent for more than a decade, helping both to maintain royalist rule and to undermine it. In the process, they had shown that they were competent and effective soldiers and not simply cannon fodder. Commanders as diverse as San Martín, Artigas, and Morillo had turned to them because of their recognized qualities. After years of service many were experienced veterans and thus even more valuable, prompting efforts to retain their services. When one slave recruit from Buenos Aires asked for his discharge after serving his required period of duty, his superiors had to comply, but they expressed the hope that he would consider reenlisting because they did not wish "to lose a good soldier." The bravery and commitment of the slave recruits had also been evident on numerous occasions on the battlefield. Antonio Lima, a runaway in the Argentine forces, fought in several battles and in one carried his captain to safety despite being shot in the knee. Captured, he managed to escape and returned to his unit. His sergeant described him as "one of the best soldiers in the corps."[31] Occasionally the recruits exhibited the "savagery" that for ages had provoked fear among whites and more recently stimulated recruiter enthusiasm. The conflict in Venezuela provides the most obvious but not the only example. In Chile, at the battle of Maipó, fought in April 1818, an observer noted that "nothing could exceed the savage fury of the Black soldiers in the patriot army; they had borne the brunt of the action against the finest Spanish regiment and had lost the principal part of their forces; they were delighted with the idea of shooting their prisoners. I saw an old Negro actually crying with rage when he perceived the officers protected from his fury."[32]

On the whole, however, blacks appear to have been no more or less brave, no more or less bloodthirsty than any other soldiers. Indeed, some commanders, such as the Argentine Manuel Belgrano, were extremely critical of them for their timidity. Writing to San Martín in 1813, he complained, rather contradictorily, that "the blacks and mulattos are a rabble who are as cowardly as they are bloodthirsty; in the five engagements that I have had with them, they have been the first to break ranks and to search for walls of bodies [to hide]."[33]

Belgrano may have been trying to divert attention from his own military failings, but his characterization was not entirely without foundation, for the slave recruits had obvious reasons to avoid battle. They had sought military service as a means to obtain their freedom, not to get wounded, captured, or killed. Their underlying motivation thus acted against bloodthirsty or valorous acts. The strategy of many seemed to be to get recruited, which secured their freedom, but then to minimize the possibility of injury. Asking for release on the basis of illness or physical ineptitude was one option (although it was far less common than seeking release for wartime injuries). Another was simply to desert. Desertion plagued every commander during the struggles for independence, a reflection of the dangers and the miserable conditions faced by the soldiers regardless of nationality or racial background. Officers everywhere reported losing troops at recruitment, during training, on campaign marches, before battles, and particularly after them, when soldiers took advantage of the breakdown in discipline, especially if they were part of the defeated army. To try to control the problem, armies offered rewards, employed bounty hunters, and imposed various penalties including imprisonment, whipping, extra years of service, reenslavement for ex-slaves, and even capital punishment. None, however, proved successful in keeping soldiers in the ranks.[34]

In a way, the desertions, like running away to enlist, were part of the increased slave assertiveness that marked the war years. The widespread destruction of property and the flight and death of owners left countless slaves on their own, and as armies began turning to them, they "discovered a sense of power."[35] Recruits obtained their own freedom and then used their status, as well as the wages they earned, to free family members. In Argentina, for example, soldiers directed part of their pay to be used for this purpose. At the same time, association with soldiers empowered many female slaves. Some accompanied their husbands or lovers as camp followers and demanded their freedom in return for their contribution. Many more made demands on the new governments, requesting the wages of their menfolk, or pensions, or charity in cases where the soldier had been killed or left an invalid as a result of wartime injuries. The passage of antislavery legislation also mobilized them into making demands on the state. In one case, an Ecuadorian slave took her request for freedom directly to Bolívar. Other slaves resorted to more disruptive acts. The unrest that marked the war years in Venezuela was replicated on a lesser scale elsewhere and continued long after the wars had ended. Slaves were accused of running away, assaulting owners, stealing, and joining the bands of highwaymen who infested rural roads. A common complaint was that they were acting as if they were free.[36]

Yet despite the slaves' activism, the freeing of recruits, and the extensive antislavery legislation of the independence era, slavery survived the wars in all but one of the former colonies. (The exception was Chile, where a combination of small slave numbers and the liberalism of the new government produced an abolition decree in 1823.) How did slavery manage to resist the wartime challenges? The most obvious reason was that these were wars of independence, not wars of abolition. Even slaves who enlisted to obtain their personal freedom very rarely if ever declared that the fight for freeing their countries should extend to freeing the slaves. Bolívar may have adopted abolition as a goal, but his was a lonely voice, drowned out by the pro-slavery chorus. There were no recognized black leaders who might have pressed the abolitionist cause because some, like Piar, did not survive the wars, and others were in no position to take on the role afterwards. Only a small proportion of those recruited returned home. Casualties were high, and others chose not to return, in some cases because they were runaways or deserters. Of the returnees, many found themselves in the courts after the wars, often for years, resisting former owners who had reclaimed them. Numerous recruits had been so seriously wounded that they were left reliant on their families or public charity for maintenance. Slaves in Gran Colombia believed they did not need to resort to militant action because they had the manumission law, which seemed to offer a route to freedom, although few actually benefited. Finally, the black population was not a united community that might have pressed the issue of abolition. They had fought on opposing sides during the wars, and even those on the same side in the patriot armies had divided along national lines, Chileans versus Argentines, Colombians versus Peruvians, and so on.[37] These divisions now intensified as the independence struggles unleashed centrifugal forces that led to renewed fighting, with contending groups struggling for control of the new nations. In Argentina fighting between federalists and centralists began before the wars of independence ended and lasted for decades. In Venezuela, liberals and conservatives engaged in frequent post-independence rebellions. In both cases slaves were recruited to serve in the new armies. Wars between states led to further recruiting. In Uruguay slaves helped defeat Brazilian troops and win Uruguayan independence in 1828. In the north, when Peru sought to challenge Bolívar's rule by declaring war on Gran Colombia in 1827, Bolivarian forces included slaves. In the following years donated slaves and runaways continued to make their way into the ranks of local armies despite prohibitions against their recruitment. As long as freedom was offered, slaves could be secured, although it was no longer offered with the frequency of the past because the number of slaves was falling and their average age was rising. Moreover, slaveholders wanted to hold on to their increasingly scarce property, and alternative soldiers were available.[38] Slave recruiting consequently declined as slavery became increasingly moribund.

Yet in at least one case slaves were called upon to serve once again and in doing so played a direct role in determining the actual date of abolition. In 1854 the president of Peru found his authority reduced to a small part of the country by the latest in a long series of civil wars. Desperate to reverse his fortunes, in November he offered freedom to any slave who enlisted in his forces for two years and extended the offer to their spouses. In response, the rebel leader and former president, Ramón Castilla, a man who claimed to represent liberal values, on December 3 issued a decree freeing every slave except those who took up arms against him. The offer attracted as many as three thousand recruits, and Castilla's military success early the following year opened the way for the nationwide application of his abolition decree.[39]

The 1850s almost saw the end of slavery in what had been Spanish South

America, the conclusion of a process that had begun with the wars of independence and the acceptance of slaves as combatants. Throughout the continent slaves had been brought into the military process, aiding in the freeing of their nations. That involvement had also served to weaken the institution that controlled them because the recruiting of slaves and their military service not only freed thousands but also changed attitudes. It aroused slaves who were noncombatants and it forced a reconsideration of the issue of slavery. Slavery was too well entrenched an institution for it to die with colonial rule, and the antislavery forces during the war years were not sufficiently strong, united, and focused to end slavery at that time, but the abolitionist process had begun. Recruiting after the wars further challenged the institution until finally slavery came to an end. Slave soldiers throughout the continent had done much to achieve this, although there are few memorials that pay tribute to their contribution.

Notes

1. Frederick P. Bowser, *The African Slave in Colonial Peru, 1524–1650* (Stanford, 1974), 97–100, 196–197; Allan J. Kuethe, *Military Reform and Society in New Granada, 1773–1808* (Gainesville, 1978); Stephen K. Stoan, *Pablo Morillo and Venezuela, 1815–1820* (Columbus, 1974), 17.

2. Ildefonso Pereda Valdés, *El negro en el Uruguay—pasado y presente* (Montevideo, Uruguay, 1965), 45, 46, 244–248; Marta B. Goldberg and Silvia C. Mallo, "La población africana en Buenos Aires y su campaña: Formas de vida y subsistencia (1750–1850)," *Temas de Africa y Asia* 2 (1993): 17, 20; John Lynch, *Argentine Dictator: Juan Manuel de Rosas, 1829–1852* (Oxford, 1981), 119; Kuethe, *Military Reform,* 29; John Lynch, *The Spanish American Revolutions, 1808–1826,* 2nd ed. (New York, 1986), 191; David G. Browning and David J. Robinson, "The Origin and Comparability of Peruvian Population Data: 1776–1815," *Jahrbuch* 14 (1977): 211.

3. José Marcial Ramos Guédez, "La insurección de los esclavos negros de Coro en 1795: Algunas ideas en torno a posibles influencias de la revolución francesa," *Revista Universitaria de Ciencias del Hombre* 2:2 (1989): 103–116; Jorge I. Domínguez, *Insurrection or Loyalty: The Breakdown of the Spanish American Empire* (Cambridge, MA, 1980), 99; Paulo de Carvalho-Neto, *El negro uruguayo (hasta la abolición)* (Quito, Ecuador, 1965), 96.

4. Tulio Halperín-Donghi, *Politics, Economics and Society in Argentina in the Revolutionary Period,* trans. Richard Southern (Cambridge, UK, 1975), 132.

5. George Reid Andrews, *The Afro-Argentines of Buenos Aires, 1800–1900* (Madison, 1980), 43, 94–95.

6. Archivo General de la Nación, Buenos Aires, Argentina (hereafter AGN-BA), Guerra, Rescate de esclavos, 1813–1817, X-43-6-7.

7. Peter M. Voelz, *Slave and Soldier: The Military Impact of Blacks in the Colonial Americas* (New York, 1993), chs. 16, 21–22.

8. "El Señor Procurador Municipal en defensa de Alexandro Campusano, esclavo, sobre se le declare exento del servicio de esclavitud," Archivo Histórico del Guayas, Guayaquil, Ecuador (hereafter AHG-G), 1826, no. 5996.

9. Andrews, *Afro-Argentines,* 39, 42–45, 47–48, 127, 132–135; Carvalho-Neto, *El negro uruguayo,* 94; Halperín-Donghi, *Politics,* 190–226; AGN-BA, Solicitudes Militares (hereafter Sol. Mil.), 1815, X-8-7-6.

10. *Gaceta de Buenos Aires,* 19 July 1810; "La morena Juliana García, esclava que fué de Don Pedro García, reclamando su libertad," 1818, AGN-BA, Administrativos, legajo (hereafter leg.) 33, expediente (hereafter exp.) 1179, IX-23-8-7; AGN-BA, Gobierno, Correspondencia del Gobierno de Buenos Aires con Elío y Vigodet, 1810–1814, X-1-5-10; AGN-BA, Representantes de la Junta, Castelli y Belgrano, Ejército del Norte y Banda Oriental, X-3-2-4, Guerra, 1811–1816, X-3-2-3; AGN-BA, Sol. Mil., 1815, X-8-7-6; Homero Martínez Montero, "El soldado negro," in Carvalho-Neto, *El negro uruguayo,* 273–274.

11. Argentina, *Registro oficial de la república argentina que comprende los documentos expedidos desde 1810 hasta 1872* (Buenos Aires, 1879), 1:168, 179, 194, 200–201, 221, 249–250, 328, 378, 383, 390–394; Rafael M. Castellano Sáenz Cavia, "La abolición de la esclavitud en las Provincias Unidas del Rio de la Plata (1810–1860)," *Revista de Historia del Derecho* 9 (1981): 90–108; AGN-BA, Cuerpo de libertos, Compra de esclavos por el estado, 1812–1814, III-37-3-22.

12. AGN-BA, Guerra, Rescate de esclavos, 1813–1817, X-43-6-7, Rescate de esclavos certificados, 1813–1817, X-43-6-8, Rescate de esclavos: Listas y ordenes del pago, 1816–1817, X-43-6-9; Andrews, *Afro-Argentines,* 48.

13. José Luis Masini, *La esclavitud negra en Mendoza: Epoca independiente* (Mendoza, Argentina, 1962), 18.

14. Andrews, *Afro-Argentines,* 117; Masini, *La esclavitud negra,* 18–34.

15. Guillermo Feliú Cruz, *La abolición de la esclavitud en Chile: Estudio histórico y social,* 2nd ed. (Santiago, Chile, 1973), 32, 33, 46, 50–57, 128, ch. 10; Núria Sales de Bohigas, *Sobre esclavos, reclutas y mercaderes de quintos* (Barcelona, 1974), 64, 76; José Antonio Ovalle y Vivanco to Sup. Director, September 5, 1817, Antonio Urrutia y Mendiburu to Junta Delegado, December 13, 1817, Archivo Nacional, Santiago, Chile, Provincia de Santiago i sus Departamentos, 1817 a 1828, Ministerio de Guerra, tomo 18, Intendencia, Santiago, vol. 1, 1817–1825, nos. 12, 41, 43, 98, 121, 173.

16. José Cevallos to Secretario de Estado y del Departamento Universal de Indias, July 22, 1815, Archivo General de Indias, Seville, Spain (hereafter AGI), Caracas 109; Lynch, *Spanish American Revolutions,* 190–199; Domínguez, *Insurrection,* 47, 174–176, 238; John V. Lombardi, *The Decline and Abolition of Negro Slavery in Venezuela, 1820–1854* (Westport, 1971), 37–39; Stoan, *Pablo Morillo,* 31, 35, 38–39.

17. "Libertad de Ramón Piñero, esclavo del Dr. Don Juan de Roxas," Archivo de la Academia Nacional de la Historia, Caracas, Venezuela (hereafter AANH-C), Civiles-Esclavos, tomo 1815-OP, exp. 5; Lynch, *Spanish American Revolutions,* 204–207; Domínguez, *Insurrection,* 177–178; Stoan, *Pablo Morillo,* 51–57.

18. Simón Bolívar, *Obras Completas* (Caracas, n.d.), 3:574.

19. "Lino Rodrígues, sargento, pide se le declare libre de servidumbre por sus servicios puestados a la República," AANH-C, Civiles-Esclavos, tomo 1825-BCGJMPRT, exp. 7;

"Juan José Ledesma, esclavo de Don Pedro Ledesma, solicitando se le de la libertad por haber militado en el Ejército de su Majestad," AANH-C, Civiles-Esclavos, tomo 1815-LM, exp. 1.

20. "El Sindico Procurador General solicita la libertad de various esclavos, 1815," Biblioteca Nacional de Colombia, Bogotá, Colombia, libro 331, no. 987, fol. 114, and "Juan Francisco Cicero, esclavo de Hacienda Saldaña," libro 329, no. 961, fol. 103; Brian Hamnett, "Popular Insurrection and Royalist Reaction: Colombian Regions, 1810–1823," in *Reform and Insurrection in Bourbon New Granada and Peru,* ed. John R. Fisher, Allan J. Kuethe, and Anthony McFarlane (Baton Rouge, 1990), 310.

21. Domínguez, *Insurrection,* 210; Stoan, *Pablo Morillo,* 67, 68, 71–72, 75, 112; Archivo General de la Nación, Bogotá, Colombia (hereafter AGN-B), Archivo Anexo, Solicitudes, tomo 5, fol. 45.

22. Morillo to Juan Bautista Pardo, June 11, 1818, AGN-B, Archivo Restrepo, caja 9, fondo I, vol. 21, fol. 195.

23. Vicente Lecuna, comp., and Harold A. Bierck Jr., ed., *Selected Writings of Bolívar,* trans. Lewis Bertrand (New York, 1951), 1:131; *Correo del Orinoco,* Angostura, October 28, 1818, no. 14; Stoan, *Pablo Morillo,* 212–213; Lynch, *Spanish American Revolutions,* 210–215; Jaime E. Rodríguez O., *The Independence of Spanish America* (Cambridge, UK, 1998), 185–186.

24. *Cartas Santander-Bolívar, 1813–1820* (Bogotá, 1988), 2:137.

25. Ibid., 2:87.

26. *Gaceta del Gobierno de Lima,* July 28, 1825, no. 8; *Cartas Santander-Bolívar,* 2:1–2, 64, 224–227, 319–323; Francisco del Pino to Minister of War, January 1, 1821, AGI, Caracas 55; "Don Juan Pablo Ayala para el Intendente solicita se le devuelvan dos esclavos pertenecientes a su hermano, que fueron empleados para el servicio de las armas," Caracas, September 6, 1822, Archivo General de la Nación, Caracas, Venezuela, Gran Colombia, Intendencia de Venezuela, tomo CVI, fol. 16, and "Representación del señor Juan José Lander al intendente," Caracas, May 6, 1822, Gran Colombia, Intendencia de Venezuela, tomo IV, fol. 338.

27. Sales de Bohigas, *Sobre esclavos,* 105; "Expediente promovido ante el Superior Gobierno por Doña María del Carmén Gómez," Archivo General de la Nación, Lima, Peru (hereafter AGN-L), Superior Gobierno, 1818, leg. 36, cuaderno 1268.

28. Timothy E. Anna, *The Fall of the Royal Government in Peru* (Lincoln, 1979), 196, 202.

29. "Alistamiento de negros," Biblioteca Nacional, Lima, Peru, Virreynato, February 18, 1821, D5985.

30. Archivo Histórico Militar, Lima, Peru (hereafter AHM-L), Correspondencia de Ministerio de Guerra y Marina con los Jefes del Ejército Unido, 1822/23, J4, and Copiador Correspondencia del Ministro de Guerra y Marina, 1821/22, L2; AGN-L, O.L. 92-10; John Miller, *Memoirs of General Miller in the Service of the Republic of Peru,* 2nd ed. (London, 1829), 1:219, 287–288, 305; Anna, *Fall of the Royal Government,* 151, 196–197; Sales de Bohigas, *Sobre esclavos,* 109–116; Lynch, *Spanish American Revolutions,* 276.

31. AGN-BA, Sol. Mil., 1815, X-8-7-5, and 1819, X-11-1-7.

32. Samuel Haigh, *Sketches of Buenos Ayres, Chile, and Peru* (London, 1831), 235.

33. Argentina, *Biblioteca de mayo. Colección de obras y documentos para la historia argentina. Guerra de la independencia* (Buenos Aires, 1963), 15:13278.

34. AGN-BA, Guerra, 1811–1816, X-3-2-3, and 1815–1816, X-39-8-5; AGN-BA, Rescate de esclavos, 1813–1817, X-43-6-7; AGN-BA, Sol. Mil., 1813, X-6-9-1, and 1817, X-10-1-1; AHM-L, leg. 7, nos. 317, 327, leg. 33, no. 8, leg. 39, no. 52; Archivo Histórico Municipal "Camilo Destruge," Guayaquil, Ecuador, Causas Militares, 1822–1829, no. 49; Lecuna and Bierck, *Selected Writings,* 2:412; Andrews, *Afro-Argentines,* 117; Dominguez, *Insurrection,* 211–213.

35. Lombardi, *Decline,* 46.

36. "Solicitando carta de libertad," AGN-BA, Administrativos, leg. 33, exp. 1144, IX-23-8-7; AGN-BA, Sol. Mil., 1814–1815, X-35-7-7, 1815, X-8-7-5, X-8-7-6, and 1818, X-10-9-5; AGN-BA, Solicitudes Civiles y Militares, 1816, X-9-2-4; Archivo Nacional del Ecuador, Quito, Esclavos, caja 23, 1825–1830, exps. 3, 6; Camilla Townsend, " 'Half my body free, the other half enslaved': The Politics of the Slaves of Guayas at the End of the Colonial Era," *Colonial Latin American Review* 7:1 (1998): 105–128; Lecuna and Bierck, *Selected Writings,* 2:512; Andrews, *Afro-Argentines,* 34; Peter Blanchard, *Slavery and Abolition in Early Republican Peru* (Wilmington, 1992), 12.

37. Andrews, *Afro-Argentines,* 117, 118, 120–127; Bowles to Croker, no. 113 Secret, October 3, 1818, Admiralty files 1/23, and Campbell to Canning, no. 102, October 7, 1826, Foreign Office files 18/28, Public Record Office, London.

38. Lynch, *Argentine Dictator,* 122; Lombardi, *Decline,* 130–131; Martínez Montero, "El soldado negro," 280–282; AGN-B, Colecciones, fondo E.O.R., caja 15, carpeta 56, fol. 9; "El Señor José Santa-Coloma reclama la entrega de su esclavo Pedro Franco, y acredita su buena conducta," AHG-G, 1830, no. 501.

39. Blanchard, *Slavery,* 190–200.

Armed Slaves and the Struggles for Republican Liberty in the U.S. Civil War

JOSEPH P. REIDY

At the start of the Civil War, most free inhabitants of the North and the South presumed that white men would settle the momentous issues that had fractured the Union. The rhetoric of preserving the Union on one side and winning independence on the other aimed to energize the respective white populations for the sacrifices that lay ahead. In the United States, black men's clamoring for a war against slavery fell on deaf ears, as did their offers of service in that cause. From the standpoint of federal officials, the black population would not affect the outcome of the contest. In the Confederate States, few failed to appreciate how enslaved African Americans would contribute to the overall mobilization as unskilled field hands and laborers, growing food-stuffs, transporting military goods, and otherwise working to support soldiers in the field and civilians on the home front. But even fewer took the potentially subversive stance of advocating the arming of slaves in pursuit of Confederate independence. On both sides of the contest, citizens and policymakers alike clung to traditional assumptions about racial roles. Arms in the hands of slaves violated the rules of civilized warfare, threatening wholesale slave revolt and a descent into barbarism.

Reality soon encroached on these assumptions, and the momentum of events carried partisans and casual observers alike in new and unforeseen directions. In the Confederacy, several hundred enslaved men (and perhaps one or two thousand free men) had served in state and Confederate military units by war's end. It is likely that one or two hundred thousand free and enslaved men (most of them the latter) provided direct support to Confederate armed forces in the capacity of servants, teamsters, and military laborers. Although the men enlisted as soldiers saw little action and consequently contributed little to the outcome, there can be little doubt that the laborers contributed significantly to the Confederate war effort.[1]

On the Union side of the contest, about 200,000 African Americans served in uniform in the army and the navy, and tens of thousands more labored in support of federal forces over the course of the war. The majority of the enlistees—perhaps 130,000 of the 179,000 soldiers and 10,000 of the nearly 18,000 sailors—had been enslaved at the start of the war.[2] The Union's African American soldiers and sailors played a significant—some have argued decisive—role in defeating the Confederacy and preserving the Union. Dispelling the doubts of their critics, they acquitted themselves well in battle and served faithfully in every capacity. By the end of the war, black units such as the Fifty-fourth Massachusetts Infantry returned home to heroes' welcomes. The veterans helped energize the postwar struggle for equal rights that, among other things, resulted in passage of the Thirteenth, Fourteenth, and Fifteenth Amendments.[3]

These achievements notwithstanding, the heroic model of African American military service does not adequately describe the complexity of the experience during the war or its variable effects after the war, even on the Union side. Men who were either born free or who had been freed before the war and who served in regiments recruited in the northern states experienced a very different war from that of formerly enslaved men recruited from the slave states. Although these regiments often served together and fraternized, the key episodes that have become emblematic of the black military experience during the Civil War—in no small measure thanks to the film *Glory,* which depicts the service of the Fifty-fourth Massachusetts Volunteers—involve northern units consisting largely of free men. To be sure, not all freeborn men shared the fruits of northern victory equally. But the freedmen from the loyal border states and the Confederate States experienced a different war and returned home to a different reception from that which greeted the freemen from the northern states. Assessing the former slaves' Civil War requires a different measure from the heroic one that fits the Massachusetts Fifty-fourth.

Confederate designs for the use of African American manpower followed traditional lines. Leaders simply assumed that enslaved men—who constituted approximately one-third of the adult men in the seceded states—would sustain the production of goods and the provision of services in the civilian economy, as they had from the introduction of slavery more than two centuries earlier. Men of unmixed European descent—slave masters, nonslaveholding yeoman farmers, and urban artisans and laborers—would carry the banner of independence into battle with the Yankees. Such a division of labor would support both the political ideology and the material requirements of the cause. Although leaders understood the need for increased vigilance on the home front, they voiced no specific fears of either rebellion or sabotage. Slaves would continue to do as directed, even if women gave the orders.

A number of Confederate citizens advanced proposals for arming the slaves early in the war and not only during its final year, when widespread manpower shortages required consideration of the option. The boldest considered this a necessary first step in the overall mobilization, one that would pay dividends on the home front as well as the battlefield. One proposed a selective mobilization "say ten or twenty placed promiscuously in each company" to relieve the threat of unrest at home and to "assist in whipping the black republicans." Although some judged the reasoning as naïve, proponents of the view argued that involving young black men in the fight on the side of the Confederacy would minimize the potential for mischief on the plantations at a time when manpower and resources were diverted to the war effort and police controls over the enslaved population correspondingly loosened.[4]

During the first two years of the war, as Confederate armies more than held their own against those of the United States, neither military nor political leaders considered a mass mobilization of black men under arms. At the same time, however, a considerable if often underestimated mobilization of black men laboring in military support capacities began. Confederate officers (like their Union counterparts) received allotments for body servants. Officers from slaveholding families frequently took young men from their slave force to serve in this capacity. Enlisted men who owned slaves often did the same, without the benefit of an allowance. Such servants typically cooked and served, cleaned laundry, tended horses and mules, and performed related camp chores. Surviving photographs often depict these servants, at times clothed in Confederate uniforms and bearing arms.[5] A smaller and less conspicuous mobilization of slave women also helped lighten the soldiers' camp chores.

The extent to which camp servants took part in armed conflicts with Union forces remains unclear. Although evidence to prove or disprove this contention definitively has been elusive, two elements bear attention. First, Confederate military camps may have fostered a spirit of camaraderie sufficiently strong to prompt such action on the part of African American men. To the extent that volunteer companies consisted of relatives and neighbors, the soldiers and the servants may have created a semblance of home — hierarchically structured, to be sure, but familiar for that very reason — that the enslaved men may have helped defend from hostile Yankee fire. Second, in the circumstance of surprise attacks, when shots rang out, the impulse of self-protection may well have prompted all men — black as well as white, enslaved as well as free — to employ weapons defensively against Union forces. The testimony of federal soldiers makes reference to such encounters, but on balance they appear to have had little impact on the outcome of military actions.[6]

The auxiliary service of enslaved African Americans served as a double-edged sword. On one side, such service contributed significantly to the field effectiveness of Confederate armies. But, on the other side, it tended to undermine slavery in the areas in which the armies operated. As early as May 1862, a Virginia slaveholder complained that Confederate troops "employ runaway negroes to cook for the mess, clean their horses, and so forth," thereby encouraging others to seek "a safe harbour in the army."[7] Soldiers rarely rebuffed black men's offers to tend their camps and cook their meals. Nor did they examine too scrupulously the claims of a man's free birth or his master's permission to be absent from home. In some cases, the carelessness aimed deliberately to spite masters for whom the war was more of an abstraction than a reality; in other cases, the desire simply to gain relief from the tedium of camp chores figured most prominently. Such actions laid bare the slaveholders' inability to provide for their people and to exert authority over them even while compromising the efficacy of slavery and its legitimacy as the foundation for Confederate independence.

Confederate naval forces also took advantage of enslaved black manpower. Prior to the war, black men had provided much of the unskilled labor associated with the maritime industry in the South. Although the bulk of the labor entailed loading and unloading ships, black men also worked on the vessels that plied the coastal and inland waterways.[8] With the outbreak of hostilities and the organization of Confederate naval forces, officials first banned the enlistment of free black men but later authorized their limited use, in numbers not to exceed one-twentieth of a ship's complement.[9] The small number of commissioned Confederate naval vessels to some extent disguises the navy's reliance on slaves as pilots and as seamen and deck hands on supply vessels. Ship owners often leased both vessel and their enslaved crewmen to Confederate or state authorities. The notable case of Robert Smalls illustrates. By managing to seize the supply vessel *Planter*, steam past the fortifications at the mouth of Charleston harbor, and surrender to the Union's blockading squadron, Smalls and his comrades achieved freedom and national notoriety. More than any other single episode, this incident revealed the Confederacy's dependence on the services of enslaved watermen.[10]

The Confederate attempt to mobilize free black men enjoyed checkered success at best. Free blacks numbering in the thousands served in support capacities as military laborers, teamsters, and the like throughout the Confederacy. Often part of defensive mobilizations in advance of Union military operations, these men were pressed into service involuntarily and felt little if any enthusiasm for the cause. By 1864, the impressments created a considerable police problem by virtue of the men's penchant for deserting—not so much to seek Yankee protection as to return home. For the remainder of the war, Confederate military authorities matched wits with impressed free black men.

Although men of African descent served the Confederacy under arms, determining their exact numbers remains a difficult task and determining their complex motives even more so. Individual free black men volunteered for military duty in every one of the Confederate states, and it is likely that hundreds actually served. In the states that bordered the Gulf of Mexico, where the tradition of free black militia service had originated under French and Spanish auspices during the colonial period, the numbers were significantly higher, particularly during the first year of the war. In Louisiana, state officials mobilized the antebellum militia of *gens de couleur*, whose various local units numbered several thousand men. The intensity of these men's support for the Confederacy varied considerably depending on their wealth and social standing, the strength of their ties with white benefactors, and the gains they expected to realize from service. As for the units raised in southern Louisiana, the Union occupation of New Orleans in the spring of 1862 enabled them to shed their allegiance to the rebellion. Incompletely organized under state officials, the free black militiamen had a negligible impact on the overall Confederate mobilization. Federal military planners took more systematic advantage of their service and eventually built a considerable force of African-descended soldiers around the core of the antebellum militia units.[11]

By 1863, as Confederate military fortunes began to flag, Confederate leaders reopened the question of the wholesale military service of enslaved men. In the mid-summer of 1863, a Mississippi slaveholder urged President Jefferson Davis to avert Confederate defeat by calling out "every able-bodied *Negro* man" of military age, confident that the men wished to join "in the frollick" and would "all go to the enemy if not taken to our own army": "Away with all squeamesness [*sic*] about employing negroes in civilized warfare," he exhorted Davis, yet Confederate officials feared the political repercussions of such a step.[12] As they faced growing—if not necessarily universal—shortages of food, war materials, and men, they had to balance military necessity against popular opinion. For another year, the potential risks involved in arming slaves appeared to outweigh any conceivable advantages.

The fall of Chattanooga late in 1863 marked an important turning point for Confederate fortunes in the western theater. Early in 1864, Major General Patrick R. Cleburne, a division commander in the Army of Tennessee, made the strategic case for arming slaves, sweeping aside philosophical and political objections. In his judgment, Confederate armies were becoming so desperate for manpower that the government could no longer refrain from mobilizing black men. He boldly concluded that freedom — for the individual soldier "and his whole race who side with us" — must reward faithful military service.[13] Cleburne's proposal eventually reached Richmond, where the president and the secretary of war ordered its suppression. Cleburne's death in battle late in 1864 silenced his dissenting voice permanently, but Confederate leaders could not so readily ignore the issues he raised. Even as public interest in the cause of arming the slaves simmered, the relation between slavery and national independence began rising to a boil.

The fall and winter of 1864–1865 proved to be especially difficult seasons for Confederate soldiers. The men in Robert E. Lee's Army of Northern Virginia — who hailed disproportionately from states east of the Mississippi River and in particular from Virginia, the Carolinas, and Georgia — showed a marked and growing propensity to desert. Early in 1865, at the dawn of another campaigning season, variants of Cleburne's proposal resurfaced and again reached Richmond. Secretary of State Judah P. Benjamin took special interest in the subject, as did President Davis. Unwilling to proceed too far out onto the political limb without support from Lee, who commanded the Confederacy's major fighting force, Davis and Benjamin arranged with Lee to poll the soldiers for their opinion about arming the slaves. Enlisted men no less than officers apparently debated the question extensively, leaving no consideration — ideological, political, social, or military — unexamined. In the end, most units in Lee's army expressed support for arming and training former slaves and rushing them to the front. Strong dissenting voices also rose to squelch the proposal, none more impassioned than that of General Howell Cobb of Georgia. "The day you make soldiers of them is the beginning of the end of the revolution," Cobb declared. "If slaves will make good soldiers our whole theory of slavery is wrong."[14] The choice of independence or slavery was difficult enough, but independence purchased with the service of slave soldiers proved unacceptable to hard-liners.

Because Lee viewed the matter through the eyes of a soldier and not those of a political ideologue, he quietly informed Davis that he and his army would welcome the men recruited from the ranks of the enslaved. Although Lee understood the need to offer freedom to slave volunteers and their immediate families, he left the details to the politicians. By March 1865, with President Davis's signature on the enabling legislation, military authorities in Richmond began recruiting and drilling a company of such men. At the time that the Confederate government abandoned the city a month later, several hundred had been uniformed and smaller numbers armed and drilled. Although some of these men reportedly engaged the Yankees in combat, the true test of Cleburne's theory of employing slave soldiers in the fight for Confederate independence never came.[15]

Perhaps not surprisingly, the surviving record contains virtually no commentary about how potential recruits and their families viewed the prospect of gaining freedom by fighting for the Confederacy, though it must have been a thoroughly — perhaps hotly — debated topic in African American communities throughout the South. As the parallel debate among free black southerners suggests, the objective was not simply to support the continuation of slavery or the success of the Confederate cause of independence. Instead, volunteers aimed to translate the public emergency into gains for themselves and their families. Free black men wished to enhance their social or political privileges; enslaved men sought the fundamental rights of free persons. Personal considerations — the need to care for an aged parent or an overwhelming sense of attachment to a place — also affected the process whereby individuals determined their next steps, mindful that they could not predict the ultimate outcome of their actions. For every circumstance in which the choice may have appeared a Faustian one between good and evil, right and wrong, there were many others in which the lines were blurred and the shadings more subtle than stark. Had the war continued beyond the spring of 1865, with growing numbers of black men either enlisting or being conscripted, the Confederacy could not have escaped the dilemma that General Cobb identified.

The debate about arming slaves in defense of the Union began from approximately the same starting point as that in the Confederacy but soon changed courses and ultimately arrived at a very different destination. By virtue of the pervasive influence of proslavery ideology in northern racial thinking, northerners sounded very much like southerners in their characterizations of African Americans, both free and enslaved. The similarity derived in part from the strong presence of the slaveholding interest in the early strategic planning on the part of the North. Because the four border slaveholding states of Delaware, Maryland, Kentucky, and Missouri had never left the Union, their politicians and citizens obliged the federal government to uphold slavery. What is more, because all four of the states occupied strategically important positions, their citizens had additional reason to expect that the government in Washington would mollify the slaveholding interest. Had Maryland seceded, the national capital in Washington would have been surrounded by Confederate territory, forcing the abandonment of the capital and tarnishing if not thoroughly corroding the Union. Had any of the other three border states allied with the Confederacy, important industrial and agricultural resources would have been denied to the United States and important routes of attack — the Mississippi, Ohio, and Delaware Rivers and Delaware Bay — would have been opened.[16]

Whether they lived in slave states proximate to the Confederate border or in the free states farther to the north, most citizens of the United States shared the notion of a white man's war. The belief derived in part from their common understanding that saving the Union, not freeing the slaves, was the chief aim. The future of slavery had no place in attempting to resolve the national emergency. President Abraham Lincoln's call for volunteers in April 1861 did not envision the service of black men; in fact, the applicable federal legislation of 1792 expressly stated that bearing arms was the responsibility (and the prerogative) of white men only.[17]

With the public eye focused on raising armies, few noticed the mobilization of black men into the navy, which actually predated the start of hostilities in April 1861.[18] From its inception in the 1790s the navy had permitted men of all ethnic and racial groups to serve. Much like the naval forces of the world's maritime powers, the navy of the United States recruited men with little regard to their race or nativity. Despite regulations first introduced in the 1840s that limited the percentage of African American recruits to 5 percent of the total, black men served. Men held as slaves at times entered naval service with the consent of their owners. At Hampton Roads, Virginia, site of a large naval base, such enlistments were routine. George Teamoh, an enslaved native Virginian who eventually escaped from bondage, served several such stints during the 1840s.[19]

The rigid structure of the naval service helps explain why the enlistment of black men — slaves included — caused such little stir. A wide chasm separated enlisted men from officers, and nested hierarchies based largely on rank situated each man relative to every other. Although naval officials generally hoped that the enlisted force might mirror the population of citizens, they also recognized that the sturdy yeoman of the Jeffersonian ideal wanted little to do with the sea. From the standpoint of officers, enlisted men were the dregs of society whose loyalty to alcohol and lewd women ran stronger than that to nation and whose obedience depended on fear of harsh punishment rather than deference to legitimate authority.[20]

By the late summer of 1861, amid a rapid and large-scale increase in the number of ships and the size of the enlisted force, naval officials began to ponder the use of black men more seriously than they had ever done before. As white men clamored to enlist in the volunteer army units, as naval enlistments faltered, and as naval vessels began operating in Confederate waters, the prospect of enlisting black men (escaped slaves not excluded) presented itself. This policy succeeded magnificently in relieving manpower shortages on vessels with crew members acclimated to the southern summer, and accordingly it served as a foundation on which later naval personnel policy rested.[21]

Few public figures outside of naval circles commented on the navy's successful enlistment of black men, and no one advocated it as a model for the army, not even the leading spokesmen for northern free blacks. To Frederick Douglass, John Mercer Langston, and other veterans of the antebellum struggles for equality, the war presented a unique opportunity to strike a blow for liberty, help save the Union, and establish an undeniable claim to manhood rights, especially the suffrage. But military and not naval service offered the path to those ends. Other men — some free-born, others formerly enslaved, and many with relatives still held in bondage — who wished to take up arms to destroy slavery added their voices to the cause. Despite the apparent indifference if not outright hostility of the government, they continued to agitate for the cause on the abolitionist speaking circuit throughout the northern states, Canada, and Europe. Although this agitation did not immediately bear fruit, it prepared the soil.[22]

First the Union had to agree to make war against slavery. This transformation occurred relatively quickly during the first year of the war. By the spring of 1862, before the first anniversary of the battle of Fort Sumter, public sentiment began reflecting this change. The federal fugitive slave act helped bring the issue into clear focus. From its passage in 1850, the law had provoked controversy, but the large mobilization of federal forces and their deployment early in the war in the border states spawned fresh concerns. Protecting the property rights of Unionist slaveholders was one thing, but not so those of Confederates. Federal troops charged with enforcing the law often experienced difficulty distinguishing between Unionist and Confederate slaveholders; both groups appeared equally determined to assure that their own interests stood paramount. Witnessing how masters mistreated apprehended fugitives both sickened volunteer soldiers and conjured up images from *Uncle Tom's Cabin*,

Harriet Beecher Stowe's sentimental novel about the inhumanity of slavery. Recounting these experiences to their families at home helped reinforce a sense of sympathy for the slaves and contempt for their masters.[23]

More to the point, soldiers quickly assessed how relieving the slaves' misfortunes could also ameliorate their own and began harboring fugitives to assist with camp chores. Certain regiments gained a reputation for such acts, with predictable results. As escaped slaves sought protection, slaveholders demanded the return of their property. Military advances into Virginia and Tennessee relaxed the political tension somewhat by removing the offending troops from states that had remained within the Union. Against the backdrop of this mobilization of convenience, citizens and policy makers alike began debating the strategic use of black men as soldiers and not simply as laborers.[24]

During the spring and summer of 1862, Congress translated this sentiment into public policy, first by exempting federal forces from the obligation to enforce the fugitive slave act and then by passing the Militia Act and the Second Confiscation Act. The former authorized the use of black men and women in support capacities to aid the Union cause. The latter offered federal protection and the hope of eventual freedom to the slaves of Confederate masters. Steps that scarcely fifteen months earlier had appeared unthinkable now took on quite a different aspect.[25]

When President Lincoln took a position on these issues during the summer of 1862, his intent was clear: preserving the Union required abandoning slavery. Yet two factors continued to hinder translating this vision into reality. The first was the continuing vitality of slavery combined with the political clout of slaveholders in the border states. The second was the possibility of a public backlash if federal officials made emancipation a war aim. Lincoln tried to appease border state slaveholders by promising monetary compensation in exchange for voluntary emancipation. As an added incentive, he proposed colonizing the freedpeople to distant lands. He clung to that notion long after its utter impracticality—and cool public reception—should have convinced him otherwise. But slaveholding Unionists refused to relinquish their property on any terms, and Lincoln's warning that the "friction and abrasion" of war would wear away at slavery began proving true.[26]

Military events in the various theaters of war also suggested the expediency of making war on slavery and employing the enslaved to further the cause. Federal operations in South Carolina and Louisiana illustrate. On assuming command of the Union occupation force based at Hilton Head, South Carolina, in the spring of 1862, General David Hunter began taking dramatic steps to make war against slavery. He proclaimed free the slaves in South Carolina, Georgia, and Florida—an action that President Lincoln promptly countermanded for procedural as well as policy reasons — and proposed to equip and train formerly enslaved men for military service against the Confederacy. Owing largely to Hunter's unbridled abolitionism, the War Department refused to grant his request for approval. He nonetheless began organizing the force, which by summer numbered in the hundreds. Increasingly skeptical that he would gain official sanction, Hunter disbanded the regiment, save for one company he assigned to his quartermaster, General Rufus Saxton, a New England abolitionist. In short order, Saxton won War Department approval and began recruiting in earnest. With the assistance of abolitionist allies, Saxton enlisted Thomas Wentworth Higginson, a renowned opponent of slavery, to command the unit. The men of the First South Carolina Volunteers (later the Thirty-third U.S. Colored Infantry) performed superbly for the remainder of the war, capitalizing on their knowledge of the local geography and the ways of the planter class. Higginson's dispatches from the front, which were published serially during the war and then under the title *Army Life in a Black Regiment* in 1870, gave stirring tribute to the men and their heroic exploits, which northern readers took as first-hand evidence that the experiment of arming black men might succeed.[27]

Reports from Louisiana pointed toward the same conclusion. Shortly after the federal occupation of New Orleans in April 1862, General Benjamin F. Butler, the Massachusetts politician commanding federal forces, became embroiled in a debate with one of his subordinates, General John W. Phelps, a Vermont abolitionist eager to make war against slavery, over the propriety of arming black men. Phelps pressed for Butler's authorization to arm and train fugitive slaves as soldiers, but Butler refused on the grounds that military necessity did not warrant the move. Butler also admonished Phelps to curb the antislavery enthusiasm of his troops and their flagrant disrespect for the property rights of Unionist slaveholders. By August Butler forced the unrelenting Phelps to resign even as he began sensing a shift in the political winds regarding the use of black men in the war effort. Recalling the offer of service to the Union made by the free men of color in the Native Guard — an offer he had originally spurned — Butler not only enlisted them but also authorized the commissioned officers to retain their ranks. In short order, African American Louisianans, enslaved no less than free, began volunteering in large numbers and continued to do so for the rest of the war.[28]

When the Confederate government did not respond favorably to his Preliminary Emancipation Proclamation, President Lincoln declared an end to slavery in the rebel states on January 1, 1863. Although critics have faulted the Emancipation Proclamation, it fundamentally transformed the nature of the war. First, it committed federal forces to destroying slavery within the Confederate states. Second, it authorized the wholesale mobilization of persons of African descent, under arms as well as in support capacities.[29] Within the short space of five months, the War Department established the Bureau of Colored Troops with special responsibility to arm, equip, and train for combat as many men of African descent as could be brought into service. General Lorenzo Thomas, the Adjutant General of the Army, personally directed the recruiting drive in the Mississippi Valley, aiming to take advantage of the heavy concentrations of slaves laboring on the plantations of the Confederate heartland.[30] Union recruiters succeeded magnificently. Of the nearly 179,000 black men who served in the Union army during the Civil War (more than 98,000 of whom were recruited within the eleven Confederate states), Louisiana accounted for more than 24,000, Tennessee for another 20,000, and Mississippi for nearly 18,000. Nearly 64 percent of the men recruited in the Confederate states and nearly 35 percent of all the black men who served in the army during the Civil War came from these three states. The vast majority of these men had been enslaved at the start of the war.[31]

The final piece of the federal mobilization of enslaved black soldiers involved the loyal slave states that had remained within the Union. Although initially placed off-limits to recruiters, the farms and plantations of Delaware, Maryland, Kentucky, and Missouri lost their exempt status in the spring and summer of 1864. As Lincoln abandoned all hope of convincing border-state slaveholders and their political representatives to embrace compensated emancipation and colonization, the War Department began seriously recruiting black men there. Federal law authorized payment of the enlistment bonus of each slave to his master, in effect offering several hundred dollars in compensation in exchange for the man's freedom. Under pressure from the enlisted former slaves and from other quarters as well, in March 1865 Congress granted freedom to the immediate families of the enlistees, thereby unloosing a new wave of enlistments that had particular impact on Kentucky, where nearly twenty-four thousand black men took up arms, many during the final weeks of the war.[32] The enlistment of enslaved black men terminally weakened the institution of slavery in the border states. Federal officials took this risk because of their desperate need for manpower and their growing acknowledgment that slavery would not survive the war. They also did so, at least implicitly, as a result of actions by the enslaved. Men ran from their masters to enlist, often traveling considerable distances and taking great risks to do so. And persons who remained on the plantations and farms pressed against the traditional boundaries of slavery.

In crude numbers, black men constituted approximately 10 percent of the

Union army's enlisted personnel during the Civil War, yet this figure underestimates the true impact of their presence. Given the small number of black troops who entered service before 1863, the influx of the African Americans began at a time when the Union's need for men was growing. Imposition of the federal draft assured a continuing flow of fresh white recruits, but conscription could not replicate either the numbers of men who volunteered at the onset of hostilities or their enthusiasm for the cause. Black soldiers helped reverse both the declining numbers and the ebbing passion, and as their numbers grew, their proportion of the effective force at the disposal of Union military strategists did likewise.[33] A similar pattern obtained in the navy. In terms of overall numbers, black sailors constituted between 15 and 20 percent of the enlisted personnel during the course of the war, but their impact grew more significant over time. In the spring of 1861 they represented less than 5 percent of the navy's fighting force; by the summer of 1862 the proportion increased to 15 percent, and during the fall of 1864 it peaked at 23 percent.[34]

The experience of formerly enslaved African Americans in the U.S. Navy during the Civil War partly overlaps that of their counterparts who served in the army. They made up more than half of the nearly eighteen thousand men who served, with particularly sizeable enlistments of men born in Virginia, Maryland, Louisiana, Mississippi, South Carolina, and North Carolina. A number of these men had had some experience with maritime life (either in coastal waters or on inland rivers), but most had not. And although the service remained impervious to the democratic tendencies that enjoyed some play in the army, African American sailors often benefited from the rigidity of naval structures. Men with similar ratings (the naval term for ranks) received the same pay regardless of race or nativity, and judicial proceedings did not overtly discriminate against black men even though the captains of individual vessels enjoyed wide latitude in how they administered naval regulations.[35]

The dynamics of individual naval vessels created miniature worlds in which the experience of formerly enslaved sailors might differ significantly from one vessel to another. The commanding officer set the tone for interactions between officers and enlisted men. If he considered black men capable of performing their duties creditably, then officers and men acted accordingly; similarly, his expressions of disdain might lead to diatribes and worse. The experience of sailors differed in other important respects from that of soldiers in the sense that the world of the vessel was defined by the rigid boundary of the hull. In the best of cases space was cramped, and men labored, ate, slept, and relaxed in close proximity to each other. Depending on the size and type of vessel, its tactical deployment, the squadron to which it was attached, and the demography of the crew, black sailors who had recently escaped from slavery interacted more or less frequently with freeborn sailors, performed more or less back-breaking labor, experienced more or less combat with Confederate forces, and enjoyed more or less likelihood of advancing in rating. Aboard the mortar schooner *Adolph Hugel* in the Potomac Flotilla, for instance, during the closing months of the war, forty-one members of the forty-eight-man crew (85 percent) were African American; their numbers included nearly all of the senior noncommissioned officers. The vessel patrolled the Potomac and Rappahannock rivers in pursuit of Confederate forces. In contrast, the supply vessel *Vermont,* whose crew was also overwhelmingly African American, remained moored to a pier at Port Royal, South Carolina, the repair and supply base of the South Atlantic Blockading Squadron. *Vermont*'s men loaded stores day in and day out, seldom going to sea or engaging the enemy.[36]

The traditions of naval service accommodated the large influx of black sailors awkwardly at best, even in the interest of helping to suppress the rebellion. During the first two years of the war, Navy Department policy relegated "contrabands" to the low-paying and low-status rating of "boy." After that restriction was lifted, enlistment officers persisted in rating the formerly enslaved at the bottom of the rating ladder. Navy Department policy also barred black men from commissioned office, and although a handful of black sailors were promoted to noncommissioned officer ratings with responsibilities of command, the numbers of such men came nowhere near the number of black noncommissioned officers in the army or their percentage of the entire enlisted force. Finally, significant numbers of contraband sailors were rated as cooks and stewards, working essentially as officers' servants. Although all shipboard personnel fulfilled assigned duties during combat — and, indeed, several contrabands merited the Medal of Honor for conspicuous acts of bravery in battle — the fact remains that formerly enslaved men largely occupied the least prestigious positions in the naval pecking order. Although they, too, fought against the forms of discrimination embedded in naval traditions and derived from the stereotypes of white officers and enlisted men, the structure of naval service was for the most part inflexible to such pressures for change. A navy court had no sympathy for Ordinary Seaman George E. Smith, who deserted to enlist in the army, where, he believed, he had a better chance for advancement than what the navy presented. In the face of such challenges, the men bided their time, kept their own counsel, performed their duty conscientiously, and awaited the day when they could return to civilian life.[37]

As the recruitment of African American soldiers intensified during the spring and summer of 1863, several black units that had been recruited earlier withstood the test of combat and helped remove the last reservations about the military potential of black men under arms.[38] Two of those units consisted largely of men who had been free before the war—the Second Louisiana Native Guard at Port Hudson, Louisiana, in May and the Fifty-fourth Massachusetts Volunteers at Fort Wagner, South Carolina, in July. But the units that fought commendably at Milliken's Bend, Louisiana, in June consisted entirely of men who had been slaves. Most were Louisiana natives recruited into service only a short time earlier. What they lacked in training, according to one after-action report, they more than compensated for in "fierce obstinacy."[39] These three battles helped dispel the doubts that men of African descent might affect the military outcome of the war.

The misgivings grew largely out of prevalent racial ideology, from which not even abolitionists were entirely immune. Colonel Thomas Wentworth Higginson of the First South Carolina Volunteers, for instance, assumed an air of paternalism toward his men, characterizing them as a "mysterious race of grown-up children." Although he did not doubt they could serve effectively, he attributed their proficiency in "drill and discipline" to their "imitativeness and docility." Despite these blind spots, Higginson clearly saw the determination with which his men fought against slavery—often in the personal terms of freeing loved ones from onerous masters—and he trumpeted the fighting ability of black men.[40] Many skeptics remained unconvinced until they, too, bore personal witness. Over the course of the next two years, more and more observers had the opportunity.

Often the soldiers from white volunteer units cast the greatest scorn, at times because they did not wish to share the laurels that they had acquired and at times because they persisted in the belief of a white man's war. First-hand observation often tempered this skepticism. White troops who fought with black men at times acknowledged their bravery, if in no other way, as the federal assault on Saltville, Virginia, in October 1864 illustrated, than by their silence. En route to the engagement black troops endured "much ridicule" as well as "jeers and taunts" from their white comrades, but after the battle, in which the black soldiers fought gallantly, "those who had scoffed at the Colored Troops on the march out were silent."[41] Even as they gave grudging respect, white soldiers also reserved the right to withhold it. What in white units might have been written off to poor leadership or bad luck was not so easily forgiven in black ones, particularly those consisting of former slaves, whose miscues on the battlefield signaled their inferiority as men.

Army officers played an ambiguous role in this process of reconfiguring racial stereotypes.[42] High-ranking officers, who had the power to shape public opinion regarding the use of black troops, sent mixed signals. Two men, Generals William Tecumseh Sherman and Ulysses S. Grant, illustrate this point. Grant clearly understood both the political and the military imperative to mobilize black manpower and did so conscientiously and effectively in the forces he commanded. He welcomed black units into his army and deployed them in combat roles. In contrast, Sherman remained skeptical throughout the war of black men's ability to fight. Although he more than welcomed their service in garrison and supply capacities, he steadfastly refused to integrate them into his combat operations.[43]

Officers who served at the company and regimental levels reproduced these tensions a thousandfold, often — but not always — based on the strength or weakness of their antislavery convictions. Even paternalistic officers who acted from selfish or careerist motives shared with their men a common need for vindication in the eyes of their comrades and the broader public. Accordingly, they often championed the men's struggles for equitable treatment from the government they served. But as both the enlisted men and the officers sympathetic to their plight testified, poor officers were capable of great mischief. Colonel James C. Beecher, brother of Harriet Beecher Stowe and commander of a regiment of native North Carolinians, protested his unit's assignment to excessive fatigue duty. Similarly situated commanders well understood the exhaustion and demoralization that ensued, as well as the deleterious effect on the men's mastery over the drill, but Beecher also identified other effects. Noting that his men "have been slaves and are just learning to be men," Beecher denounced the "so-called 'gentleman' in uniform of U.S. Officers" who addressed the troops as "'d——d Niggers.'" Such treatment "simply throws them back where they were before and reduces them to the position of slaves again."[44] With General Sherman signaling that black soldiers were nothing more than military laborers, small wonder that regimental and company officers treated them as drudges.

White officers of an antislavery bent, like their counterparts in civilian life, took every opportunity to contrast the arbitrary authority of slavery with the rule of law practiced in free institutions. They had difficulty explaining — especially to the men who served under them — the elements of caprice and contradiction that this allegedly impartial rule of law often displayed. The soldiers who had been freed from bondage at enlistment or shortly before did not necessarily need the prodding of officers to perceive the army as different from the plantation, yet they also learned quickly that the two were not necessarily polar opposites. Most important, formerly enslaved soldiers also came to understand that individual officers and the army as an institution were vulnerable to the comparison with slavery, and pressing that point might warrant a hearing if it did not necessarily produce the desired results.

In addition to combating doubts about their military effectiveness, black soldiers faced other challenges, perhaps none so fully chronicled as their struggle for equal pay. In June 1863, when the War Department ruled that black soldiers were entitled to earn only $10 per month (less clothing) rather than the $13 per month (plus clothing) that white soldiers earned, black troops inaugurated a protest campaign that lasted more than a year until the government abolished the distinction. The disability affected all soldiers equally. It insulted their manhood and devalued their part in the struggle against the Confederacy whether they were freeborn or formerly enslaved. Soldiers of every antebellum status and from all geographical regions resented the distinction and protested as best they could. Indeed, the one soldier executed for opposing unequal pay was a former slave: Sergeant William Walker of the Third South Carolina Volunteers. Walker led his men to stack their arms before the tent of their company commander. Although the regimental commander sympathized with the men's objection to inferior pay, he nonetheless preferred charges against Walker for mutiny; the court found him guilty and sentenced him to death.[45]

A testament to the men's widespread resentment to second-class treatment, Walker's execution also illustrates how the experience of formerly enslaved men differed from that of their freeborn comrades. Lacking access to both the tools of literacy and strong advocates inside and outside the service, Walker acted on his convictions in ways that left him vulnerable to harsh military regulations. In contrast, the protesting soldiers in the Fifty-fourth and Fifty-fifth Massachusetts Volunteers employed the printed and spoken word and the support of various advocates to help advance their cause. In one of the most eloquent petitions of the entire war, James Henry Gooding, a freeborn corporal serving in the Fifty-fourth, wrote to President Lincoln protesting the injustice of unequal pay. At once a blistering refutation of the logic of inequality and a stirring appeal for justice based on the men's loyalty and sacrifice, Gooding posed the critical issue: "We have done a Soldiers Duty. Why cant we have a Soldiers pay?"[46] The soldiers' advocates, who included officers in the Massachusetts regiments, elected officials, abolitionists, and journalists, amplified the case, citing a spectrum of reasons ranging from "their self respect" as men to the government's abrogation of its contract.[47]

Beyond simply illuminating different modes of expressing dissent accessible to men of northern and southern birth, the pay controversy also hints at deeper divisions. Gooding's letter contrasted the government's relation with freeborn men to its relation with former slaves. While not wishing to rate "our Service, of more Value to the Government, than the service of the exslave," he insisted that the Massachusetts men "were not enlisted under any 'contraband' act" whereby the federal government assumed a role of "temporary Gaurdian" over "slaves freed by military necessity." Gooding pointedly distanced the freemen from the freedmen, saying that the former were "freemen by birth, and consequently, having the advantage of *thinking,* and acting for ourselves, so far as the Laws would allow us."[48] Other freeborn northerners advocated on behalf of the formerly enslaved without drawing the distinction that Gooding did. Simon Prisby, for instance, a freeman from Pennsylvania, took up the case of the men in the Twenty-fifth Army Corps whose abusive officers struck with their swords anyone who lacked proficiency in military drills. Prisby argued that "men who has Been in Bondage" cannot be expected "to Do as well as a man that has Been free."[49]

Freemen from southern states likewise denounced the policy of unequal pay as unjust, but they did not contrast themselves with their slave-born comrades to quite the extent that Gooding did. William J. Brown, a black sergeant from Kentucky, for example, also argued for "our Just Rights" respecting equal pay. Yet in characterizing himself as "Freeborn and Educated to some extent" and distinguishing himself from the rest of his regiment — "a *coloured* one of Southern Birth consequently have no education," he did not suggest their ineligibility for the entitlements of freemen.[50] Almost in the nature of the case, the interactions between freeborn men and men who had been enslaved moved along a spectrum ranging from mutual solidarity to mutual suspicion.

When Confederate forces captured black soldiers in battle, they did not necessarily treat freemen differently from former slaves. From the time of the first deployment of black soldiers in federal military operations beginning in the summer of 1862, Confederates had threatened to treat captured black soldiers as rebellious slaves rather than prisoners of war. By the following spring, the growing mobilization of black men enabled Confederate soldiers to make good on the threat. With the authorization of the Secretary of War, Confederate troops were permitted to summarily execute captured black soldiers, inasmuch as "[t]hey cannot be recognized in any way as soldiers subject to the rules of war and to trial by Military Courts."[51] Subsequent orders required captors to remand black captives to state authorities for proper disposition according to the laws of the respective states; the white commanding officers deserved the same fate on the grounds that they were leading "armed slaves in insurrection."[52] The assault on Fort Wagner in July 1863, in which scores of men from the Fifty-fourth Massachusetts Volunteers were captured and their slain commander, Robert Gould Shaw, was allegedly buried "with the Negroes that fell with him," created a public outcry in the North.[53] President Lincoln did, in fact, issue orders on July 31, 1863, denouncing the Confederate policy as "a relapse into barbarism, and a crime against the civilization of the age" and threatening to retaliate against Confederate prisoners.[54] For the remainder of the war, Confederate troops on occasion executed black prisoners — most notoriously at Fort Pillow, Tennessee, and Saltville, Virginia, in 1864 — without federal retaliation. Yet not all of the African American captives were executed. Some prisoners of Fort Wagner remained incarcerated in Charleston until the city fell into Union hands late in the war, and most of the black men confined at Andersonville survived the ordeal, perhaps, as a recent study suggests, because their assignment to labor details afforded them "[t]he opportunity for exercise and extra rations."[55]

Black soldiers' relationships with their families also followed the fault line of slavery. Men from the free states of the North legitimately feared for the well-being of their loved ones. Given their marginality in the northern economy, families often relied on networks of kinfolk and neighbors to meet their necessary expenses. As the Massachusetts men pondered an appropriate response to the government's offer of inferior pay, the potential impact on their families loomed large. That notwithstanding, the men decided to refuse inferior pay, and the predictable suffering ensued.[56] Yet the men whose families were still enslaved — in the border slave states of the Union as well as the states of the Confederacy — had stronger causes for concern.

Black men from the slave states considered liberating their loved ones the best remedy against abusive masters. Sergeant Joseph J. Harris from Bayou Sara, Louisiana, for instance, wrote to General Daniel Ullman, the antislavery commander of a brigade of African American soldiers operating near his home. Harris asked Ullman for "a Small favor," namely, to visit his home plantation to "take a way my Farther & mother & my brothers wife with all their Childern," harbor them at his headquarters, and notify Harris so that he could "Send after them." It would be better for the children to be in school than serving their mistress, he argued.[57] Spotswood Rice, a former slave who had served as a manager on tobacco plantations, wrote directly to the owner of his children demanding their release. In an impassioned statement that drew as much on his faith in a vengeful God as his confidence in federal arms, Rice told Kitty Diggs — addressing her directly, without employing the customary "Miss Kitty" as a sign of deference — that "where ever you and I meets we are enmays to each othere I offered once to pay you forty dollars for my own Child but I am glad now that you did not accept it Just hold on now as long as you can and the worse it will be for you."[58] More typically, black soldiers had little knowledge of their families' fate and less ability to influence it.

With varying degrees of self-sufficiency and dependence, soldiers' families faced the promises and perils of freedom apart from their menfolk. In areas occupied by federal forces, families often lived in contraband camps more or less distant from or off-limits to the men. There they encountered military and government officials, missionaries, teachers, philanthropists, and private citizens with varying motives for working among the freedpeople.[59] Families of soldiers still in the hands of slaveholders faced even greater challenges. Masters required women to perform the labor previously done by the men, deprived them of privileges, whipped them, and threatened them with worse out of spite for the soldiers' having enlisted. In some locales, owners reportedly locked up their field hands' "clothing, boots and shoes" at night to prevent them from running away.[60] "I have had nothing but trouble since you left," Martha Glover wrote her husband from Mexico, Missouri, in late 1863. "You need not tell me to beg any more married men" to enlist, she informed him. "I see too much trouble to try to get any more into trouble too."[61] Patsy Leach of Woodford County, Kentucky, testified that after her husband enlisted, her master "treated me more cruelly than ever whipping me frequently without any cause and insulting me on every occasion."[62]

Women had to assume the additional physical and emotional burdens attendant on their new circumstances. Such experiences fostered a developing sense of freedpeople's rights that in many respects paralleled what the men experienced. They sought justice as well as protection from federal authorities. Though not adverse to labor, those in Union-occupied areas of the Confederacy did not wish to continue working like slaves. Those in the border states expected the government to make good its March 1865 grant of freedom to the families of black soldiers. Growing awareness of these rights and the struggles to achieve them helped lay the foundation for an expansion of such efforts after the war.[63] Yet evidence from recent wars offers a sobering perspective on the vulnerability of civilian populations in war zones to general and specific traumas and the likelihood of post-traumatic stress.[64] Without necessarily extinguishing the quest for freedom, these experiences tempered the sense of jubilation.

In the end, the men no less than their families learned the painful lesson that the federal government was an institution, whose representatives — whether military or naval officers, civilian officials, teachers, missionaries, or philanthropists — displayed the full range of human foibles. Freedom would be an ongoing process rather than a single, earth-shattering event. It affected private lives as well as the body politic, in the northern free states no less than the southern slave states. The true heroism of the Civil War generation lay in their persisting in the struggle even after the myths of the Day of Jubilee and the Promised Land were shattered.

Endurance in the struggle depended on mastering such skills of citizenship as literacy, a connection that soldiers from slave states, which generally prohibited slaves from learning to read and write, perceived with special clarity.

First Sergeant John Sweeny, a free Kentuckian, wished to establish a school in his regiment inasmuch as "we Stand deeply in need of instruction the majority of us having been slaves." Fearing that his lack of education might "cast a cloud over my future life," he also expressed "heart ache to see my race of people . . . neglected And ill treated on the account of the lack of Education being incapable of putting Thier complaints or applications in writing."[65] During the last year of the war, men in virtually all the black units benefited from regimental schools, often through a combination of their own exertions and those of military officers and northern missionaries and teachers. The chaplain of one Louisiana black regiment described a remarkable growth in literacy skills: early in 1864 "not more than fifteen in the regiment knew the alphabet thoroughly"; a year later "but *one* person . . . does not know the alphabet."[66] In another, "the men seem to regard their books as an indespensable portion of their equipments, and the cartridge box and spelling book are attached to the same belt."[67] Men born in the free states of the North often had the rudiments of an education. They could communicate with loved ones through the mails and read (and, if the spirit moved them, write letters to) the New York *Anglo-African* or the *Christian Recorder,* the organ of the African Methodist Episcopal Church. Perhaps most important, they could employ their mastery over the written word as a weapon in the struggle for equal rights.[68]

For all these reasons, no less than for their understanding of the place of literacy in the constellation of attributes that free persons enjoyed, former slave soldiers placed a high premium on access to education and took advantage of every opportunity to master the skills of reading, writing, and spelling.[69] They carried this passion into the postwar period, passing it on to their children and grandchildren, while often contending against former masters who desired to keep them ignorant. As the freedpeople learned, literacy provided access to much more than simply the political culture of the republic; it also opened access to the Scriptures and offered a measure of protection against those who used the written word to swindle the unschooled.[70]

Such proponents of black military service as Frederick Douglass had argued from the start that soldiering would lead inexorably to citizenship rights, including the suffrage, and during the closing months of the war, certain key indicators began pointing in a promising direction.[71] President Lincoln proposed that Louisiana Unionists consider granting limited suffrage rights to African American men, and one version of the proposed Thirteenth Amendment that Congress was considering, to ensure that Lincoln's Emancipation Proclamation would withstand the end of hostilities, contained an express guarantee of equal rights to all citizens.[72] At the same time, antislavery politi-

cal factions gained ascendancy in several of the border states and began taking
the steps that would eventually result in the abolition of slavery in Maryland,
Missouri, and Tennessee between November 1864 and February 1865.[73]

A remarkable petition from African American residents of Nashville, Tennessee, to the Unionist state convention assembled to form a new state government illustrates the ways in which military service invigorated the struggles for
human and citizenship rights. The petitioners claimed "freedom as our natural
right" by virtue of membership in "the great human family, descended from
one great God, who is the common Father of all, and who bestowed on all
races and tribes the priceless right of freedom." In light of the fact that the
Emancipation Proclamation exempted Tennessee from its provisions, the petitioners urged the convention "to cut up by the roots the system of slavery," one
of "the greatest crimes in all history" and the source of the rebellion. Their un-
wavering fidelity to the Union, as illustrated by the service of nearly "200,000
of our brethren . . . in the ranks of the Union army," merited citizenship: "If
we are called on to do military duty against the rebel armies in the field,
why should we be denied the privilege of voting against rebel citizens at the
ballot-box?"[74]

On balance, enslaved men under arms contributed significantly to the Union's
victory in the Civil War. They helped alleviate a shortage of manpower at
precisely the time that white northerners began seriously questioning the level
of sacrifice that the federal government asked of its citizens. Moreover, their
strong commitment to emancipation helped to counterbalance white soldiers'
lukewarm support for — not to mention outright opposition to — the Emancipation Proclamation. Although they generally lacked the public forums and
the literary tools for expressing their understanding of the war, their surviving
explanations evoke the principles of loyalty, equality, and justice. Even as they
placed implicit faith in Abraham Lincoln to lead the nation out of the throes of
slavery into the Promised Land of freedom, they also recognized — as Frederick Douglass and others had exhorted — that he who would be free must
himself strike the first blow.

Looking forward to the return of peace and the end of human bondage,
formerly enslaved soldiers and sailors expected assistance from the federal
government. They did not necessarily wish to keep their former masters down,
but neither did they desire to have the disabilities of slavery retard their progress as freed people. In the circumstances, they desired protection for themselves and their families, schools for their children and, insofar as possible,
government assistance in acquiring land or securing employment.

Taking inspiration from their knowledge of their role in preserving the

Union and from the struggles for equality in which they had engaged while in the service, African American veterans intended to exercise the rights of free men. Although most did so without fanfare, a significant number built on the skill and experience they had gained in uniform to serve their communities on returning home. Former slaveholders did not always appreciate such initiative, and the Ku Klux Klan and similar vigilante bands frequently targeted black veterans for attack. In instances where the veterans had access to weapons, armed clashes at times resulted, and not always to the advantage of the terrorists. In the end, however, without strong government protection, black veterans — like the freed people generally — realized that they could do little against the armed wrath of the former masters.[75]

Politics offered hope of influencing public policy for the common good. Predictably, former soldiers viewed manhood suffrage as a means both to guarantee government protection against the whims of vindictive former masters and to exert positive influence on the legislative process. Although formerly enslaved soldiers may not have sought public office with quite the determination that freeborn African Americans did, they nonetheless contributed substantially toward promoting political awareness and support for the Republican Party during the early postwar years. By virtue of their sheer numbers, the formerly enslaved soldiers who returned to their homes in the former Confederate states lent a powerful impetus to the movement for black manhood suffrage, first made possible in the Reconstruction Acts of 1867 and then in the Fourteenth and Fifteenth Amendments of 1868 and 1870. Civil War veterans provided the backbone of the Republican Party in such former Confederate states as Louisiana, Mississippi, and Tennessee throughout Reconstruction and beyond. In the process, they contributed handsomely to grassroots democratic movements that have been a hallmark of the political tradition in the United States from the beginning.[76]

Less heroically, however, formerly enslaved soldiers often returned to their homes and engaged in the mundane struggle for survival in a harsh environment wherein their federal service constituted a liability rather than an asset. Because the war resulted in the destruction of slavery, former masters held a special grudge against the men whose service helped achieve that end. Slaveholders in the border states showed special animus, particularly when the Thirteenth Amendment took effect in December 1865. In Kentucky, where approximately sixty-five thousand persons were still enslaved at that time, masters unleashed a virtual reign of terror against persons of African descent, the presumed beneficiaries of the federal government's alleged betrayal of its loyal white citizens. Soldiers and their families suffered most.[77]

In such a political climate, African American veterans of military and naval service made no secret of their true colors to their families and neighbors but weighed the risks of expressing their political beliefs publicly outside the framework of the Grand Army of the Republic.[78] That notwithstanding, they applied for federal veterans' pension benefits in roughly the same proportion as did their white comrades. Although not insubstantial, the benefits were far from princely; they did, however, enable the recipients to exert a measure of independence from white employers, literally and figuratively.[79] Notwithstanding the manifold challenges that freedom presented, the veterans could take pride in knowing that they helped destroy slavery, save the Union, and establish republican liberty and the rule of law throughout the land. The memory of those accomplishments carried them and their children a long way.

Notes

1. See Ervin L. Jordan Jr., *Black Confederates and Afro-Yankees in Civil War Virginia* (Charlottesville, 1995), chap. 11; Richard Rollins, ed., *Black Southerners in Gray: Essays on African-Americans in Confederate Armies* (Redondo Beach, CA, 1994); James H. Brewer, *The Confederate Negro: Virginia's Craftsmen and Military Laborers, 1861–1865* (Durham, 1969).

2. The approximation for service in the army derives from Ira Berlin, Joseph P. Reidy, and Leslie S. Rowland, eds., *The Black Military Experience*, ser. 2 of *Freedom: A Documentary History of Emancipation, 1861–1867* (Cambridge, UK, 1982), p. 12, table 1, which indicates that more than 98,000 men were recruited from the states of the Confederacy and nearly 42,000 additional men from the slaveholding states that remained within the United States; it is unlikely that more than 10,000 of this 140,000 were free men. For the navy, see Joseph P. Reidy, "Black Men in Navy Blue during the Civil War," *Prologue: Quarterly of the National Archives and Records Administration* 33:3 (Fall 2001): 155–67, esp. 156.

3. For an assessment of the impact of black soldiers on the Union's war effort, see Berlin, Reidy, and Rowland, *Black Military Experience;* Joseph T. Glatthaar, *Forged in Battle: The Civil War Alliance of Black Soldiers and White Officers* (New York, 1990); and Joseph T. Glatthaar, "Black Glory: The African-American Role in Union History," in *Why the Confederacy Lost,* ed. Gabor S. Boritt (New York, 1992), 135–62. Of the numerous works on the Fifty-fourth Massachusetts, particularly noteworthy are Luis F. Emilio, *A Brave Black Regiment: History of the Fifty-Fourth Massachusetts Volunteer Infantry, 1863–1865,* 2nd ed. (Boston, 1894), and Martin H. Blatt, Thomas J. Brown, and Donald Yacovone, eds., *Hope and Glory: Essays on the Legacy of the 54th Massachusetts Regiment* (Amherst, 2001).

4. Excerpt from John J. Cheatham to the Hon. L. P. Walker, May 4, 1861, in Berlin, Reidy, and Rowland, *Black Military Experience,* 282.

5. See representative photographs in Jordan, *Black Confederates,* following p. 181.

6. Ibid., 223–24, and chap. 10 generally.

7. L. H. Minor to [Secretary of War], May 2, 1861, in Ira Berlin, Barbara J. Fields, Thavolia Glymph, Joseph P. Reidy, and Leslie S. Rowland, eds., *The Destruction of*

Slavery, seri. 1, vol. 1 of *Freedom: A Documentary History of Emancipation* (Cambridge, UK, 1985), 698.

8. See David S. Cicelski, *The Waterman's Song: Slavery and Freedom in Maritime North Carolina* (Chapel Hill, 2001); Thomas C. Buchanan, "The Slave Mississippi: African-American Steamboat Workers, Networks of Resistance, and the Commercial World of the Western Rivers, 1811–1880" (Ph.D. diss., Carnegie Mellon University, 1998).

9. John M. Coski, *Capital Navy: The Men, Ships, and Operations of the James River Squadron* (Campbell, CA, 1996), 176; Jordan, *Black Confederates, 187.*

10. James A. Miller Jr., *Gullah Statesman: Robert Smalls from Slavery to Congress, 1839–1915* (Columbia, 1995), chap. 1.

11. See James C. Hollandsworth Jr., *The Louisiana Native Guard: The Black Military Experience During the Civil War* (Baton Rouge, 1995); Manoj K. Joshi and Joseph P. Reidy, " 'To Come Forward and Aid in Putting Down This Unholy Rebellion': The Officers of Louisiana's Free Black Native Guard During the Civil War Era," *Southern Studies* 21 (Fall 1982): 326–42; and Mary F. Berry, "Negro Troops in Blue and Gray: The Louisiana Native Guards, 1861–1863," *Louisiana History* 8 (Spring 1967): 165–90.

12. O. G. Eiland to President Davis, July 20, 1863, in Berlin, Reidy, and Rowland, *Black Military Experience,* 284 (emphasis in original).

13. Robert F. Durden, *The Gray and the Black: The Confederate Debate on Emancipation* (Baton Rouge, 1972), 60. See also Charles H. Wesley, "Employment of Negro Troops as Soldiers in the Confederate Army," *Journal of Negro History* 4 (July 1919): 239–53.

14. Durden, *Gray and the Black,* 184.

15. Jordan, *Black Confederates,* 246–51.

16. James M. McPherson, *Battle Cry of Freedom: The Civil War Era* (New York, 1988), chaps. 1, 9; Russell F. Weigley, *A Great Civil War: A Military and Political History, 1861–1865* (Bloomington, 2000), 36–49.

17. Berlin, Reidy, and Rowland, *Black Military Experience,* 5–6.

18. Herbert Aptheker, "The Negro in the Union Navy," *Journal of Negro History* 32 (April 1947): 169–200; Harold D. Langley, "The Negro in the Navy and Merchant Service, 1798–1860," *Journal of Negro History* 52 (October 1967): 273–86; David L. Valuska, *The African American in the Union Navy: 1861–1865* (New York, 1993); Joseph P. Reidy, "Black Men in Navy Blue During the Civil War," *Prologue: Quarterly of the National Archives and Records Administration* 33 (Fall 2001): 155–67. For first-hand glimpses into this experience, see William B. Gould IV, ed., *Diary of a Contraband: The Civil War Passage of a Black Sailor* (Palo Alto, CA, 2002), and Paul E. Sluby Sr. and Stanton L. Wormley, eds., *Diary of Charles B. Fisher* (Washington, DC, 1983).

19. George Teamoh, *God Made Man, Man Made the Slave: The Autobiography of George Teamoh,* F. N. Boney, Richard L. Hume, and Rafia Zafar, eds. (Macon, GA, 1990), 82–84.

20. Harold D. Langley, *Social Reform in the United States Navy, 1789–1862* (Urbana, 1967) treats naval culture before the Civil War.

21. Valuska, *African American in the Union Navy,* chaps. 2–3.

22. The best recent overviews of the war are McPherson, *Battle Cry of Freedom,* and Weigley, *Great Civil War.* See also James M. McPherson, *The Negro's Civil War: How*

American Negroes Felt and Acted During the War for the Union (New York, 1965); David W. Blight, *Frederick Douglass' Civil War: Keeping Faith in Jubilee* (Baton Rouge, 1989); C. Peter Ripley et al., eds., *The Black Abolitionist Papers,* 5 vols. (Chapel Hill, 1985–92), esp. vol. 5; and Philip S. Foner and George E. Walker, eds., *Proceedings of the Black State Conventions, 1840–1865,* 2 vols. (Philadelphia, 1979–80), which survey the field of African American political agitation in the Civil War era. For a brief account by Douglass of his role in these developments see *Life and Times of Frederick Douglass Written by Himself* (Hartford, 1881), chaps. 11–12.

23. On *Uncle Tom's Cabin,* see Marcus Wood, *Blind Memory: Visual Representations of Slavery in England and America, 1780–1865* (New York, 2000), chap. 4. For a subtle analysis of public sentiment toward the freedpeople during the Civil War, see Alice Fahs, *The Imagined Civil War: Popular Literature of the North and South, 1861–1865* (Chapel Hill, 2001), esp. chap. 5.

24. See Berlin, Reidy, and Rowland, *Black Military Experience,* chaps. 3–4; Berlin, Fields, Glymph, Reidy , and Rowland, *Destruction of Slavery,* chaps. 1, 6–9.

25. Berlin, Reidy, and Rowland, eds., *Black Military Experience,* 4–5.

26. On Lincoln, see Mark E. Neely Jr., *The Last Best Hope of Earth: Abraham Lincoln and the Promise of America* (Cambridge, 1993); LaWanda Cox, *Lincoln and Black Freedom: A Study in Presidential Leadership* (Columbia, 1981).

27. Thomas Wentworth Higginson, *Army Life in a Black Regiment* (1870; reprint, New York, 1984).

28. See Berlin, Reidy, and Rowland, *Black Military Experience,* 41–44, 62–67; Hollandsworth, *Louisiana Native Guard,* chap. 2.

29. See John Hope Franklin, *The Emancipation Proclamation* (Garden City, NY, 1963).

30. See Michael T. Meier, "Lorenzo Thomas and the Recruitment of Blacks in the Mississippi Valley, 1863–1865," in John David Smith, ed., *Black Soldiers in Blue: African American Troops in the Civil War Era* (Chapel Hill, 2002), 249–75.

31. Berlin, Reidy, and Rowland, *Black Military Experience,* 12.

32. *U.S. Statutes at Large, Treaties, and Proclamations* (Boston, 1866), 13:571.

33. See Glatthaar, "Black Glory," esp. 158.

34. Reidy, "Black Men in Navy Blue," 157–58, 165, n. 5.

35. In addition to the sources noted in n. 18, see Dennis J. Ringle, *Life in Mr. Lincoln's Navy* (Annapolis, 1998); and Donald J. Canney, *Lincoln's Navy: The Ships, Men and Organization, 1861–65* (Annapolis, 1998).

36. Reidy, "Black Men in Navy Blue," 158–63; Roger A. Davidson Jr., "Yankee Rivers, Rebel Shore: The Potomac Flotilla and Civil Insurrection in the Chesapeake Region" (Ph.D. diss., Howard University, 2000); Lisa Y. King, "Wounds That Bind: A Comparative Study of the Role Played by Civil War Veterans of African Descent in Community Formation in Massachusetts and South Carolina, 1865–1915" (Ph.D. diss., Howard University, 1999).

37. Reidy, "Black Men in Navy Blue," 160–61.

38. The definitive treatment of black soldiers' battlefield performance during the Civil War is Noah Andre Trudeau, *Like Men of War: Black Troops in the Civil War, 1862–1865* (Boston, 1998), but see also the essays in Smith, *Black Soldiers in Blue.*

39. Brigadier General Elias S. Dennis to Colonel John A. Rawlins, June 12, 1863, in

Berlin, Reidy, and Rowland, *Black Military Experience,* 533. On Port Hudson, see Lawrence Lee Hewitt, "An Ironic Route to Glory: Louisiana's Native Guards at Port Hudson," Smith, in *Black Soldiers in Blue,* chap. 2, and Stephen J. Ochs, *A Black Patriot and a White Priest: André Cailloux and Claude Paschal Maistre in Civil War New Orleans* (Baton Rouge, 2001), in addition to Hollandsworth, *Louisiana Native Guards,* chap. 5. On Fort Wagner, see Trudeau, *Like Men of War,* 71–90. On Millikens Bend, see Richard Lowe, "Battle on the Levee: The Fight at Milliken's Bend," in Smith, *Black Soldiers in Blue,* chap. 3.

40. Higginson, *Army Life* (quotations on 41 and 51). See also Keith Wilson, "In the Shadow of John Brown: The Military Service of Colonels Thomas Higginson, James Montgomery, and Robert Shaw in the Department of the South," in Smith, *Black Soldiers in Blue,* 306–35; George M. Fredrickson, *The Black Image in the White Mind: The Debate on Afro-American Character and Destiny, 1817–1914* (New York, 1971), 169–71.

41. Colonel James S. Brisbin to Brig. Gen. L. Thomas, October 20, 1864, in Berlin, Reidy, and Rowland, *Black Military Experience,* 557–58.

42. Glatthaar, *Forged in Battle,* offers a superb overview of the relations between white officers and their troops.

43. On Sherman's opposition to the use of black soldiers, see Anne J. Bailey, "The USCT in the Confederate Heartland," in Smith, *Black Soldiers in Blue,* 227–48.

44. Colonel James C. Beecher to Brig. Gen. Edward A. Wild, September 13, 1863, in Berlin, Reidy, and Rowland, eds., *Black Military Experience,* 493.

45. For general treatments of the struggle against unequal pay, see Berlin, Reidy, and Rowland, *Black Military Experience,* chap. 7; Dudley Taylor Cornish, *The Sable Arm: Negro Troops in the Union Army, 1861–1865* (New York, 1956), 181–96.

46. Corporal James Henry Gooding to Abraham Lincoln, September 28, 1863, in Berlin, Reidy, and Rowland, *Black Military Experience,* 385–86, quotation on 386. See also Virginia M. Adams, ed. *On the Altar of Freedom: A Black Soldier's Civil War Letters from the Front* (Amherst, 1991); Donald Yacovone, ed., *A Voice of Thunder: The Civil War Letters of George E. Stephens* (Urbana, 1997); Donald Yacovone, "The Fifty-Fourth Massachusetts Regiment, the Pay Crisis, and the 'Lincoln Despotism,' " in Blatt, Brown, and Yacovone, *Hope and Glory,* 35–51.

47. Colonel E. N. Hallowell to Governor John A. Andrew, November 23, 1863, in Berlin, Reidy, and Rowland, *Black Military Experience,* 387; Higginson, *Army Life,* appendix D. On the importance of contracts in the Civil War era, see Amy Dru Stanley, *From Bondage to Contract: Wage Labor, Marriage, and the Market in the Age of Slave Emancipation* (Cambridge, 1998).

48. Gooding to Lincoln, September 28, 1863, in Berlin, Reidy, and Rowland, *Black Military Experience,* 386 (emphasis in original).

49. Simon Prisby to E. M. Stanton, July 20, 1865, in Berlin, Reidy, and Rowland, *Black Military Experience,* 424. In commenting on a similar incident, another soldier observed, "The treatment we Receive from Our Pretended Friends I think is very Rough and I hope God will Save me from Such friends." Late Q.M. Sergt. Charles H. Davis to Capt. E. D. Kennedy, February 21, 1866, in ibid., 429.

50. William J. Brown to the Honourable Secretary of War, April 27, 1864, in Berlin, Reidy, and Rowland, *Black Military Experience,* 377–78 (emphasis in original).

51. James A. Seddon to Gen. G. T. Beauregard, November 30, 1862, in Berlin, Reidy, and Rowland, *Black Military Experience,* 571–72.

52. M. I. Bonham to General G. T. Beauregard, July 22, 1863, in Berlin, Reidy, and Rowland, *Black Military Experience,* 579–80.

53. Quoted in Benjamin Quarles, *The Negro in the Civil War* (Boston, 1953), 18.

54. General Orders No. 252, War Department, Adjutant General's Office, July 31, 1863, in Berlin, Reidy, and Rowland, *Black Military Experience,* 583.

55. See William Marvel, *Andersonville: The Last Depot* (Chapel Hill, 1994), 155. For treatments of the massacres of black troops at Fort Pillow and Saltville, see John Cimprich, "The Fort Pillow Massacre: Assessing the Evidence," in Smith, *Black Soldiers in Blue,* 150–68; Thomas D. Mays, "The Battle of Saltville," in ibid., 200–226. See also Trudeau, *Like Men of War,* 156–69, 269–75.

56. See Yacovone, "Fifty-Fourth Massachusetts Regiment," esp. 41–42, which also notes the negative impact that the families' troubles had on the morale of the men.

57. First Sgt. Joseph J. Harris to Gen. Ullman, December 27, 1864, in Berlin, Reidy, and Rowland, *Black Military Experience,* 691–92.

58. Spotswood Rice to Kitty Diggs, [September 3, 1864], in Berlin, Reidy, and Rowland, *Black Military Experience,* 690.

59. See Ira Berlin, Thavolia Glymph, Steven F. Miller, Joseph P. Reidy, Leslie S. Rowland, and Julie Saville, eds., *Wartime Genesis of Free Labor: The Lower South,* ser. 1, vol. 3 of *Freedom: A Documentary History of Emancipation, 1861–1867* (Cambridge, UK, 1990); Ira Berlin, Thavolia Glymph, Steven F. Miller, Joseph P. Reidy, Leslie S. Rowland, and Julie Saville, eds., *Wartime Genesis of Free Labor: The Upper South,* ser. 1, vol. 2 of *Freedom: A Documentary History of Emancipation, 1861–1867* (Cambridge, UK, 1993). See also Patricia C. Click, *Time Full of Trial: The Roanoke Island Freedmen's Colony* (Chapel Hill, 2001); Leon F. Litwack, *Been in the Storm So Long: The Aftermath of Slavery* (New York, 1979), esp. 64–103; Herbert G. Gutman, *The Black Family in Slavery and Freedom, 1750–1925* (New York, 1976), esp. 363–431.

60. Colonel A. Jackson to Major Genl. Rosecrans, February 17, 1864, in Berlin, Reidy, and Rowland, *Black Military Experience,* 241.

61. Martha Glover to My Dear Husband [Richard Glover], December 30, 1863, in Berlin, Reidy, and Rowland, *Black Military Experience,* 244.

62. Affidavit of Patsy Leach, March 25, 1865, in Berlin, Reidy, and Rowland, *Black Military Experience,* 244, 268.

63. For representative works illustrating the postwar manifestations of African American women's struggles for citizenship, see Elizabeth Regosin, *Freedom's Promise: Ex-Slave Families and Citizenship in the Age of Emancipation* (Charlottesville, 2002); Laura F. Edwards, *Gendered Strife and Confusion: The Political Culture of Reconstruction* (Urbana, 1997); Leslie A. Schwalm, *A Hard Fight for We: Women's Transition from Slavery to Freedom in South Carolina* (Urbana, 1997); Elsa Barkley Brown, "Negotiating and Transforming the Public Sphere: African American Political Life in the Transition from Slavery to Freedom," *Public Culture* 7 (1994): 107–46.

64. For a pioneering study of post-traumatic stress in Civil War soldiers, see Eric T. Dean, Jr., *Shook Over Hell: Post-Traumatic Stress, Vietnam, and the Civil War* (Cambridge, 1997).

65. First Sergeant John Sweeny to Brigadier General Fisk, October 8, 1865, in Berlin, Reidy, and Rowland, *Black Military Experience*, 615.

66. Chaplain C. W. Buckley to Lt. Austin R. Mills, February 1, 1865, in Berlin, Reidy, and Rowland, *Black Military Experience*, 623.

67. Chaplain E. W. Wheeler to Brig. Genl. Ullmann, April 8, 1864, in Berlin, Reidy, and Rowland, *Black Military Experience*, 618.

68. Studies of regiments from the northern states include Versalle F. Washington, *Eagles on Their Buttons: A Black Infantry Regiment in the Civil War* (Columbia, 1999); Edward A. Miller Jr., *The Black Civil War Soldiers of Illinois* (Columbia, 1998); James M. Paradis, *Strike the Blow for Freedom: The 6th United States Colored Infantry in the Civil War* (Shippensburg, PA, 1998); James Kenneth Bryant II, "The Model 36th Regiment: The Contribution of Black Soldiers and Their Families to the Union War Effort, 1861–1866" (Ph.D. diss., University of Rochester, 2001).

69. White officers of Colored Troop regiments had a vested interest in promoting literacy as well. Illiterate noncommissioned officers might still lead the men serving under them, but they could not complete the paperwork that made up a large part of the responsibilities of their counterparts in regiments where literacy was the norm. As a result, officers often had to assume the burden.

70. Theodore Rosengarten, *All God's Dangers: The Life of Nate Shaw* (New York, 1974), 266–68, recounts an incident during the 1920s in which Ned Cobb's literate wife advised him against signing mortgage papers that would have subjected all they possessed to seizure.

71. Quarles, *Negro in the Civil War*, 184, quotes Douglass. For insights into the broader history of citizenship rights in the nineteenth century, see Alexander Keyssar, *The Right to Vote: The Contested History of Democracy in the United States* (New York, 2000), chaps. 1–4; Eric Foner, *The Story of American Freedom* (New York, 1998), chaps. 2–5.

72. Cox, *Lincoln and Black Freedom*; Michael Vorenberg, *Final Freedom: The Civil War, the Abolition of Slavery, and the Thirteenth Amendment* (Cambridge, 2001), 102–7, 130–33, 137–38, 181–91.

73. For Maryland, see Charles L. Wagandt, *The Mighty Revolution: Negro Emancipation in Maryland, 1862–1864* (Baltimore, 1964); Barbara Jeanne Fields, *Slavery and Freedom on the Middle Ground: Maryland During the Nineteenth Century* (New Haven, 1985). For Missouri, see William E. Parrish, *Turbulent Partnership: Missouri and the Union, 1861–1865* (Columbia, 1963). For Tennessee, see John Cimprich, *Slavery's End in Tennessee, 1861–1865* (University, AL, 1985). Two neighboring states provide fascinating contrasts: for that of Kentucky, see Victor B. Howard, *Black Liberation in Kentucky: Emancipation and Freedom, 1862–1884* (Lexington, 1983); for that of Iowa, see Robert R. Dykstra, *Bright Radical Star: Black Freedom and White Supremacy on the Hawkeye Frontier* (Cambridge, 1993).

74. Andrew Tait et al. to the Union Convention of Tennessee, January 9, 1865, in Berlin, Reidy, and Rowland, *Black Military Experience*, 811–16, quotations at 811–12.

75. Eric Foner, *Reconstruction: America's Unfinished Revolution* (New York, 1988) treats the Ku Klux Klan (425–44) and general political development among the freedpeople (77–123).

76. Eric Foner, *Freedom's Lawmakers: A Directory of Black Officeholders During Reconstruction* (New York, 1993), xi–xxxii; King, "Wounds That Bind."

77. See Berlin, Fields, Glymph, Reidy, and Rowland, *Destruction of Slavery,* 493–659; Vorenberg, *Final Freedom,* 216–18, 231–32.

78. See David W. Blight, *Race and Reunion: The Civil War in American Memory* (Cambridge, 2001); Nick Salvatore, *We All Got History: The Memory Books of Amos Webber* (New York, 1996); Stuart McConnell, *Glorious Contentment: The Grand Army of the Republic, 1865–1900* (Chapel Hill, 1992).

79. Donald R. Schaffer, "Marching On: African-American Civil War Veterans in Postbellum America, 1865–1951," Ph.D. diss., University of Maryland, College Park, 1996.

Armed Slaves and Anticolonial Insurgency in Late Nineteenth-Century Cuba

ADA FERRER

On October 10, 1868, Carlos Manuel de Céspedes, a lawyer, sugar planter, and slaveholder in eastern Cuba, gathered the slaves on his sugar mill, La Demajagua, and granted them their freedom. "You are as free," he told them, "as I am." Then, addressing them as "citizens," he invited them to help "conquer liberty and independence" for Cuba. Thus began the first war for Cuban independence: with an act that highlighted the central link between the institution of slavery and the process of national liberation, between armed slaves and anticolonial struggle.

The existence and importance of this link should come as little surprise. As Robin Blackburn has shown for the late eighteenth and early nineteenth centuries, freedom from slavery and freedom from colonial rule may have been two distinct political and social projects, but in the Age of Revolution they often became intertwined as "successive challenges to the regimes of colonial slavery [led] to the destruction either of the colonial relationship, or of the slave system, or of both, in one after another of all the major New World colonies."[1] In the case of Cuba, the preservation of colonial rule had long been linked to the institution of slavery. During the Age of Revolution, when almost every other Spanish territory freed itself from imperial rule, Cuba survived as Spain's "ever-faithful isle." The preservation of sugar, slavery, and the prosperous plantation economy they engendered depended, elites agreed, on the continuation of the colonial bond. To opt for independence was to risk social upheaval and economic annihilation. This association between slavery and colonial order remained strong for much of the nineteenth century. Thus when in 1868 creole elites decided to challenge the colonial regime, slavery became a major issue in their efforts, as nationalist insurgency and the institution of slavery each threatened to disrupt the other in significant ways.

The centrality and complexity of the link between slavery and insurrection assumed multiple forms. First, slaves themselves became enmeshed in the process of anticolonial struggle, as both the colonial army and the nationalist rebels mobilized them for their respective causes. But alongside the arming of slaves by contending political camps emerged the symbolic use of the figure of the armed slave in colonial and anticolonial discourse. The conflicts that arose from that unprecedented military and discursive mobilization — as slaves took up arms, fled plantations, freed their peers, or burnt sugar cane, and as they were written into emerging narratives of nationhood — profoundly shaped the course of Cuban independence and the possibilities for black political action in postemancipation Cuba. This chapter analyzes both aspects of this revolutionary arming of slaves: first, the military mobilization in support of independence and then their discursive mobilization, also in support of independence. Throughout, it highlights the limits and contradictions of this dual process, as rebel leaders and the enslaved struggled to define the boundaries, meanings, and implications of the arming of slaves.

When the principal conspirators of October 10, 1868, declared Cuban sovereignty, they began by freeing and mobilizing their own slaves for war. The initial leadership of the war against Spain came from the ranks of slaveowning whites in eastern regions such as Bayamo and Manzanillo, where slavery was becoming less central to the economy and where the slave population was a relatively small proportion of the total population (between 3 and 9 percent depending on the jurisdiction).[2] The declining position of slavery in these regions helps explain the leaders' willingness to risk social upheaval and their ritualized freeing and arming of their own slaves in the first public act of rebellion. Yet this revolutionary arming of slaves had obvious limits. Prominent leaders liberated their slaves immediately, but the movement as a movement advocated only a very gradual abolition. This abolition, moreover, would indemnify owners, and it would occur only after the successful conclusion of the war.[3] This hesitation betrayed the contradictions inherent in the position and mission of the local leadership of the early period of the war. From the start, Céspedes and his colleagues recognized that they would have to reconcile their need to attract slaves, so as to have the soldiers necessary to wage war, with their need to attract slaveholders, so as to have the resources required to finance that war. They had to portray their movement as in the best interest of two groups whose objectives were apparently irreconcilable. The early leaders of the movement believed that the solution to this quandary lay in the exercise of restraint, and the leaders' expression of a "desire for abolition, gradual and indemnified" exemplified that moderation. If justice demanded the emancipation of slaves, argued insurgent leaders, then fairness also required that cooperative slaveholders be compensated for their loss.[4]

Nationalist leaders admitted that the initial hesitation regarding slavery was, in part, the result of political strategy. Thus Céspedes explained to fellow nationalists that although he was "a staunch abolitionist, the need to remove all obstacles to the early progress of the revolution forced [him] to delay the immediate emancipation of slaves and to proclaim in [his] manifesto a gradual and indemnified [abolition]."[5] At the same time, his explanation of the delays in enacting a more comprehensive program for emancipation reveals something of his misgivings about the exercise of full political and social freedom by men and women who had lived their lives enslaved. Thus he explained to those same colleagues: "The emancipation of slavery is not yet a *fait accompli* because I have wanted to prepare it so that as the new citizens enter into the full exercise of their rights, they do so at least modestly trained to understand the proper meaning of true liberty."[6] Abolition, therefore, would be gradual and cautious, and the transition from slavery to freedom would be conducted under the tutelage of rebel leadership in the battles against Spain.

The policy concerning abolition adopted on October 10, precisely because it was so modest, had obvious tactical advantages. It offered, above all, the potential to appease the groups whose support for war was most necessary. For in the promise of a gradual and indemnified emancipation, slaveholders heard that no financial loss would occur for the time being and that whatever loss might occur at some later moment would be compensated. Meanwhile, slaves, whose only promise of freedom prior to October 10 had been in manumission or in a risky attempt at flight, heard that a rebellion had started and that, should the rebels win, they would all be free.

This cautious balancing act, born of the need to make the war feasible, became one of the first casualties of that war. The limited and carefully maneuvered intentions of a handful of leaders could not determine the direction the rebellion would take once initiated. Spanish authorities immediately observed this gap between the initial designs of the conspirators and the actions of the rebels. Only two weeks after the start of the insurrection, the island's Spanish governor observed: "I have no doubt that the instigators of the uprising, conceived of something limited . . . but the fact that shortly after their uprising, they began to burn sugar mills and take the slaves as free men, in effect rais[ed] the issue of the social question and arous[ed] . . . the spirit of people of color."[7] Leaders tried to curb the dangers of social unrest that might be unleashed by their declarations and to reassure landowners whose support they courted that their property, in people and in land, would be spared by the insurrection. Days after the outbreak of rebellion, Céspedes promised that the rebel army would respect the lives and property of all and treat everyone with equal consideration.[8] At the end of the first month of war, he expressly forbade officers to accept any slaves into their ranks without his own permission or that of their masters.[9] Two weeks later he went further, decreeing that any rebel caught stealing from peaceful citizens or raiding farms to take slaves or to incite them to rebellion would be tried and, if found guilty, sentenced to death by the rebel administration.[10]

These measures and reassurances, however, did not entirely work. Céspedes's decree did not prevent insurgents on the ground from taking slaves to the insurrection against the wishes of hesitant slaveholders. All over the rural outskirts of Santiago — an eastern region more invested in slavery and where landowners did not lead or heed the call to rebellion in 1868 — owners who tried to maintain production on their coffee and sugar farms saw their efforts thwarted by insurgents who burnt their fields and liberated and took their slaves.[11] Across the regions of Santiago and Guantánamo, insurgents attacked estates and farms, and — with or without the consent of the slaves themselves — liberated slaves so that they might in some manner aid the cause of insurrection. In December 1868, a group of 153 rebels stormed the coffee farm San Fernando, outside Guantánamo, and took thirty able-bodied slaves. In January 1869, insurgents invaded the sugar estate Santísima Trinidad de Giro near Cobre, set fire to the cane fields, and took all eighty-seven slaves. Countless others were taken in the same manner.[12]

Slaves, however, did not necessarily require prodding in order to abandon the farms of their masters; they could, on their own or in small groups, flee their farms and volunteer their services to the rebellion. The slave Pedro de la Torre, for example, presented himself at a rebel camp near Holguín expressing "his desire to sustain the Holy Cause."[13] José Manuel, a slave on the coffee farm Bello Desierto near Cobre, went further, fleeing of his own volition to join the insurrection and then appearing on neighboring farms with copies of rebel handbills and proclamations of freedom in order "to seduce" other slaves.[14]

The forced and voluntary induction of large numbers of slaves meant that leaders could theoretically count on a larger pool of recruits and reap the military advantages of a growing army. In practice, however, the relationship between insurgent structures and potentially politicized slaves was less clear-cut. For insurgent leaders, the emancipation of slaves and their incorporation into armed struggle required that slaves labor, productively and quietly, in supportive roles. Labor in this fashion would materially aid the rebellion and also allay fears of social unrest. The tasks given slave men and women in the insurgency tend to reflect this desire on the part of leaders. In fact, most slaves who were freed from coffee and sugar farms by insurgents and who were later questioned by authorities testified that they had been put to work building trenches, clearing paths, and doing a variety of other menial tasks. Few mentioned actual combat experience. The sixty-year-old African-born Marcos, "one-eyed and old," was given the job of peeling plantains for the insurgents. Many others functioned as servants or *asistentes* (assistants) whose primary role was to serve the officers to whom they were assigned, cooking, washing, and attending to their needs.[15] Still, though many slaves were not the protagonists of armed combat, many appear to have exercised their newfound freedom by embracing the rebel cause perhaps more fervently than their recruiters imagined they would. Some new libertos were beginning to see themselves not as menial laborers but as free persons engaged in armed political struggle. A freed slave named after his owner, Francisco Vicente Aguilera, who rose through the ranks to become a lieutenant colonel, for example, clearly did more than play the part of a dutiful servant. So did the slave José Manuel, who not only joined the movement but also recruited other slaves by publicizing the rebellion's stance on antislavery. A slave identified as Magín faced disciplinary measures for attempting to take more political initiative than leaders wanted to concede. Given the straightforward task of delivering a message to an officer at another rebel camp, Magín decided to confiscate a horse in order, perhaps, to complete his mission more expeditiously. When challenged, he proclaimed unrepentantly that "he was a rebel chief and that nobody could interrupt his journey."[16] That he proudly declared himself to be a rebel leader with control over his time and movement, if not that of others, suggests that the insurgency was producing new forms of self-identification for the people it recruited. At the very least, the insurgency seems to have offered men such as Magín and Aguilera an arena in which they could assert a degree of mobility and independence they could not have asserted as rural slaves, even if every recruit did not have the opportunity or desire physically to take up arms.

These new recruits, however, were singularly problematic figures for the rebel leadership. Were they free men and women willing to choose the path of independence? Or were they slaves who could be taken, as rebels took other property, and forced to work and fight in battlefields, as they had earlier been coerced to labor in cane and coffee fields? In the uncertainty of 1868 and beyond there was no simple answer to this question. But one fact soon became clear: the growing visibility of slave supporters began to make certain questions unavoidable—among them questions about the nature of slaves' incorporation into the armed struggle for sovereignty and into the nation itself. As the growing presence of slaves made these questions more and more pressing, the leaders' tenuous ideological balancing act became more and more fragile. And within months of the start of the insurgency, rebel leaders realized that the transition from slavery to freedom could not be postponed until the end of the rebellion, as they had first planned.

Thus, only three months into the war, the leadership modified its original position regarding abolition, moving beyond the vague promise of indemnified emancipation to occur after the victory of the independence struggle and outlining several ways in which enslaved men and women could gain immediate freedom. The first formal step was taken on December 27, 1868, when Céspedes decreed that all slaves belonging to enemies of their cause would be considered free and their owners not subject to compensation. Slaves who presented themselves to rebel authorities with the consent of pro-Cuban owners would be declared free and their owners compensated for their financial loss. Separatist slaveholders also reserved the power to "lend" their enslaved workers to the insurgent cause, and in so doing they preserved their rights of ownership until the rebel republic decreed full abolition at some unspecified moment. Finally, the document stated that runaway slaves presenting themselves to or captured by rebel forces would be returned to their owners, provided that the owners were supporters of the Cuban cause.[17]

Though the decree listed multiple paths to immediate freedom, overall, it offered only a limited emancipation, accessible only to a fraction of slaves and, in many cases, valid only with the consent of their masters. Ultimately, slaveholders who supported the Cuban cause reserved the right to decide, on a case-by-case basis, whether they would free their slaves. Though individual conspirators may have undertaken the dramatic act of freeing their own slaves and addressing them as citizens, the formal policy of the revolution in December 1868 encouraged only manumission, a regular feature of slave society, and thus, by default, condoned slavery.

The December 1868 decree concerning abolition—cautious, ambiguous, faltering—had, however, enormous power to attract enslaved men and women to the cause of national independence. And even this most hesitant of moves produced among its slave audience, who only months earlier had had little prospect of freedom, "great excitement" and "indescribable enthusiasm." As a result, slaves joined the Cuban forces, wrote Céspedes in January 1869, by the thousands; "they marched in companies shouting cries of long live Liberty and [long live] the whites of Cuba, who only yesterday had governed them with the harshness of the whip and who today treat them as brothers and grant them the title of free men."[18]

Had Céspedes been able to, he might have chosen to stop time at that very moment, to give permanent life to that instance of mutual satisfaction and consensus. But instead with every week and month that passed the relations between slaves and insurgents became more and more complex and the connections between antislavery and anticolonialism more and more entwined. Modest promises of eventual freedom drew an ever-increasing number of slaves to the insurrection; their participation then pushed leaders to do more about abolition. But then, the closer leaders came to the emancipation of slaves, the more slaves joined; and the larger the number of slaves who joined, the more urgent and central they made the issue of abolition. The result, then, was an almost infinite and two-way circle of slave and insurgent initiatives and responses leading — gradually and fitfully — to a speedier and more thorough emancipation than leaders envisioned at the outset and to the consolidation of an army with growing numbers of slave soldiers.[19]

In this continual back-and-forth between slaves and insurgents and between slavery and freedom, few policies concerning slaves had limited effects and few remained in place for long. The conservative decree of December 1868, for example, was superseded only months later by the rebel constitution drafted in Guáimaro in April 1869. This constitution declared, unequivocally, that "all inhabitants of the Republic [were] entirely free." Article 25 further specified that "all citizens of the republic [would be] considered soldiers of the Liberation Army."[20] Here, then, was legal recognition for the transformation of enslaved workers into citizens and soldiers of a new republic.

But the path to absolute emancipation in rebel territory was slow and indirect, and just as the presence of slave soldiers could hasten the formal progress of abolition, so, too, could it produce the opposite reaction, as leaders saw their carefully laid plans for a gradual and tightly supervised abolition unraveled by the actions and desires of a growing population of slave-insurgents. Thus in July 1869 the leadership backtracked, curtailing the potential effects of the constitutional proclamation of freedom approved only three months earlier. First, the rebel legislature amended Article 25. Rather than recognize all citizens as soldiers, the constitution now required that "all citizens of the republic" lend their "services *according to their aptitudes*."[21] No longer would officers be formally required to accept slaves as combatants; now they could, with the legal sanction of the rebel republic, require them to work in agriculture in camps set up in support of the insurgency or as servants for rebel leaders or their families.

Later that same month the rebel legislature drafted the Reglamento de Libertos, which further circumscribed the freedom granted to slaves in the constitution of Guáimaro by requiring all libertos in the insurrection to work without compensation. The reglamento conceded to libertos the right to abandon the homes of their (former) masters. But it went on to state that it was the responsibility, indeed, the obligation, of such slaves immediately to report to the Office of Libertos so that they might be assigned to "other masters" whose side they were not to leave "without powerful reasons previously brought to the attention" of authorities. In this way, the leadership preserved its access to the time, labor, and bodies of enslaved men and women. Pro-Cuban owners or newly assigned masters meanwhile retained the right to slaves' labor and, with it, the right to "reprimand" them when necessary, so long as they did so "fraternally."[22] Elite rebel leaders, exhibiting their desire to placate more of their class, thus aggressively attempted to manage the status and mobility of slaves and slave recruits in rebel-controlled territory. The multifarious regulations on the labor and movement of slaves persisted until Christmas Day 1870, when Céspedes formally ended the forced labor of libertos, arguing that although they had been unprepared for liberty in 1868, "two years of contact with the pageantry of our liberties have been sufficient to consider them already regenerated and to grant them independence." Even on paper, however, this freedom emerged as conditional, for Céspedes added that under no circumstances would freed slaves be allowed to "remain idle."[23] Activity and movement remained subject to insurgents' control.

The rebel leadership's early vacillation regarding abolition and slave participation in armed rebellion manifested itself clearly in formal rebel policy. But the lapses and bursts in abolitionist initiatives from the rebel leadership resulted not only from ideological conviction or political calculation. They also emerged from the interaction of slaves and insurgents, and between commanders and subalterns, in the camps and battlefields of rebel territory. This interaction could be strained and volatile, for at issue was not only the meaning of the freedom promised by insurgents and sought by slaves but also the question of who would define its boundaries.

When Céspedes originally deferred the abolition of slavery, he confided in private that he believed that Cuban slaves were not yet trained for freedom. The war, he implied, would have to serve as a classroom where newly freed slaves would be "trained to understand the proper meaning of true liberty."[24] Céspedes's choice of words should not be surprising, for white emancipators—whether British policymakers in Jamaica or northern soldiers in the U.S. South—nearly always spoke of the transition from slavery to freedom with metaphors of learning; hence the name "apprenticeship" to denote the transitional period between slave and free labor in the British colonies. The emancipators' tutelage focused customarily on teaching slaves to sell their labor to others for a wage.[25] But in Cuba, in the midst of armed rebellion for national sovereignty and surrounded everywhere by their own declarations of freedom and equality, nationalist leaders attempted to modify the customary sphere of that tutelage. They were not primarily training free laborers. Leaders saw themselves as training free (and industrious) soldiers and citizens. In their efforts, however, insurgent and republican leaders revealed the extent to which they sought to distinguish the freedom of former slaves from their own. They revealed it, as we have seen, in assigning libertos to masters, in establishing offices to supervise their movements, and in writing laws requiring them to work. They also revealed it in their daily contact with slave-insurgents.

Direct contact between slaves and insurgents often began at the moment of recruitment. In inducting slaves into the movement, military leaders regularly found themselves in the position of explaining the objectives of the rebellion to the new recruits. For example, when insurgents entered estates to mobilize slaves, they assembled the slave forces and gave speeches about the meaning of the insurrection and its relation to the abolition of slavery. Military leaders, initially anxious for the support of landholders, attempted to exert a moderating influence during these talks. Given the opportunity, then, many represented the revolution and emancipation in ways that would appeal to slaves' desire for emancipation yet also temper the freedom they promised. Thus, early in the rebellion, two leaders whose forces included many liberated slaves, Máximo Gómez and Donato Mármol, in return for the cooperation of slaveholders, promised slaves eventual freedom but also explained to them the "insurmountable problems that sudden abolition would create for them and the immense benefits that would come with gradual, but prompt, abolition — an abolition ennobled by and ennobling of work, honesty, and well-being."[26] In recruiting slaves with this sort of preamble, leaders asked them for patience in their desire for freedom. They also provided something of a partial definition of freedom: freedom from slavery and participation in armed insurgency did not imply the freedom not to work.

The insurgent colonel Juan Cancino, who owned one slave, was somewhat more subtle in the way he proposed to address potential slave recruits. He explained to fellow insurgents that he planned to "attract some slaves from Manzanillo to [their] ranks by promising them that if they take up arms against Spain they will be free, given that it was that very government which had enslaved them."[27] Cancino's plan had the advantage of attracting slaves by identifying a common enemy in Spain. More important, however, the plan had the advantage of portraying the rebels as benevolent liberators who would end the rule of the enslavers and grant freedom to all the slaves. Implicitly, then, mobilized slaves owed gratitude to their liberators.

This strategy — like Gómez and Marmol's speeches — represented more than insurgent abolitionism. It also represented a means of enlarging the rebel army and a potential avenue for managing newly freed slaves by encouraging gratitude and subservience to rebel leaders and structures. To represent themselves as liberators and to encourage the indebtedness and patience of slaves-turned-soldiers was to attempt to control and mediate the transition from slavery to freedom.

Insurgents' messages of gratitude, restraint, and forbearance, however, were less discernible to slaves than was the message of emancipation. And when slaves later described these talks by insurgent leaders, what appeared to impress them most was the promise of freedom. Public authorities recognized as much when they reported that slaves were being "forcibly extracted" from their farms not with guns and threats but with "deceit and promises."[28] When Zacarías Priol, a suspected insurgent and a former slave on a coffee farm near Santiago, was captured by the Spanish, he offered his captors routine testimony: he and other slaves on the farm had been taken by force by Cuban insurgents.[29] Priol implied, as had many other captured slaves, that he had merely obeyed the insurgents' order to leave as promptly as he had earlier obeyed his master's order to stay and work. Slaves were not alone in making such claims. Almost all individuals caught and tried by Spanish authorities for participating in the rebellion attempted to avoid punishment by testifying that they were taken against their will and under threats of death by bands of insurgents.[30]

The details Priol provided his interrogator about that seemingly forcible extraction demonstrated, however, that a much more complex and ambiguous process was unfolding. Priol explained to his Spanish audience that the rebel general Donato Mármol arrived on his farm, gathered about forty of the male slaves, and made them take a vow to the Caridad del Cobre (later the patron saint of Cuba), presumably to show that they understood that "if the insurrection triumphed all the slaves would be free." After taking their vow, "they all followed [the general] to Sabanilla," where the insurgents had assembled about nine thousand people. In giving his testimony, Priol chose to say that the slaves "went with" rather than "were taken by" the rebels and that it was the rebel promise of freedom that precipitated their flight. Though Mármol specified to them that freedom would come only with the triumphant end of the insurrection, this could be little consolation to the slaveholders whose slaves had just become insurgents. Thus even Mármol, one of the officers who had promised to encourage forbearance among slaves, was unable to mute the essence of the rebel message: that anticolonial rebellion had suddenly made freedom from slavery a palpable prospect.

Much to the dismay of unconverted owners, other rebel leaders were significantly less discreet in the way they represented imminent freedom to enslaved workers. At the *ingenio* (sugar mill) San Luis, near Santiago, a small group of insurgents arrived and, with the help of the *mayoral* (overseer), took some of the estate's slaves (including women and children) to the insurrection. One of these slaves, Eduardo, was later caught with "weapons in his hands." Not surprisingly, he testified — much as Zacarías Priol had — that the insurgents had taken him and the others by force. The insurgents, he added, had forced them all to carry weapons: "They had no choice but to take them," he insisted. He explained that the insurgents gave each slave one machete, which they were "to sharpen every day, as much for working as for killing the *patones*." (Patones, literally "big-feet," was a pejorative label used by Cubans to describe Spaniards.) This insurgent leader defined slaves' freedom as the obligation to labor but also as the privilege to make war. Eduardo also testified that the rebels told them to "kill all the *patones* in Cuba, so that they would all be free and then they would no longer have to say *mi amo* or *mi Señor*" (my master or my lord).[31] Rebels promised slaves their freedom and then produced examples of its day-to-day exercise. The slave who described this speech did not dwell on any appeals for patience and moderation. Rather, his interpretation of the rebels' public statements led him to believe that his actions now, in labor and in combat, would produce new conditions — conditions under which he would no longer have to be subservient to the men who had formerly ruled over him. His recollection of the rebel sermon captured perfectly the multiple and often contradictory messages contained in rebels' call to arms for slaves: the promise of a freedom that would entail the right to fight and the opportunity to shed some of the habits of deference and submission central to slave society, but a freedom defined as well by unremunerated labor.

Insurgent leaders and slave recruits clearly disagreed about the boundaries of the new freedom, and these differences of opinion made the question of discipline a major concern of rebel practice. The Liberation Army established a disciplinary apparatus that mirrored the Spanish system of military tribunals. Insurgents caught stealing, deserting, or showing disrespect to their officers were tried in *consejos de guerra*.[32] Slaves, though technically subject to this system of discipline, were also likely to receive punishment outside this formal legal network. Slaves questioned by colonial authorities made frequent references to being put in stocks in insurgent camps, and rebel officers, anxious to control slaves' behavior, often referred to the need to punish wayward *libertos* publicly, even suggesting giving them "a good beating as an example" to the others.[33] Insurgent leaders thus punished new behaviors encouraged by novel conditions with old and familiar methods of slave discipline.

These methods, which epitomized leaders' attempts to limit slave autonomy and to regulate the transition from slavery, in fact, produced the contrary effect. Disciplinary measures encouraged the very behavior insurgent leaders sought to suppress. For as slaves saw that insurgents who had promised them freedom now sought to delay its practice, they were moved to flee from rebel camps. Individual and small groups of slaves moved through the countryside, anxious to avoid capture by insurgents, only to be seized by the Spanish. For example, in only four days Spanish troops picked up 108 slaves who were identified as having fled from eastern coffee farms.[34] Not only did the insurgents lose these potential soldiers and workers, they often lost them to Spanish troops, who used them in "services appropriate to the condition of slaves."[35] In mid–1870 the captain general of the island reported to the colonial minister that, in one case, 32 slaves had surrendered to Spanish authorities, allegedly "saying unanimously that they preferred by far to be *Spanish slaves than to be free mambís.*"[36]

Although this alleged statement certainly would have served the slaves' interests at the moment of surrendering to the Spanish, some slaves did, in fact, serve in the Spanish army. Many served in roles not unlike those they had had in the Cuban rebel army: stretcher-bearers, cooks, or trench diggers. Slaves who served in the Spanish army were potentially eligible for their freedom after lengthy interrogations by authorities. In fact, it appears that many of those serving the colonial army had first been drafted into the war by the rebels and then ended up — by choice, circumstance, or force — switching sides and serving in the Spanish army.[37]

Most slaves who fled from the insurrection, however, struggled just as energetically to avoid the Spanish military camps. Some formed small communities of ex-slaves or joined *palenques,* preexisting communities of fugitive slaves living in mountainous regions outside the control of both the plantations and the rebel state. The relations between these groups of fugitive slaves and the Cuban insurgent movement highlights the contradictions that emerged in the relations between slaves and insurgents more generally. Céspedes's decree of December 1868 had accorded freedom to palenque slaves, giving them the right to join and live with the insurgents or, if they preferred, to remain in their own communities, "recognizing and respecting the Government of the Revolution."[38] In practice, however, relations between these fugitives and insurgent military officers were very strained.

Rebel leaders, knowing of the existence of the palenques, preferred that the services of these groups aid them rather than their Spanish enemies. They also hoped that by initiating the *apalencados* (palenque members) into the struggle for independence, they would also inculcate in them the habits of a republican polity. Thus insurgents became increasingly intolerant of what they perceived as the palenques' continued lack of discipline, their refusal of civilization. According to one rebel officer, the maroons "were more given to chanting than to fighting and became such a dangerous and fatal plague" that insurgent leaders were soon forced to capture their leaders and publicly and summarily try them in military tribunals. The officer added that these maroons "were hunted energetically to force them to lend services to the republic, since from miserable slaves they had come to be free citizens."[39] This Cuban officer captured perfectly the nature of the relationship between the white separatist and the black slave. The separatist saw himself proudly as a liberator who had taken "brute" slaves and converted them to "citizens, patriots, and soldiers of liberty."[40] Yet the separatist clearly saw the slave as a special sort of citizen — one who, in some instances, was still subject to being hunted and, in all, was still subject to the appropriation of his or her labor and time in the service of nationhood.

The process of arming slaves in the context of anticolonial insurgency in Cuba shares certain features with other cases examined in this book. As in the French Antilles during the Age of Revolution or the U.S. South during the Civil War, the "armers" of slaves (of various political persuasions) sought to manage and control the process of arming them, to use the power of armed slaves for their own interests in defense, war-making, or state formation. Consistently, they sought to delimit the power that slaves acquired from their mobilization. Whether slaves were armed by the state to defend a colony or by rebels to wage war against a colonist, they were to serve loyally, in a way that preserved or secured the power of those who armed them but that did not allow them to overstep the cautious freedoms granted them in the process. Consistently, however, armed slaves sought to push against the limits set by their armers, using their service to argue for greater rewards, taking initiatives to secure or expand newfound privileges, and redefining on the ground and in daily practice the boundaries of the freedom suggested in the very process of arming them.[41]

Yet the story of the arming of slaves in revolutionary Cuba cannot end there. For the arming of slaves, already a complex and contentious process in and of itself, unfolded within a broader colonial context. Contention and conflict over this arming affected the very course of insurgency. But the arming of slaves produced contention and uncertainty not only in the daily practice of war. It also produced a broader argument about the consequences of that mobilization for the construction of nationhood itself. Spanish authorities, faced with the widespread and unprecedented mobilization of enslaved black men for anticolonial ends, responded by constantly invoking the charge of racial warfare and resurrecting the image of a Haitian-style apocalypse. And white insurgents were capable of being swayed by such arguments. Indeed, over the course of ten years of warfare, and in the peace and subsequent armed attempts that followed, a good number of white Cubans rejected independence on the basis of its alleged links to racial warfare. Cuban opponents of independence, as well as former insurgents turned loyalists, when placed in the position of explaining their own political choices, tended to characterize the independence movement as black. And it was precisely in that blackness that some white insurgents located the rebellion's threat to the future of Cuban society. Thus if the arming of slaves served key strategic and ideological purposes, it also raised issues and anxieties that threatened the cohesiveness and clarity of the bid for independence.

This pattern crystallized at several key moments in the history of anticolonial insurgency. For example, in 1870–71 in Puerto Príncipe, a key theater of the war and immediately west of where the war began, a crisis ensued as more and more rebels abandoned the rebellion and a good number offered their services to the colonial state. In purporting to explain the reasons for their surrender to Spanish authorities, repentent insurgents gave center stage to the question of race. According to one declaration made by surrendering insurgents, the powerful local rebel movement, which had counted on three or four thousand armed men and thirty to thirty-five thousand sympathizers in the countryside, had been reduced to three or four hundred men, "blacks in their majority."[42] And it was this state of affairs — the literal blackening of insurgency — that many surrendering insurgents in the region highlighted when explaining their decision to retreat from insurgency. Colonial appeals to racial fear and white anxiety about political power were perhaps now more resonant than ever, given that they were made in the context of a rebellion that mobilized slaves and free people of color.

Though this pattern was particularly dramatic and noticeable in Puerto Príncipe in the early 1870s, the insurgency's crisis in that region cannot be seen as a singular aberration, for controversy and division over issues of slave mobilization and multiracial insurgency manifested themselves, to different degrees and in different forms, even in areas and among leaders unwilling to renounce the cause of independence. Céspedes, for example, who began the rebellion and who fought until his death in 1874, was not immune to doubts and not unwilling to act on his misgivings. In this case, however, acting on those misgivings entailed not surrender but the search for protection from the

United States. Thus in 1869 Céspedes wrote to nationalist colleagues in the United States: "[I]n the minds of a majority of Cubans . . . is always the idea of annexation as a last resort, in order to avoid the abyss of evils which they say would lead to a war of the races." And a week later he described the state of the rebellion in these words: "The blacks in large numbers are fighting in our ranks; [and] those of us with weapons in our hands are convinced that [it] is becoming necessary to ask for annexation to those important States."[43] The scourge of surrenders may have been particular to Puerto Príncipe, but the doubts and worries that motivated them seemed to be present in the very center of the revolution.

The revolution, however, survived the crisis and lasted until 1878. The treaty that ended the war, which was accepted by rebel leaders, mainly white, in Puerto Príncipe and rejected by many black and mulatto leaders from farther east, granted neither abolition nor independence. It granted freedom only to the slaves who had served either in the insurrection or in support of the Spanish colonial army.

Although the rebellion had failed to achieve abolition, by freeing and mobilizing slaves it had altered forever the social relations of slavery. Spanish authorities recognized that slave-insurgents, if forced to return to their farms, were likely to "demoralize the slave forces and become fugitives."[44] They sought to diminish the problem by freeing slaves who had served in the Cuban army. But this policy created profound contradictions. As one prominent sugar planter had asked earlier: "What logic, what justice can there be in having those [slaves] who were loyal to their owners remain in slavery, while their malicious companions, instead of receiving the severe punishment that their wicked conduct deserves, get instead the valuable prize of liberty?"[45] Despite these objections, the freedom of rebel slaves was enacted by Spain; the policy freed about sixteen thousand slaves.[46] The process set in motion by the insurgency and the peace treaty had committed Spain to abolish slavery sooner rather than later—a fact which meant that slaves could associate emancipation as much with nationalist insurgency as with any abolitionist policy of the colonial state. And, in fact, after final emancipation came by law in 1886, former slaves were said to proclaim proudly that they were freed not by the government's decree of emancipation but by their own participation in the war and by the *convenio* of 1878, which recognized their liberty as a reward for that participation.[47] Decades later two former slaves named Genaro Lucumí and Irene would gather neighborhood children in the small town of Chirigota in Pinar del Río to tell them stories about the end of slavery and about Antonio Maceo, the famous mulatto general who began the war in 1868 as a private, rose through the ranks almost immediately, and died in battle in 1896 during Cuba's third war of independence against Spain. Still others heard stories about another former slave who, having acquired his freedom, changed his name to Cuba.[48] Insurgency and nationalism had become central to former slaves' efforts to give meaning to their freedom; the link between antislavery and anticolonialism was inviolably established.

The war transformed Cuban society in other ways as well. The insurrection had emerged from and erupted into a colonial slave society in which race and nation had been negatively associated. The Cuban "race question" had been used to provide an automatic and negative answer to the Cuban "national question": the numerical significance of the nonwhite population and the economic significance of slavery necessitated the continuation of a colonial bond with Spain. With the outbreak of the insurrection in 1868, the link between race and nation was thrust to the foreground, demanding fresh resolution. The initiators of the rebellion attempted to resolve it by introducing cautious measures toward achieving abolition. These partial measures were soon superseded by the day-to-day practice of insurgency, as slaves joined rebel forces of their own volition and as local leaders emancipated them without the consent of central rebel authority. The movement seemed to suggest that slaves could become soldiers and citizens and that a slave colony could become a free nation.

As the rebellion progressed, however, it became clear that the relation between race and nation could not be transformed without struggle and dissent. The response to widespread black participation (and to the emergence of powerful black and mulatto leadership) was, for many white insurgents, withdrawal from and condemnation of the rebellion as destructive of Cuba's best interests. Although insurgents who surrendered were still partial to the idea of Cuban independence, they rejected the early movement's implications for racial politics in post-independence Cuba.

When a new anticolonial insurgency erupted a year later in August 1879, this tension between black mobilization and white fear again assumed a central role. The new war, known as the Guerra Chiquita or Little War because it lasted less than a year, again mobilized massive numbers of slaves. In this insurrection, slave mobilization and black leadership assumed an even more important role than they had in the earlier war. First, black slaves who remained on plantations and farms saw their fellow slaves who had rebelled in 1868–78 freed for their participation in armed insurgency. With that precedent set, the payoffs of rebellion seemed larger and surer than ever before. In 1879, then, eastern slaves were said to profess that they wanted "their freedom like the *convenidos*," the slaves freed in the treaty ending the first war. In the first two months of the new war, almost 800 slaves escaped their workplaces to join the insurrection. Rebels, meanwhile, put the total number of fugitive slaves at five thousand. From the outset, then, slaves played a more prominent role in this insurrection than in the first. Likewise, the principal military leaders on the island were men of color. As the war went on, Spanish opponents increasingly used the issue of racial warfare to detract from the movement and to alienate potential white support. Published lists of captured insurgents strategically omitted the names of white rebels so that, according to the local Spanish governor, white Cubans would see race and not independence as the crux of the armed movement. They used such tactics to elicit white surrenders and then went further, making pardon on surrender contingent on the whites' public denunciation of the "racist" motives of their comrades of color. This tactic, which responded in part to the perceived "blackness" of the rebellion, then helped make the rebellion that much blacker, which led to more surrenders, and then to stronger evidence of its blackness, in turn.

The failures of these two insurrections, though complex and multifaceted, revealed the effective power of the label of racial warfare. Spanish officials and their Cuban allies used the allegation that the independence movement was a black movement — a real threat of another Haiti. They used the allegation because it worked; that is, it served to qualify support for insurrection. In the aftermath of two failed insurgencies, rebels came to realize that in order to succeed at anticolonial insurgency they had to invalidate traditional claims about the racial risks of rebellion; they had to construct an effective counterclaim to arguments that for almost a century had maintained that Cuba was unsuited to nationhood. "The power to represent oneself," they had come to realize, was "nothing other than political power itself."[49] The struggle for that power of representation required that nationalist leaders reconceptualize nationality, blackness, and the place of people of color in the would-be nation. In the process, black, mulatto, and white patriot-intellectuals constructed powerful and eloquent expressions of a new and antiracist nationality. In this reconstruction the figure of the armed slave played a preeminent role.

As part of a response to the Spanish portrait of the Cuban rebellions as race wars, separatist writers in the interlude between the second and third insurrections and in the years following final emancipation in 1886 conducted a sweeping reevaluation of the role of the black insurgent in the process of making the nation. This act of reexamination involved, on one hand, telling stories about the everyday activities of unknown slave insurgents in the Ten Years' War. On the other hand, it involved the formulation of an ideal black insurgent who rose above others in acts of selfless (and, as we shall see, "raceless") patriotism. In the process, the figure of the slave insurgent, dreaded emblem of race war and black republic, was neutralized and made an acceptable — indeed, central — component in the struggle for Cuban nationhood.

One apparent beneficiary of this process of neutralization was an elderly slave named Ramón, who went from being the cause of the death of Carlos Manuel de Céspedes, the leader of the first insurrection, to being a faithful and trustworthy slave with no connection to the "father of the patria." In the 1870s and 1880s, the conventional account of Céspedes's death maintained that his whereabouts had been revealed to Spanish troops by an aging former slave named Ramón, who betrayed the liberator of slaves in exchange for his personal freedom. (One variant of the story held that a slave named Robert had denounced Céspedes in exchange for his life when captured by Spanish forces). In the 1890s, as independence activists prepared the ideological and political groundwork for a new rebellion, several new accounts appeared to disavow these theories. The new accounts maintained that the elderly Ramón, known to everyone in the area as "Papá Ramón," did not know Céspedes and played no role whatsoever in his death. The Spanish soldiers who killed Céspedes were, in fact, surprised to learn that they had killed the president of the Cuban Republic. And this surprise, the new theories maintained, revealed that Céspedes's whereabouts could not have been disclosed by a slave or by anyone else.

The reformulation of the story is significant within the context of the 1890s. Céspedes, though censured by some of the independence movement for favoring the military rather than the civilian elements of the revolution, was still recognized as the heroic father of the incipient nation. His most compelling act had been the granting of freedom to his slaves, who then joined the new Cuban army. That he might have been murdered as a result of betrayal by an ungrateful slave could only help sustain those who invoked the dangers of insurrection and independence. In the retelling of the story in the nineties, the elderly soldier "wept desperately" over his role in Céspedes's death, but everyone around him consoled him, certain of "the honor" and "total innocence" of the "poor and valiant old man."[50] Thus Ramón — suspected Judas — was reappropriated and transformed into the benign Papá Ramón.

The slave insurgent portrayed in proindependence writings of the 1890s was, however, more than merely safe or unthreatening; he was also a Cuban hero and patriot. Examples of depictions of slave insurgents as benign heroes abounded at this time.[51] Among the most eloquent perhaps was the 1892 portrayal of a black insurgent named José Antonio Legón by rebel-turned-author Ramon Roa. Roa described a childlike and submissive slave-turned-insurgent. He represented the pre-war Legón thus: "This, our José Antonio Legón, [was] of average stature, astounding agility, imponderable sagacity, and an audacity, of which he himself was unaware, just as a child is unaware of his mischief. When the revolution began in Sanctí Spíritus he was a '*negrito*,' the slave of a Cuban who supported ideas of independence for his native land." Roa explained that Legón fought with valor and enthusiasm for the Cuban cause until his master was killed by Spanish forces. Then he became "taciturn and preoccupied, concerned only with destroying his enemy, as if he wanted to avenge a personal offense." Still, he fought fearlessly, and soon scars everywhere "interrupted the blackness of his skin." He was eventually captured by the Spanish and, given the option of deserting and saving his life, he responded: "Well, when my master — who raised me and who was good — passed away, he told me: 'José Antonio, never stop being Cuban,' and the poor man left this world for another. Now I comply by being Cuban until the end. . . . You can kill me if you want."[52] And kill him they did. But the soldier they murdered was not the same slave who had joined the rebellion months earlier. For in the course of fighting the war, Legón had gone from being "*un negrito*" and a slave to being simply Cuban. Even his black body had been lightened by the numerous scars of Cuba Libre. He had not, however, demanded this transformation from black slave to Cuban soldier and citizen for himself. Rather, he was freed by a benevolent master who, on his death, expressed his wish that Legón be and remain Cuban. By resisting the authority of Spain, he was thus consecrating the wishes of his master. In this manner, the rebellion of the armed slaves was rendered unthreatening because their military action was represented as an outcome of their masters' will and not of personal initiative or political conviction.[53]

Opponents of independence, and even some of its proponents, had long characterized the black insurgent as a threat. In the 1890s, independence propagandists painted a different insurgent of color: one who felt himself to be, and who was recognized by his fellow soldiers as, Cuban. And as a Cuban, who naturally loved his country, he fought valiantly. Furthermore, when the slave's master was a Cuban insurgent, his love of country could be portrayed as an extension of his love for his former master. Like Legón, the armed slaves that populated nationalist writings of the period were all characters who obediently complied with their duties as soldiers — and as servants — of the Cuban nation. Politically, they would be incapable of imagining a black republic.

Moreover, they posed no threat of social disorder. Even with weapons in his hands, the black insurgent of the pro-independence writings respected the norms that relegated him to an inferior social status. Thus Manuel Sanguily, a prominent Havana journalist and a white veteran of the Ten Years' War, painted a vivid portrait of deferential black insurgents. Writing of the daily interactions between white and nonwhite insurgents in the war, he argued that "boundaries were never confused, nor were natural differences erased, nor was equilibrium lost for a single instant. Each one occupied always his proper place. Different spheres remained independent from one another, without anyone having to demand it or even comment on it."[54] Thus Sanguily and others constructed a world in which the enslaved man could violate enough prescriptions of colonial society to threaten the colonial order, but not enough to overturn traditional norms of social interaction. Such representations were predicated, in part, on a division between political and social spheres. In the political sphere the slave was allowed enough agency to become a submissive insurgent. But in daily social contact between those identified as white and those identified as black, the norms of racial etiquette were always maintained. Thus the "regime of equality" that Sanguily said was produced in the fields of the insurrection could coexist with the "most profound order."[55] They could coexist without contradiction because that "regime of equality" was seen as something the black slave neither demanded nor constructed for himself. Equality was cast as a gift of the white leadership, and the black slave, knowing it was a gift, enjoyed it respectfully and obediently. The transgression of boundaries that allowed him to challenge colonialism and slavery was, in these writings, less a transgression than an extension of his subservience to a white insurgent master.[56] And his heroism was one grounded in gratitude and unrelated to black political desire.

In fact, the black insurgent's desirability within the national project was predicated on the erasure of any hint of his own desire. Thus the black insurgent in the prose of independence appeared to lack not only political will but also any trace of sexual desire. Indeed, the absence of sexuality was essential to the portrayal of his political passivity and deference. Spanish representations of dangerous black insurgents often included allusions to black men seducing white women, so figures such as Guillermo Moncada and Rustán, both black officers in the Ten Years' War, were discredited with stories about defiled white womanhood. In the late 1880s and early 1890s, however, pro-independence writers explicitly countered such images, painting a black insurgent incapable of posing any sexual threat. Sanguily wrote: "[N]ever did the black man [el negro] even dream of taking possession of the white woman [la blanca]; and there [in the war] living in the midst of wilderness, never did we hear of any crime of rape, or of any attempt against the woman, forsaken in the loneliness of the mountains."[57] Even with clear opportunity, Sanguily suggested, the black insurgent showed no inclination to subvert racial and gender hierarchies. Nowhere was white recognition of the absence of that desire more visible than in José Martí's 1894 description of Salvador Cisneros Betancourt, the aging insurgent-aristocrat who during the Ten Years' War decided to bury his white daughter in the same grave as his own black male slave. In this moment, which Martí exalts as emblematic of the revolution, unity between black and white, between slave and master, was given literal and permanent form in the union of the bodies of a white woman and a black man.[58] Yet that union posed no threat—not only because it occurred in death, but also because it represented not black will but white benevolence and generosity.

In the years before the final war, writers, officers, and readers looked back on the armed slave of the 1870s and conferred on him the traits of loyalty and submissiveness to the cause of Cuba Libre. It was impossible for any of these figures to betray the cause of Cuba, to threaten white women, to harbor hatred for their former white masters, or to support the idea of a black nation. Compare this image with that prevalent in the 1870s and early 1880s of the black insurgent leader Guillermo Moncada. One correspondent from the United States recounted some of the rumors that prevailed about the black general in the 1870s: he was "a man . . . as ferocious in disposition as terrible in aspect," who was said to kill every white man who fell into his hands and to keep women (white and otherwise) in "harems."[59] Yet by 1888 a popular compilation of insurgents' biographies described the general as "good and trustworthy" and as proof of what "strong allies" men of color could be if nurtured and educated "only in virtues" from an early age.[60] By the early 1890s the black insurgent had been reconfigured: the terrible Guillermón had given way to the loyal Legón and the innocent Papá Ramón.[61]

But though the figure of the armed slave was rendered "safe" in the prose of insurgency, that figure was also made central to the very process of nation making. He appears as the central figure in poems such as "1868" by Enrique Hernández Miyares, in which the protagonist, a heroic and self-sacrificing black soldier on horseback, is defined as the very essence of the rebel effort, or in stories such as "Fidel Céspedes," in which the armed slave hero sacrifices his life to save the lives of fellow Cubans. And in numerous political essays published by white and nonwhite authors, the arming and liberating of slaves is identified as a principal achievement of the independence movement, which is distinguished by its commitment to antislavery and, in many cases, antiracism.[62]

Clearly, then, the mobilization of slaves proceeded on two fronts. In armed rebellion against Spain, slaves actively engaged themselves, answering and in many ways surpassing the cautious call to arms issued by creole patriots. But their very presence called into being a whole set of arguments about the racial character of rebellion and the racial character of the nation that the rebellion sought to found. Thus alongside the arming of slaves for war came a mobilization of a different sort: the invocation of the figure of the armed slave in a new prose of independence, a new set of writings that made the armed slave welcome and central in the national project. Though both the military and the discursive mobilization of slaves may have been at times tactical and calculated, once the mobilization had begun slaves and former slaves could call on their participation in the military to make bold claims for political rights in the postemancipation republic erected at the end of the century.

Notes

1. Robin Blackburn, *The Overthrow of Colonial Slavery, 1776–1848* (London, 1988), 3.

2. For a discussion of the regional and class dimensions of the leadership of the rebel movement, see Ada Ferrer, *Insurgent Cuba: Race, Nation, and Revolution, 1868–1898* (Chapel Hill, 1999), 17–23, 54–58.

3. "Manifiesto de la Junta Revolucionaria," October 10, 1868, in Hortensia Pichardo, ed., *Documentos para la historia de Cuba* (Havana, 1968), 1:358–62. See also Cepero Bonilla, "Azúcar y abolición," in *Escritos Historicas* (Havana, 1989), 92–95.

4. "Manifiesto de la Junta Revolucionaria," 1:361; "La situación de Cuba," *Boletín de la Revolución,* December 16, 1868, in Biblioteca Nacional (Madrid), Manuscritos (hereafter BNM), MSS/20283/1 (10).

5. Carlos Manuel de Céspedes, "Comunicación diplomática encargando explorar la opinión norteamericana sobre la anexión," January 3, 1869, in Céspedes, *Escritos* (Havana, 1982), 1:142–46.

6. Ibid.

7. Captain General Lersundi, October 24, 1868, in Archivo Histórico Nacional, Spain (hereafter AHN), Seción Ultramar (hereafter SU), leg. 4933, 1a parte, book 1, doc. no. 55.

8. Carlos Manuel de Céspedes, October 17, 1868, in "Criminal contra Don Manuel Villa," in Archivo Nacional de Cuba (hereafter ANC), Fordo Comisión Militar (hereafter CM), leg. 125, exp. 6, 136–37.

9. "Ordén del día," Bayamo, October 29, 1868, in Céspedes, *Escritos,* 1:117.

10. Carlos Manuel de Céspedes, "Bando de 12 de Noviembre de 1868," in Justo Zaragoza, *Las insurrecciones en Cuba* (Madrid, 1872–73), 2:732. See also Cepero Bonilla, "Azúcar y abolición," 94.

11. "Informe referente a que sería injusto fijar cuota de contribución . . . a las fincas rústicas del Departamento Oriental," in ANC, Fondo Asuntos Políticas (hereafter AP), leg. 59, exp. 7.

12. "Diligencias formadas para averiguar si es cierto que una partida de insurrectos se llevaron junto con los esclavos de la Hacienda San Fernando del Dr. Fernando Pons el negro emancipado nombrado Martín," in ANC, AP, leg. 57, exp. 18; petition of E. G. Schmidt in U.S. National Archives, Record Group 76, Entry 341, U.S. and Spanish Claims Commission, Claim no. 81. Though historians and rebels often describe these assaults on farms as the liberation of slave forces, it is very important to note that insurgents sometimes freed or took only partial slave forces, and sometimes only the men.

In the case of Santísima Trinidad de Giro, rebels took men, women, and children alike, but in many other instances women and children were left behind on the estates. See, e.g., "Expediente en averiguación de los servicios prestados por el negro esclavo Zacarías Priol," ANC, AP, leg. 62, exp. 34.

13. Comandante Andrés Brisuelos to Gen. Julio Grave de Peralta, December 3, 1868, in AHN, SU, leg. 5837. For other examples of individual slaves freely offering their services to the rebellion, see the documents relating to captured insurgents in AHN, SU, leg. 4457.

14. "Sumaria instruida contra el negro esclavo José Manuel por el delito de insurrección," February 1869, in ANC, AP, leg. 58, exp. 44. For an example of a rebel handbill directed at slaves, see the proclamation in AHN, SU, leg. 4933, 2a parte, book 4, doc. no. 96. For a discussion of the ways in which slaves who remained on plantations used the uncertainty created by war to exercise more autonomy and agency, see Rebecca Scott, *Slave Emancipation in Cuba: The Transition to Free Labor, 1860–1899* (Princeton, 1985), ch. 2.

15. For slaves taken from farms by insurgents and made to do menial work in support of the rebellion, see the documents relating to captured insurgents in AHN, SU, legs. 4439, 4457, 5837, 5844. Many of these slaves went on to serve the Spanish army in similar roles. See the individual files in ANC, AP, legs. 61–70.

16. On Francisco Vicente Aguilera, see Ramiro Guerra y Sanchez, *La Guerra de los Diez Años* (Havana, 1950–52), 1:108n. On José Manuel, see ANC, AP, leg. 58, exp. 44. On Magín, see AHN, SU, leg. 4439.

17. Carlos Manuel de Céspedes, Decreto, December 27, 1868, in Pichardo, *Documentos para la historia de Cuba*, 1:370–73.

18. Céspedes, "Comunicación diplomática."

19. Numbers of slave participants were not recorded or preserved systematically. There would have been significant variation by region and period over the course of the ten years of war. There is no single roster of soldiers for the rebel army in this war.

20. "Constitución de Guáimaro," in Pichardo, *Documentos para la historia de Cuba*, 1:376–79.

21. Quoted in Cepero Bonilla, "Azúcar y abolición," 107. Emphasis mine.

22. "Reglamento de libertos," in Pichardo, *Documentos para la historia de Cuba*, 1:380–82.

23. Carlos Manuel de Céspedes, December 25, 1870, in Pichardo, *Documentos para la historia de Cuba*, 1:388.

24. Céspedes, "Comunicación diplomática."

25. See especially Thomas Holt, *The Problem of Freedom: Race, Labor, and Politics in Jamaica and Britain, 1832–1938* (Baltimore, 1992), ch. 2; Julie Saville, *The Work of Reconstruction: From Slave to Wage Laborer in South Carolina* (Cambridge, UK, 1994).

26. Donato Mármol and Máximo Gómez, "Alocución a los hacendados de Cuba," December 31, 1868, reprinted in Emilio Bacardí y Moreau, *Crónicas de Santiago de Cuba* (Madrid, 1973), 4:79–81. Many of the slaves taken from coffee and sugar farms were later captured by or presented themselves to Spanish authorities. See their case files, scattered throughout ANC, AP, legs. 61–70.

27. Colonel Juan M. Cancino to Campamento provisional de Palmas Altas, December

30, 1868, in AHN, SU, leg. 4457; "Esclavos embargados, Bayamo, 1874," in ANC, BE, leg. 200, exp. 6.

28. "Expediente instruido sobre la averiguación y conducta del negro esclavo agregado a este Batallón, Juan de la Cruz (a) Bolívar," in ANC, Fondo Bienes Embargados (hereafter BE), AP, leg. 62, exp. 32.

29. See his testimony in ANC, AP, leg. 62, exp. 34.

30. The incorporation of slaves into rebel forces was even referred to as "forced recruitment." See Francisco de Arredondo y Miranda, *Recuerdos de las guerras de Cuba* (Havana, 1962), 97. For testimony given by slaves other than Priol regarding their forced extraction by insurgents, see ANC, CM, leg. 129, exp.27, and the following files in ANC, AP: 62/23, 62/32, 62/36, 62/77–79. For testimony of free people making similar claims about their forced induction into rebel forces, see the following files in ANC, CM: 125/6, 126/1, 126/13, 126/17, 126/30, 127/7, 127/17, 129/12, 129/27, 129/30.

31. See his testimony in ANC, CM, leg. 129, exp. 27.

32. See, e.g., the files on *consejos de guerra* during the final years of the war in ANC, Fondo Donativos y Remisiones, 463/18, 469/15, 577/28, 577/51.

33. See, e.g., "Criminal contra D. Emilio Rivera, et al." in ANC, CM, leg. 129, exp. 27; Gen. P. Rebustillo to [name crossed out], Los Cocos [Santiago], July 28, 1869, and Com. José Ruiz to Cor. José C. Sánchez, Camp San Nicolás, March 30, 1870, both in AHN, SU, leg. 4439.

34. "Diario de Operaciones, Regimiento de la Habana No. 6 de Infantería, 1er Batallón," in Servicio Histórico Militar, Sección Ultramar, Colección Microfilmada Cuba, reel 1, leg. 5.

35. See "Expediente del moreno Andrés Aguilera," in ANC, AP, leg. 62, exp. 19. For other cases of slaves' requesting their freedom for having served Spain, see the petitions in ANC, AP, legs. 61–70.

36. Captain Gen. Caballero de Rodas to Min. de Ultramar, May 16, 1870, in AHN, SU, leg. 4933, 2nd part, book 5, doc. no. 99. Emphasis in original. The term *mambí* was a common name for the insurgents. Some have defined it as literally the offspring of a monkey and a vulture, others as the Indian term for rebels against the first Spanish conquerors. Though the term may have originated as a pejorative label for the rebels, sources agree that insurgents came to use the name proudly to refer to themselves. See esp. Miguel Barnet, *Biografía de un cimarrón* (Havana, 1986), 169; Antonio Rosal y Vásquez, *En la manigua: Diario de mi cantiverio* (Madrid, 1876), 248; Fernando Ortiz, "Un afrocubanismo: El vocablo mambí," in *Etnía y sociedad* (Havana, 1993), 102–3.

37. For individual cases of slaves' requesting their freedom for having served Spain, see the petitions in ANC, AP, legs. 61–70.

38. Carlos Manuel de Céspedes, Decreto, December 28, 1868, in Pichardo, *Documentos para la historia de Cuba*, 1:370–73.

39. Ramón Roa, quoted in Pichardo, *Documentos para la historia de Cuba*, 318–19.

40. "10 de Octubre," *La Revolución* (New York), October 13, 1869, clipping in AHN, SU, leg. 4933, 2a parte, book 4, doc. no. 88.

41. See Dubois, Reidy, and Morgan and O'Shaughnessy in this volume.

42. AHN, SU, leg. 4935, 1a parte, book 11, doc. no. 11. For more on the Puerto Príncipe crisis, see Ferrer, *Insurgent Cuba*, ch. 2.

43. Carlos Manuel de Céspedes, "Comunicación diplomática" and "Comunicación sobre el estado crítico de la revolución," both in Céspedes, *Escritos,* 1:144, 147.

44. Martínez Campos letter, February 18, 1878, AHN, SU, leg. 4936, 2a parte, book 17, doc. no. 202.

45. Francisco Ibañez, Junta Central Protectora de Libertos, to Gobernador General, September 22, 1874, AHN, SU, leg. 4882, tomo 3, exp. 49.

46. Scott, *Slave Emancipation in Cuba,* 115; Carlos M. Trelles y Govin, *Biblioteca histórica cubana* (Matanzas, 1922–26), 3:553; "Convenio del Zanjón," in Pichardo, *Documentos para la historia de Cuba,* 1:403–4.

47. Manuel Moreno Fraginals, *Cuba/España, España/Cuba* (Barcelona, 1995), 255.

48. George Vecsey, "Cuba Wins; Therefore, Cuba Wins," *Washington Post,* August 4, 1991, sec. 8, p. 2. Stories about Genaro Lucumí and Irene were told to me by my mother, who was among the children to whom they told their stories.

49. Partha Chaterjee, *The Nation and Its Fragments: Colonial and Postcolonial Histories* (Princeton, 1993), 76.

50. Bibliófilo [pseud.], *El negro Ramón y la muerte de Céspedes* (San Antonio de los Baños, 1894), 20–22; Fernando Figueredo Socorrás, *La toma de Bayamo* (San Antonio de los Baños, 1893), 30–31; Socorrás, *Revolución de Yara, 1868–1878, Conferencias* (1902; reprint, Miami, 1990), 43n. All refute the claim of the slave's betrayal of Céspedes. The latter, though published in 1902, is composed of lectures given by Figueredo in the 1880s and was originally scheduled for publication in 1894.

51. For additional examples and discussion, see Ferrer, *Insurgent Cuba,* ch. 5.

52. The clipping appears in ANC, DR, leg. 287, exp. 28. The article, and another with the same title about a black insurgent named Joaquín Júa, were published in *La Igualdad* on September 21, 1892, and October 1, 1892, respectively, and reprinted later in Ramón Roa, *Con la pluma y el machete* (Havana, 1950), 1:248–51. Roa also published a short article about the patriotic services of a black woman, Rosa la Bayamesa, in the same newspaper in 1892. The article was reprinted as a chapter titled "Rosa la Bayamesa" in his *Calzado y montado* in *Con la pluma y el machete,* 1:189–92. Roa was also the author of a vivid description of insurgent *matiabos*—the African maroon communities that lent services to the Cuban leaders of 1868. Although that description, in which the black insurgent is painted as foreign and dangerous, was written in the 1890s as part of the same collection as the portrait of Rosa la Bayamesa, it did not appear until the publication of his collected works in 1950.

53. Note that Roa's description of Legón first appeared in the black newspaper *La Igualdad,* suggesting that the audience for these writings was made up of not only white Cubans whose fears they sought to allay but also black Cubans whose support was also courted by the colonial state and the autonomist party. Legón's story demonstrates that point particularly well, for it appeared in numerous publications accessible to white and nonwhite audiences. For example, Manuel de la Cruz told Legón's story in his *Episodios de la revolución cubana* (Havana, 1911) and Serafín Sánchez, veteran of the Ten Years' War and the Guerra Chiquita, authored a short biography of Legón in his book *Heroes humildes y poetas de la guerra,* published in New York in 1894. Sánchez's account chronicled the same transformation, explicitly identifying Legón as African-born. Thus he was transformed from a black African slave (not merely a black slave) to a Cuban

patriot. See Cruz, *Episodios de la revolución cubana,* 126–27; and Serafín Sánchez, *Heroes humildes y los poetas de la guerra* (Havana, 1981), 41–50.

54. Manuel Sanguily, "Negros y blancos," *Hojas Literarias,* January 31, 1894, reprinted in Manuel Sanguily, *Obras de Manuel Sanguily* (Havana, 1925), vol. 8, bk. 2, 137–38.

55. Sanguily, *Obras,* vol. 8, bk. 2, 137.

56. Although the introduction and the maintenance of the institution of slavery on the island are attributed to the Spanish, individual slaveowners are often portrayed as benevolent, pro-independence Cubans.

57. Sanguily, "Negros y blancos."

58. José Martí, "Los cubanos de Jamaica," in Martí, *Obras completas* (Havana, 1946), 1:494–95.

59. James O'Kelly, *The Mambi-Land, or Adventures of a* Herald *Correspondent in Cuba* (Philadelphia, 1874), 124. See also Manuel Suarez's letter of October 1, 1879, in Archivo Nacional de Cuba, *Documentos para servir a la historia de la Guerra Chiquita* (Havana, 1949–50), 2:252.

60. *Album de El Criollo* (Havana, 1888), 200–204.

61. In this process of reconfiguration, the most prominent black insurgents in the war are relatively absent from the public prose of independence. Few black insurgents appear in Martí's biographical portraits of independence leaders, and he seems to have published no biographical sketches of men such as Quintín Bandera or Guillermo Moncada. His profile of Antonio Maceo is interesting precisely because Maceo remains surpisingly absent. Purportedly a profile of Maceo, it devotes significantly more attention to Maceo's mother. Maceo appears in the beginning of the portrait as an intelligent and industrious farmer waiting for orders from others before taking part in a revolution. See "Antonio Maceo,""Mariana Grajales," and "La Madre de los Maceo," which were all published in *Patria* in 1893 and 1894 and reprinted in Martí, *Obras completas,* 1:586–89, 617–18.

62. Enrique Hernández Miyares, "1868," in *Obras completas* (Havana, 1915–16), 1:33; Cruz, *Episodios de la revolucion cubana,* 29–31. See also the discussion of essays by José Martí, Manuel Sanguily, Juan Gualberto Gomez, and Rafael Serra in Ferrer, *Insurgent Cuba,* ch. 5.

The Arming of Slaves in Comparative Perspective

CHRISTOPHER LESLIE BROWN

Slaveholders sometimes entrusted slaves with the use of deadly force. But the arming of slaves, as a practice, has yet to become the subject of sustained comparative analysis. The neglect follows, in part, from the difficulty of the task. Effective comparisons across space and time require command of a vast number of customs, institutions, and specific historical settings. "It is perhaps the variety of times and places where slave soldiers have appeared," the historian Douglas H. Johnson has written, "which inhibit a clear focus on the continuity and character of the institution itself."[1] The practice of arming slaves, moreover, varied widely enough to resist broad assessments of its character, to discourage hasty generalizations about its nature and tendencies. Perhaps it has seemed that such assessments could yield only abstracted ideal types — "the armed slave" and "the arming of slaves" — too remote from the specific experiences of masters and bondsmen and too imprecise to have value for historical analysis. For these reasons, few investigators have wished to do more than allude in passing to how specific practices differed from the arming of slaves elsewhere.[2] Indeed, most have not gone even this far, electing instead to present the particular instances in their particularity and isolate them from wider historical contexts. Ambitious attempts at sustained comparisons, as a consequence, have been exceptionally rare.[3]

The juxtaposition in this book of thirteen very different histories, however, should indicate the possibilities that careful comparisons across time and space may present. The particular histories begin to look less peculiar. The divergent traditions expose problems for explanation. An awareness of the wider contexts facilitates more precise questions about the individual cases. Plantation slavery has long attracted comparative research that links regions, hemispheres, oceans, and continents. The comparative history of abolition, emancipation, and post-emancipation societies has received increasing attention, too. The arming of slaves, as a subject of study, stands to benefit from similar experiments in cross-cultural analysis. For, despite their significant differences, the individual cases present certain common features that make comparison useful: they each treat enlistment in the context of enslavement, and they each consider captivity as the basis for recruitment.

The chapters of this book take up a complex and varied subject. The number of cases under consideration could easily be extended to include almost every known slave society. It would require a second volume of comparable length to treat each of the major instances of slave arming in respectable detail. In ancient Rome, as in ancient Greece, for example, political authorities recruited slaves in moments of crisis, particularly in the Punic Wars and during the last decades of the republic. When Hannibal threatened Rome in the third century B.C., Livy later recorded, the Romans responded by purchasing with public funds the freedom of eight thousand slaves willing to serve in exchange for liberty. At roughly the same time, during the Han Dynasty (206 B.C.–A.D. 25), nobles employed armed slaves as a way to fortify their authority. The Chinese gentry now and again directed their bondsmen to terrorize commoners, murder enemies, and confront state officials. In a similar way, "prominent Romans of the late Republic," the historian Keith Bradley has written, "commonly used their gladiators as personal security guards." In medieval Korea, as in the Roman republic, officials liberated slaves en masse to defend the state against attack from Mongol raiders in the mid-thirteenth century, Japanese threats in the late sixteenth century, and, finally, Manchu invaders in the seventeenth century. These crises encouraged the establishment of permanent regiments in which slaves and commoners served side by side, a practice that contributed to the gradual decline of slavery in eighteenth- and nineteenth-century Korea. Slaves constituted approximately a third of the fighting force in sixteenth-century Russia, primarily as cavalry in their owners' service. "Muscovite combat slaves," the historian Richard Hellie has written, "were as responsible as free men for the victories and losses of early modern Russian arms." By the late seventeenth century, slave soldiers had become essential infantrymen in the war-making power of the Russian state.[4]

The arming of slaves in western Africa, which John Thornton surveys here, persisted long after the abolition of the Atlantic slave trade. Slave soldiers filled the ranks in Dahomey and in the Yoruba states prominent in the first half of the nineteenth century in the regions that Europeans had known as the Bight of Benin and the Bight of Biafra. Slave armies, sometimes organized as private militias, policed the enslaved agricultural workers who labored near the Atlantic coast to produce palm oil for European markets.[5] The European governments that partitioned Africa at the end of the nineteenth century would rely, in turn, on African soldiers of slave origin in order to establish the political authority of colonial governments. In several instances they liberated, conscripted, or purchased bondsmen in order to seize control from local elites. The *Tirailleurs Senegalais,* who enabled French conquest of the western Sudan in the late nineteenth century and who subsequently defended France itself during World War I and World War II, represent only the most famous example of the several colonial armies founded through the enlistment of slaves.[6] The Portuguese use of Chikunda slaves as instruments of state authority in colonial Mozambique, as assessed here by Allen Isaacman and Derek Peterson, represents just one instance of a common practice among European colonizers in Africa.

The mamlūk system, described in Reuven Amitai's chapter, had institutional legacies across the Muslim world. The ghulams (Turkish military slaves) who served the Delhi sultanate during the thirteenth and fourteenth centuries arrived from the same regions that supplied bondsmen for the mamlūks.[7] "In the early seventeenth century the sultans of Acheh" in Muslim Indonesia "were served by 500 royal slaves born abroad and trained in warfare in their youth," Geoffrey Parker reports, citing the work of Anthony Reid. In the modern era, slave warriors participated in the raids for slaves that produced laborers for the Sulu sultanate in the present-day Philippines.[8] The Ottoman Empire that took shape in the eastern Mediterranean during the fourteenth century owed its military power to the janissaries, a professional army of slave soldiers established first through wars of expansion and subsequently through levies on dependent Christian villages in the Balkans. This was the most sophisticated system of military slavery to emerge in the Muslim world in the late medieval and early modern periods. If the gradual inclusion of free men in the jannisary corps during the seventeenth and eighteenth century prepared the way for the formal demise of the system in 1826, slaves continued to serve in the middle and upper ranks of the Ottoman army until the final collapse of the empire in 1918.[9] The institution of military slavery persisted in the region throughout the nineteenth century, especially once invigorated and intensified by the Ottoman general Mehmed Ali Pasha, who raided and then conquered the Sudan to create a modern army manned by slave soldiers, the jihadiya. The result was what Douglas H. Johnson has characterized as "the most extreme and important example" of military slavery "in modern African history."[10]

The essays published in this book, therefore, represent case studies of a global phenomenon, instances of a set of practices more or less characteristic of numerous societies where slaveholding became common. Considered together, they make apparent the variety of issues the subject presents and the range of questions that a comparative study of the arming of slaves could profitably address. There are, first, the social and political facts regarding the arming of slaves: the occasions that put slaves in arms, the mode of recruitment and enlistment, the quality of their preparation for battle, the absolute and relative numbers involved, and the responsibilities assigned to slave soldiers. A second topic relates to the experiences of slave soldiers, the ways military service shaped the ways they regarded their circumstances, opportunities, and themselves, as well as the ways those slave soldiers related to the state, the political elite, free peoples, and other slaves. The chapters also document transformations in slavery: the impact of slave soldiers on slave societies, the civil status of slave soldiers in the aftermath of war, the relation between military service and manumission (as well as other forms of social incorporation), the emergence of elite slaves, and the weakening or strengthening of slave systems through the deployment of slave soldiers. In these three ways, the arming of slaves becomes an essential aspect of the history of slavery itself. And yet, at the same time, the arming of slaves emerges as well as a vital topic, even more broadly, in the history of warfare and the acquisition and mobilization of political power.

Statecraft and Recruitment

The arming of slaves took a wide variety of forms, from the hasty provision of weapons to specialized training for battle. And it could occur more or less routinely, from the arming of slaves in moments of crisis to the systematic employment of slave soldiers in permanent regiments. Initiated in each instance by political or military elites, the arming of slaves must be distinguished analytically from the many moments when slaves armed themselves to achieve retribution, liberation, or independence. In this way, the subject differs from the history of slave resistance. The practice, in most instances, represented instead an effort among certain elites to turn their influence over bondsmen to political advantage. If plantation slavery provided landholders with a way to accumulate wealth, the arming of slaves provided political elites (or those hoping to become political elites) with a way to accumulate power. To this extent, the arming of slaves represented to slaveholders an instrument of

statecraft. At the same time, the use of slaves in warfare could, in some instances, award political standing and political importance to those who had
been armed, vesting the slave (or former slave) with the range of options
usually available to military elites hoping to establish for themselves independence, autonomy, and power. If the arming of slaves rarely proved dangerous
to political elites in the short term, in the long run the practice could (and often
did) complicate questions of power and powerlessness among both the enslaved and the free, by placing the dependent in a position of power and, in
turn, the powerful in a state of dependence.

The ambitious armed slaves in order to advance every conceivable agenda,
as the chapters, taken together, make clear. Governments sometimes found the
arming of slaves useful when extending their spheres of authority. Slaves assisted the expansion of empires. The Spartans of classical Greece employed the
subject Helots extensively when fighting distant campaigns. The expansion of
Islam owed much to the superior military capacity of mamlūk slaves in service
to the Islamic states in the Middle East. Slaves in arms had an important role in
European expansion in the Americas, particularly to the Spanish, for whom
enslaved Africans provided some of the muscle for the Spanish conquest of the
Indies in the sixteenth century.[11] During the era of the Haitian Revolution,
European combatants enlisted enslaved men for expeditions designed to capi-
talize on the troubles in Saint Domingue. Jacobin agents hoping to export the
French Revolution to the West Indies liberated slaves in Guadeloupe, Laurent
Dubois explains, in order to launch a campaign of conquest in the Eastern
Caribbean. The British established their well-known West India Regiments
with the aim of annexing the plantation colonies possessed by France and the
Netherlands. In each of these instances, the arming of slaves allowed officials
to undertake military campaigns that would have been inconceivable without
the mobilization of slave labor.

Governments also enlisted slaves to discourage or suppress political opposition. In much of Africa and the Islamic Middle East, rulers armed slaves (or,
rather, acquired slaves in order to arm them) so that they could centralize
power and discourage political resistance. The practice became a favored option as well for elites in the Americas facing the dissolution of their authority.
British commanders resorted to this expedient during the American Revolution in the hopes of retaining the thirteen colonies. Royalist agents in early
nineteenth-century Venezuela and Peru liberated enslaved men and women to
fight against colonial rebels to preserve those settlements for the Crown. The
United States government armed tens of thousands of enslaved men to preserve the federal union during the American Civil War. When imperial governments proved incapable of protecting their overseas colonies from attack

by European rivals, the colonists sometimes turned to their slaves in self-defense. Morgan and O'Shaughnessy show this to have been an especially common practice in the Caribbean, where the ratio of blacks to whites was greatly unbalanced and where European troops often proved ineffective in sustained fighting on the ground. Colonists of every nationality in the seventeenth-century Caribbean armed slaves reluctantly but routinely to defend their nascent settlements. Thereafter, "trusted" enslaved men served regularly in the island militias.[12] By the end of the eighteenth century, British and French planters counted on enslaved men for assistance in preserving control of their estates, even as insurrections by former slaves lay the wealthiest colony in the Caribbean to waste. Sustaining political authority in the Americas often meant entrusting slaves with the use of force, notwithstanding the anticipated risks.

Enslaved men sometimes served as the defenders of the social order. In several societies outside of the Americas, the use of slaves as internal police became systematic. Enslaved Scythian archers kept the peace in classical Athens. Mamlūks provided security for the caliphs and other rulers in the Islamic Middle East. The slave army established in the early eighteenth century, the 'Abid Al Bukhari, provided the infrastructure for the highly centralized Moroccan state.[13] In East Africa, the elite Chikunda slaves of Portuguese proprietors monitored the indigenous peasant proprietors on behalf of their overlords. In most of these instances, control over the social order extended to control over the economic order. Mamlūks and Chikunda not only policed the free population. They used their monopoly over the legitimate use of force to control economic resources within the regimes. They regulated commerce, collected taxes, and seized booty for their owners and themselves. The use of military power to bolster economic power figures in countless instances where slave soldiers came to prominence. The nobility of Muscovy chose to deploy slaves in combat roles because, in part, the extra hands could assist the transport of valuable goods from the field of battle.[14] The royal slaves who served as military commanders in the Sokoto Caliphate of northern Nigeria in the early twentieth century also supervised tax collection and the management of state plantations.[15]

Armed slaves figured in campaigns of political resistance, too. For provincial elites and for the leaders of states at the peripheries of far-flung empires, the arming of slaves could help prevent absorption and preserve local autonomy. Officials in Minas Gerais, Hendrik Kraay indicates, discouraged the arming of slaves in the Brazilian hinterland because they feared that the practice would make slaveholders there even more difficult to govern. Arab traders operating in the Nile River basin under European direction kept private armies of slave soldiers to facilitate raids for ivory, cattle, and African captives in the late nineteenth century. Those soldiers, subsequently, became important in the Arab traders' ultimately unsuccessful resistance to colonial rule in the southern Sudan.[16] The arming of slaves in the Americas, as in Africa, sometimes figured significantly in campaigns for political independence. This was especially the case in Spanish America, where wars of liberation became deeply entwined with and heavily dependent on the mobilization of the enslaved population. The victories of San Martín in Argentina and Bolívar in Venezuela are incomprehensible, as Peter Blanchard makes clear, without reference to the contributions made by slave soldiers. In Cuba, too, as Ada Ferrer details, resistance to colonial rule in 1868 began with the liberation of certain slaves for battle. Indeed, the arming of slaves in some instances enabled the pursuit of political ambitions that otherwise would have been impossible to realize. Neither the Portuguese in seventeenth-century Angola nor the Republicans of early nineteenth-century Brazil, for example, could have achieved political power without first enlisting enslaved men and women in their cause.

In institutional terms, the arming of slaves expressed itself in one of two ways — military slavery (which prevailed in much of Africa and the Middle East) and the less sophisticated schemes for the arming of slaves particularly common to the Americas. The contrasts are striking. Muslim and African rulers depended on armed slaves because, in societies where kinship often shaped political allegiance, slaves represented a particularly dependable source of loyal service. Slave soldiers, by definition, possessed no family ties and, as professional warriors, rarely had a role in economic production. Political elites acquired these involuntary soldiers in systematic fashion, through conquest, long-distance slave trades, or levies on subject peoples. Often they displayed a preference for those they regarded as "martial races," for nomadic peoples who depended on their military prowess for survival and who lived in communities vulnerable to exploitation by more powerful states — although, in some crucial instances, slave armies were formed from the indigenous population. Recruiters sought adolescent boys especially, if not exclusively, those young enough to be retrained in loyalty to a new patron. Their preparation for service usually began with ceremonies of ritual death and rebirth that left them dependent on their new patrons for their status within society. Authorities typically housed the new slave soldiers in encampments distant from the rest of the slave and free population. There they received a specialized education in the art of war and developed, in the process, a corporate identity rooted in their position as elite bondsmen of the ruler. These military slaves, frequently numbering in the thousands, were often regarded as members of the royal household. In this way, military slaves became a highly vulnerable elite, able to possess and exercise substantial political authority because of their special relationship with the powerful, and yet, as slaves, unable to reproduce their social position through their heirs. Their ranks instead were sustained through continual imports of newly enslaved boys from vulnerable populations.

In the Americas, the arming of slaves typically took on a very different dynamic. Elites enlisted slaves less to acquire loyal subjects than to address shortages of manpower. Recruitment took place, as a consequence, in a more haphazard fashion, as a response to the sudden perception of a need, as a reaction in moments of insecurity. Europeans in the Americas did not purchase slaves with the intention of deploying them in military service. Instead, slaveholders had to reassign agricultural and domestic workers to military roles, or colonial authorities had to appropriate the enslaved workforce when faced with the prospect of war. Sometimes, in the Americas, the initiative originated with the enslaved themselves. Fugitives from slavery, as volunteers in search of liberty or favor, offered their service in time of war, in some instances before the combatants sought out their assistance. In these instances, the arming of slaves functioned also as a consequence of — and further encouragement to — slave flight, particularly during the American Revolution, the Haitian Revolution, and the Spanish American Wars of Independence.[17] Because they were enlisted and deployed in a hurry, armed slaves in the Americas rarely received the sustained training characteristic of military slavery in the mamlūk kingdoms or the Ottoman Empire. Men, not boys, represented the ideal recruit. And the new soldiers, as members of a much larger colonial or imperial army, very rarely became a separate military and political elite as the mamlūks and their descendants did in late medieval Egypt. If slaves that entered service in the Americas could sometimes expect to obtain freedom in exchange for their labor, only in rare instances did they escape the stigma associated with their slave origins.

These broad institutional resemblances, of course, mask significant and substantial differences in practice. No two systems of military slavery were exactly alike. They diverged from each other in a variety of ways, especially in the numbers of men involved, the character of their preparation for warfare, and the manner in which those bondsmen became slave soldiers. Investigators will learn as much from the differences that distinguish the mamlūks of late medieval Egypt from the jahidiya of the Turco-Egyptian Sudan or from the warrior slaves of Segu in the Niger valley as they will from their similarities. A single system of military slavery, moreover, could change radically over time. The janissary corps of the Ottoman Empire in the eighteenth century look very different from the corps of the sixteenth century, since, in the interim, free men (those without slave origins) had begun to occupy a major place in these regiments. Systems of military slavery were not static institutions. The same holds true for the more haphazard practice of arming slaves in the Americas. Traditions varied from region to region, sometimes from colony to colony, and took different shapes over time. Caribbean practices departed from the conventions that developed in North America and departed again from the traditions that developed in Brazil. The age of revolutions led to unrivaled innovation and improvisation in the military roles allowed to enslaved men in the Americas; it marked a sharp break from the past.

The opportunities for comparison, then, lie within specific traditions as well as between them. The evolution and transfer of institutions, in particular, need more careful scrutiny. The origins and influence of the mamlūk phenomenon in the Middle East and in South Asia have become reasonably well known through the work of David Ayalon, Richard Pipes, and Andre Wink, among many others. But its precise relation to military slavery elsewhere in the Muslim world, and beyond, remains obscure. It is not yet apparent, for example, whether military slavery, which seems to have been universal in the Muslim world, developed from a particular sequence of institutional influences or, instead, from more general tendencies peculiar to Muslim societies. The character of institutional development is even less clear for the history of Atlantic slave systems. Like the more familiar plantation complex, which Philip Curtin and other historians have traced from the Mediterranean to the Atlantic,[18] the arming of slaves has an institutional history in the Americas. The practice migrated across space and adapted to new needs over time. As Jane Landers indicates, there was a pattern of influence from military slavery in Muslim Spain and during the Christian reconquista to the Spanish employment of enslaved men in the Indies and the subsequent use of slaves as combatants throughout the Caribbean. This institutional history remains difficult to relate in detail, however, and, as a consequence, difficult to mark through its various stages.

In one instance, as David Geggus shows in this book, the patterns of development are especially clear. The power of precedent, and the impulse to imitate and adapt, became especially apparent during the Haitian Revolution, as those long reluctant to arm slaves for battle hurried to recruit bondsmen into service and thereby attain prominence in the colony. Free coloreds in the Port au Prince region enlisted the "Swiss" — fugitive slaves from nearby sugar estates — in order to assert their claim to political power. French radicals in the colonial city responded by establishing their own corps of armed slaves, the Compagnie des Africains, who launched raids against free colored strongholds on the Cul de Sac plain. In the midst of this crisis, slave owners, both white and mixed-race, armed their own slaves to defend their estates. At the same time, the British government, beginning in 1793, began to systematically enlist slaves — the "Chausseurs" — into its ranks in order to restore the plantation economy. Similar dynamics took shape in the Eastern Caribbean during the era of the Haitian Revolution and, during the ensuing decades, in South America. The arming of slaves by one set of combatants could lead to the arming of slaves by another, a tendency that further study perhaps would reveal in other moments of warfare in the Caribbean basin or elsewhere in the Americas.

In the present state of research, the "facts" about the arming of slaves may be identified and compared but not as easily linked. The details pertaining to recruitment and deployment become increasingly clear; the way that slave soldiers assisted exercises in statecraft are apparent. But how a specific set of practices in one place affected comparable institutions elsewhere remains, in most instances, vague and obscure, though suggestive leads abound throughout the existing scholarship. The Spanish, for example, had a long and vexed history with the Ottoman Empire, in part because of their contest for supremacy in the Mediterranean. As a consequence, the Spanish knew well the importance of the janissaries to the defense of the Ottoman frontiers and to the power of Ottoman rulers. That example of captives in the service of empire seems to have influenced the concepts and strategies attractive to Spanish officials in colonial New Mexico during the late seventeenth and eighteenth centuries. They designated the Indian captives whom they assigned to police the frontier outposts as "genizaros," the Spanish word for janissaries.[19]

Armed Slaves

As a form of labor, military service bears comparison with the other labor regimes in which men of slave origins worked. In the first place, this form of labor was highly gendered. In its uneven demographic proportions the practice represents the inverse of sexual slavery, for which women were acquired in equally disproportionate numbers.[20] In the Americas, this meant, among other consequences, that enslaved men possessed a route to manumission not open to enslaved women.[21] In the more developed systems of military slavery in the eastern Mediterranean, the imbalance reflected a more general pattern of segregation, which was often regarded in Muslim societies as of crucial importance. In the Sudanese sultanate of Dar Fur, to give just one example, male and female slaves entered the palace through separate doorways.[22] Like other forms of labor — like task labor, like gang labor, like domestic service — the arming of slaves produced a characteristic social dynamic. The practice tended to elevate the dishonored. It awarded a measure of power to the otherwise dispossessed, creating a class of what the scholarly literature has tended to classify as "elite slaves," bondsmen vested with certain rights and privileges typically reserved for the free. In Muslim states, in fact, slave soldiers often enjoyed benefits and privileges not available to the free as a consequence of their service in the royal household. The mamlūk ruling elite of medieval Egypt presents only the most familiar example. Sean Stilwell, writing of the Kano emirate in the Sokoto caliphate during the late nineteenth century, has emphasized that the advantages enjoyed by royal slaves not only included access to wealth and power but included as well access to knowledge about the workings of the state. If the soldier of slave origins, in theory, remained vulnerable to the whims of his patron, he also, in most instances, possessed special value to the regime. The murder of a "hamba raja" — a Malay royal slave — was treated by law more severely than the murder of an ordinary slave or a commoner.[23]

Enslaved men did not acquire a similar elite status in the Americas through military service; slave soldiers did not become administrators, governors, or members of the political elite. Instead, in most instances, they escaped bondage itself; for those that survived, service in war typically led to or was preceded by a release from slavery. The prospect of social advancement meant, in turn, that bearing arms could be experienced as an opportunity to display courage and merit, even for those who, at first, found themselves bearing arms unwillingly. Where the arming of slaves became somewhat common, in the Caribbean in particular, one result was the growth of free black communities, which, generally, thought of themselves as distinct from and superior to those that remained in slavery. In American slave societies where the arming of slaves was less systematic, the more rigid definitions of what slaves could do meant, in most instances, that enslaved men who went to war, because they went to war, could no longer be slaves. In societies where military slavery was common, by contrast, the arming of slaves contributed to wide varieties of status *within* the enslaved population, as well as, in some instances, manumission through military service.

Military service not only affected the social position of the captive. It also affected how those captives thought about each other and themselves. Often alienated from the communities in which they had been born, then isolated within corps dedicated to warfare and in some instances forced to reside in remote camps or barracks, slave soldiers typically developed a pronounced group identity that, at once, distinguished them from other enslaved men and women as well as the community of the free. Recruiters and rulers often encouraged this sense of distinctiveness because it reinforced the dependence of soldiers on a patron or the state. Those elevated in this way tended to identify with and find their interests in the needs of those in power, because the state provided uniforms, salaries, rank, the means of subsistence, and opportunities for plunder. The mamlūks were not unusual in developing deep loyalty to their former masters even after manumission. This identity as bondsmen trusted with the use of force also developed its own dynamic, however, as armed soldiers of slave origin defined for themselves distinctive rituals, customs, and languages through which they fostered a sense of brotherhood. Among the Ottoman military elite, for example, slave origins became a point of pride.[24] The results, in some instances, were new ethnic identities that were defined, in most instances, by the members' shared history of captivity and military service, even as the experience itself receded with each passing generation. Those interested in comparative history of slavery and post-emancipation societies perhaps could learn a great deal by examining such groups — the Tirailleurs Senegalais, the Nubi of the Sudan, the Chikunda of Mozambique, and the West India Regiments of the British Empire, to take just a few examples — within a single analytical framework.[25] Despite their considerable differences, the members of each group shared the experience of slavery, military service, and the construction of new corporate identities from the memory of service in warfare.

The consequences of these identities-forged-through-battle for gender conventions and gender expectations within these communities would benefit from sustained investigation. An opportunity to bear arms, in some instances, meant an opportunity for enslaved men to assert control over women, both slave and free. A rebel leader during Russia's civil war of the early seventeenth century, "The Time of Troubles," told the bondsmen who joined him that they could take the daughters of estate owners as their wives.[26] There is evidence that the commanders of slave soldiers in West Africa, to take another set of examples, sometimes secured the loyalty of their military slaves by guaranteeing them access to dependents — women and children — of their own. The crystallization of a warrior identity, moreover, could affect gender relations within particular communities. The Chikunda ethnicity, with its emphasis on military prowess and spectacular feats of courage, produced substantial innovations in gender norms among the peoples that became Chikunda. Most important, it encouraged a population that had been captured from predominantly matrilineal cultures to adopt patrilineal modes of kinship. That history hints that much may be learned from pursuing in greater depth the legacies of military service in the households of former slaves. Several of the chapters in this book point out that newly freed soldiers purchased or petitioned for the liberty of a spouse or a family. There are instances here, as well, in which the widows of slave soldiers sought from the government the right to the property and the status of the deceased, as occurred, for example, in the aftermath of the U.S. Civil War and the Spanish American wars of independence.[27] But more research is needed on the gendered meaning of liberty in communities that recognized courage in warfare as the principal path to freedom or social advancement.

A no less crucial set of relations concerns the interactions between soldiers and the state they served. If the arming of slaves established communities that owed their social standing to the patronage and protection of the political elite, the arrangement, even with its benefits, could place those same rulers in a bind. The arming of slaves both enabled and encouraged additional claims on the state for privileges and rights — rights to freedom, rights in property, rights as citizens, and rights to recognition. The black auxiliaries of Carlos IV, Jane Landers shows, continued to demand recognition of their service to the Crown even after their exile from Santo Domingo. Joseph Reidy emphasizes that freedmen and freedwomen after the U.S. Civil War treated their service as the basis for claims for pensions, for land, and for education. A reluctance to honor such requests could prove risky when the military depended heavily, if not exclusively, on soldiers recruited from slavery. There are countless instances in which armed slaves mutinied when they felt their privileges vulnerable or their positions threatened. A British West Indian regiment in Dominica revolted in 1802 when it looked to them as if the state planned to return them to the sugar plantations. The Chikunda of Mozambique rebelled against their Portuguese masters not long afterward, when the prazeiros tried to sell the Chikunda into the Atlantic slave trade or force them into agricultural labor. The Sudanese slave soldiers of Kasala turned on their Turco-Egyptian masters in 1865 as their pay fell in arrears and their overlords failed to meet their obligations as patrons and protectors.[28] Those armed by the state could not be disarmed by the state without risking a substantial threat to social and political stability. Slaveholders never exposed themselves to greater danger than when they demoted, humiliated, or disregarded those who had won liberty or rights through military service.

In much of West Africa and the Middle East, slave soldiers often mobilized their considerable military might to sustain their power and influence. Since that power usually depended on the security of their patron or the preservation of the state, these slave elites often proved to be determined defenders of the established order. The mamlūks took control of the sultanates of Egypt and Syria in the thirteenth century when it looked as if new caliphs would remove them from office and diminish their influence. The Ceddo soldiers in the Bambara state of Segu placed themselves in office in the late eighteenth century when a succession crisis seemed to put their social position and access to power at risk. A rebellion by Muslim slaves in the military figured in the collapse of the Oyo Empire in the early nineteenth century.[29] "Those sultans who tried to defy their slaves," one historian of the Ottoman Empire has written, "soon found themselves deposed."[30] In one memorable instance in the Americas, an army forged in the crucible of slavery placed itself in power, as Muslim slave soldiers had done several times before. Toussaint's "black Jacobins" ruled revolutionary Saint Domingue on behalf of France until the government of the first consul decided to return the liberated to slavery. Toussaint's army responded to this threat by seizing control of the colony and establishing Haitian independence. In this way, independent Haiti emerged as, in some respects, an American variant on the mamlūk state.

Slave soldiers usually had every incentive to fight to the death. Armed slaves captured in battle typically faced an unpleasant fate, since the victors, particularly in the Americas, rarely tried to return such soldiers to agricultural labor or domestic service. Some veterans, such as the black loyalists that served the British army during the American Revolution or the Tropas Auxiliaries that served Charles IV in Santo Domingo, faced exile and resettlement. The less fortunate found themselves abandoned to the enemy. This was the experience of black troops the British recruited in 1794 and 1795 in an unsuccessful bid to seize Saint Domingue. Others, such as the Afro-Brazilian defenders of Sabinada or the revolutionary army of Victor Hugues, were simply massacred. In much of the Islamic world, overthrowing a ruler typically meant disposing of the elite slaves who served him. At the outset of their conquest of Egypt in the early sixteenth century, Ottoman conquerors systematically disposed of the mamlūk elite. The Ottomans honored private property and safeguarded cooperative civilians. The mamlūks they decapitated. These events repeated themselves almost three centuries later, after the revival of mamlūk power during an era of Ottoman decline. When the Ottoman general Muhammad Ali took control of Egypt in the early nineteenth century, he decided that his independence as a leader would depend on removing the mamlūks from power. He slaughtered them in 1811 in order to replace one set of slave elites with his own. Few events better illustrate the precarious position of even the most privileged of bondsmen whose position depended entirely on their relationship to the state.[31]

A research agenda that intends, then, to elucidate the position of the armed slave has a variety of questions to consider. In addition to the work that slave soldiers performed, in addition to the ways they were prepared for duty and deployed for battle, there were a constellation of relationships that affected what being an armed slave meant. These relationships with the free, with the state, and among each other helped decide the character of the military experience. If the history of slave arming is in part the history of slaves and statecraft, that history must also be a study of the social and political life of the enlisted bondsmen.

Transformations in Slavery

The arming of slaves often had lasting consequences for the institution of slavery itself, as well as for the enslaved. It figured in the comprehensive emancipations in the French Caribbean in the late eighteenth century and in the United States of America in the mid-nineteenth century, as well as during the wars of independence in republican Venezuela and Peru. In these cases, mobilizing manpower for public ends often meant liberating bondsmen from private ownership. Liberated soldiers often proved to be the most committed to ensuring that these wartime exigencies became the basis for permanent changes in law. Bondsmen in arms, particularly in the Americas, often became abolitionists by means of military service. In other instances, the arming of slaves helped initiate a slow death for slavery, by allowing slaves liberty in exchange for service, by eroding the property rights of slaveholders, by creating opportunities for escape among enslaved men and women, or by blurring the customary boundaries (such as race) that distinguished the enslaved from the free. This pattern prevailed, for example, in the late eighteenth- and nineteenth-century British empire, where, inadvertently in the West Indies and deliberately in West Africa, British demands for power and manpower compromised the position of slaveholding elites.[32] In either case, through rapid and radical change or through slow erosion, when European authorities armed slaves, the typical result was the erosion of slaveholders' authority. It was this dynamic that Orlando Patterson had in mind when he treated slaves in military service under the more general rubric of "patterns of manumission."[33]

In other situations, however, the arming of slaves could produce the opposite effect. A demand for slave soldiers often encouraged the enslavement of boys and men and promoted the trade in bondsmen. In the long run, European governments helped cause an end to slavery in Africa in the late nineteenth and early twentieth century by drawing off slave labor into their colonial armies and by refusing legal recognition to established forms of slavery. In the short run, however, those same colonial powers encouraged local elites to take new captives to replace those they lost to European regiments. As the historian Taj Hargey has explained, to give just one example, the British government "fostered fresh slave acquisition" in the Sudan when it enlisted manumitted and fugitive slaves into the army in the early twentieth century "as owners sought to replace those conscripted."[34] The arming of slaves had an even more profound effect on slavery in the Mediterranean, the Balkans, and the Caucusus in the medieval and early modern eras. Slave trades in those regions emerged *because* of the demand for slave soldiers in North Africa and the Middle East. Across the Islamic world, from the ninth through the nineteenth centuries, Muslim rulers instituted or supported slave markets in order to attain a sufficient number of slaves for elite regiments. Linda S. Northrup has recently argued that ensuring the steady supply of slaves represented a prime diplomatic imperative for a mamlūk ruler.[35] If the Atlantic slave trade came into being to meet the demand for plantation labor in the Americas, slave raiding expanded in the Nile Valley during the nineteenth century to provide the Turco-Egyptian state (and then its Sudanese competitors) with slave soldiers. Feeding and sustaining these armies typically required the intensification of agricultural production, and, sometimes as a consequence, the intensification of agricultural slavery. This was true not only in the Sudan but in the warrior states of West Africa as well. If the arming of slaves, then, sometimes contributed to the end of slavery in the Americas, elsewhere the practice encouraged slave trading and caused it to flourish.[36]

These differences — between military slavery in the Middle East and large parts of Africa, and the occasional deployment of slaves for battle in the Americas — often have drawn comment but rarely extended consideration. Those most interested in the comparative questions have tended to focus on the circumstances that made military slavery distinct and, by implication, aberrant. It is sometimes assumed that military slavery developed only in regions and eras subject to Muslim influence.[37] But military slavery, though common in Islamic states, was not unique to them. It developed in several societies beyond the reach of Islam, in much of sub-Saharan Africa, and in early modern Russia and Korea, as well as briefly in the Caribbean, where, at the end of the eighteenth century, the British established a major, if short-lived, system of military slavery. The British West India regiments shared many of the features of military slavery elsewhere. The British government purchased slaves through the Atlantic slave trade with the explicit purpose of arming them for battle. They trained the captives for warfare and housed them in encampments separate from the rest of the enslaved population. These slave soldiers, in theory, served for life. They did not earn their freedom, at least initially, in service to the Crown. The example of the British West India regiments, therefore, marks out the path not taken by European governments in the Americas and elsewhere, though it should be noted that French officials in Senegal and Dutch officials in Java both purchased hundreds of slaves from traffickers in the early nineteenth century in order to deploy those bondsmen in colonial armies.[38] The familiar problem regarding the "peculiar character" of slavery in the Islamic world and much of Africa, then, might be turned on its head. The interesting question has not been asked — Why did military slavery, which otherwise prevailed in much of the slaveholding world, fail to develop in the Americas?

Those in the Americas opposed to the arming of slaves frequently described such a step as a "dangerous expedient." That assessment conforms to the expectations that prevail in contemporary historical scholarship, with its characteristic emphasis on the tendency of enslaved peoples to resist, and violently, when opportunity offered. The commitment among slaves to an elevation in status and ultimately to social and political standing need not be questioned. In practice, however, the arming of slaves does not seem to have been distinctively dangerous, at least for those who did the arming. Mutinies and desertions by slave soldiers punctuate the history of military slavery in the Middle East and East Africa, from the Zanj rebellion of the ninth century to the revolts within the Sudanese army in the nineteenth.[39] It is not clear, however, that soldiers of slave origin turned on authorities more frequently than did armies composed of "free" men; indeed, it would be valuable to have a systematic analysis of particular instances. Most important, those who did arm slaves rarely seem to have regretted the choice. The practice, in fact, would seem to have had the apparently paradoxical effect, in some cases, of discouraging violent resistance to slavery rather than promoting insurrection. Often the arming of slaves connected bondsmen more closely to the established order instead of deepening their alienation. Prospects for honor, distinction, liberty, and status may have mattered more to the bondsmen than opportunities for violent retribution. If the dynamics in such situations are not better understood, it will remain difficult to comprehend why ship captains could confidently assign armed captives to keep watch over disarmed captives on late seventeenth-century British slaving ships, a phenomenon that historian David Eltis has recently described.[40] Fears about what slaves would do if armed may tell more about the anxieties and needs of the slaveholding class in the Americas than about the likely behavior of enslaved men. Such anxieties, perhaps, arose as much from prejudice and ideology as from a careful measure of probable outcomes.

Ideology, in fact, may have mattered as much as fear in discouraging the arming of slaves in the Americas. Making soldiers into slaves promised a violation of conventions, a dramatic innovation in what it meant to be a soldier and what it meant to be a slave. The arming of slaves seemed at once to accord enslaved men respect and degrade the honor traditionally associated with military service. In both respects, classical precedents proved influential in the Americas. The ideal soldier in Greece and Rome was a free citizen.

Military service was a privilege as much as a duty. It drew on and conveyed honor. Those ideals, as Peter Hunt has argued here and elsewhere, led ancient chroniclers to understate the extent to which slaves served in the Athenian army and navy.[41] And that tradition of excluding slaves from service and minimizing the service that slaves actually rendered, provided an institutional legacy of its own for European settlers in the Americas in the early sixteenth century and after. This kind of explanation, of course, with its emphasis on cultural traditions, merely restates the problem in a different form. It does not make clear why ancient precedents should have been so powerful. The comparatively rapid rise and fall of military slavery in Korea and Russia during the early modern period demonstrates the possibilities for significant institutional change in methods of recruitment and mobilization of manpower, even in the face of established traditions.[42] The power of institutional legacies also fails to explain why military slavery failed to develop in Europe, despite centuries of exposure to the powerful example presented by the mamlūk state and the Ottoman Empire. In short, the question of why opposition to the systematic arming of slaves had such a long life in European states would benefit from further reflection. It may be that a study of European perception of military slavery in Islamic and African states would reveal much about the ideological restraints on institutional innovation within Europe during the medieval and early modern eras.

It would seem, in any case, that the economic origins and economic orientation of slavery in the Americas must have been especially important to inhibiting the use of slaves in military roles, perhaps as important as the fear of slave revolts and perhaps as important as received ideals about the social roles of slaves and the proper character of the soldier. Europeans acquired slaves from Africa and transported them to the Americas in order to make money, not war, a fact that limited the options available to those later interested in the arming of slaves for battle. Diverting the workforce from profitable labor into military service always looked to slaveholders like a threat to their investment, especially since a prolonged tour of duty seemed to render bondsmen unfit for agricultural labor in the aftermath. This was why colonial and imperial governments that hoped to enlist slaves for battle offered slaveholders compensation. Without compensation, the arming of slaves represented not only a threat to an investment but also an expropriation of property, a severe and involuntary tax. And it should be noted, in this regard, that compensation figured centrally in the arming of slaves in situations as diverse as the late Roman Republic, late seventeenth-century Morocco, and the Paraguayan War in nineteenth-century Brazil.[43] For even with compensation, slaveholders could still regard the arming of slaves as a violation of their rights, since property in slaves was sometimes understood as distinct from property in things, from property in other forms of transferable wealth. Slaveholders often thought of enslaved men and women as dependents, as well as property. For this reason, they could experience the appropriation of slaves by the state in time of war as a violation of the household, as a challenge to their patrimonial rights. Even in times of need, as a consequence, slaveholders in the Americas often insisted that only they had the right to vest slaves with arms. In this way, opposition to the arming of slaves in the Americas could serve as a protest against an aggrandized state or against a threat to aristocratic autonomy, as an expression, in short, of political and economic interests, more than an articulation of fears or social ideals.

The importance of slaveholder opposition highlights a crucial but overlooked obstacle to the arming of slaves in the Americas. The governing authorities — imperial, federal, colonial, and local — usually possessed no slaves of their own. That situation stands in sharp contrast to the circumstances obtaining in much of Africa and the Islamic world, where military slaves, by definition, were usually the slaves of the state or the personal slaves of the ruler, senior officers, or warlords. Crown slaves existed in limited proportions in the Spanish and Portuguese colonies, where they served primarily in public works. Spanish officials purchased from Atlantic merchants more than four thousand African captives, most of whom were men, and assigned those slaves to the reconstruction of Cuban forts after the British occupation of Havana in 1762 and 1763. The British state, as well, possessed more than ten thousand slaves of its own in the West India Regiments by the early nineteenth century.[44] But for reasons that need further research, the crowns of Europe seem not to have considered purchasing slaves en masse to advance the ends of state. The expense alone may have been prohibitive. The imperial and colonial governments almost certainly would have found it beyond their capacity to compete with slaveholders in the Americas for the labor of enslaved men. Such innovations, moreover, may have seemed unnecessary at the time. The manpower available through more conventional channels perhaps answered the demands decided by restricted ambitions. The British, for example, organized the West Indian Regiments only in a moment of acute need. Yet need, of course, is a matter of subjective perception rather than objective fact. Slaveholders in the Americas elected to accept defeat in countless instances rather than systematically admit slaves into the ranks. The choices made by the Confederacy during the American Civil War demonstrate clearly how an honorable defeat could be understood as preferable to a dishonorable victory won with the assistance of slaves. The widespread employment of slaves could have enabled military and political options that authorities in the Americas never contemplated. But such possibilities were hampered severely by the institutional barriers that discouraged the creation of various forms of government slaveholding.

Ultimately, the arming of slaves as a subject of historical analysis needs to be situated within broader questions regarding the mobilization of manpower, the resources available to the state, and the conventions of warfare. At the same time the subject opens up new ways to approach the now-familiar problems regarding the dynamics of power within slave societies, the nature of domination and resistance, and the paradoxes of mastery and enslavement. If the basic outlines of the individual histories have become familiar, the opportunities for cross-cultural study remain abundant. The institutional legacies and influences must still be traced. The complex social position of the soldier of captive origins, in most instances, needs more searching scrutiny. The political consequences of placing slaves in arms can still be pursued with more rigor and nuance in almost every case. The arming of slaves occurred too frequently, it shaped institutions and societies too fundamentally, to be treated as a noteworthy exception. Students of slavery will understand their subject better when they begin to see the arming of slaves as predictable and explicable, rather than as a paradox or a problem, when they understand, as Peter Hunt recently has written, that "there is nothing inherently contradictory about the use of slaves in warfare."[45]

Notes

I am pleased to thank Indrani Chatterjee, Hilary-Anne Hallett, Ken Himmelman, and the contributors to this volume for advice and guidance on this chapter. All references are to chapters of this book except where indicated. A preliminary version was presented to the annual meeting of the Organization of American Historians in Memphis, Tennessee, in the spring of 2003.

1. Douglas H. Johnson, "Sudanese Military Slavery from the Eighteenth to the Twentieth Century," in *Slavery and Other Forms of Unfree Labor* (London, 1988), 142.

2. For notable recent attempts to place particular cases in broader context, see Roger Norman Buckley, *Slaves in Red Coats* (New Haven, 1979), viii–x; Daniel Pipes, *Slave Soldiers and Islam: The Genesis of a Military System* (New Haven, 1981), 24–45; Richard Hellie, *Slavery in Russia* (Chicago, 1982), 472–473; Peter Hunt, *Slaves, Warfare, and Ideology in the Greek Historians* (Cambridge, 1998), 206–218; John Edward Philips, "The Persistence of Slave Officials in the Sokoto Caliphate," in Miura Toru and John Edward Philips, *Slave Elites in the Middle East and Africa: A Comparative Study* (London, 2000), 216–222, 232–234; James Brooks, *Captives and Cousins: Slavery, Kinship, and Community in the Southwest Borderlands* (Chapel Hill, 2002), 127–128.

3. For sociological assessments of the practice, see H. J. Nieboer, *Slavery as an Industrial System: Ethnological Researches* (New York, 1908; 2d rev. ed., 1971), 398–403; Orlando Patterson, *Slavery and Social Death: A Comparative Study* (Cambridge, Mass.,

1982), 287–293. For a highly detailed study of free black and enslaved military service in the Americas during the colonial period, see Peter M. Voelz, *Slave and Soldier: The Military Impact of Blacks in the Colonial Americas* (New York, 1993).

4. Norbert Rouland, *Les esclaves romains en temps de guerre* (Brussells, 1977); Adrian K. Goldsworthy, *The Second Punic Wars* (London, 2000), 219; C. Martin Wilbur, *Slavery in China During the Former Han Dynasty* (Chicago, 1943), 187–193; Keith Bradley, *Slavery and Rebellion in the Roman World, 140 B.C.–70 B.C.* (Cambridge, 1989) 90; Patterson, *Slavery and Social Death*, 288–289; James B. Palais, *Confucian Statecraft and Korean Institutions: Yu Hyongwon and the Late Choson Dynasty* (Seattle, 1996), 226–228, 249–252; Richard Hellie, *Enserfment and Military Change in Muscovy* (Chicago, 1971), 267; Hellie, *Slavery in Russia*, 467–474 (estimate on page 468, quotation on page 471); Hellie, "The Manumission of Russian Slaves," *Slavery and Abolition*, 10, no. 3 (1989): 32–33.

5. Paul Lovejoy, *Transformations in Slavery: A History of Slavery in Africa*, 2d ed. (Cambridge, 2000), 176–182; Claude Meillassoux, *The Anthropology of Slavery: The Womb of Iron and Gold*, translated by Alide Dasnois (Chicago, 1991), 166–169, 227–230; Babatunde Agiri, "Slavery in Yoruba Society in the 19th Century," in Paul Lovejoy, ed., *Ideology of Slavery in Africa* (London, 1981), 131–136. See also Funso Afolayan, "Warfare and Slavery in 19th Century Yorubaland," in Adeagbo Akinjogbin, ed., *War and Peace in Yorubaland, 1793–1893* (Ibadan, Nigeria, 1998), 407–419, who stresses that the acquisition of slave soldiers through warfare brought individual warlords to political and economic power.

6. See, e.g., Myron Echenberg, "Slaves into Soldiers: Social Origins of the Tirailleurs Senegalais," in Paul Lovejoy, ed., *Africans in Bondage: Studies in Slavery and the Slave Trade* (Madison, 1986), 311–334; Echenberg, *Colonial Conscripts: The Tirailleurs Senegalais in French West Africa, 1857–1960* (Portsmouth, N.H., 1991). Also see David Northrup, "The Ending of Slavery in the Eastern Belgian Congo," and Allen Isaacman and Anton Rosenthal, "Slaves, Soldiers, and Police: Power and Dependency Among the Chikunda of Mozambique, ca. 1825–1920," in Suzanne Miers and Richard Roberts, eds., *The End of Slavery in Africa* (Madison, 1988), 470, 239–244. For European dependence, more generally, on men of slave origin during the conquest of Africa, see Lovejoy, *Transformations in Slavery*, 258–259, 269.

7. Salim Kidwai, "Sultans, Eunuchs and Domestics: New Forms of Bondage in Medieval India," in Utsa Patnaik and Manjari Dingwaney, eds., *Chains of Servitude: Bondage and Slavery in India* (Madras, 1983), 81–84; André Wink, *Al-Hind: The Making of the Indo-Islamic World*, vol. 2, *The Slave Kings and the Islamic Conquest, 11–13th Centuries* (Leiden, 1997), 112–115.

8. Geoffrey Parker, *The Military Revolution: Military Innovation and the Rise of the West, 1500–1800*, 2d ed. (Cambridge, 1996), 125; James Francis Warren, "The Structure of Slavery in the Sulu Zone in the Late Eighteenth and Nineteenth Centuries," *Slavery and Abolition*, 24, no. 2 (2003):116, 123.

9. The historian Virginia Askan has recently bemoaned "the appalling lack of systematic studies" of the janissaries. Askan, "Whatever Happened to the Jannissaries? Mobilization for the 1768–1774 Russo-Ottoman War," *War in Society* 5, no. 1 (January 1998): 26n. My discussion draws primarily from Askan, "Janissaries," in Paul Finkelman

and Joseph C. Miller, eds., *Macmillan Encyclopedia of World Slavery* (New York, 1998), 443–444; Ehud Toledano, *Slavery and Abolition in the Ottoman Middle East* (Seattle, 1998), 20–28; M. L. Bush, *Servitude in Modern Times* (Cambridge, 2000), 168–172; and Dror Ze'evi, "*Kul* and Getting Cooler: The Dissolution of Elite Collective Identity and the Formation of Official Nationalism in the Ottoman Empire," *Mediterranean Historical Review* 11, no. 2 (1996), 177–195.

10. Johnson, "Sudanese Military Slavery," 142. From a very large and sophisticated literature, see also Johnson, "The Structure of a Legacy: Military Slavery in Northeast Africa," *Ethnohistory* 36, no. 1 (1989): 72–88.

11. In addition to the chapter by Jane Landers in this book, see Matthew Restall, "Black Conquistadores: Armed Africans in Early Spanish America," *The Americas* 57, no. 2 (2000): 171–205.

12. In addition to Morgan and O'Shaughnessy, see Jerome Handler, "Freedmen and Slaves in the Barbados Militia," *Journal of Caribbean History* 19, no. 1 (1984): 1–25.

13. Allen R. Meyers, "Slave Soldiers and State Politics in Early 'Alawi Morocco, 1688–1727," *International Journal of African Historical Studies* 16, no. 1 (1983): 40. Also see the chapter by John Thornton in this book.

14. Hellie, *Slavery in Russia*, 472.

15. Sean Stilwell, " 'Amana' and 'Asiri': Royal Slave Culture and the Colonial Regime in Kano," *Slavery and Abolition* 19, no. 2 (1998): 170.

16. Robert O. Collins, "The Nilotic Slave Trade: Past and Present," in Elizabeth Savage, ed., *The Human Commodity: Perspectives on the Transaharan Slave Trade* (London, 1992), 147–149.

17. European invaders would have a similar impact elsewhere during the late nineteenth and early twentieth centuries as wars for empire led some slaves in Africa to escape their bondage by volunteering to serve in colonial armies. Samson P. Ukpabi, "Military Recruitment and Social Mobility in Nineteenth Century British West Africa," *Journal of African Studies* 2, no. 1 (1975): 87–107; Richard Roberts, "The End of Slavery in the French Soudan, 1905–1914," in Miers and Roberts, *End of Slavery in Africa*, 284; Martin Klein, *Slavery and Colonial Rule in French West Africa* (Cambridge, U.K., 1998), 74.

18. Philip D. Curtin, *The Rise and Fall of the Plantation Complex*, 2d ed. (Cambridge, U.K., 1998); William D. Phillips Jr., *Slavery from Roman Times to the Early Transatlantic Trade* (Minneapolis, 1985); Robin Blackburn, *The Making of New World Slavery: From the Baroque to the Modern* (London, 1998).

19. Brooks, *Captives and Cousins*, 123–142, esp. 127–129.

20. The notable exception is nineteenth-century Dahomey, where women, many of slave origins, also served as soldiers and palace guards. See, most recently, Robin Law, "The 'Amazons' of Dahomey," *Paideuma* 39 (1993): 245–260; Stanley B. Alpern, *Amazons of Black Sparta: The Women Warriors of Dahomey* (New York, 1998); Edna Bay, *Wives of the Leopard: Gender, Politics, and Culture in the Kingdom of Dahomey* (Charlottesville, 1998).

21. Maria Elena Diaz, *The Virgin, the King, and the Royal Slaves of El Cobre* (Palo Alto, 2000), 256–260.

22. R. S. O'Fahey, "Slavery and Society in Dar Fur," in John Ralph Willis, ed., *Slaves and Slavery in Muslim Africa*, vol. 2, *The Servile Estate* (London, 1985), 88.

23. Sean Stilwell, "The Power of Knowledge and the Knowledge of Power: Kinship, Community and Royal Slavery in Pre-Colonial Kano, 1807–1903," and John Edward Philips, "The Persistence of Slave Officials in the Sokoto Caliphate," in Toru and Philips, *Slave Elites in the Middle East and Africa,* 117–156, 216–217. Philips draws his assessment from V. Matheson and M. B. Hooker, "Slavery in the Malay Texts: Categories of Dependency and Compensation," in Anthony Reid, ed., *Slavery, Bondage, and Dependency in Southeast Asia* (St. Lucia, Queensland, 1983), 182–208.

24. Ze'evi, "*Kul* and Getting Cooler," 182–185.

25. On the Nubi of the Sudan, see Johnson, "Structure of a Legacy," 82–84.

26. Hellie, *Slavery in Russia,* 576; Meillassoux, *Anthropology of Slavery,* 169, 171–173, 194.

27. Peter Blanchard, "The Language of Liberation: Slave Voices in the Wars of Independence," *Hispanic American Historical Review* 82, no. 3 (2003): 519.

28. Roger N. Buckley, *Slaves in Red Coats: The British West India Regiments, 1795–1815* (New Haven, 1979) 57; Ahmad Alawad Sikainga, "Comrades in Arms or Captives in Bondage: Sudanese Slaves in the Turco-Egyptian Army, 1821–1865," in Toru and Philips, *Slave Elites in the Middle East and Africa,* 197–214.

29. Agiri, "Slavery in Yoruba Society in the 19th Century," 136–138.

30. Ze'evi, "*Kul* and Getting Cooler," 183.

31. David Ayalon, "Mamluk Military Aristocracy During the First Years of the Ottoman Occupation of Egypt," in C. E. Bosworth, C. Issawi, R. Savory, and A. L. Udovitch, eds., *Islamic World from Classical to Modern Times: Essays in Honor of Bernard Lewis* (Princeton, 1989), 414, as reprinted in Ayalon, *Islam and the Abode of War: Military Slaves and Islamic Adversaries* (Aldershot, 1994); Khaled Fahmy, *All the Pasha's Men: Mehmed Ali, His Army and the Making of Modern Egypt* (Cambridge, U.K., 1997), 82–84. The reemergence and terminal decline of the mamlūk in Ottoman Egypt may be traced in the essays by Michael Winter, Jane Hathaway, Daniel Philip, and Daniel Crecelius in Thomas Phillip and Ulrich Haarmaan, eds., *The Mamluks in Egyptian Politics and Society* (Cambridge, U.K., 1998), chaps. 5–8.

32. Buckley, *Slaves in Red Coats,* 142–144; Paul E. Lovejoy and Jan S. Hogendorn, *Slow Death for Slavery: The Course of Abolition in Northern Nigeria, 1897–1936* (Cambridge, U.K., 1993).

33. Patterson, *Slavery and Social Death,* 287–293.

34. Taj Hargey, "*Festina Lente:* Slavery, Policy and Practice in the Anglo-Egyptian Sudan," *Slavery and Abolition* 19, no. 2 (1998): 253.

35. Linda S. Northrup, *From Slave to Sultan: The Cause of Al-Mansur Qalawun and the Consolidation of Mamluk Rule in Egypt and Syria, 678–689* A.H./*1279–1290* A.D. (Stuttgart, 1998), 190.

36. For telling examples that detail the macro and micro dimensions of this trade see, respectively, Andrew Ehrenkreutz, "Strategic Implications of the Slave Trade Between Genoa and Mamluk Egypt in the Second Half of the Eighteenth Century," in A. L. Udovitch, ed., *The Islamic Middle East, 700–1900: Studies in Economic and Social History* (Princeton, 1984) 335–345; Douglas H. Johnson, "Recruitment and Entrapment in Private Slave Armies: The Structure of the *Zara'ib* in the Southern Sudan," in Elizabeth

Savage, ed., *The Human Commodity: Perspectives on the Trans-Saharan Slave Trade* (Portland, Ore., 1992), 162–173.

37. This is the point of departure, for example, for two well-known works: Pipes, *Slaves and Soldiers,* and Patricia Crone, *Slaves on Horses: The Evolution of the Islamic Polity* (Cambridge, U.K., 1980).

38. Echenburg, *Colonial Conscripts,* 8–10; Anthony Reid, "The Decline of Slavery in Nineteenth-Century Indonesia," in Martin A. Klein, ed., *Breaking the Chains: Slavery, Bondage, and Emancipation in Modern Africa and Asia* (Madison, 1993), 72–73.

39. Jere L. Bacharach, "African Military Slaves in the Medieval Middle East: The Cases of Iraq (869–955) and Egypt (868–1171)," *International Journal of Middle East Studies* 13 (1981): 473; Johnson, "Sudanese Military Slavery," 145–146.

40. David Eltis, *The Rise of African Slavery in the Americas* (Cambridge, U.K., 2000), 228–229.

41. In addition to his chapter in this book, see Hunt, *Slaves, Warfare, and Ideology in the Greek Historians.*

42. It might be observed, moreover, that in Russia, as elsewhere, slaves served as fighters because commoners, as productive laborers, were deliberately discouraged from military service. Hellie, *Slavery in Russia,* 473.

43. Hunt, *Slaves, Warfare, and Ideology in the Greek Historians,* 207; Ahmad Alawad Sikainga, "Slavery and Muslim Jurisprudence in Morocco," *Slavery and Abolition* 19, no. 2 (1998): 63; Hendrik Kraay, "Slavery, Citizenship and Military Service in Brazil's Mobilization for the Paraguayan War," *Slavery and Abolition* 18, no. 3 (1997): 228–256.

44. Hendrik Kraay notes the small number of Crown slaves in nineteenth-century Brazil in Kraay, "Slavery, Citizenship and Military Service," 235–236. Crown slavery in Spanish America is treated most recently in Maria Elena Diaz, *The Virgin, the King, and the Royal Slaves* and Evelyn Powell Jennings, "State Enslavement in Colonial Havana," in Verene Shepherd, ed., *Diversity in Caribbean Economy and Society Since the 17th Century* (Gainesville, 2002), 152–182. See also Jennings, "In the Eye of the Storm: The Spanish Colonial State and African Enslavement in Havana, 1763–1790," *Historical Reflections/Réflexions Historiques* 29, no. 1 (2003): 159–162. In addition to the work of Roger N. Buckley, see, for the British Caribbean, Alvin O. Thompson, *Unprofitable Servants: Crown Slaves in Berbice, Guyana, 1808–1831* (Barbados, 2002).

45. Hunt, *Slaves, Warfare, and Ideology,* 206.

Contributors

REUVEN AMITAI is Eliyahu Elath Professor of the History of the Muslim Peoples at the Institute of Asian and African Studies at the Hebrew University of Jerusalem.

PETER BLANCHARD is professor of history at the University of Toronto.

CHRISTOPHER LESLIE BROWN is associate professor of history at Rutgers University.

DAVID BRION DAVIS is Sterling Professor of History emeritus at Yale University.

LAURENT DUBOIS is associate professor of history at Michigan State University.

ADA FERRER is associate professor of history at New York University.

DAVID GEGGUS is professor of history at the University of Florida.

PETER HUNT is associate professor of classics at the University of Colorado at Boulder.

ALLEN ISAACMAN is Regents Professor of History at the University of Minnesota and director of the Interdisciplinary Center for the Study of Global Change.

HENDRIK KRAAY is associate professor of history at the University of Calgary.

JANE LANDERS is associate professor of history at Vanderbilt University.

PHILIP D. MORGAN is the Sidney and Ruth Lapidus Professor of the American Revolutionary Era at Princeton University.

ANDREW JACKSON O'SHAUGHNESSY is Saunders Director at the Robert H. Smith International Center for Jefferson Studies at Monticello.

DEREK PETERSON is lecturer in African history at Cambridge University and a fellow of Selwyn College.

JOSEPH P. REIDY is professor of history at Howard University.

JOHN THORNTON is professor of history and African American studies at Boston University.

Index